CHARLES DICKENS
AND THE MID-VICTORIAN PRESS
1850-1870

CHARLES DICKENS
AND THE MID-VICTORIAN PRESS
1850-1870

Edited by Hazel Mackenzie and Ben Winyard

The University of Buckingham Press

First published in Great Britain in 2013 by

The University of Buckingham Press
Yeomanry House
Hunter Street
Buckingham MK18 1EG

© DJO

A CIP catalogue record for this book is available at the British Library

ISBN 9781908684202

Printed and bound in Great Britain by
Marston Book Services Ltd, Didcot, Oxon

Contents

Section 4

Acknowledgements

The Editors gratefully acknowledge the Leverhulme Trust for its generous funding of our postdoctoral posts and of the *Dickens Journals Online* project. For generous financial assistance in the organisation and hosting of the conference, we gratefully acknowledge the Department of English and the Humanities Research Institute at the University of Buckingham and the International Dickens Fellowship. We would also like to extend our thanks to the hard-working and ever-helpful administrative, IT, catering and support staff at the University of Buckingham, without whom the conference could not have taken place.

We would like to thank the University of Leicester, especially Holly Furneaux, Gail Marshall and Joanne Shattock, for generously co-organising the conference and providing indispensable support and guidance.

We would also like to thank the following individuals for their invaluable assistance in various aspects of managing the conference: Anthony Burton; David Paroissien; Tony Williams; and Johan Ehlers. Lastly we would like to thank John Drew, the originator, architect and champion of the *DJO* project, for his constant enthusiasm, support and generosity.

Laurel Brake is Professor Emerita of Literature and Print Culture at Birkbeck College, University of London.

Koenraad Claes lectures at University College Ghent and is guest professor at Ghent University.

Iain Crawford is Associate Professor in the Department of English at the University of Delaware.

Daragh Downes lectures in the School of English at Trinity College, Dublin.

John Drew is Professor of English Literature at the University of Buckingham and Director of the Dickens Journals Online project.

Judith Flanders is the author of *A Circle of Sisters* (2001), *The Victorian House* (2004), *The Invention of Murder* (2011) and *The Victorian City; Everyday Life in Dickens's London* (2012).

Laura Foster is a doctoral student in English Literature at Cardiff University.

Holly Furneaux is Reader in Victorian Literature at the University of Leicester.

Ignacio Ramos Gay is Senior Lecturer in French Literature at the University of Valencia.

Clare Horrocks is Senior Lecturer in Media and Cultural Studies at Liverpool John Moores University.

Louis James is Emeritus Professor of Victorian and Modern Literature at the University of Kent.

Patrick Leary is President of the Research Society for Victorian Periodicals.

Hannah Lewis-Bill is a doctoral student at the University of Exeter.

Helen Mckenzie is a doctoral student at Cardiff University

Pete Orford is editor of *Dickens on London, Dickens on Poverty* (forthcoming 2013), *Dickens on Theatre and Dickens on Travel* (Hesperus, 2009-11), and Honorary Research Fellow in the School of Humanities, University of Buckingham.

The late David Parker was Honorary Research Fellow at Kingston University and, formerly, Curator of the Charles Dickens Museum. David died unexpectedly during the production of these proceedings; he will be much missed.

David Paroissien is Emeritus Professor of English at the University of Massachusetts, Amherst, and Honorary Professorial Research Fellow in the School of Humanities, University of Buckingham

Robert L. Patten is Lynette S. Autrey Professor in Humanities at Rice University

Jasper Schelstraete is a doctoral student at Ghent University.

Paul Schlicke is Emeritus Senior Lecturer at the University of Aberdeen and Honorary Professorial Research Fellow in the School of Humanities, University of Buckingham

Joanne Shattock is Emeritus Professor of Victorian Literature at the University of Leicester

Michael Slater is Emeritus Professor of English Literature at Birkbeck College, University of London.

John Tulloch is Professor of Journalism and Head of the Lincoln School of Journalism at the University of Lincoln

Catherine Waters is Reader in the School of English at the University of Kent and Honorary Senior Research Fellow in the School of Humanities, University of Buckingham

Foreword

Michael Slater

B. W. MATZ'S forty-volume 'National Edition' of the works of Charles Dickens included, in 1908, two volumes called *Miscellaneous Papers* in which Matz gathered together as much as he could identify of Dickens's uncollected journalism and fugitive pieces such as the pamphlet *Sunday under Three Heads* (1836). These volumes could not be individually purchased, nor could the two called *Collected Papers* that formed part of the deluxe 'Nonesuch Dickens' subscription edition of 1937, edited by Walter Dexter and that included all the material in *Miscellaneous Papers*. Shortly afterwards, in his ground-breaking *The Dickens World* (1941), Humphry House drew extensively on Dickens's journalism in such periodicals as *The Examiner* and, in particular, articles from his weekly magazines *Household Words* and *All the Year Round*. The great majority of House's readers, however, would have had no access to this material, other than what Dickens himself had collected and republished during his own lifetime in *Reprinted Pieces* (1858) and *The Uncommercial Traveller* (1861, etc.).

This remained the case when, in the 1960s, Philip Collins published his two major studies of Dickens's writings on social themes, *Dickens and Crime* (1962) and *Dickens and Education* (1963). Then, in 1968, there appeared Harry Stone's two meticulously edited (and richly illustrated) volumes called *Charles Dickens's Uncollected Writings from Household Words, 1850-1859*. Ironically, however, these consisted of what Stone calls 'composite' articles, i.e., those only partly written by Dickens in collaboration either with his sub-editor W. H. Wills, or with another staff-writer or contributor. Meanwhile, all of Dickens's sole-authored articles, apart from what appeared in *Reprinted Pieces* and *the Uncommercial Traveller*, remained accessible only in the National and Nonesuch Editions, or in the increasingly rare original volumes of *Household Words* and *All the Year Round*.

When J.M. Dent, publishers of my *Dickens and Women* (1983), proposed to me in 1990 that I should become the General Editor of their projected 'Everyman Paperback' edition of Dickens's works (reprinting the texts of the old hardback Everyman Dickens volumes with new introductions, notes, etc.), I saw a great opportunity to bring back into circulation a representative selection from the riches of Dickens's out-of-print journalism. I suggested that the two volumes of this Edition devoted to journalism should comprise, in addition to *Sketches by Boz* and selected essays from *Reprinted Pieces* and *The Uncommercial Traveller*, a number of pieces taken from *Miscellaneous Papers*. These volumes, I argued, would fill a big gap in provision not only for Dickens studies but for Victorian studies in general. Dent accepted my suggestion, also that I should write head-notes for each sketch or essay, rather than footnote them, and should provide a subject index/glossary at the end of each volume. This format was retained after Weidenfeld and Nicolson had become the owners of the Dent imprint and had subsequently been incorporated into the Orion Publishing Group (1991). By this time the two journalism volumes had been separated from the Everyman Paperback Dickens and were now envisaged as four uniform hardback volumes. They would contain a very generous selection of Dickens's journalism but still not all of the available material. In addition there would be a complete listing at the end of each volume showing what had been included in it and what had been omitted. By 1993 the series title had been established as The Dent Uniform Edition of Dickens' Journalism (see illustration).

The first volume appeared in 1994, and was widely and enthusiastically reviewed in both the British and the American Press. Writing in the *Sunday Times*, John Carey welcomed the 'first ever annotated edition of Dickens's journalism', noting the 'immense debt' that nineteenth-century fiction owed to newspapers and magazines. The volume was 'a wonderful introduction to that great urban world which Dickens created', enthused Peter Ackroyd in *The Times*, and the series would 'comprehensively define this most important aspect of [Dickens's] genius'. Reporting that he 'gobbled up these essays greedily, hardly believing at the end that they take up 550 pages', Paul Foot commented (*The Spectator*) that 'their most extraordinary quality is their durability'. Subsequent volumes, published in 1996, 1998, and 2000 respectively, were equally well received. Reviewers of Volume 2 hailed Dickens's 'prodigious feats of journalism' (*The Times*) and how he had 'defied the restraints imposed on [him] by the medium' (*The Independent*); in Volume 3, Robert McCrum called Dickens the 'greatest and most visible journalist of an age rich in journalistic talent' (*The Observer*), while John Gross celebrated

Jacket images of the four volumes of the Dent Uniform Edition of
Dickens' Journalism 1994-2000

the 'literary power' of his writing in this genre, concluding that he would 'still be remembered as a great journalist' even if he had never written a word of fiction. Volume 4, which I co-edited with John Drew and which was published at the dawn of the new millennium, drew yet higher accolades from the British press, as if modern journalists were delighted to bask in reflected glory. 'There has never been a greater novelist than Dickens', concluded Philip Hensher in *The Spectator*, 'and it seems entirely unfair that he should so unarguably, so effortlessly, have acquire the mantle of the greatest journalist along the way'. Within academia, over a similar period, the growth and achievements of periodical studies in charting the richness of the Victorian press were also increasing our wider understanding of the immense significance of the medium in which Dickens was writing and publishing. Thus, at the close of the twentieth century, Dickens's work as a journalist as well as his role as editor were objects of widespread and eager appreciation and enquiry.

However, without the contextual evidence available in the columns of the periodicals Dickens 'conducted' and in which his writings appeared, such enquiries could be only very limited. The volumes of *Household Words* and *All the Year Round* are thus a crucial resource but a print re-issue of them has never been considered a viable proposition. Well may we all be grateful, therefore, that under the auspices of the University of Buckingham's *Dickens Journals Online* project, a freely accessible digital edition of both journals is now available. *DJO* offers readers a 'uniform edition' of the totality of Dickens's own contributions to them as well as of the thousands of other contributions by other writers known and still unknown, many of which were carefully copy-edited and altered/improved upon by Dickens himself. That this material is rich in interest to both an existing and a new generation of readers and scholars was amply evident at the project's launch conference in March of this year and is reflected in the selection of essays which follows.

Michael Slater
Birkbeck College, October 2012

John Drew

Journalism is most appreciated when it turns into a nonjournalistic phenomenon.

Barbie Zelizer[1]

IN April 1868, as Michael Slater describes in the definitive biography of recent years, an ill and exhausted Charles Dickens arrived, limping, an hour late, at 'the grand Farewell Banquet given to [him] by the New York press at Delmonico's [restaurant...] with the Pickwickian-looking Horace Greeley, editor of the *New York Tribune* in the chair'.[2] During one of the after-dinner speeches—'the best', Dickens later said, 'he had ever heard'—the essayist and journalist George W. Curtis claimed that nowhere could he and his colleagues (who comprised over 200 representatives of more than thirty American newspapers in different states) 'study the fidelity, the industry, the conscience, the care, and the enthusiasm which are essential to success in our profession more fitly than in the example of the editor of *All the Year Round*'. As far as the much-vaunted power of the press was concerned, Curtis continued:

> [L]et us remember that the foundations of its power as a truly civilizing influence are, first, purity, then honesty, then sagacity and industry [...]. It is impossible to determine the limits or the merits of individual agency, but there is no doubt that among the most vigorous forces in the elevation of the character of the Weekly Press

---

[1] Barbie Zelizer, *Taking Journalism Seriously: News and the Academy* (Thousand Oaks, CA: Sage Publications, 2005), p. 1.
[2] Michael Slater, *Charles Dickens* (New Haven and London: Yale University Press, 2009; repr. 2011), p. 582.

ha[ve] been *Household Words* and *All the Year Round*; and since the beginning of the publication of *Household Words*, the periodical literature of England has been born again.[3]

Grand words, and worth quoting at the start of this collection of new essays on the relationship between those journals and the wider publishing world in which, apparently, they had effected a Renaissance. The confident emphasis on the purity and other transcendent virtues of the press sounds, in the current climate of suspicion and corruption enquiries, incongruous.

In his speech of thanks earlier that evening, Dickens attributed his own professional success '[t]o the wholesome training of severe newspaper work, when I was a very young man', commenting that he had accepted his hosts' invitation 'in loyal sympathy towards a brotherhood which, in the spirit, I have never quitted'.[4] Nor, he could have added, in the flesh: but this, perhaps, would have been to acknowledge the extent to which his status as 'Author' and man of letters was, and always had been, ambivalently bound up with the periodical press, as indivisibly as mind and body. A few years earlier, in a speech to the reconstituted Newspaper Press Fund in London, Dickens had described the relationship in almost psychosomatic terms, explaining how his 'fascination' for his 'old pursuit' of shorthand reporting remained so strong and involuntary within him that '[t]o this present year of my life' while listening to public speeches he would find himself, 'mentally following the speaker in the old way; and sometimes, if you can believe me, I even find my hand going on the tablecloth, taking an imaginary note of it all'.[5] It is not on record whether his hand was tracing marks on the cloth at Delmonico's while Curtis spoke, but it is nonetheless a compelling episode in the life of the writer, combining as it does the developmental arc of Dickens's relationship with America with a kind of alpha and omega of his own career, which had begun nearly four decades before with the listening to, and recording of, speeches and here was at its zenith. Curtis's later comment about the value of Dickens's work to reporters, and 'the numberless instances in which a word from Dickens, by a sort of stenographic system of allusions and characterizations well comprehended by a universal public, saves you whole columns of writing' is eloquent also of

---

[3] Cited in Frederic Hudson, *Journalism in the United States, from 1690 to 1872* (New York: Harper & Brothers, 1873), p. 664.

[4] K. J. Fielding (ed.), *Speeches of Charles Dickens* [1960] (Hemel Hempstead: Harvester Wheatsheaf, 1988), p. 379.

[5] 'Newspaper Press Fund, 20 May 1865', in *Speeches*, p. 348.

the peculiar interplay between the Dickens imaginary and journalistic reality that obtained throughout his writing career, and which persists today in scarcely less perplexing symbiosis.[6] 'The press made Dickens—then Dickens made the press' is the strap-line of the relationship.

*

To those with more critical distance from this cosy reciprocity, the starting premise for this collection—that somehow a single contributor and the entirety of a complex cultural phenomenon can be handled on the same plane of analysis—begs a number of questions. There is surely a kind of epistemological mismatch between our construction of the individual 'Life' and individual agency, and our way of conceptualising an abstraction such as 'The Press', a rhetorically convenient but wide-angled metonymy for a set of social, literary and industrial practices so wide-ranging and impersonal as almost to defy definition.[7] An anonymous reviewer, writing in the influential Whig quarterly *Edinburgh Review* in 1855 (a high water mark in press history) makes as valiant an effort as any:

> In common with everything of signal strength, Journalism is a plant of slow and gradual growth [...]. It has created the want which it supplies. It has obtained paramount influence and authority partly by assuming them, but still more by deserving them. Of all *puissances* in the political world, it is at once the mightiest, the most irresponsible, the best administered, and the least misused. And, taken in its history, position, and relations, it is unquestionably the most grave, noticeable, formidable phenomenon—the greatest FACT of our times.[8]

---

[6] Hudson, *Journalism in the United States*, p. 664; *Speeches*, p. 665. For lively and perceptive recent readings of the relationship between shorthand, voice recording and the norms of parliamentary journalism during Dickens's time in the press gallery, see Ivan Kreilkamp's *Voice and the Victorian Storyteller* (Cambridge: Cambridge University Press, 2005), Chapter 2, pp. 69-88 and Nikki Hessell, *Literary Authors, Parliamentary Reporters* (Cambridge: Cambridge University Press, 2012), Chapter 5, pp. 129-66.

[7] Well illustrated by the excerpts in Paul Fyfe's 'The Random Selection of Victorian New Media', *Victorian Periodicals Review*, 42:1 (2009), 1-23.

[8] [William Rathbone Greg], 'The Newspaper Press', *Edinburgh Review*, No. 102 (October 1855), 470-98 (p. 470), partially excerpted in Andrew King and John

To set Dickens, 'poor little man' (Carlyle's description), on the other side of the see-saw from a Behemoth so described seems almost ill-conceived, until one notes how the passage moves uneasily between Adam Smithian and Shakespearean phrasing before finding its surest footing in a peroration worthy of Thomas Gradgrind.[9] Rhetorically and materially, perhaps Dickens and the Victorian press really are commensurate?

In any case, there are multiple precedents for this approach. Marching through the latter half of twentieth-century Anglophone criticism is a series of well-regarded monographs whose titles begin with the words *Dickens and* … which set the writer up as a supposedly sufficient counterweight for a surprising variety of significant modern concerns: crime, education, charity, money and society, the city, religion, women, popular entertainment, race, and so forth.[10] No other writer of his era has been afforded quite this treatment, and in this bicentenary of the year of his birth, Dickens's stature, not just in the academy but in popular culture, seems as great as if he had been a statesman, premier or crowned prince.[11] Like Shakespeare's Caesar or Mark Antony, he has somehow usurped his position and bestrides the narrow world like a Colossus. As for his widely-recognised catalogue of artistic flaws and personal failings, we have perhaps indulgently concluded,

---

Plunkett, *Victorian Print Media. A Reader* (Oxford: Oxford University Press, 2005), p. 44, and in Alexander Andrews, *The History of British Journalism* (London: Richard Bentley, 1859), pp. 6-7. Both volumes offer exemplary context in which to situate the discussion of *Household Words* and *All the Year Round* presented in this collection.

[9] 'To Jane Welsh Carlyle, 6 July 1844', in *The Collected Letters of Thomas and Jane Welsh Carlyle*, ed. by Charles R. Sanders, Kenneth J. Fielding, Brent E. Kinser and others, 39 vols (London and Durham NC: Duke University Press, 1970-2011), Vol. 18, pp. 108-09; *The Carlyle Letters Online* <DOI: 10.1215/lt-18440706-TC-JWC-0> [accessed 15 July 2012].

[10] Philip Collins, *Dickens and Crime* (London: Macmillan, 1962) and *Dickens and Education* (London: Macmillan, 1963); Norris Pope, *Dickens and Charity* (London: Macmillan, 1978); Grahame Smith, *Dickens, Money and Society* (Cambridge: Cambridge University Press, 1978); F. S. Schwarzbach, *Dickens and the City* (London: Athlone Press, 1979); Dennis Walder, *Dickens and Religion* (London: Allen & Unwin, 1981); Michael Slater, *Dickens and Women* (London: Dent, 1983); Paul Schlicke, *Dickens and Popular Entertainment* (London: Allen & Unwin, 1985); Laura Peters, *Dickens and Race* (Manchester: Manchester University Press, 2012).

[11] Michael Hollington's edited collection *The Reception of Charles Dickens in Europe*, 2 vols (London: Continuum, forthcoming 2013), surveying the writer's critical fortunes across a swathe of continental, non-Anglophone countries and his impact on major European authors, seems likely to give further substance to this impression.

with Lepidus, that his 'faults in him seem as the spots of heaven, / More fiery by night's blackness'.[12] Carlyle, in first promoting in English the notion of the hero as man of letters, may be as much to blame as anyone for this cultural exaltation, in which the collaboration of posterity is refracted back into the perceived brilliance of the originator:

> He, with his copy-rights and copy-wrongs, in his squalid garret, in his rusty coat; ruling (for this is what he does), from his grave, after death, whole nations and generations who would, or would not, give him bread while living,—is a rather curious spectacle! Few shapes of Heroism can be more unexpected.[13]

Lecturing here on Johnson, Rousseau and Burns, Carlyle is clearly aware of the oddity of this exercise of power, and how it inherits its kingdom after death. Carlyle also saw something 'very good and gifted' in 'poor little Dickens', detecting some kind of latent heroism, so that 'in his lot are tragic elements enough capable of unfolding themselves'. This process of posthumous unfolding would appear to be still in full swing, in spite of our supposed post-Romanticism.[14]

There is a further paradox which obtains specifically when the periodical press is the element in which the literary hero must sink or swim. In the mid-nineteenth century, when Dickens 'ruled' as editor, the practice of anonymity was a much contested one (as it is now, in online rather than print media), and particularly widespread in the weekly and daily press. Together with the use of the editorial 'We', the practice was observed, flouted, exploited and misread in ways that increased blood pressures and animosities no less than circulation. Dickens himself blew hot and cold on the matter.[15] Other journalistic norms applied stylistic pressure on reporters and narrators to

---

[12] William Shakespeare, *Julius Caesar* [*c.* 1599], Act I, Sc. 2, 134-35; *Antony and Cleopatra* [1623], Act V, Sc.2. 88-90; *Antony and Cleopatra*, Act I, Sc. 4, 13-14.

[13] Thomas Carlyle, *On Heroes, Hero-Worship, & The Heroic in History. Six Lectures* (London: James Fraser, 1841), p. 250.

[14] Carlyle, *On Heroes*, p. 250; a more nuanced discussion of such terms and attitudes than space here allows can be found in Claudia Moscovici's call-to-arms *Romanticism and Post-Romanticism* (Plymouth: Lexington Books, 2007), Chapters 6 and 7 in particular, and Christine Haynes's survey of the 'historiography of authorship' in 'Reassessing "Genius" in Studies of Authorship: The State of the Discipline', *Book History*, 8 (2005), 287-320 (p. 287).

[15] See Paul Schlicke, 'Our Hour' below, pp. xxx-xxx; also, John M. L. Drew, *Dickens the Journalist* (Houndsmill: Palgrave Macmillan, 2003), pp. 117-118, 151.

render themselves invisible in the service of graphic transcription or the transmission of others' voices, or to surrender individual opinion and idiolect to the priorities of a group ideology and a 'house' style.[16] *Fraser's* 'Maga' (1830-1882) and *Punch* (1841-2002)—to mention only two publications whose composite identities far outweighed the impact of a single contributor—were at the height of their influence during the formative years of Dickens's career, and in his much-quoted 'Shadow' proposal for the weekly journal that became *Household Words*, sent to John Forster in October 1849, he can clearly be seen searching for the nirvana of a narrative perspective that would 'get a character established as it were which any of the writers may maintain without difficulty'.[17] This from a writer who styled himself 'the Inimitable' clearly raises some complex issues for the study of literary distinction, editorial approach and collaborative authorship. Exploration of the tension, then, between the virtues of imitability versus those of inimitability (to present the matter as a simple binary) is particularly appropriate in Dickens's case. We believe that this collection of new enquiries has something helpful to say on this score perhaps greater even than the sum of its individual parts.

*

No student of periodical and authorship studies over the last thirty years will be unfamiliar with the names of some of the scholars contributing to this volume, whose work has defined those fields, both in broad terms and with specific reference to Dickens. Intermingled with the rich harvest of this experience are the green shoots of a rising generation of interdisciplinary

---

[16] See Hessell, *Literary Authors*, p. 169: '[E]ach of the authors examined in this book [Johnson, Coleridge, Hazlitt, Dickens] was, throughout his career, a natural collaborator, always adjusting to the rhythms and routines of different forms of writing and relationships with other people in the literary marketplace as he had done in the [reporters'] gallery'.

[17] To John Forster, [7 October 1849], *The Letters of Charles Dickens*, ed. by Kathleen Tillotson, Graham Storey and others, Pilgrim Edition, 12 vols (Oxford: Clarendon Press, 1965-2002), Vol. V, pp. 622-23. Two outstanding recent studies focus on the 'birth' and 'invention' of Dickens-as-author in a world still dominated in the 1830s and 1840s by publishers, booksellers and the ethos of edited, mediated authorship: see Robert L. Patten, *Charles Dickens and 'Boz': The Birth of the Industrial-Age Author* (Cambridge: Cambridge University Press, 2012), and Robert Douglas-Fairhurst, *Becoming Dickens* (London: Belknap Press, 2011).

scholars, finding new textual and theoretical spaces in which to flourish, thanks in no small part to the schooling of such predecessors. This was a notable and pleasurable feature of the conference that stands behind this collection.[18] Twenty-two of the thirty-six papers read at that conference are present here, rearranged in a way that is intended to balance and brace text against context, appreciation with critique, singularity against conformity, and that acknowledges at least some of the tensions identified above.

Thus, the first of four sections groups wide-ranging synoptic essays examining the publishing scene in the 1850s and 1860s, and the kinds of competition—commercial, aesthetic, ideological—encountered by *Household Words* and *All the Year Round*, the two weekly journals edited by Dickens during these decades.[19] Scrutiny detects rivalry and anxiety of influence in unexpected places, as well as complementarity: between *All the Year Round* and its own younger incarnation; between *Household Words* and its own supplements, substantively discussed here for the first time in print; even between the different formats and periodicity in which material from the same journal was released. It says much about the breadth and range of their appeal, and the strength of their networking amongst widely different communities of readers, that they withstand the searching comparisons instigated here across the gamut of periodical publishing in this period, from 'penny bloods' through to the shilling monthlies and the most august of quarterly reviews.[20]

Section Two considers the journals' handling of a number of central 'Condition of England' questions, and hence their participation in the circulatory systems of discourse surrounding science, public health and social policy, as well as the trademark rhetorical and narrative strategies which the editorial team encouraged. To start with a keynote Dickensian theme, a close

---

[18] 'Charles Dickens and the Mid-Victorian Press, 1850-1870', University of Buckingham, UK, 28-31 March 2012.

[19] See chapters by Joanne Shattock (pp. 1-10), Laurel Brake (pp. 11-33), Louis James (pp. 35-54) and Koenraad Claes (pp. 55-67) below.

[20] Iain Crawford attributes this in part to Dickens's modelling of 'his own version of the role of the periodical editor' on Francis Jeffrey, pioneering editor of *The Edinburgh Review* ('"Faithful Sympathy": Dickens, *The Edinburgh Review*, and Editing *Household Words*', *Victorian Periodicals Review*, 44:1 (2011), 42-68 [p. 45]); Lorna Huett has argued convincingly for a deliberate hybridity in the design, paper texture and formats of the journals Dickens edited, in order to increase their reach in the marketplace ('Among the Unknown Public: *Household Words*, *All the Year Round* and the Mass-Market Weekly Periodical in the Mid-Nineteenth Century', *Victorian Periodicals Review*, 38:1 (2005), 61-82).

reading of a trio of articles on workhouses reveals how specific institutions and policies are opened up to public debate and deliberation. Directing the gaze of readers to the shadowy corners of the workhouse space, dramatising the human suffering within, the articles call for the power of inspection to be placed not with Poor Law authorities but in the hands of a public that implicitly includes the readers of the journal.[21] Parochial British thinking and practice in town planning, whether of parks or slaughterhouses, is frequently exposed, and in spite of their developing suspicion of the expansionist pretensions of the Second French Empire under Napoleon III (1852-70), the journals make frequent trips across the channel to report positively on French alternatives. The Swiftian satire of Dickens's 'A Monument of French Folly', for example, demonstrates a complex reading of nature that combines biblical discourse with contemporary environmental axioms.[22] Rather than romantic iconography, Dickens's description of public gardens and vegetation in Amiens can be seen to endorse rational Enlightenment views—a conclusion that may hold good for much satire in the journals, given the strong influence of *The Examiner* on the editorial team.[23]

Such enquiries argue for the need to scrutinise the complex role of the journals Dickens edited in the multifarious mid-Victorian campaign for sanitary and social reform, above and below the ground and in public and private spaces.[24] *Household Words* in particular adopted a crusading,

---

[21] See Laura Foster (pp. 71-80) below.

[22] [Charles Dickens], 'A Monument to French Folly', *Household Words*, Vol. II, No. 50 (8 March 1851), 553-558; See Ignacio Ramos Gay (pp. 81-94) below.

[23] Dickens hailed Albany Fonblanque, editor of *The Examiner* from 1830 to 1847, as 'another Swift' (To Lady Holland, 11 July 1842, *The Letters of Charles Dickens*, Vol. III, p. 266); he learned the craft of reviewing and leader-writing on the paper. John Forster and Henry Morley were successively editors of the paper 1847-56 and 1861-67 and at the same time crucial figures in the founding and editorial positioning of *Household Words* and the *Household Narrative of Current Events* and, in Morley's case, of *All the Year Round*; see Drew, *Dickens the Journalist*, p. 104 and Chapter 6 as well as Downes, pp. 185-200 below.

[24] In 'What Lies beneath Great Expectations, in "Underground London"' (unpublished panel paper presented at 'Charles Dickens and the Mid-Victorian Press, 1850-1870', University of Buckingham, UK, 28-31 March 2012), Megan Burke Witzleben suggested the viability of a subterranean connection between the series of 'Underground London' papers appearing in *All the Year Round* and the reading experience of parallel instalments of *Great Expectations*. Meanwhile, Bethan Carney addressed the keen interest shown by the journals Dickens edited in inspecting

proselytising stance which was in itself a method for public inspection through the vehicle of the periodical press.[25] Aside from this recurring emphasis on modes of inspection, the 'detection' of disease figures as a powerful narrative and rhetorical device, and one which naturally aligns itself with another area of discussion in which *Household Words* took a pioneering and distinctive role—as Philip Collins long since recognised in *Dickens and Crime*—namely, its presentation of the detective police. The next chapter thus explores the history of relations between Charles Dickens as a journalist and the detective branch of London's Metropolitan police and reflects on their contemporary relevance, in the light of the issues that have given rise to the 2012 Leveson Inquiry into the culture, practice and ethics of the press. It takes the *Household Words* articles by Dickens and Wills as case studies through which to explore the development of one dominant model of police/press relations: in which both journalist and detective bring to the table a set of permanent, mutual needs.[26] The 'Dickens model', depending on mutual esteem and sociability, as well as discreet inducements, remains significant but one to be regarded with suspicion, even if, in Dickens's exceptional case, it can result in some wonderful journalism. These implicitly Foucauldian readings invite further discussion of the extent to which the journals themselves, and not just the novels serialised within their columns, helped constitute a disciplinary regime that policed the domestic sphere, and how hard or soft such forms of inspection and regulation are felt to be.[27]

Standing as a representative of the journals' engagement with the balance of power in world politics, and the expansion of the British Empire, the final chapter in this section tracks a growing interest in China in a social, political and geographical sense. Despite the protestations of *Household Words* staff

---

popular amusements and evaluating their cultural significance, in 'Holding the Mirror up to Joe Whelks: Theatre-Going, Class and the Looking-Glass Curtain'.

[25] See Clare Horrocks (pp. 95-106) below.

[26] See John Tulloch (pp. 107-122) below.

[27] D.A. Miller's seminal *The Novel and the Police* (Berkeley and Los Angeles: University of California Press, 1988) focused on two Wilkie Collins novels serialised in *All the Year Round*, and on Dickens's *Bleak House* (1852-53), serialised simultaneously with *Household Words*, but has little to say about their periodical context; Miller's disciplinary claims for the Victorian novel and the British, as opposed to continental, state are progressively modified by Lisa Rodensky (*Crime in Mind: Criminal Responsibility and the Victorian Novel* [Oxford: Oxford University Press, 2003]) and Lauren Goodlad (*Victorian Literature and The Victorian State* [Baltimore: Johns Hopkins University Press, 2003]), who, of the three critics, has the most perceptive things to say about Victorian and Dickensian journalism.

writers about Chinese stasis and lack of progress, the inward-looking nature
of the Celestial Empire could be both desirable and threatening. The reason
for the journal's ambivalence, far from revealing a disinterest, points instead
to an interest heightened by the threat China posed, albeit from afar, through
a lack of conformity to British expectations of economic development.[28]
This kind of underlying tension inheres in much of the coverage of foreign
affairs provided by Dickens's journals, which, given their global reach, aided
by widespread excerpting and reprinting of articles in the colonial press,
represented an important mapping of ideas of 'Englishness', 'foreignness'
and nationhood at a crucial moment in the economic rise of the West.[29]

Indeed, for the postcolonial historian—whether proclaiming the
triumphs of industrialised free market democracies or tracing reasons for the
progressive disillusion of Asian thinkers with the mindset of Western
modernity across the nineteenth and twentieth century—there are numerous
avenues of research to be pursued in this area.[30] Theses wait to be written on
the representation of Italy, America, Australia, India, Turkey, no less than
France, in *Household Words* and *All the Year Round*. Useful work is already
underway on the sentimentalised presentation of Polish affairs in *All the Year
Round* leading up to and following the failure of the January Uprising in
1863.[31] At the same time, however, analysis of separate series of articles
about Russia and Russian life in these journals is not necessarily going to
reveal a consistent presentation of brutal Cossack enemies tyrannising over
an innocent, oppressed neighbour. Mixing messages is partly what a
miscellany does. For all that Dickens is held to have been a tight-fisted hand
at the editorial grindstone, the collective scrutiny of the contents of the
journals which this collection carries forward, is starting to reveal how much
room there was for the play of opinions and the voicing of discrete,
sometimes jostling, occasionally jarring, perspectives. A weekly magazine
with over 450 contributors could scarcely, over a twenty-year period,

---

[28] See Hannah Lewis-Bill (pp. 123-132) below.
[29] An argument ably developed by Sabine Clemm in *Dickens, Journalism, and
Nationhood: Mapping the World in Household Words* (London: Routledge, 2009).
[30] See, for example, Niall Ferguson's *Civilization: The West and the Rest* (London: Allen
Lane, 2011) and Pankaj Mishra's revisionary *From the Ruins of Empire: The Revolt against
the West and the Remaking of Asia* (London: Allen Lane, 2012).
[31] Aleksandra Budrewicz-Beratan "'The Ghost from Poland Shrugged his
Shoulders...": Poland in *All the Year Round* and *Household Words*', unpublished panel
paper presented at 'Charles Dickens and the Mid-Victorian Press, 1850-1870',
University of Buckingham, UK, 28-31 March 2012.

ventriloquise a single set of views, and some of Dickens's more despotic outbursts in letters to contributors are—as Shu Fang Lai has cogently argued—to be read more as tokens of executive frustration than any real intent to impose ideological uniformity.[32] The editor (with a small *e*) may attempt to streamline and merge the flow of letterpress, but the best Editors are—perhaps unconsciously—aware that the latter's eddies and counter-currents may be exactly what attracts an individual reader.

With this in mind, Section Three sets out to give some sense of how different contributors responded to the challenge of working for magazines so conspicuously 'Conducted by' the most popular writer of their generation: the hierarchy and power relations; the sense of unequal partnership and rewards, and of gratified ambition compounded with frustration; the struggle to assert a personal rather than a choric voice; to write to taste rather than to order—all become apparent in these reconstructions of contributor/editor exchanges, even if few contributors dared, like Andrew Halliday, to make it the overt substance of a submission.[33] The journals show a sophisticated awareness of the ironies and contradictions involved in the mass production of the personal touch that was crucial to their market success, so the first two chapters in this section explore how *Household Words* and *All the Year Round* represent the literary profession and the models of authorship—industrialised, collaborative, creative—they reproduced.[34] Chapters then follow on five writers, focalised through their contributions and concerns: Harriet Martineau, George Augustus Sala, Henry Morley, Henry Vizetelly and Fitzjames O'Brien (Elizabeth Gaskell being considered in a postscript to the first essay in Section One).[35] The last two essays in the section present cases for the attribution of articles whose authors are not known from any extant external evidence, and throw into relief the important forensic, not less than theoretical, work that remains to be done on the body of anonymous work in both magazines and *All the Year Round* in particular. The ascription of articles to O'Brien, for example, is patiently and diligently

---

[32] See Shu Fang Lai, 'Fact or Fancy: What Can We Learn about Dickens from His Periodicals *Household Words* and *All the Year Round*?', *Victorian Periodicals Review*, 34:1 (2001), 41-53.

[33] See [Andrew Halliday], 'My Pantomime', *All the Year Round*, Vol. X, No. 238 (14 November 1863), 272-83.

[34] See Helen Mckenzie (pp. 135-145) and Jasper Schelstraete (pp. 147-156) below.

[35] See essays by Iain Crawford (pp. 157-173), Cathy Waters (pp. 175-184), Daragh Downes (pp. 185-200), David Parker (pp. 201-209) and Pete Orford (pp. 211-231) below.

carried out by traditional qualitative methods, as much as by quantitative analysis. In attribution studies, the latter is increasingly achieved through computer-based approaches such as computational stylistics, and not the least exciting consequence of having *Household Words* and *All the Year Round* in an accurate digital form lies in the ongoing application and interrogation of such techniques.[36]

The half-dozen contributors profiled here are little more than a handful; we can only refer readers curious for more information to the scrupulously-researched profiles in Anne Lohrli's *Household Words* [...] *Table of Contents, List of Contributors and Their Contributions* (1973), a generous proportion of which are reproduced on the *Dickens Journals Online* website, by kind permission of the University of Toronto Press; or, for penetrating discussion of the contributor/editor relationship in the case of Wilkie Collins and Dickens, to Lillian Nayder's *Unequal Partners* (2002).[37] Other figures, central and peripheral, are coming into clearer focus, thanks, perhaps, to the increased accessibility of the journals. John Hollingshead and Charles Allston Collins, for example, were 'regulars' on *Household Words* and *All the Year Round* respectively, each with distinctive and eccentric reporting personae, whose strategies of bearing journalistic witness were nevertheless central to the journals' forms of engagement with the contemporary scene. Published studies of their roles and writings for these journals specifically are to be looked for.[38] The same could be said of Eliza Lynn Linton, Robert Bulwer

---

[36] See John Drew and Hugh Craig, 'Did Dickens write "Temperate Temperance"?: An Attempt to Identify Authorship of an Anonymous Article in *All the Year Round*,' *Victorian Periodicals Review*, 44:3 (2011), 267-90, for a preliminary report on the method. A series of further tests is underway.

[37] Anne Lohrli, *Household Words: A Weekly Journal 1850-1859, Conducted By Charles Dickens. Table of Contents, List of Contributors and their Contributions* (Toronto: University of Toronto Press, 1973); Lillian Nayder, *Unequal Partners: Charles Dickens, Wilkie Collins, and Victorian Authorship* (Ithaca, NY: Cornell University Press 2002); John Sutherland spoke eloquently on the same writerly rivalry in 'Great Expectations and All the Year Round: What did Dickens Learn from Wilkie?' in an unpublished plenary presented at 'Charles Dickens and the Mid-Victorian Press, 1850-1870', University of Buckingham, UK, 28-31 March 2012.

[38] Fionnuala Dillane discussed 'John Hollingshead on the Author and his Audience: Embodied Authenticity versus "Counterfeit Presentment"' and Sarah Dougherty tackled C. A. Collins in '"It Is *Not* A Fish, and It Does *Not* Talk": "Our Eye-Witness and Empathetic Anthropomorphism' in unpublished panel papers presented at 'Charles Dickens and the Mid-Victorian Press, 1850-1870', University of Buckingham, UK, 28-31 March 2012

Lytton (whose verse contributions to *All the Year Round* turn out to be substantial), Adelaide Anne Procter, the enigmatic R. H. Horne and numerous others.[39] Last, but far from least, in so far as the day-to-day management and ordering of issues is concerned, William Henry Wills merits far greater attention than this volume is able to offer. Often portrayed as the anchor and engine of the editorial team, punctual, steady, unimaginative—Charlie Watts to Dickens's Jagger—Wills was a hugely versatile and skilled literary craftsman, whose collected contributions, republished and otherwise, likewise await serious academic attention. Again, Anne Lohrli has pointed the way, although she omits from her biographical profile of Wills the tantalising hint of a dark side reported by Henry Vizetelly in his autobiography, namely that as a young man Wills had 'drifted into literature, under the wing' of Margaret Wilson (1797-1846), 'a magazine poetess of the period, whose patronage he ill-requited in a fashion that imperilled his liberty, and something like a cloud hung over him for several years afterwards'.[40] Speculation, as they say, runs rife.

The man Wills worked for, by contrast, has had his dark sides explored and exposed by commentators with great assiduity, and has emerged from under various critical and biographical clouds with almost added lustre. The fourth and final section of this volume presents essays that tackle the 'Chief' (as he was referred to by both Hollingshead and George Dolby) as a journalist and man of letters who by 1850 was already difficult to 'know' as anything other than a media creation,[41] an unstable projection every bit as

---

[39] Peter Stiles discussed 'Truth and Mendacity in "The Manchester Marriage", by Elizabeth Gaskell' (Gaskell's contribution to 'A House to Let', the Extra Christmas Number of *Household Words* for 1858) in an unpublished panel paper presented at 'Charles Dickens and the Mid-Victorian Press, 1850-1870', University of Buckingham, UK, 28-31 March 2012.

[40] Henry Vizetelly, *Glances Back through Seventy Years*, 2 vols (London: Kegan Paul, Trench, Trübner, 1893), Vol. I, p. 247. This nugget appears instead in Lohrli's profile of Wilson's daughter, Florence (born *c.* 1823), see Lohrli, p. 470. See also Sandra Spencer, 'The Indispensable Mr Wills', *Victorian Periodicals Review*, 21:4 (1988), 145-51 and [John M. L. Drew], 'Wills, William Henry', in *The Oxford Reader's Companion to Dickens*, ed. by Paul Schlicke (Oxford: Oxford University Press, 1999; repr. 2011), pp. 598-600.

[41] See Hollingshead's 'Fifty Years of *Household Words*' in the *Household Words* 'Jubilee Number' No. 26 (May 1900), 1-2, cited in Drew, *Dickens the Journalist*, p. 150; George Dolby, *Charles Dickens as I Knew Him: The Story of the Reading Tours in Great Britain and America, 1866-1870* (New York: Charles Scribner's Sons, 1912), Chapter 1 'My First Tour with the Chief' and throughout.

elusive as the mysterious 'Shadow' in his letter to Forster: 'a kind of semi-omniscient, omnipresent intangible creature [...] a sort of previously unthought-of Power going about'.[42] For all that, some stability can be found by, as Curtis had done in his eulogy at Delmonico's, stressing how a fiction-writer can be thought of as a kind of reporter-at-large, operating on a similar set of journalistic principles. The first chapter here thus re-emphasises the heavy traffic and crisscrossing between fiction and non-fiction in Dickens's reporting of city slums and the continuity of commitment in his work across the decades to their public airing—a commitment amplified but not reinvented in *Household Words* and *All the Year Round*.[43] From this perspective, Dickens's Christmas Books of the hungry forties, such as *A Christmas Carol* and *The Chimes*, can be read as tracts on urban poverty, and by the same token, the fanciful stories in the 'Extra Christmas Numbers' of *Household Words* and *All the Year Round* (1850-67)—themselves multi-authored within a framework, like a newspaper—can be viewed journalistically. The 'conscientious approach' and 'compassion for the poor' evinced by the Dickensian 'Christmas Number' (as opposed, say, to the satirical playfulness if not cynicism of *Punch*) towards this widely-imitated mid-Victorian press phenomenon, is noteworthy.[44]

The following chapter takes up the conscientious and compassionate orientation of the Christmas numbers by reading Dickens's own contribution to *The Seven Poor Travellers* (Christmas 1854) within the context of the broader press response to the Crimean War, particularly that of *Household Words* itself. In telling the story of Richard Doubledick and his veneration for Captain Taunton, Dickens is seen to emphasise the virtue of male bonds, capable of overcoming a long history of national antagonism and reworking a private desire for vengeance, in a way that allows for a complex response to the cry

---

[42] *The Letters of Charles Dickens*, Vol. V, pp. 622-23.

[43] See Judith Flanders (pp. 235-244) below. 'What are novelists?' Curtis had asked; 'They are men commissioned by nature to see human life and the infinite play of human character, and write reports on them' (cited in Hudson, *Journalism in the United States*, p. 663).

[44] Olivia Malfait (Ghent University), 'Serious or Satire? Victorian Christmas Portrayals in *Household Words*, *All the Year Round* and *Punch*', unpublished panel paper presented at 'Charles Dickens and the Mid-Victorian Press, 1850-1870,' University of Buckingham UK, 28-31 March 2012; see also [John M. L. Drew], 'Christmas Issues', *Dictionary of Nineteenth-Century Journalism in Britain and Ireland*, ed. by Marysa Demoor and Laurel Brake (London: Academia Press/British Library, 2009), pp. 117-18.

for administrative reform of the armed forces and civil service that the war was already provoking.[45] In his own leaders for *Household Words* in 1854 and 1855, some of Dickens's most searing invective is reserved for administrative incompetence and corruption in national life, yet these articles are interspersed with charming familiar and semi-autobiographical essays from the editor's pen. Yet titles for both kinds of paper often begin with the possessive 'Our' ('Our French Watering Place', 'Our Commission') and this discrepancy leads to another wide-ranging discussion, both stylistic and ideological, of Dickens's complex use of the editorial plural.[46] From a classical rhetorical perspective, the striking differences in approach might be containable within the Horatian and Juvenalian traditions of satire, but in Dickens the ironic undercutting of positions through parody and imitation is such that, often, no such scholastic division is possible. 'We' remains as elusive and shadowed a concept as 'I.'

Part of the problem—part of the richness of the problem—lies in Dickens's refusal to co-opt his writing self to any pre-existing social or community grouping, even, it can be argued, when he appears to set off firmly to promote or denounce a particular cause. As a journalist writing in *All The Year Round* of which he was both editor and owner, Dickens was a free electron, and never freer, perhaps, than when writing under the variable (dis)guise of 'The Uncommercial Traveller'. Accordingly, the next chapter proposes an important and highly original take on Dickens's methods in this collection of essays, and how they attempt to bring private and highly idiosyncratic perception into conversations with larger aggregations and categories, in order to produce something like an account of the nation. In this reading, the 'Uncommercial' can operate anywhere on a spectrum between Banksy and the Registrar General, and in doing so, lays down a challenge to both governments and journalists that is still highly relevant.[47]

This powerful flexibility could be attributable to our sense that conscientiousness and compassion in Dickens coexist with anger and aggression and the way the latter seem to sublimate into the atmosphere of

---

[45] See Holly Furneaux (pp. 245-259) below. The leader in *The Times* of 25 December 1854 ran: 'If we have transported England to the Crimea in one sense, we have not in the sense of English humanity, prudence, mechanical genius, and variety of resources. Will it be believed that the authorities in the Crimea will neither take proper care of the sick and wounded themselves, nor allow others to do it for them?' (p. 6).
[46] See Schlicke, 'Our Hour', (pp. 261-295) below.
[47] See Robert L. Patten (pp. 277-295) below.

his writing projects in similarly complex ways. The attitude of the journals he edited to a range of contemporary developments was importantly inflected by a palpable anger with history: for example, at the treatment of the common man under the twin tyrants of absolute monarchy and the unreformed Church. Purchasers of the four-penny *Household Words Almanac* in 1856 may have been surprised to find, amongst the calendars of dates and holidays and homely medical prescriptions for how to dress children in warm weather, etc., standing items ironically entitled 'Chronicles of Progress' (which reveal the barbarities of bygone ages) and 'Remarkable Predictions' (which modern times completely contradict). As Koenraad Claes points out, Henry Morley probably drafted these, but the 'ideological programme' (below, p. 66) is characteristic of the *Household Words* stable—and one that the parent journal had set out at some length in the forty-five instalments of Dickens's curiously overlooked foray into history-writing, *A Child's History of England*. Serialised between 1851 and 1853, the first instalment (and the one most obviously written in simplified language for younger persons) occupied the 'leader' slot below the masthead. Dickens's authorship was revealed after only the fourteenth instalment.[48] The penultimate essay in this collection explores both the genesis and the (generous?) anger of *A Child's History*, which functioned almost as a third supplement to *Household Words*, yet was contained within it. Previous criticism has, perhaps unjustly, neglected or decried the work, but when it is restored to its periodical context, it develops ramifications and resonances. After all, Samuel Johnson, with characteristic ponderousness, had dubbed journalists 'diurnal historiographers', so the link with Dickens's other journalistic ventures is perhaps now easier to see.[49]

Our final offering shows the master-minder of both *Household Words* and *All the Year Round* in all his complexity and mass, from a radically different

---

[48] An advertisement for the first volume of the *History*, 'to be completed in three volumes' by publishers Bradbury and Evans, followed the 14th instalment on *Household Words*, Vol. V, No. 107 (10 April 1852), p. 92.

[49] Drew (*Dickens the Journalist*, p. 126) blithely dismisses the Child's History as 'all too puerile'; few critics apart from Barry Westburg ('"His Allegorical Way of Expressing It": Civil War and Psychic Conflict in *Oliver Twist* and *A Child's History*', *Studies in the Novel*, 6 [1974], 27-37) and Rosemary Jann ('Fact, Fiction, and Interpretation in *A Child's History of England*', *Dickens Quarterly*, 4:4 [1987], 199-205) deal with it in detail. Johnson uses the expression in *The Rambler*, No. 145 (6 August 1751) and claims '[a] journalist is an historian' in the opening manifesto he was commissioned to write in 1758 for [*Payne's*] *Universal Chronicle* (1758-60), and in which his own 'Idler' essays appeared; see *Samuel Johnson, The Major Works*, ed. by Donald Greene (Oxford: Oxford University Press, 1984; repr. 2000), pp. 231, 544.

perspective.[50] All through the volume (and appropriately for one that takes the physical materiality of the Victorian press very seriously), questions of composition, control, form, representation and imposition have been raised and discussed. The osmotic exchange between the public and the domestic spheres through the medium of print has been crucial. The last word here is therefore given to an expert analysis of how Dickens's painful separation from his wife became matter for comment in the newspaper press all over the English-speaking world. Spreading all over Britain within a few days of Dickens's supposedly slander-scotching announcement (the *Household Words* leader titled 'Personal'), news of the scandal crossed the Atlantic in less than a fortnight, and spread far and wide, before returning in various altered forms.[51] Now, the shadowy editor whose publications had trespassed on hidden byways of public life (think Charles Foster 'Citizen' Kane), the media owner whose publications had intruded into the personal spaces of thousands of individuals, in fictional form (think News International), was himself in the press equivalent of the dock, and vulnerable to media intrusion of his own privacy. From this unromantic perspective, the affair reads like the end of the tale of the biter bitten. For believers in the heroic man of letters, however, mindful of the reasons for the closure of *Household Words* and the founding of *All the Year Round*—it turns out to be just the beginning.

---

[50] See Patrick Leary (pp. 305-325) below.
[51] Charles Dickens, 'Personal', *Household Words*, Vol. XVII, No. 429 (12 June 1858), 601.

Map

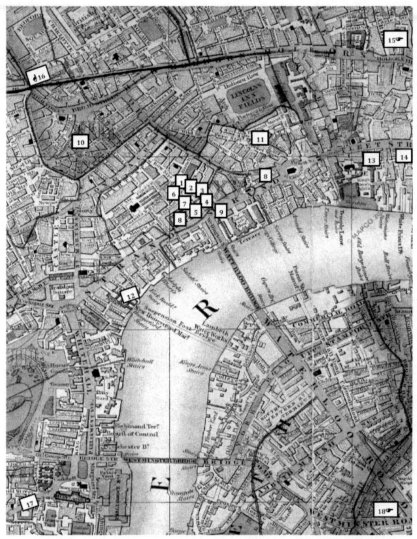

MAP: Cheek by jowl: The London periodical press and London's poor

SECTION 1

Household Words and the 'Community of Print' in the 1850s

Joanne Shattock

ARISING from her research on the print culture network that existed on Wellington Street, near the Strand, Mary L. Shannon has noted that from the *Household Words* office at 16 Wellington Street North, Dickens could see the office of the weekly *Athenaeum* (1828-1921) at Number 14, the office of the *Morning Post* (1772-1937) at Number 18, that of the *Examiner* (1808-81), edited by his friend John Forster at Number 5, and the office-cum-residence of G. W. M. Reynolds, proprietor of *Reynolds's Miscellany* (1846-69), at Number 7. Situated nearby were Lacy's Theatrical Bookshop and the Lyceum theatre. The location of the journal's newly-established office was obviously congenial, apart perhaps from the proximity of Reynolds, combining as it did Dickens's literary and theatrical interests. As Shannon observed, it gave substance to the reference in 'A Preliminary Word' in the first issue of *Household Words* (30 March 1850) to those 'tillers of the field into which we now come [...] whose high usefulness we readily acknowledge and whose company it is an honour to join'.[1] The inhabitants of Wellington Street were his fellow writers, editors and proprietors, part of the 'community of print' to which his new weekly miscellany was to be a spectacularly successful addition.

Shannon could have gone on to point out the offices of Bradbury and Evans, the publishers of *Household Words* and the proprietors of *Punch* (1841-2002), at nearby Bouverie Street, where the weekly dinners of the *Punch* staff

---

[1] [Charles Dickens], 'A Preliminary Word', *Household Words*, Vol. I, No. 1 (30 March 1850), 1-2 (pp. 1-2). I am grateful to Mary L. Shannon for this insight in her paper, 'Dickens's Networks on Wellington St. Strand', presented at the British Association for Victorian Studies conference at the University of Sheffield in September 2011. See below, p. 44, for Dickens's reasons for distancing himself from Reynolds, and the Map on p. xxiii for a number of these landmarks.

were held. On the other side of the Strand, at 142, the radical publisher John Chapman was soon to enter into negotiations to purchase the *Westminster Review* (1824-1914) in 1851. Moving further towards the City, on Fleet Street, Eliza Cook had established the office from which she conducted *Eliza Cook's Journal* from 1849 to 1854. In the other direction, across Trafalgar Square at 22 Pall Mall, the Edinburgh publisher William Blackwood had opened his London office in 1840. *Blackwood's Magazine* (1817-1980) continued to be edited and printed in Edinburgh but from 1852, when his son John Blackwood became head of the firm as well as editor of the magazine, the London office became increasingly important for its dealings with London-based authors and contributors. The Edinburgh firm of W. & R. Chambers had opened a London office in 1842 for the same reason. Elsewhere in London in 1850 G. H. Lewes and Thornton Hunt were raising funds to establish their radical weekly *The Leader* (1850-60; see **Map**, p. xxiii).[2]

Not all of these publications were direct competitors of *Household Words* but their proliferation in the early 1850s emphasises two important points: the propitious timing of *Household Words* and the concentration of journal production in London. In his 1976 study of *Victorian Novelists and Publishers*, John Sutherland identifies the 1850s as a period in which improvements in communications (the railways and the penny post), the technological advances in printing and book production, the increase in the spending power of the middle classes and the newly acquired literacy of the lower classes came together to produce ideal circumstances for fiction publishing.[3] The same could be said for periodical publishing, and in particular for periodicals selling for under a shilling.

---

[2] *The Small Edition of the Post Office London Directory, 1852,* 53rd edn. (London: F. Kelly [1851]) also gives the following publishers and periodicals operating on or near Wellington Street: *Gardeners' Chronicle & Agricultural Gazette Newspaper* (5 Upper Wellington St), *United Service Gazette* (6 Wellington St), *Spectator* (9 Wellington St), the *Leader* (10 Wellington St), William Tweedie, publisher (11 Wellington St), *Mirror of the Time* (11A Wellington St North), *Guardian Newspaper* (12 Wellington St North), *Morning Chronicle* & *Evening Chronicle* Office (332 Strand); see the *Historical Directories Searchable Digital Library*, a University of Leicester Project (www.historical directories.org). Following the Metropolitan Management Act (1855, Wellington Street was re-numbered in April 1860; prior to this it had been divided into Wellington Street South and Wellington Street North (overlapping with 'Upper Wellington Street', itself a renaming of Charles Street which, by 1844, had become notorious for brothels), with inconsistent numbering.

[3] J. A. Sutherland, *Victorian Novelists and Publishers* (London: Athlone Press, 1976), pp. 63-65.

Another factor in the success of *Household Words* was the availability of writers, both male and female, professionals who actively sought paid work from the press and expected to earn a living from it. A frequently cited article by G. H. Lewes in *Fraser's Magazine* (1830-82) for March 1847, 'The Condition of Authors in England, Germany, and France', underlined a gradual change in literary life. 'Literature has become a profession', Lewes wrote. 'It is a means of subsistence, almost as certain as the bar or the church'. 'The real cause', he went on, was 'the excellence and abundance of periodical literature'.[4]

I have argued elsewhere that this professional literary life, which brought with it social respectability and some financial security, operated through intricate networks of writers, editors, publishers and proprietors, networks that were more elaborate and extensive at mid-century than in earlier periods. They also included more women writers. The way *Household Words* tapped into these networks is one of the aspects of the journal I want to explore.[5]

As Michael Slater points out in the headnote to 'A Preliminary Word' in the second volume of the *Dent Uniform Edition of Dickens' Journalism*, Dickens wanted to distinguish *Household Words* from mass circulation publications like *Reynolds's Miscellany*, and *Lloyd's Weekly Newspaper* (1842-1931) with their 'villainous' [his word] sensational fiction on the one hand and *Chambers's Edinburgh Journal* (1832-1956) on the other.[6] *Chambers's*, Dickens wrote, was 'a somewhat cast-iron and utilitarian publication as congenial to me, generally, as the brown paper packages in which Ironmongers keep Nails'.[7] Yet as both John Drew and John Sutherland note, *Chambers's* was in many ways the inspiration for *Household Words*, its influence apparent in the physical similarity of the layout of their double column pages, a fact which Drew

---

[4] [G. H. Lewes], 'The Condition of Authors in England, Germany, and France', *Fraser's Magazine for Town and Country*, Vol. XXXV, No. 207 (March 1847), 285-95, (p. 288).

[5] Joanne Shattock, 'Professional Networking: Masculine and Feminine', *Victorian Periodicals Review*, 44:2 (Summer 2011), 128-40.

[6] *The Dent Uniform Edition of Dickens's Journalism*, ed. by Michael Slater and others, 4 vols (London: J. M. Dent, 1994-2000), Vol. II, pp. 75-76.

[7] To Mrs S. C. Hall, 23 April 1844, *The Letters of Charles Dickens*, ed. by Kathleen Tillotson, Graham Storey and others, Pilgrim Edition, 12 vols (Oxford: Clarendon Press, 1965-2002), Vol. IV, pp. 110-11

attributes to W. H. Wills having been formerly assistant editor of *Chambers's*.[8] Unlike the *Penny Magazine* (1832-45), founded at the same time, *Chambers's* contained fiction and it aspired to reach a middle-class as well as an artisan and lower-middle-class audience.

There were other cheap and highly successful weeklies that serialised fiction. The *London Journal; and Weekly Record of Literature, Science and Art* (1845-1928) was a penny publication with a circulation of half a million at its peak in the 1850s. Some of its fiction was original, but it also published reprints of older novelists including Walter Scott. *The Family Herald or Useful Information and Amusement for the Million* (1842-1940), its chief competitor, favoured historical romances and domestic fiction, most of it anonymous or pseudonymous. Both publications were more respectable than those published by Lloyd and Reynolds, but the weekly penny magazine, or 'penny novel journal' as Wilkie Collins referred to them in his article 'The Unknown Public' (21 August 1858), was a tainted form.[9] Margaret Oliphant identified the *Family Herald* and the *London Journal* by name in her *Blackwood's* article 'The Byways of Literature: Reading for the Million' published in the same month as 'The Unknown Public' and making the same points as Collins.[10]

Weeklies directed at a similar readership but with a social agenda had a different reputation. *Howitt's Journal* (1847-48), a self-proclaimed magazine of 'popular progress' along with its precursor, the *People's Journal* (1846-48), sold for one-and-a-half pence and contained fiction by Elizabeth Gaskell, Harriet Martineau and Eliza Meteyard and contributions by Samuel Smiles. The Howitts were a well-connected literary couple at the centre of several networks. Mary Howitt in particular was known for her patronage of younger women writers. In 1849 she had recruited Harriet Martineau and Elizabeth Gaskell, two writers whom Dickens also set out to attract to *Household Words*, to write for *Sartain's Union Magazine* (1848-52), a Philadelphia-based monthly. In the same year, 1849, she was busy recruiting

---

[8] See John Drew, '*Household Words*', in *Dictionary of Nineteenth-Century Journalism*, ed. by Laurel Brake and Marysa Demoor (Ghent and London: Academia Press and the British Library, 2009), pp. 292-3 and John Sutherland, *The Longman Companion to Victorian Fiction*, 2nd edn (Harlow: Pearson Education, 2009), p. 111.

[9] [Wilkie Collins], 'The Unknown Public', *Household Words*, Vol. XVIII, No. 439 (21 August 1858), 217-22.

[10] [Margaret Oliphant], 'The Byways of Literature: Reading for the Million', *Blackwood's Edinburgh Magazine*, Vol. LXXXIV, No. 514 (August 1858), 200-16, repr. in *Selected Works of Margaret Oliphant*, Vol. I, ed. by Joanne Shattock (London: Pickering & Chatto, 2011), pp. 179-202.

writers for her protégé Eliza Cook's new journal. In the case of Elizabeth Gaskell, this time she was unsuccessful. *Eliza Cook's Journal* sold for between a penny and a penny-and-a-half, and published work by Julia Kavanagh, Samuel Smiles, Eliza Meteyard and Cook herself. *Sharpe's London Magazine* (1845-70), promising 'Entertainment and Instruction for General Reading', was aimed at the same readers as *Household Words*, 'the middle and lower walks of society'. It was a sixteen-page weekly, containing fiction and selling for a halfpenny, but it became a shilling monthly in 1848 (the title changed to *Sharpe's London Journal*. It was edited for a while by the novelist Frank Smedley, and serialised several of his novels, and then by Anna Maria Hall, wife of Samuel Carter Hall.[11]

Like the Howitts, Anna Maria Hall and her husband were very well networked. Anna Maria actively recruited writers for *Sharpe's*, for *Chambers's Journal*—she was responsible for recruiting Dinah Mulock, another *Household Words* contributor, for *Chambers's*—and she wrote for it herself. Later she recruited writers for the *St. James's Magazine* (1861-1900) which she edited between 1861 and 1868.

Many of the writers for *Household Words* were drawn from these existing networks. In her analysis of the contributors to *Household Words*, Anne Lohrli divided the 390 known contributors into several groups. The first was the inner core of staff comprising the sub-editor, W. H. Wills, R. H. Horne, Henry Morley, who wrote the largest number of articles of all (300), and Wilkie Collins. After that there were some thirty-five regulars, not all of whom remained for the full nine years of the weekly's run. But the majority of contributions to *Household Words*, and this was Lohrli's important point, came from little known writers who sent in articles unprompted, just as they might have done to *Chambers's Journal*, *Sharpe's*, *Bentley's Miscellany* (1837-68), *Ainsworth's Magazine* (1842-54) or to *Fraser's Magazine*.[12]

In terms of the invitations he extended to individuals, Dickens's judgement was astute. Elizabeth Gaskell was known to him through Forster and through the Chapman and Hall connection. She had in fact been introduced to Chapman and Hall by William Howitt. The Howitts, whom he knew from their *Journal*, were also invited to write for *Household Words*. They were both flattered and grateful although in the end they did not contribute

---

[11] Graham Law, '*Sharpe's London Magazine*', in *Dictionary of Nineteenth-Century Journalism*, pp. 568-69 (p. 569).
[12] Anne Lohrli, *Household Words: A Weekly Journal 1850-1859, Conducted By Charles Dickens. Table of Contents, List of Contributors and their Contributions* (Toronto: University of Toronto Press, 1973), pp. 24-34.

much. In 1850 Harriet Martineau was an established figure on the literary scene and like Gaskell was an inspired choice. Gaskell proved to be surprisingly adept in responding to the challenge of writing for the miscellany, although, as is well known, she was uncomfortable with the demands of weekly serialisation. Others like Geraldine Jewsbury, Eliza Lynn (later Linton) and Dinah Mulock (later Craik) wrote occasionally. All three were sound choices. Dickens also invited Tom Taylor and Douglas Jerrold, both of whom refused.

Why then was *Household Words* so successful, in comparison with the other journals, many of whom had some of the same contributors? The two reasons usually given are the quality of the original fiction—novels and stories by Gaskell, Wilkie Collins, Lynn Linton, Harriet Parr and James Payn, all of whom were, or would become, significant writers, and of course fiction by Dickens. By contrast, much of the fiction in the competing magazines was anonymous, some of it was reprinted from earlier periods, and much of it was by little-known writers.

The second reason was Dickens himself. He was a celebrity editor of a kind that had not been seen before. None of the other eponymous journals had a 'Conductor' with such pulling power, certainly not Douglas Jerrold, or the Howitts or Eliza Cook. Writers wanted to be published in Dickens's journal, and then to republish their essays, stories and articles, as having been 'first published in *Household Words*'. The office received, according to report, 'whole sacks' of material, much of which was rejected, all of which had to be read and sifted.[13] Reading Michael Slater's account of the effort Dickens put into his journal—rewriting or altering many of the articles submitted, keeping a hold on the proceedings, including the finances, while also writing *David Copperfield* (1849-50), *Bleak House* (1852-53), *Little Dorrit* (1855-57), undertaking public readings and amateur theatricals, one can only marvel at his energy.

In her recent book, *Women's Authorship and Editorship in Victorian Culture* (2011), Beth Palmer argues that Dickens, as the 'Conductor' of his two journals, was regarded as a role model by the novelists Mary Elizabeth Braddon, Ellen Wood and Florence Marryat when they took charge of *Belgravia* (1867-99), *Argosy* (1865-1901) and *London Society* (1862-98) respectively in the 1860s and 1870s. Such was his prestige as the celebrity novelist-cum-editor she suggests, that these women novelist-editors looked

---

[13] Percy Fitzgerald, *Memories of Charles Dickens, with An Account of 'Household Words' and 'All the Year Round' and of the Contributors Thereto* (Bristol: J. W. Arrowsmith, 1913), p. 4.

back to him, rather than to the more recent successes of George Smith's *Cornhill Magazine* (1860-1975) under Thackeray and his successors or to *Macmillan's Magazine* (1859-1907). They sought to emulate Dickens's 'performance' as editor and the control he exerted over the form, content and style of *Household Words* and *All the Year Round*. Palmer also suggests that Samuel Beeton's emphasis on 'the editress', in other words Mrs Beeton, in the *Englishwoman's Domestic Magazine* (1852-79) from 1854 onward, was another attempt to replicate Dickens's all embracing 'conducting' of *Household Words*.[14]

Lohrli makes the point that the non-fictional content of *Household Words* did not differ in subject from that of other general miscellanies, and that in its social purpose it resembled the content of publications such as *Eliza Cook's Journal*, or *Chambers's Journal*. After reading Catherine Waters' *Commodity Culture in Dickens's Household Words*, I would add a third factor in the success of *Household Words*: the innovative nature of its non-fiction. Waters provides a compelling 'tour' or 'excursion' through these articles— many of them by *Household Words* regulars like Sala, Morley and Martineau— demonstrating their imaginative take on their subjects and the virtuoso performances of the writers.[15]

Household Words copied one particularly important feature of *Chambers's Edinburgh Journal*. Like the earlier weekly, it was a hybrid, available in weekly issues of twenty-four double-column pages selling for two pence (*Chambers's* had sixteen pages and sold for one-and-a-half pence) and in nine-penny monthly numbers with wrappers, and more substantial bound biannual volumes, the last two aimed at middle-class purchasers and readers.

Lorna Huett, in her illuminating article 'Among the Unknown Public: *Household Words*, *All the Year Round* and the Mass-Market Weekly Periodical in the Mid-Nineteenth Century', shows how in the format of his periodical Dickens carefully hedged his bets—deliberately choosing the cheaper paper, the dense type face and crowded double-column page layout of the cheap weeklies, but also the smaller crown octavo size of the more expensive periodicals.[16] By means of the physical appearance of the miscellany and by

---

[14] Beth Palmer, *Women's Authorship and Editorship in Victorian Culture: Sensational Strategies* (Oxford: Oxford University Press, 2011), pp. 18-48.

[15] Catherine Waters, *Commodity Culture in Dickens's Household Words: The Social Life of Goods* (Aldershot: Ashgate, 2008).

[16] Lorna Huett, 'Among the Unknown Public: *Household Words*, *All the Year Round* and the Mass-Market Weekly Periodical in the Mid-Nineteenth Century', *Victorian Periodicals Review*, 38:1 (Spring 2005), 61-82.

its carefully judged contents Dickens attracted both the new readerships of the lower-middle and artisan classes and a middle-class family readership. Waters' reading of the non-fiction is that it was aimed specifically at a middle-class readership. The 'commodity culture' it interrogated was one with which the middle classes of the 1850s were familiar, and in so doing it paved the way for the shilling monthlies aimed at a middle-class readership that would follow in the 1860s.

I want to conclude this paper by talking briefly about Elizabeth Gaskell's non-fictional contributions to *Household Words*, about which very little has been written, and which are good examples of the way in which the contents of *Household Words* bridged the gap between the middle-class family readers that Dickens set out to attract and the less well educated artisan and lower-middle-class readers in whose price range the miscellany positioned itself.

Much has been written about Dickens's hands-on approach to Gaskell's first story, 'Lizzie Leigh' (1850), his suggestions for the ending of 'The Old Nurse's Story' (1852), which she ignored, and their falling out over the serialisation of *North and South* (1854-55). In contrast Dickens rarely commented on her essays and book reviews, except to acknowledge them, often enthusiastically, in retrospect, and to pay her at above-average rates. Unlike her novels and stories, the essays and reviews were anonymous. 'The Schah's English Gardener' (1852) was in the vein of real life experiences that relay knowledge of life in foreign parts. 'Traits and Stories of the Huguenots' (1852) blended essay and story and dealt with a period in French history that Gaskell knew well. 'Cumberland Sheep-Shearers' (1853) combined travel narrative, fiction, and autobiography.[17] Dickens told Wills he was 'delighted to hear of Mrs Gaskell's contributions' apropos of his injunction to 'Keep Household Words Imaginative!' in a letter written in mid-November 1852.[18] Two of Gaskell's articles are book reviews but in the *Household Words* mode are couched as general articles—'Modern Greek Songs' and 'Company Manners'.[19] Gaskell was an accomplished reviewer. She wrote for the *Athenaeum* in the early 1850s at the same time she was writing for *Household*

---

[17] [Elizabeth Gaskell], 'The Schah's English Gardener', *Household Words*, Vol. V, No. 117 (19 June 1852), 317-21; 'Traits and Stories of the Huguenots', *Household Words*, Vol. VIII, No. 194 (10 December 1852), 348-54; 'Cumberland Sheep-Shearers', *Household Words*, Vol. VI, No. 148 (22 January 1853), 445-51.
[18] To W. H. Wills, 17 November 1853, *The Letters of Charles Dickens*, Vol. VII, p. 200.
[19] [Elizabeth Gaskell], 'Modern Greek Songs', *Household Words*, Vol. IX, No. 205 (25 February 1854), 25-32; 'Company Manners', *Household Words*, Vol. IX, No. 217 (20 May 1854), 323-31.

Words, and she would become a regular reviewer for the *Reader: A Review of Science, Literature and Art* (1863-67), a weekly published by Macmillan. In 'Company Manners', she took as her subject a series of articles on Madame de Sablé, the seventeenth-century French salon hostess, which were originally published in the *Revue des Deux Mondes* (1829-) by Victor Cousin, and turned it into an essay on entertaining, contrasting the intellectual sparkle and vigour of the French salons, of which she had first-hand experience, with the ostentation and tedium of English middle-class dinner parties. Five months later Marian Evans reviewed the same work for the *Westminster Review*, the essay now known as 'Woman in France: Madame de Sablé', a celebration of the intellectual role French women play in their society, in contrast to the cramping restrictions imposed on their English counterparts.[20] It is fascinating to compare these two reviews of the same book, one written by a novelist at the top of her game, the other by a novelist in the making, both of them judging perfectly the audience of their respective journals.[21] Less than five years after *North and South* was serialised and 'Company Manners' appeared, *Household Words* came to an abrupt end and was succeeded by what Gaskell called 'this new Dickensy periodical'. Her newly-minted adjective has been over-worked and quoted out of context ever since. In a letter to her friend Charles Eliot Norton she expressed anxiety about the story she was currently writing, which was not going well. 'I know it is fated to go to this new Dickensy periodical', she wrote '& I did so hope to escape it'.[22] She did not escape, and 'Lois the Witch', one of her best stories, was published in three parts in *All the Year Round* in October 1859.[23] Gaskell clearly regarded the new periodical as less prestigious than George Smith's *Cornhill Magazine*, which was launched in January 1860 and to which she also contributed. Gaskell critics, notably Linda K. Hughes, who

---

[20] [Marian Evans], 'Woman in France: Madame de Sablé', *Westminster Review*, Vol. LXII, No. 122 (October 1854), 448-73.

[21] Gaskell's review was of the articles published in the *Revue des Deux Mondes*; Marian Evans reviewed the biography, based on the collected articles, which Cousin published several months later. See Joanne Shattock, 'Gaskell and Eliot on Women in France', in *Victorian Turns, Neo-Victorian Returns: Essays on Fiction and Culture*, ed. by Penny Gay, Judith Johnston and Catherine Waters (Newcastle upon Tyne: Cambridge Scholars Publishing, 2008), pp. 59-67.

[22] *The Letters of Mrs Gaskell*, ed. by J. A. V. Chapple and Arthur Pollard (Manchester: Manchester University Press, 1966; repr. 1997), p. 538.

[23] [Elizabeth Gaskell], 'Lois the Witch', *All the Year Round*, Vol. I, Nos. 24-26 (8-10 October 1859), 564-71, 587-97, 609-24.

has edited her stories from both periodicals, are less certain that the *Cornhill* stories are superior, or that she sent her 'sensational' tales to *All the Year Round* and what she considered her more enduring ones to the *Cornhill*. I have argued that Gaskell was not 'trading up', as the editors of her *Further Letters* have suggested, when she eagerly accepted an invitation from Smith to contribute to his magazine.[24]

The broader question of the quality of the original fiction in *All the Year Round* versus that in the *Cornhill* and of the relative positions of the two publications must be left for another time. I want merely to note that in her phrase 'this new Dickensy periodical', Gaskell was inadvertently paying its 'Conductor' a great compliment. She intended her comment to be dismissive, if not slightly contemptuous. But she was in fact articulating what the reading public already knew—that the Dickens 'brand' of periodical was now firmly established on the literary scene, and its distinctiveness was undeniable.

---

[24] See 'Introduction' in *Further Letters of Mrs Gaskell*, ed. by John Chapple and Alan Shelston (Manchester: Manchester University Press, 2000; repr. 2003), pp. xi-xxiii; *The Works of Elizabeth Gaskell*, ed. by Joanne Shattock and others, 10 vols (London: Pickering & Chatto, 2005-06), Vol. IV: *Novellas and Short Fiction III: Cousin Phillis and Other Tales from All the Year Round and the Cornhill Magazine 1859-1864*, ed. by Linda K. Hughes (2006), pp. vii-xxiv; Vol. I: *Journalism, Early Fiction and Personal Writings*, ed. by Joanne Shattock (2005), pp. xxiii-xxv.

Second Life: *All the Year Round* and the New Generation of British Periodicals in the 1860s

Laurel Brake

THIS paper will approach *All the Year Round* comparatively in the context of other journals of the 1860s and not primarily from the perspective of its publisher, 'conductor', proprietor and frequent contributor. There we have the difference between *All the Year Round* and most of its contemporaries—the conflation of these journalism functions and agents essentially into a single figure. A second difference is what John Drew characterises as Dickens's 'elaborate vision of how a multi-authored journal might project a powerful single personality'.[1] So there is a formal organisational conflation of roles and a particularly active editorial mediation of copy that homogenise the journal's discourse. Together these inhibit the approach I am proposing, both of comparison and of seeing around, behind, beyond 'Dickens'. A third impediment to a comparison and concomitant commentary is the 'success' of *All the Year Round*—its longevity (until 1895), its circulation (three times that of *Household Words*), its reach (across continents) and its position at the centre of other titles by Dickens. These elements of success complicate what we take to be the identity of the journal, which is inevitably multiple across the years, continents, and in the context of Dickens's life, within it and external to it. Attempts to focus on Dickens's two journals thus tend to oscillate between the man (*his* name and brand), his contributions (*their* names and brand), his other publications and activities, and the journal (*its* name and generic contents).

***

All the Year Round was one of a plethora of well-known British serials established from 1855, in a burst of titles that constituted new variations on

---

[1] John M. L. Drew, *Dickens the Journalist* (Houndmills: Palgrave Macmillan, 2003), p. 106.

extant forms of daily newspapers, weeklies, monthly magazines and reviews. It was an outcrop that followed the gradual removal of the newspaper taxes, or taxes on knowledge, between 1853 and 1861. These sources of government revenue, which included a tax on each advertisement, stamp duty on each newspaper sheet and a tax per pound of paper, had conspired since the late eighteenth century to keep the price of dailies and news weeklies high. Energised by favourable market conditions—no tax on paper or advertisements and no stamp duty—the diverse new titles shared one characteristic: cheaper cover prices. At the inception of *Household Words*, before the taxes were rescinded, its character, as well as its cost, was the result of the conditions of the press at the time: it was the absence of news that exempted it from paying stamp duty and thus enabled its two-pence per issue cost. In 1850 *Household Words* took the route of avoiding politics in news form in order to be economically accessible to, and circulate among, poorer readers—artisans and the lower middle classes. *All the Year Round* continued this policy, despite the repeal of the taxes.[2]

To explore this argument, what follows is divided into two parts: a comparison of *All the Year Round* with other journals; and an assessment of its undoubted success, despite the new generation of titles and formats.

Among the new generation of weeklies and monthlies founded in and after 1855 were the *Saturday Review*, a weekly news title that featured an acerbic critical register; two new-look monthly magazines, *Macmillan's Magazine* and *Cornhill Magazine*, which were cheap at a shilling; and two illustrated weeklies, *Once a Week* from Dickens's former publisher, Bradbury and Evans, and *Good Words,* a Sunday magazine initially from Scotland. 1855-65 was a decade of change, when nineteenth-century serials of a variety of types renewed themselves through the refashioning of established genres. The number of dailies increased both in the metropolis and the regions; newspapers and monthly magazines became cheaper, and even cheap, reflecting the loss of the tax; extant weekly newspapers increased their frequency and new titles were launched, especially regionally and locally. Weekly miscellanies introduced woodcuts and other forms of graphics; weeklies were also published monthly. The 'Review' genre moved from quarterly to monthly or fortnightly; the price dropped to under half that of the previous generation of quarterly Reviews, and the incidence of fiction was significantly increased, especially in monthly magazines, but also in new

---

[2] It is beyond the scope of this paper to assess the effect, if any, of the repeal of the conditions of stamp duty on both *Household Words* and *All the Year Round*, but it is an interesting research question.

Reviews such as the *Fortnightly*. As a new title, *All the Year Round* may appropriately be compared with other new titles of this decade, but how new was Dickens's follow-on from *Household Words*? It is arguable that *All the Year Round* is largely not a new journal like the other new titles of its time, but the results of a merger with an extant title—a common mode of transition in serials in that period and in our own.

I. The New Generation

Issued on 30 April 1859, *All the Year Round* preceded the launch dates of four journals that invite close comparison. They comprise two weeklies—*Once a Week* and *Good Words*—which came out in July 1859 and January 1860 respectively, and two shilling monthly miscellanies—*Macmillan's Magazine* and *Cornhill Magazine*—that appeared in November 1859 and January 1860. So, one might observe that Dickens and W. H. Wills, his deputy editor, did not have to deal with them initially in planning *All the Year Round*, but rather the newcomers had to deal with it.

Insofar as *All the Year Round* savoured a new freedom in its manifesto, what was envisaged by the other new titles? What distinctive elements did they pursue, how did they benefit from the example of *Household Words* and the infant *All the Year Round*, how did they withstand the force of the Charles Dickens personal/periodical nexus, and how if at all, did *All the Year Round* respond to them? Issues include signature, illustration, balance of fiction and non-fiction, frequency, format and size, price, the nature of the miscellany and the serial 'voice'. Lastly, taking Dickens's lead in dismissing his publisher, how did the publishers of these new titles figure in their content and fortunes?

By the time *Once a Week* appears in July 1859, Dickens's former publishers and printers Bradbury and Evans, with a gap in their list and in their production schedule, had ample opportunity to see the greater emphasis on serial fiction that *All the Year Round* was offering. *Once a Week* imitates that, along with *All the Year Round*'s motto, design, weekly/monthly frequency and relatively low price (it dropped to three-pence quickly, from sixpence), but *Once a Week* trumps these with what quickly became lavish illustration, perhaps imitating as well as rivalling Cassell's *Illustrated Family Paper* and *All the Year Round*. Bradbury and Evans were also far more generous with signature in *Once a Week* than Dickens and Wills in *All the Year Round* and, while the latter published attributions for all of the major serial fiction, not only Dickens's as in *Household Words*, the rest of the articles—

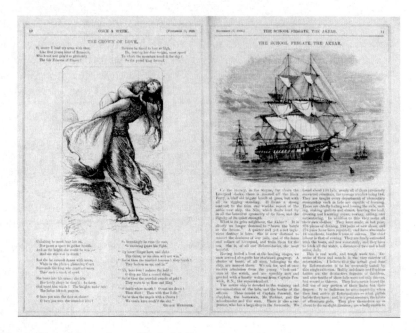

Fig. 1. Spread from *Once a Week,* 31 December 1859, with signed articles by George Meredith and Jelinger C. Symons.

which are signed in *Once a Week*—remain anonymous in *All the Year Round* (see **Fig. 1**). This self-conscious commitment to signature in *Once a Week* is also seen in the other new journals of the day, which are not only unencumbered by an editor alert to the draw of his name, but are also gradually willing to cede the uniform branding of the serial title to multiple authorial and artists' signatures.

Good Words (established January 1860) is similarly cheap and issued weekly at one-and-a-half pence and monthly at sixpence, but only for the first year, after which it opts exclusively for monthly publication, adjusting to the increasing prevalence among journals of monthly frequency. It also similarly incorporates a motto and includes fiction, but not always of novel length or on the first page.[3] By 1862 it names the editor on each opening— like *All the Year Round*. However, it appears on Sundays, rather than

---

[3] Interestingly, like *All the Year Round*, *Good Words* had an immediate predecessor, the weekly *Christian Guest*, which was edited by Rev. Norman MacLeod, February-December 1859. See the *Waterloo Directory to English Newspapers and Periodicals* <www.victorianperiodicals.com>.

Saturdays and it adopts a stronger Christian register, in keeping with its Scottish location and a named clerical editor. Thus, it clearly distinguishes itself from *All the Year Round* by register and day of issue, but, from number four onward, also by illustration, again like *Once a Week* by well-known artists named on its annual Contents page and cover.[4] From number five, illustrations began to appear on the opening of page one and, by December, illustrations and fiction are combined in that first position in the weekly issue. Gradually, it begins to include full-length but carefully selected serial fiction. From the first, its annual volume cover is graphically ornate. However, it continues to adapt itself to the market in the early 1860s, claiming more insistently that although it is suitable for Sunday reading, its aim is to be read throughout the week. Its weekly and then monthly feature, of prayers for each day, is soon abandoned and the journal becomes less ostensibly religious and more secular, thus competing more effectively with the shilling monthlies. By the 1870s at its height, it had the largest sales of all monthlies.[5] The argument for a prominent place for serial fiction, exemplified by *All the Year Round* and probably the *Cornhill Magazine,* proves irresistible in these first two decades after the repeal of stamp duty.

Cornhill Magazine, the second of the shilling monthlies to be launched, also appeared in January 1860. Competing with *All the Year Round*'s monthly issue costing nine-pence, with a difference of only three-pence, it is similarly committed to full-length serial fiction—even more than *All the Year Round*. Like Dickens's journal, it unevenly acknowledges authorship and largely for fiction. However, it is illustrated, eventually richly, with an unruled page and, being monthly, it is adorned with a graphically-striking golden yellow cover. The main debt to *All the Year Round*, in addition to the above, is its celebrity editor—significantly, Dickens's main rival as a novelist, W. M. Thackeray— whom Smith and Elder, its publisher, not only contracted to write fiction and a monthly personal column for each issue, but also encouraged to situate the monthly as a 'family' journal like Dickens's titles, but with a variety of rules which make certain types of copy off-limits. Thus, while it is not personally dominated to the degree that Dickens inflected *All the Year Round*, *Cornhill* creates a space—'Roundabout Papers'—to introduce a personal voice to rival Dickens's. By comparison with Dickens's two titles, the *Cornhill* nevertheless materialises as a half-hearted attempt by Thackeray and his

---

[4] As in the 1860 Library Edition annual volume.

[5] Sally Mitchell, 'Good Words', in *British Literary Magazines Vol. 3: The Victorian and Edwardian Age, 1837-1913*, ed. by Alvin Sullivan (Westport, CT and London: Greenwood Press), p. 145.

publisher, but it seems to be one to which Dickens responds robustly, by the introduction of 'The Uncommercial Traveller' into *All the Year Round* from 28 January 1860, as the impact and character of the first number of *Cornhill*, that had appeared only a month before, became clear. Sixteen articles in Dickens's series appear irregularly between January and October 1860, but Dickens persists with them, publishing another spurt of twelve between May and October 1863, by which time Thackeray abandons his 'Roundabout Papers' and *Cornhill*, having published thirty-four 'Papers' to Dickens's twenty-eight. The similar numbers reflect the rivalry. However, five years after Thackeray's death, Dickens resumes the travelogues, from October 1868, producing a last group of eight, under an adjusted title—'New Uncommercial Samples'—for the launch of the new series of the weekly, which was clearly occasioned by the success of the shilling monthlies as a genre, with or without Thackeray. Also, *All the Year Round* had no problem matching Thackeray's novels serialised in the *Cornhill* with fiction by Dickens and Wilkie Collins.

Although *Macmillan's Magazine* (from November 1859) was the earliest of the new generation of shilling monthlies, it seems less influenced by Dickens's titles than *Once a Week*, *Good Words*, or the *Cornhill*. *Macmillan's* is monthly, cheap and illustrated—but less than the *Cornhill*. Not only does it lack a personal note, it prides itself on a collective editing group allied to Christian Socialism, which materialised in a short-lived 'Colloquy of the Round Table' at the end of its first two issues. Presumably, the title of Thackeray's end-piece in the *Cornhill* echoes it, responding to its predecessor in the shilling monthly market, but hinting at the notion of travel in its version of '*Roundabout* Papers', which Dickens alters in turn to 'The Uncommercial *Traveller*' a month later. With respect to its general contents, it is less likely to publish full-length serial fiction prominently and regularly than either the *Cornhill* or *All the Year Round*: it favours a cluster of serious articles on topical issues. However, initially acknowledging the place of fiction in *All the Year Round* and *Once a Week* at its launch, its first issue has a novel in a prominent position by one of its Christian Socialist adherents, who is already on its publisher's list.[6]

---

[6] Instalments of *Tom Brown at Oxford* by Thomas Hughes appear in the second position in each of the first three issues in 1859-60, which begin true to the emphasis in *Macmillan's* with articles on contemporary social and political issues. Hughes was part of the editorial collective, as well as a *Macmillan's* author. His *Tom Brown's Schooldays* appeared in 1857 on the *Macmillan's* list.

In December 1861 *Macmillan's* publishes an article in favour of signature, early in this debate, in contrast to *All the Year Round*.[7] An important difference between the two shilling monthlies and Dickens's and Wills's new title is the extent to which both of their publishers are to the fore. Significantly, the principal name associated with *Macmillan's Magazine* is the publisher's, with the *Magazine* explicitly its house journal; while consciousness of the publisher Smith and Elder (in the person of George Smith) sits right alongside Thackeray in the profile of the *Cornhill*, as its title references the street which the publishing office of Smith and Elder overlooks. Thackeray leaves the *Cornhill* as editor in May 1862 and for a while it was edited by successive groups of two or three, all of which included Smith, in a long interregnum that ended only when Leslie Stephen was appointed in 1871, after Dickens's death. Once Smith began to act in the capacity of editor, he remained a significant co-editor to whoever nominally held the reins, at least until Stephen took over. If these two shilling monthlies lack a visible editor, such a figure is replaced, particularly in the *Cornhill*, by the figure of the publisher, whose participation Dickens was so anxious to exclude from *All the Year Round*.

In the context of the new generation of British journals, *All the Year Round* appears a product of a merger with a predecessor, where continuity is more evident than change in the new title, rather than a new journal in the mode of other start-ups of its day. It is recognisably a *second* life of its progenitor: eschewing illustration, remaining cheap, resisting the taste for attribution and multiple signatures, and remaining weekly while stubbornly refusing to develop its monthly identity in line with the increasing dominance of monthly magazines. Formally, *All the Year Round* appears slightly archaic in the sixties, despite the sustaining delight of its readers in some of the best fiction of the day, its signature travel sketches and the Dickensian aura of its other, anonymous copy.

II. Success

This comparison of *All the Year Round* with other serials of the 1860s shows the degree to which the new title was not the result of rethinking the periodical market in 1859, as so many others were doing after the repeal of the newspaper taxes. Nor was Dickens fully attending to the potential of new

---

[7] Thomas Hughes, 'Anonymous Journalism', *Macmillan's Magazine*, 5 (December 1861), 157-68.

technologies or the taste for illustration that had developed in the wake of the pictorial journalism of 1840s titles such as *Punch* (1841), the *Illustrated London News* (1842), the *London Journal* (1845) and the *Pictorial Times* (1843), and of 1850s titles such as *Cassell's Illustrated Family Paper* (1853) and the *Illustrated Times* (1855). Mainly, *All the Year Round* resembles other mergers or replications resulting from sudden, often enforced change (of publisher, editor, political orientation or cash liquidity), the glance of which is largely backward. Its roots in a genre established not only by its immediate predecessor, and its success, may also be traced to a hugely successful title from even earlier in the century.

This is *Chambers's Journal*, a fifth title important to *All the Year Round* that preceded *Household Words* by eighteen years. This weekly—called *Chambers's Edinburgh Journal* for its first twenty-two years (1832-54)—was one that Dickens's deputy, Wills, had edited in the early 1840s and to which he was still contributing in 1849, just before *Household Words* was founded. If *Chambers's* retained a muted Scottish note even after it became a national title early on, so *Household Words* had a detectable presence of Englishness. In *Dickens the Journalist* (2003) John Drew adumbrates the many debts *of Household Words* to this established weekly: its page size, font, design, exclusion of news, dual remit of instruction and entertainment, and low price, with the important difference that Dickens insisted on 'fancy'—the imaginative element—in *Household Words*. Nevertheless, the material similarities between the two titles are striking, but because of the durability of *Chambers's*—managed through a canny policy of updating itself every ten years, with new series in 1844, 1854 and 1864—the second Dickens weekly had to contend with it as well, at its founding in 1859 and later in 1864. *Chambers's* innovations in 1854 had included a deletion of *Edinburgh* from its title so that it became simply *Chambers's Journal*, to shed any geographical identity that might limit circulation, and a change of its subtitle to feature 'Popular Literature' above 'Science, and Art' (see **Fig. 2**). This signalled a notable shift of its remit to include more fiction, expressed by the redesigned graphics of its volume title page and through the font size of the three terms 'Popular Literature, Science, and Art'. The new series of *Chambers's* in 1854 also afforded greater prominence to its already extant monthly format that catered for its foreign readership, with a wrapper and lucrative adverts not attached to the weekly.

Like *Household Words* before it, *All the Year Round* adopted aspects of the *Chambers's* business model and Dickens announced that he would update *Household Words*, given the opportunity that the re-launch afforded. Like

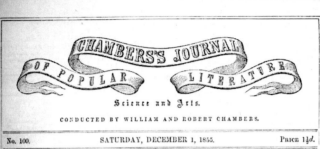

Fig. 2. *Chambers's Journal*, masthead 1 December 1855.

Chambers's from 1854, *All the Year Round* shows a significantly greater emphasis on fiction from 1860, in its new commitment to the serialisation of novels and enhanced attention to foreign sales.[8]*All the Year Round* continued the practice of *Household Words* of appearing in both weekly numbers and monthly parts that carried wrappers and adverts, as did the monthly issues of *Chambers's*. However, in *All the Year Round*, the rhythm of the monthly parts of the journal was initially reinforced by monthly parts of the first of the two novels Dickens wrote for his weekly—*A Tale of Two Cities* (1859)—being issued as they were serialised. So at the end of each month in which the novel appeared weekly in *All the Year Round*, it reappeared in the monthly aggregation of the issues, *and* in monthly instalments of the novel portion of the journal, uniform with monthly instalments of earlier novels by Dickens.

The weekly and monthly iterations of the journal were supplemented each December from 1859 through to 1867 by an Extra Christmas number, two weekly issues in length. Their blue covers, with adverts on the reverse of the front cover and both recto and verso of the back covers, echoed the covers of the monthly parts, and they seem to have been circulated with both weekly and monthly issues to paying subscribers and sold independently by 'booksellers and newsmen', as the cover states.[9] Moreover, editions of various Dickens/Chapman and Hall titles are advertised through tipped-in slips in the Christmas Extras; for example, the 1864 Extra has a tipped-in slip for the first volume of *Our Mutual Friend* (1864-65), to appear 20 January 1865 at 11 shillings, with advance orders to the publisher (see **Fig. 3**). It had been published in monthly parts, not in *All the Year Round*. Other wrappers for monthly parts (more graphically elaborate from 1868) are available via the Internet Archive's open access text archive.[10]

Additionally, a small rectangle of space on the last page of individual weekly issues, which did not carry other adverts, was normally dedicated to *All the Year Round*-related adverts. There, on 31 December 1859, a one-volume edition of *A Tale of Two Cities*, priced nine shillings, with sixteen illustrations by 'Phiz' (Hablôt Knight Browne), is announced, the novel

---

[8] *Household Words* over 10 years, published only four novels, one by Dickens.

[9] The cover of monthly part thirty-two in the British Library indicates that it comprised the four December numbers plus the double Christmas extra, which brought the price to one shilling, one pence.

[10] See http://archive.org/details/mrslirriperslega64dickrich (accessed 14/09/2012).

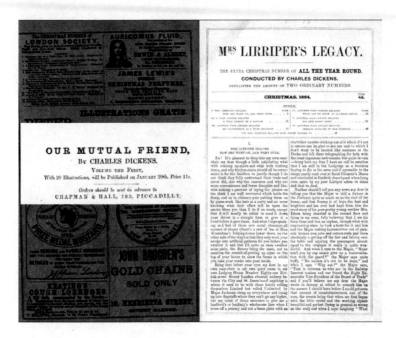

Fig. 3. *Mrs Lirriper's Legacy. All the Year Round* Extra Number for Christmas, 1864. Inner cover and masthead, with flier tipped in.

having recently finished its weekly instalments in *All the Year Round*.[11] The high price of this volume, relative to that of the tuppence weekly, draws attention to its added value, including the presence of illustrations, absent from the weekly and monthly issues and appearing only exceptionally in the Christmas Extras (see **Fig. 4**). Their absence makes *All the Year Round*, especially in the 1860s in which woodcut illustrations flourished, look austere. If one condition of the low price of Dickens's weeklies was the absence of news, a second was the absence of illustrations which, if they were to be of high quality (and not like those of the weekly *London Journal*), would have also raised the cost per issue. Bradbury and Evans's illustrated periodical, *Once a Week*, cost three-pence in 1859, but by 1868 the price had dropped to tuppence, reflecting perhaps its continued competition with *All*

---

[11] *All the Year Round*, Vol. II, No. 36, p. 236.

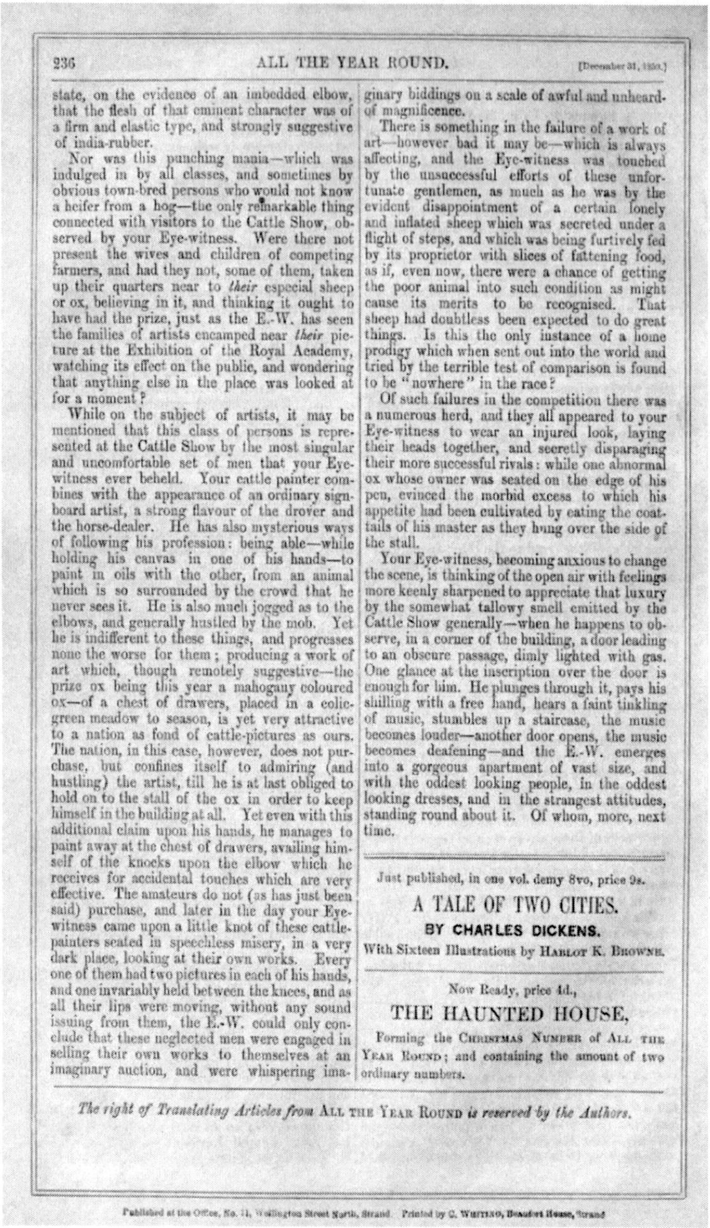

state, on the evidence of an imbedded elbow, that the flesh of that eminent character was of a firm and elastic type, and strongly suggestive of india-rubber.

Nor was this punching mania—which was indulged in by all classes, and sometimes by obvious town-bred persons who would not know a heifer from a hog—the only remarkable thing connected with visitors to the Cattle Show, observed by your Eye-witness. Were there not present the wives and children of competing farmers, and had they not, some of them, taken up their quarters near to *their* especial sheep or ox, believing in it, and thinking it ought to have had the prize, just as the E.-W. has seen the families of artists encamped near *their* picture at the Exhibition of the Royal Academy, watching its effect on the public, and wondering that anything else in the place was looked at for a moment?

While on the subject of artists, it may be mentioned that this class of persons is represented at the Cattle Show by the most singular and uncomfortable set of men that your Eye-witness ever beheld. Your cattle painter combines with the appearance of an ordinary sign-board artist, a strong flavour of the drover and the horse-dealer. He has also mysterious ways of following his profession: being able—while holding his canvas in one of his hands—to paint in oils with the other, from an animal which is so surrounded by the crowd that he never sees it. He is also much jogged as to the elbows, and generally hustled by the mob. Yet he is indifferent to these things, and progresses none the worse for them; producing a work of art which, though remotely suggestive—the prize ox being this year a mahogany coloured ox—of a chest of drawers, placed in a colic-green meadow to season, is yet very attractive to a nation as fond of cattle-pictures as ours. The nation, in this case, however, does not purchase, but confines itself to admiring (and hustling) the artist, till he is at last obliged to hold on to the stall of the ox in order to keep himself in the building at all. Yet even with this additional claim upon his hands, he manages to paint away at the chest of drawers, availing himself of the knocks upon the elbow which he receives for accidental touches which are very effective. The amateurs do not (as has just been said) purchase, and later in the day your Eye-witness came upon a little knot of these cattle-painters seated in speechless misery, in a very dark place, looking at their own works. Every one of them had two pictures in each of his hands, and one invariably held between the knees, and as all their lips were moving, without any sound issuing from them, the E.-W. could only conclude that these neglected men were engaged in selling their own works to themselves at an imaginary auction, and were whispering imaginary biddings on a scale of awful and unheard-of magnificence.

There is something in the failure of a work of art—however bad it may be—which is always affecting, and the Eye-witness was touched by the unsuccessful efforts of these unfortunate gentlemen, as much as he was by the evident disappointment of a certain lonely and inflated sheep which was secreted under a flight of steps, and which was being furtively fed by its proprietor with slices of fattening food, as if, even now, there were a chance of getting the poor animal into such condition as might cause its merits to be recognised. That sheep had doubtless been expected to do great things. Is this the only instance of a home prodigy which when sent out into the world and tried by the terrible test of comparison is found to be "nowhere" in the race?

Of such failures in the competition there was a numerous herd, and they all appeared to your Eye-witness to wear an injured look, laying their heads together, and secretly disparaging their more successful rivals: while one abnormal ox whose owner was seated on the edge of his pen, evinced the morbid excess to which his appetite had been cultivated by eating the coat-tails of his master as they hung over the side of the stall.

Your Eye-witness, becoming anxious to change the scene, is thinking of the open air with feelings more keenly sharpened to appreciate that luxury by the somewhat tallowy smell emitted by the Cattle Show generally—when he happens to observe, in a corner of the building, a door leading to an obscure passage, dimly lighted with gas. One glance at the inscription over the door is enough for him. He plunges through it, pays his shilling with a free hand, hears a faint tinkling of music, stumbles up a staircase, the music becomes louder—another door opens, the music becomes deafening—and the E.-W. emerges into a gorgeous apartment of vast size, and with the oddest looking people, in the oddest looking dresses, and in the strangest attitudes, standing round about it. Of whom, more, next time.

The right of Translating Articles from ALL THE YEAR ROUND *is reserved by the Authors.*

Published at the Office, No. 11, Wellington Street North, Strand.   Printed by C. WHITING, Beaufort House, Strand.

Fig. 4. Final page and advertising section, *All the Year Round*, 31 December, 1859.

the Year Round and changing technology that made the printing of illustrations cheaper.

The dogged persistence of *All the Year Round* under the editorship of Charles Dickens Jnr. in continuing without illustration, particularly in light of the importance it gave to fiction, which often attracted illustration, does suggest that the arrangements suited its conductors.[12] Was the prevailing model entirely economically driven (focus on a niche market?), or might Dickens have valued this space, which permitted him to publish his prose, and that of others, without the distractions and reinterpretations of visual art and artists? The graphic austerity of the two titles, until the slight thaw of the new series of 1868, implies a similar insouciance, even indifference, to the design of the journal, even in the face of the beautiful *Cornhill*.

However, to an extent, Dickens and Wills *did* address the challenge of the monthly *Cornhill*. Although the journals remained resolutely austere, their spin-offs did not. In issue one, in the back-page advertising space, there is an advert for the first monthly part of *A Tale of Two Cities*—which was clearly in the business plan from the first. It was expensive at a shilling and it was illustrated. It catered for a different, more bourgeois reader than the weekly journal, which cost eight (four issues) or ten pence (five issues) per month with its monthly number at nine or eleven pence (for four or five weekly numbers, respectively), although the prices are very similar. There is a nuanced range of consumption catered for, monthly, which takes in the appetite of *Cornhill* readers for fiction and illustration and rivals it. The joint publishers here—Dickens and Chapman and Hall—got their shilling, as Smith and Elder did for *Cornhill* numbers, plus the income for the weekly and monthly parts of the *All the Year Round*.

The severely limited advertising rectangle in the weekly issues also alerts us to the volume format of *All the Year Round*, which was for sale at half-yearly intervals. In 1859 and 1860 these volumes, in which the more ephemeral formats of weekly and monthly issue pass into the safe keeping of the 'library' and cease to be 'ephemera', cost five shillings and sixpence and covered April-October and October-April. They are advertised as 'always' available and are not confined to the date stamp of when they are issued.

These spin-offs from *All the Year Round*—the monthly collation, the monthly novel part, the Christmas Extra and the bi-annual volumes—indicate another similarity between the publishing pattern of Dickens and the business of the Chambers brothers (who were, like Dickens, the publishers

---

[12] Dickens's son, who represented himself for over a decade as Charles Dickens Junior, succeeded to the editorship after the death of his father in 1870.

of their weekly). Dickens's journals with their spin-offs are located at the centre of his publications, insofar as they provided a regular and stable monthly income, while the fees he received from his fiction, trips and readings were irregular payments attached to intermittent occasions of production and performance. *Household Words* and *All the Year Round* also kept Dickens, week after week, visible and in contact with his readers. For the last two decades of his life, they might be viewed as the economic and material base on which his other and various activities were built. Even before he founded his own magazine, he regarded any future journal of his in this light, writing to Bradbury and Evans that he was seeking a journal that would yield 'Chambers-like-profits'.[13] In the case of the Chambers brothers, their journal was the centre not of their own literary work, although they both contributed to it, but of a vast array of publishing projects— Dictionaries, Encyclopaedias, 'Libraries' and educational pamphlets which hovered around the hive of their weekly. Both business profiles resulted in considerable financial success and a breadth of publishing possibilities (see **Fig. 5**).

Before ending this consideration of the 'success' of *All the Year Round*, I want to look briefly at the implications of monthly reissues of weekly titles, a publishing strategy adopted by a number of weeklies in the nineteenth century (see **Fig. 6**). The main benefits of an additional monthly reissue of a 'weekly' are at the supply and distribution end of the process, not at the production end, although monthly parts do provide more work for printers, binders and publishers. Like each periodical format—whether a library edition, a re-issue, a second or third edition or a digital re-mediation— monthly numbers have distinctive features; in the case of *All the Year Round* a wrapper afforded space on its cover (verso) for a Table of Contents of the part, and it also accommodated advertisements, with their potential for additional revenue (see **Figs 7** and **8**). The adverts also provide an opportunity for free advertising for the publisher, for work by Dickens, and for *All the Year Round*, developments or news.

The frequency and format of monthly numbers of *All the Year Round* boosted foreign sales, making it cheaper and safer to ship abroad weekly issues in multiples of four or five, protected by the wrapper. This market is addressed on the back cover of the Christmas Extra for 1865, which includes sixteen

---

[13] Drew, p. 106.

SELECTED PUBLICATIONS.

Chambers's Encyclopædia; A DICTIONARY OF UNIVERSAL KNOWLEDGE FOR THE PEOPLE. Of this important and comprehensive work seven volumes have been issued. It is confidently anticipated that nine volumes will complete the undertaking.

Published Weekly, at 1½d.; Monthly, at 7d.; and in Volumes, at 9s. each.

☞ Illustrated by hundreds of Wood Engravings, and by Maps beautifully printed in colours.

The Book of Days. A Miscellany of Popular Antiquities in connection with the Calendar, including Anecdote, Biography, and History; Curiosities of Literature, and Oddities of Human Life and Character. Edited by ROBERT CHAMBERS, LL.D.

Two Volumes, price One Guinea.

Elaborately illustrated by quaint Wood Engravings.

'*There is, in truth, a rich supply of entertainment in its pages. Let the reader get the volumes of* Mr CHAMBERS *for himself; he must be of a peculiar temperament if he does not find in them lasting sources of pleasure.*'—TIMES, December 28, 1864.

The Cyclopædia of English Literature. *New Edition.* Edited by ROBERT CHAMBERS, LL.D. A Critical and Biographical History of English Writers in all departments of Literature; illustrated by specimens of their Writings, and numerous Wood Engravings.

In Two Volumes, 16s.

The Pictorial Bible. A New and Improved Issue. This work is splendidly Illustrated with Steel Engravings, Wood-cuts, and Maps, with numerous Notes by JOHN KITTO, D.D., F.S.A.

In 4 Volumes, cloth lettered, at........................£1 16 0

————, *morocco, or calf extra, gilt edges,*......3 12 0

The Gallery of Geography. A Pictorial and Descriptive Tour of the World. By the Rev. T. MILNER. Illustrated by 354 high-class Wood Engravings, and further embellished by 6 Steel Engravings, and 12 Maps, beautifully printed in Colours. The work is accompanied by an elaborate Index.

In One, or Two Volumes, price One Guinea.

☞ For Students and others who are interested in the study of Geography, the above work is specially recommended.

Shakspeare's Works. Chambers's Household Edition, purged of all Impurities and Objectionable Phrases; with Introductions and Copious Notes. Edited by ROBERT CARRUTHERS and WILLIAM CHAMBERS. Illustrated by KEELEY HALSWELLE. Post 8vo.

In 10 Volumes, cloth, at 30s.

☞ An Edition of the Works of Shakspeare, designed to be read aloud in the Family Circle.

Domestic Annals of Scotland, from the Reformation to the Revolution. Edited by ROBERT CHAMBERS, LL.D. In 3 Vols. demy 8vo. *Second Edition.* Price 40s.

W. & R. CHAMBERS, London and Edinburgh. [*Over.*

Fig. 5. Advertisement for the Chambers suite of publication, in the *All the Year Round* Advertiser (July 1865).

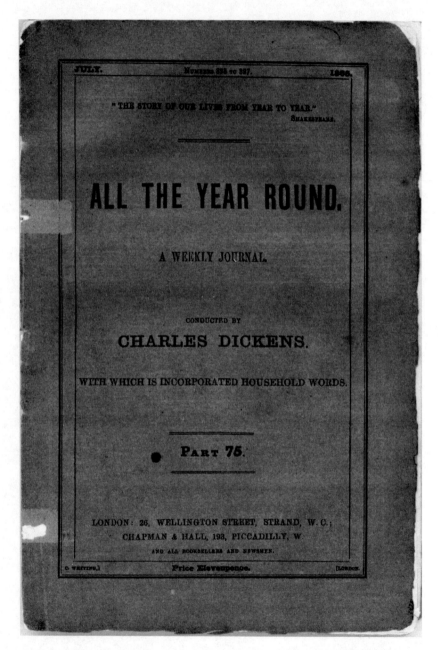

Fig. 6. Front wrapper of a monthly number of *All the Year Round* (July 1865).

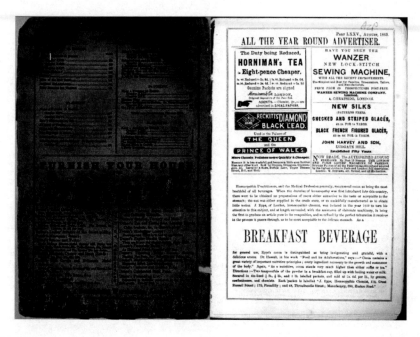

Fig. 7. Verso of *All the Year Round* monthly wrapper (July 1865) and p. 1 of the 8-page 'Advertiser'.

heraldic shields of different countries, to augment sales to foreign visitors (see **Fig. 9**).

Domestically, the monthly reissue broadens the reach of the journal's purchasers to a different (middle) class who are more attuned to the purchase of monthly magazines than to weeklies. Many adverts in the Christmas Extras suggest comfortable bourgeois readers, including women who might buy pianos, expensive furniture and drapery, female equestrian costumes, and so forth (see **Fig. 10**). Dickens refers to monthly parts in a letter quoted by Bob Patten in *Dickens and his Publishers* (1979), as the form in which back issues were supplied, reminding us that monthly parts increase the number of sales points in time, from four to five per month, increasing circulation for sheets that are part of the weekly print run.[14] *All the Year Round* enhanced this to six, as already mentioned, by the issue of monthly novel parts that Dickens contributed (but not other contributors), and to

---

[14] Robert L. Patten, *Dickens and his Publishers* (Oxford: Oxford University Press, 1979), p. 277.

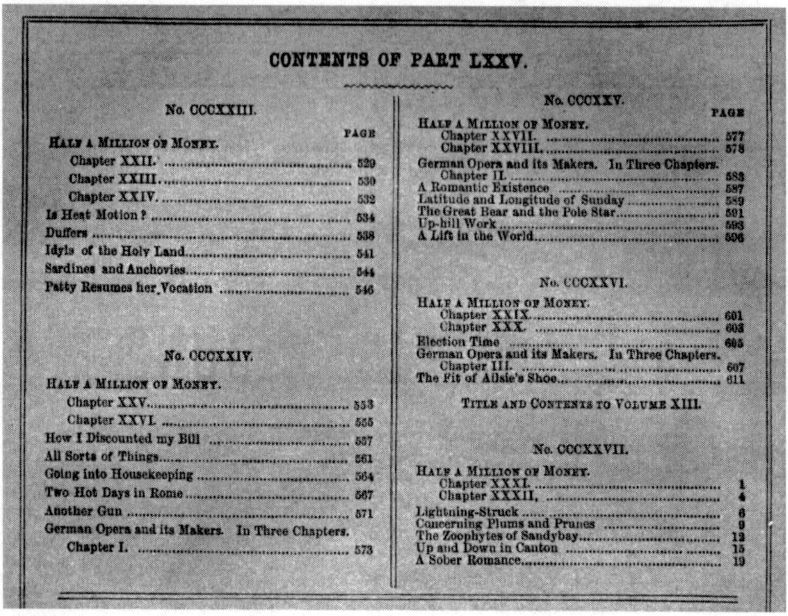

CONTENTS OF PART LXXV.

Fig. 8. Close up of **Fig. 7** cover verso, showing list of contents.

seven each December. Monthly novel parts also afford readers a larger 'bite' of fiction than that offered by the weekly 'teaspoonful'. This *might* have comforted authors, in that their fragmented texts would be read in a more liberal swathe of continuous prose and larger episodes. Thus, novelists may have been writing with both instalment lengths in mind, especially since they would appear monthly as well as weekly.

So, although *Household Words* and *All the Year Round* stated prominently on their mastheads that they were in the weekly periodical market, they were also monthlies, competing for middle-class readers with monthly titles such as *Fraser's* and later shilling magazines such as *Cornhill* and *Temple Bar*. However, it cannot be said the British editions of *All the Year Round* developed their monthly editions to compete with the new generation of weeklies or monthlies. The covers of the *All the Year Round* monthly edition insist that it is a *weekly* magazine; nowhere is the word 'monthly' used, only 'Part' followed by a number. In 1865, for example, the monthly's formal contents are indicated on the cover in the small space of the frame at the

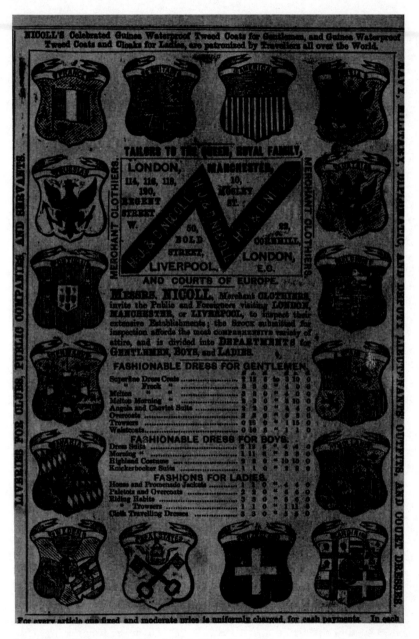

Fig. 9. Back wrapper of the *All the Year Round* Extra Number for Christmas, 1865 (*Doctor Marigold's Prescriptions*).

top, by the naming in very small font of the month, the year and the numbers included On the verso of the front cover the contents of the numbers are listed, separately by successive numbers (see Figs 6, 7, 8). There is little effort made to remediate the weekly parts into a monthly number. So *All the Year Round* and its conductor might be thought to have regarded its monthly appearance as a clear by-product of the weekly journal, *not*, as other titles did, as a format to be embraced and as a valuable commodity in its own right.

To summarise, although commentators are tempted to see Dickens's journals as above all 'personal', it is useful to examine the ways Dickens's journals resembled and compared with other journals of their day to see what, if anything, we see afresh. Specifically, while the origins of *All the Year Round* may appear idiosyncratic and personal, given the end of Dickens's marriage and the row with Bradbury and Evans, they also exemplify a common model of serial growth and development in the nineteenth century, in which titles splinter, merge and 'twin'. Examples of splinters that are also mergers, where staff and editors move to a new title include: *Punch* and the *Tomahawk*; the *Illustrated News* and new rivals the *Graphic, Pictorial Times* and the *Illustrated Weekly Times*; the *Nineteenth Century* and the *Contemporary Review* in 1877; and the *Westminster Gazette* and the *Pall Mall Gazette* in 1880.

In the prospectus for *All the Year Round* that appeared in *Household Words* and elsewhere, Dickens emphasised the continuities between the present title and its replacement (which incorporated the title *and* the staff), in an effort to reassure readers that they should transfer their loyalties and pennies to the new title; and not stick with the current publisher. The prospectus also gestured vaguely toward changes, cemented by a change of title and the reassurance, which might not have meant much to readers, that 'no publisher' was to be involved. There is a strong sense however that the new enterprise would stick closely to the appearance, price, contents and conduct of the old publication, which was after all only discontinued because of its conductor's ire at his publisher, not because of any dissatisfaction with the extant title. That is, the stress on continuities between the titles was as much to its conductor's taste as it was for reassurance of its readers. I would add to that a general contextual note: the prodigiously successful marriage between fiction and the periodical press in the second half of the nineteenth century and their symbiotic relationship, which promulgated the fortunes of both. In this process *All the Year Round* might be seen as a direct descendent of one of the brokers of this engagement: *Household Words*. *Household Words* along with *Blackwood's Magazine* are among the main publishers of fiction in the

Fig. 10. Advertisements for mustard, furniture, drapery, pills &c. from the monthly *All the Year Round* Advertiser (July 1865), p. 3.

periodical press before the new generation, in which fiction became a ubiquitous if uneven ingredient. [15]

Nevertheless, more than nearly all journals I know of in the nineteenth century, Dickens's titles are associated with a single author, under whose aegis they create a reading community with his imprimatur. Charles Dickens, the conductor of *All the Year Round*, is not a ludic third-party figure, with a visual representation such as Mr Punch, or *Fraser's* Oliver Yorke, or even contained in Dickens's avatars Master Humphrey or Mr Pickwick; the presiding spirit is a personae of Charles Dickens himself, an editorial personality that he augmented by moving *himself* as well his *fiction* to stages across Britain during the run of *All the Year Round*, with his readings. Charles Dickens is a celebrity editor like very few others in nineteenth-century Britain; W. T. Stead is the only parallel I can think of. Dickens not only lent himself to being the named 'conductor' of his journals—he relished it. When Stead railed against the 'old journalism' as he touted the new in the mid-1880s, he defended 'personal journalism' as though it was the antithesis of current or earlier practice. But he had forgotten Dickens's example, with which his career just overlapped. From this perspective, the personal nature of the issue that occasioned the disruption of *Household Words* and the launch of *All the Year Round*—Dickens's expectation that his publisher and fellow editors would similarly see journalism as personal and publish an address to his public about himself—appears understandable, as others have also argued. The disconnect in this crisis between Charles Dickens and the developing profession of journalism—personal in its advocacy of interviews, but impersonal in its commitment to investigation and fact—was not isolated or aberrant in Dickens's case; as others have noted, it is of a piece with the strong personal 'voice' of his journals.

Undoubtedly, 'Dickens' was an important factor in the success of both journals. Even though his contributions to *All the Year Round* were notably fewer than to *Household Words*, and the second journal reads as less personal than the first, the branding work of 'Charles Dickens' was successfully established earlier, by diverse cultural phenomena: *Household Words*; the success of his earlier fiction in monthly numbers, and volumes; the pirated parts and stage productions of the latest Dickens publications; and the first series of Dickens's public readings. Moreover, *All the Year Round* was launched with a strong showing of two novels by its conductor, bastioned by

---

[15] See Laurel Brake, 'The Advantage of Fiction: The Novel and the "Success" of the Victorian Periodical', in *A Return to the Common Reader: Print Culture and the Novel*, ed. by Beth Palmer and Adelene Buckland (Farnham: Ashgate, 2011), pp. 9-21.

a similarly robust serial, *The Woman in White* (1859-60). And the personal note *was* struck very effectively in the spurts of travel narratives by 'The Uncommercial Traveller' (1860, 1863 and 1868-69). *All the Year Round* was a financial success; profits were particularly buoyant, as it was sold legally in the US through agents—unlike *Household Words*, which had been pirated. To that extent, the success of the journals built on each other; and the continuities may be an important part of this success. Together they are the heart of Dickens's publications between 1850 and his death, a pattern also found in the Chambers brothers' publishing business. Like Dickens, they generated and published a huge number of publishing satellites to *Chambers's Journal*, which were advertised in its pages and in turn advertised it. For Dickens to have shed the necessity to deal with a publisher of his weekly, not only permitted him a greater share of the profits, but also the freedom to fashion a second life for his original plan, with relatively small changes, rather than to wholly rethink his project in light of the new generation of the magazine in the 1860s.

A 'Hopeful Congeniality' between Mr Whelks and the Duchess? *Household Words* in a Journalistic Context

Louis James

ON the night of 29 January 1850, Dickens invited Daniel Maclise to join him at the Royal Victoria Theatre on the Waterloo Road to watch 'a Melo Drama'.[1] A month later, on 2 March, Dickens ventured into working-class Hoxton in the East End of London to watch a performance at the Royal Britannia Saloon, where the bill was headed by another melodrama, George Dibdin Pitt's, *Lady Hatton; or, the Suicide's Tree* (1850).[2] The visits formed the basis for a two-part *Household Words* essay, 'The Amusements of the People' (30 March and 13 April 1850), in which Dickens imagines taking a working-class lad, 'Mr Joe Whelks', to serve as Weller to his Pickwick in his venture into working-class theatre.[3] Although a *Theatrical Journal* editorial of 2 May thought Dickens's account patronising and dismissive, Dickens was clearly fascinated by the experience. The climax of the melodrama brought a minor epiphany:

> When the situations were very strong indeed, they were very like what some favourite situations in the Italian opera would be to a profoundly deaf spectator [...]. So do extremes meet; and so there is

---

[1] The melodrama was *May Morning; or, the Mystery of 1715*, playing at the Royal Victoria Theatre from 28 January until 13 February 1850. To Daniel Maclise, [?29 January 1850], *The Letters of Charles Dickens*, ed. by Kathleen Tillotson, Graham Storey and others, Pilgrim Edition, 12 vols (Oxford: Clarendon Press, 1965-2002), Vol. VI, p. 21 and n.

[2] To Daniel Maclise, 2 March 1850, *The Letters of Charles Dickens*, Vol. VI, pp. 51-52 and see also p. 52, n. 1.

[3] [Charles Dickens], 'The Amusements of the People [i]', *Household Words*, Vol. I, No. 1 (30 March 1850), 13-15; 'The Amusements of the People [ii]', *Household Words*, Vol. I, No. 3 (13 April 1850), 57-60.

some hopeful congeniality between what will excite MR WHELKS, and what will rouse a Duchess.[4]

As Dickens made these visits when he was working on 'A Preliminary Word' to *Household Words* (30 March 1850), and placed the first part of the 'Amusements' essay in the opening issue, it is reasonable to suppose they relate to Dickens's intentions for his journal as a whole. If he were to appeal to Mr Whelks (and his family), he himself had to find a 'happy congeniality' between the contents of his periodical and the vitality and strength of feeling to be found in popular theatre.

As he wrote to Morley:

> The indispensable necessity of varying the manner of narrations as much as possible, and investing it with some little grace or other, would be very evident to you if you knew as well as I do how severe the struggle is, to get the publication down to the mass of the readers, and to displace the prodigious heaps of nonsense, and worse than nonsense, which suffocate the better sense.[5]

Dickens believed rival cheap journals had either ignored or crudely exploited this culture. *Chambers's Edinburgh Journal*, launched in 1832 and continuing, with title variations, until 1956, was the one major survivor of the massive expansion of popular publishing sparked by 'the March of the Intellect'. Dickens had earlier found *Chambers's* 'a somewhat cast-iron and utilitarian publication (as congenial to me, generally, as the brown paper packages in which Ironmongers keep Nails').[6] It offered sixteen densely printed pages, without illustrations, for a penny and a half. Its circulation, which had peaked in the 1840s at 90,000, was declining: in 1849 it was estimated at between 60,000 and 70,000.[7] It offered a solid diet of articles on science, geography and history, and miscellaneous literary essays, a weekly poem and sober short stories. These were typically on domestic themes and maintained a primly anti-Romantic stance. An Editorial 'Proposals for a Reform in Light Literature', attacked as 'a horrid stupidity this constant straining to bring

---

[4] [Dickens], 'The Amusements of the People [ii]', p. 60.

[5] To Henry Morley, 31 October 1852, *The Letters of Charles Dickens*, Vol. VI, pp. 790-91 (p. 790).

[6] To Mrs S. C. Hall, 23 April 1844, *The Letters of Charles Dickens*, Vol. IV, pp. 110-11 (p. 110 and n.).

[7] Richard D. Altick, 'English Publishing and the Mass Audience in 1852', *Studies in Bibliography*, Vol. VI (1954), 3-24 (p. 9 and n.).

about a marriage between two commonplace young people, with which a curtain may at last be allowed to drop'.[8]

As the circulation of *Chambers's* slipped, the field of cheap popular journals became dominated by two massively popular serials, the *Family Herald: or, Useful Information and Amusement for the Million* (1842-1940) and the *London Journal; and Weekly Record of Literature, Science and Art* (1845-1928). The first had been founded in 1842 by the millenarian socialist James Elishama Smith to promote the virtues of domesticity. Its manager and printer, John Biggs, used the technical advances powering the expansion of popular literature to make it the first journal to be typeset, printed by steam-press and bound throughout entirely by machine. (Its labour-cutting production methods provoked an early strike by its work force.) Cheap methods of production, and a circulation reaching 300,000 by mid-century, enabled Biggs to offer its sixteen pages at a penny, against the penny-half-penny of *Chambers's*. Eschewing all illustrations other than a few diagrams, it provided a diet of recreational family reading, aimed particularly at women in the rapidly expanding middle and lower middle classes, where many now had servants and time on their hands. Its banner heading of Britannia seated beside a bale of periodicals before an ocean-going ship reflected its awareness of a rapidly expanding audience in Britain's colonies (**Fig. 1**).[9]

In the *Daily News*, William Hepworth Dixon noted that the *Family Herald* 'is a purely domestic magazine; and is also decidedly the least offensive of its class'.[10] Roughly half the content consisted of short 'useful and entertaining' paragraphs, grouped under such headings as 'Family Matters', 'Scientific and Useful', 'Statistics', 'Random Readings' and 'The Riddler' (puzzles and charades). 'To Correspondents' gave a wide range of advice on household and personal topics, with guidance on the conduct of romantic affairs. So 'Triesta' was advised that, 'Ladies may and ought to show preferences to

---

[8] [Anon.], 'Proposals for a Reform in Light Literature', *Chambers's Edinburgh Journal*, n.s. Vol. XI, No. 268 (17 February 1849), 97-98 (p. 97).

[9] In New South Wales, Australia alone, in the 1860s, the *London Journal* and the *Family Herald* were selling 1,500 copies and 900 respectively. See J. Don and Rosemary T. Van Arsdel (eds), *Periodicals of Queen Victoria's Empire: An Exploration* (Toronto: University of Toronto Press, 1996), p. 51.

[10] [William Hepworth Dixon], 'The Literature of the Lower Orders [iii]', *Daily News*, Tuesday 9 November 1847. There were five articles in this series, running on 26 October and 2, 9, 25 and 29 November 1847. I am indebted to Mary L. Shannon for this reference.

Fig. 1. Masthead of the *Family Herald*, 14 August 1847.

gentleman they prefer', but was warned that, 'Showing preferences and making advances are two very different things'.[11] In spite of the socialist convictions of 'Shepherd' Smith its founder, its editorials on women's issues were conservative. One condemned female emancipation movements as 'the raving of Utopian criticism [...]. The two sexes are widely separated from one another in the intercourses of life by the rules of propriety and decorum'.[12] Another editorial, 'Progress; or, Whither Are We Going?' warned against the dangers of Radical agitation, declaring that social inequality required moral, not political solutions.[13] The miscellany's fiction, which relied heavily on translations from French *feuilleton* writers, including Alexandre Dumas, Frédéric Soulié and Eugène Sue, was more romantic and sensational that anything allowed in *Chambers's*. This received less approval from Dixon, writing in the *Daily News*, who found Sue's *Martin the Foundling; or, the*

---

[11] The *Family Herald: A Domestic Magazine of Useful Information and Amusement*, Vol. V, No. 238 (27 November 1847), p. 174.

[12] The *Family Herald: A Domestic Magazine of Useful Information and Amusement*, Vol. VI, No. 278 (2 September 1848), p. 283.

[13] The *Family Herald: A Domestic Magazine of Useful Information and Amusement*, Vol. V, No. 242 (25 December 1847), pp. 541-42.

Adventures of a Valet de Chambre (1847) 'disgusting' and quite unsuitable for young ladies to read.[14]

When Dickens launched *Household Words* in 1850, the *London Journal* was estimated to have a weekly circulation of some 500,000.[15] Like the *Family Herald*, it offered sixteen pages of dense print in three columns for a penny, providing an entertaining miscellany of essays, with pieces on history, science and contemporary events. It also ran a column 'Notices to Correspondents'. However, unlike the *Family Herald*, this and its other contents had no particular female focus and were directed to readers of either sex. It was launched by George Stiff, by profession an engraver who had worked on the illustrations to G. W. M. Reynolds's *Mysteries of London* (1844-48), and also differed in featuring prolific illustrations. The first twenty-eight issues of the *London Journal* alone featured nearly ninety illustrations, excluding diagrams and smaller inserts.

Their style owed much to the *Illustrated London News* (1842-1989), whose success had come from the profuse use of graphic illustrations made possible by developments in wood engraving. Indeed, the two periodicals were to share several artists and engravers, notably the prolific (later Sir) John Gilbert.[16] Dickens excluded the potential attraction of such illustrations from *Household Words*, preferring the sober, serious image of *Chambers's Journal*. But he may have had another reason for keeping his journal without illustrations. His early fiction had seamlessly integrated with the multi-layered illustrations of George Cruikshank and Hablot Knight Browne. But the new style of illustration was related to the mid-century preference for more realistic representation, as seen in early photography and the Pre-Raphaelite concern with literal detail so hated by Dickens as banishing 'the light of fancy' from narrative art.[17]

In practice, although many of the *London Journal*'s illustrations were ostensibly documentary—portraits, historical scenes, architecture and the like—they differed from the educational graphics central to the success of Charles Knight's earlier *Penny Magazine* (1832-35). A geographical panorama

---

[14] [Dixon], 'The Literature of the Lower Orders [iii]'.

[15] Andrew King, *The London Journal, 1845-83: Periodicals, Production and Gender* (Aldershot: Ashgate, 2004), p. 845.

[16] King, p. 99.

[17] See [Charles Dickens], 'Old Lamps for New Ones', *Household Words*, Vol. I, No. 12 (15 June 1850), 265-67, which attacks Millais's painting, 'Christ in the House of His Parents' (1849-50).

Fig. 2. Cover page of the *London Journal*.

accompanying 'Travels in the East' on one cover page, for example, shows a caravan passing beneath the skeletons of impaled robbers; on another, an account of the methods of the Spanish inquisition features a beautiful woman being hideously tortured (see **Figs 2** and **3**).[18]

The explanatory text beneath an apparently innocuous scene of clerks reading mail in a city office, on yet another cover page illustration, reveals it as showing government spies opening private mail in 'The Secret Chamber in the General Post'. The scene hovers between fact and fiction, for it illustrates a quotation from Reynolds's *Mysteries of London* (**Fig. 4**).[19] If the new wood engraving banished the more stylised narrative art of Hogarth, Cruikshank and Browne, illustrators like George Stiff and John Gilbert found ways to import the old iconographies into the new 'realism'. As Brian Maidment has shown, the illustrators of the *London Journal* and *Reynolds's Miscellany* drew on 'a variety of generic allusions, pulling in caricature, reportage, the theatre, the gothic and melodrama'.[20]

By March 1850, the character of the *London Journal* was becoming identified with the massively successful fiction of John Frederick Smith, its leading serial novelist.[21] The title of Smith's first serial, *Stanfield Hall* (1849-50) capitalised on public interest in the sensational contemporary murder in November 1848 of two Norfolk landowners, Isaac Jermy and his namesake son, by James Blomfield Rush, a disgruntled tenant farmer. But the novel avoided the crime and its background of rural unrest. Instead, Smith used the location as the setting for a three-part novel in the style of Walter Scott, using fiction to explore the history of the English peoples. It begins in the mid-eleventh century, with the conflicting loyalties developing between Saxons and Normans, and ends just after the Restoration on the theme of national reconciliation with extraordinary scenes in which the poet Milton frustrates a plan by Charles II to desecrate Cromwell's body.

---

[18] The *London Journal*, Vol. I, No. 4 (22 March 1845), p. 49; the *London Journal*, Vol. I, No. 8 (19 April 1845), p. 113.

[19] 'The Secret Chamber in the General Post Office', the *London Journal*, Vol. I, No. 3 (15 March 1845), pp. 33-34; G. W. M Reynolds, the *Mysteries of London*, 4 vols (London: G. Vickers, 1845), Vol. I, chapter 6.

[20] Brian Maidment, 'The Mysteries of Reading: Text and Illustration in the Fiction of G. W. M. Reynolds', in *G. W. M. Reynolds*, ed. by Ann Humpherys and Louis James (Aldershot: Ashgate, 2008), pp. 227-46 (p. 234).

[21] King, pp. 104-09.

THE

LONDON JOURNAL;

And Weekly Record of Literature, Science, and Art.

NO. 8. VOL. I.　　　　FOR THE WEEK ENDING APRIL 19, 1845.　　　　[PRICE ONE PENNY.

THE MYSTERIES OF THE INQUISITION.

PROLOGUE.

TOWARDS the middle of the sixteenth century, during the reign of Charles V., the population of Seville—that gay and charming capital of Andalusia—had become sombre, silent, and mournful.

Vainly did the Moorish city, with its vast terraces shaded by verdant plants and gorgeous flowers, court the rays of the resplendent orb of light: gloom spread over scenes once so laughter-loving; and a mysterious melancholy pervaded the elegant balconies, where creeping vines, red passion-flowers, and Virginian jessamine, with large corallas of golden hue, imparted perfume and freshness to the air, and charmed the eye.

And by night—mystic hours of love and adventure in the sunny south—no longer were heard, beneath those balconies, the voices of amorous cavaliers and courtly gallants,—voices that were wont to mingle with the dulcet sounds of the guitar. And if, when the sun had sunk to rest, and the heavens shone with myriad stars,—if, at that delicious time, a few timid maidens ventured to appear upon the terraces, to inhale the fresh and perfumed breeze which blew from the banks of the Guadalquiver, they moved hither and thither with the silence and solemnity of visionary shadows; while no sound, save peradventure a stifled sigh, escaped their lips—sighs in the place of the joyous

laughter and the harmonious melody of language which, in the mouth of woman, gives the Spanish tongue a semblance of a sonorous music.

For a long time had terror reared its mournful standard in Seville!

There were no more familiar gossipings—no more patriarchal meetings: distrust and fear paralysed the sweetest and softest sentiments of the soul.

The father looked with suspicion upon the son; the brother cast a searching glance upon the brother; the friend seemed to doubt the friend; for at that epoch every one trembled lest he should discover a traitor and a spy in him who was nearest and dearest to him.

No one was assured of his fortune and his life. People lived from day to day, daring to place confidence in nothing—crushing, stifling all generous feelings and noble sentiments at the bottom of their hearts. They sought no consolation, and placed no hope in the exercise of religion. The face of the Almighty seemed averted from them; —for none could safely venture to invoke his name with freedom of conscience, because there was a possibility of expressing a prayer or manifesting a faith not recognised by the law!

And, at that epoch, there was a "Sacred Usurper" of all religious rights and privileges, according to whose system Man was to worship God

only in one settled form, and according to whose principles its own establishment upon the earth was a reflection of the divine supremacy. This institution arrogated to itself infinite power, and exercised a despotic control over soul and body,— a pitiless tyrant that sought, by all possible means, to reach its one grand aim—UNIVERSAL DOMINION! For the Inquisition was at that epoch in the zenith of its power!

Its chief was the Cardinal Alphonso Manrico Archbishop of Seville.

CHAPTER I.

THE GRAND INQUISITOR AND HIS GUESTS.

THE palace of the Grand Inquisitor, Peter Arbuez, was an immense and sumptuous Moorish edifice, formerly inhabited by the King of Seville. A magnificent garden, planted with the most lovely flowers and the choicest trees, communicated with an isolated pavilion that had originally served as a bathing-establishment. The voluptuous Arbuez had turned it to another use.

This pavilion, situate at a distance from the main building, and concealed as it were amidst a dense mass of foliage, was the place where the Grand Inquisitor revelled with his most favoured friends. Bishops and monks—men as dissolute as

Fig. 3. Cover page of the *London Journal*.

THE

LONDON JOURNAL;

And Weekly Record of Literature, Science, and Art.

No. 3. Vol. I.   FOR THE WEEK ENDING MARCH 15, 1845.   [Price One Penny.

THE SECRET CHAMBER IN THE GENERAL POST OFFICE.

SAINT MARTIN'S LE GRAND.

THE immense sensation that has been produced throughout the country, for a year past, by the publicity given to the system of opening letters in the General Post Office, Saint Martin's Le grand, has induced us to present our readers with a faithful representation of the interior of the Secret Chamber where this proceeding takes place. With the propriety of that proceeding we have nothing to do, the policy of any measure of government not being a subject for discussion in the columns of a journal devoted to literary and scientific purposes. The Secret Chamber is situate in the northern London" thus describes the process of opening letters—an explanation which we are inclined to quote, because, upon enquiry, we have ascertained it to be correct to the very letter:—

"The door of the room was carefully bolted. At one end of the table was a large black tray, covered with an immense quantity of bread seals of all sizes. Perhaps the reader may recall to mind, that amongst the pursuits and amusements of his school days, he diverted himself with moistening the crumb of bread, and kneading it with his fingers into a consistency capable of taking and retaining an accurate impres- others wafered, stood upon that end of the table at which the elderly gentleman was seated. The occupation of these five individuals may be thus described in a few words. The old gentleman took up the letters one by one, and bent them open, as it were, in such a way that he could read a portion of their contents, when they were not folded in such a manner as effectually to conceal all the writing. He also examined the addresses, and consulted a long paper, of an official character, which lay upon the table at his right hand. Some of the letters he threw, after as careful a scrutiny as he could devote to them without actually breaking the seals or wafers, into a large

Fig. 4. Cover page of the *London Journal*, 15 March 1845.

Between 1849 and 1855 Smith wrote a succession of highly successful novels for the *London Journal*, exploiting interest in topical events and issues while skilfully defusing political issues through suspenseful plotting and melodramatic scenes of resolution. *Amy Lawrence* (1851-52) evokes the world of Elizabeth Gaskell with its account of suffering Manchester workers, but moves on to breathless adventures in London and Moscow. The much-dramatised *Minnigrey* (1851), with its virtuous Spanish heroine, is set in the Peninsular Wars (1808-14), but slips away from national or racial issues to a Romantic ending between English lovers. In contrast to Reynolds, Smith's

Gothic fiction even manages to sidestep condemning the excesses of the Spanish Inquisition.

But it was *Reynolds's Miscellany* (1846-69), that Dickens had in mind when, in his 'A Preliminary Word' to *Household Words*, he attacked the 'Bastards of the Mountain, draggled fringe on the Red Cap, [who] Panders to the basest passions of the lowest natures'.[22] Reynolds's publications were almost certainly the 'perilous stuff' Dickens referred to in October 1852, 'circulating six times the amount of Household Words'.[23] As Dickens and Reynolds, as Mary L. Shannon has noted, had their editorial offices situated in Wellington Street on either side of the Strand, and since their periodicals were so closely identified with their editors, it is worth spending a moment on Dickens's hated rival.[24] Dickens's feud with Reynolds began in the 1830s, with the appearance of Reynolds's *Pickwick Abroad; or, the Tour in France* (1838-39) in the *Monthly Magazine*. Reynolds insisted his work was a continuation, not a plagiarism of Dickens's novel, and indeed the sometimes louche account of the Pickwickians enmeshed in the seamy side of Paris society is very different from the original. It met with some success, reappearing under different imprints until as late as 1864, and Reynolds followed it with 'Noctes Pickwickiana' in his journal the *Teetotaler* (1840) and a short story 'Pickwick Married' in his Dickens-inspired serial, *Master Timothy's Bookcase* (1841-42).[25]

Then, on 6 March 1848, Reynolds took the chair at an illegal Chartist demonstration in Trafalgar Square against the introduction of income tax, which ended with Reynolds addressing a cheering crowd from the balcony of his house in Wellington Street. The demonstration was followed by minor rioting and an attempted march on Buckingham Palace. To Dickens, this demonstrated that Reynolds was not only an unscrupulous plagiarist, but also a middle-class agitator who exploited working-class causes for his own ends. When, in 1849, Dickens discovered that Reynolds was subscribing to a fund to help an arrested Chartist, he insisted that Reynolds be removed from the list, for his was 'a name with which no lady's, and no gentleman's, should be

---

[22] [Charles Dickens], 'A Preliminary Word', *Household Words*, Vol. I, No. 1 (30 March 1850), 1-2 (p. 2).

[23] To Henry Morley, 31 October 1852, *The Letters of Charles Dickens*, Vol. VI, pp. 790-91 (p. 790 and n. 4).

[24] Mary L. Shannon, paper given at 'Orality and Literacy' seminar, King's College London, 17 March 2012.

[25] Humpherys and James, p. 274.

associated'.[26] Dickens, although no Republican or Socialist, also campaigned against social abuses and considered himself a true Radical. 'I feel strongly for the genuine working men who are Chartists', he wrote of Reynolds, 'but have no sympathy whatever with the amateurs'.[27]

Reynolds was less of an 'amateur' in working-class matters than Dickens knew. Although he was born the son of a well-to-do Kentish post-captain's family with a long tradition of naval service, Reynolds's claims to have inherited a substantial family fortune, and to have become a French citizen and served in the Paris National Guard after the July Revolution in 1830, were fabrications.[28] In reality, in September of 1830, scarcely aged seventeen, he had abruptly left the Royal Military Academy at Sandhurst for unspecified reasons. With little financial means of support, he appears to have gone to ground in the underworld of London Radical publishers, where his first work, the pamphlet *The Errors of the Christian Religion Exposed*, was published by Richard Carlile in 1832. By 1835 he was working in a bookshop in Paris. That year he married an English girl, Susannah, probably aged seventeen to his twenty-one, at the British Embassy; a son was born six months later. In Paris he lost what money he possessed and in 1837 returned to England, bankrupt. In 1840, now with a wife and two children, Reynolds was sharing a tenement with five other families in Bethnal Green, one of the poorest areas of London, struggling to make a living by his pen.[29] Reynolds, who had his own 'blacking factory' experience to hide, in his turn attacked, 'That lick-spittle hanger-on to the skirts of Aristocracy's robe—"Charles Dickens Esq."—originally a dinnerless penny-a-liner on the *Morning Chronicle*.'[30]

As an editor, Reynolds, like Dickens, identified closely with his periodical, seeing it as his personal campaign to improve the lot of the working classes. He placed his portrait at the head of the first issue. He wrote the main serials, signed leading articles and entered a weekly dialogue with his readers through the 'Notes to Correspondents'. He made a

---

[26] To W. C. Macready, 30 August 1849, *The Letters of Charles Dickens*, Vol. V, pp. 603-04.

[27] *The Letters of Charles Dickens*, Vol. V, p. 603 and n.

[28] G. W. M. Reynolds, *The Modern Literature of France* [1838], revised and enlarged edition (London: George Henderson, 1841), pp. ii-iii.

[29] Dick Collins, 'George William Macarthur Reynolds: A Biographical Sketch', in *The Necromancer* [1857], by George W. M. Reynolds, ed. by Dick Collins (Kansas City, MO: Valancourt, 2007), p. xvii.

[30] G.W.M Reynolds, 'Charles and Dickens and the Democratic Movement', *Reynolds's Weekly Newspaper*, 8 June 1851, p. 7.

sustained effort to address the needs of the largely urban working classes. Well-written articles, ranging from geography and history to contemporary science, addressed the interests of self-educating artisans. Reynolds distanced himself from middle-class 'improving' journals for the masses; he wished to empower, not direct, his readers, because 'BY EDUCATION PEOPLE BECOME EASY TO LEAD, BUT DIFFICULT TO DRIVE; EASY TO GOVERN, BUT IMPOSSIBLE TO ENSLAVE'.[31] If the readers of his series 'Etiquette for the Millions' would have found little of relevance in the sections on fashionable dining protocol, Reynolds included a warning against following inappropriate customs or neglecting one's own class values. 'No one can possibly move in all societies', Reynolds argued, declaring that a self-respecting working man is superior to a conventionally polite aristocrat. He insisted that all good behaviour, finally, was based on consideration of others.[32]

In his *Miscellany* Reynolds introduced a series of 'Letters to the Industrious Classes', drawing on writers with inside knowledge of specific areas of working life, from cotton-spinners, needle-women and agricultural workers to teachers.[33] But the political issues central to a sister paper, *Reynolds's Political Instructor* (1849-50), were largely absent from *Reynolds's Miscellany*. Reynolds asserted that the French Revolution had opened up an era of progress towards greater social equality, but declared that while reform was needed in England, there was also the need to maintain law and order— 'After all, Government is a necessary evil.' While his journals were hostile to the repressive rule of European monarchies, Reynolds remained respectful of Queen Victoria and the British royal family.[34]

If Dickens hated Reynolds's politics, he believed Reynolds's fiction 'pander[ed] to the basest passions of the lowest natures'. In 1845, as its first editor, Reynolds startled the readers of the *London Journal* with a translation of a lurid contemporary French serial, *The Mysteries of the Inquisition* (1845) by 'M. V. De Féréal' (the pseudonym for an Iréne de Suberwick). The first

[31] G. W. M. Reynolds, 'Letters to the Industrious Class. Letter I: General Address', *Reynolds's Miscellany*, Vol. I (30 January 1847), p. 199.
[32] G. W. M. Reynolds, 'Etiquette for the Millions. 1 – Introductory Remarks', *London Journal* Vol. 1, (12 April 1845), p. 104. The series ran for seventeen weekly articles until number seventeen 'The Lady' (30 August 1845).
[33] Seven 'Letters to the Industrious Classes' were published in *Reynolds's Miscellany* between Vol. I (30 January 1847), 199–200 and Vol. II (15 May 1847), 11–14.
[34] G.W.M. Reynolds, 'The Queen, Prince Albert, and Their Children', *Reynolds's Miscellany*, Vol. I (5 December 1846), 73–74 (p. 73).

chapter described, in lingering detail, monks administering water torture to a bound woman victim, with a graphic wood engraving of the scene. Reynolds's *Faust* (1845-46), the historical romance that followed, was less disturbing, but also included scenes of cruelty, some of which were also set around the Spanish Inquisition.

In 1847 Reynolds left the *London Journal* to start *Reynolds's Miscellany* and, while Dickens was preparing the launch of *Household Words*, the *Miscellany* was running Reynolds's serial *The Bronze Statue; or, the Virgin's Kiss*.[35] The innocent-sounding title referred to a magnificent hollow statue of the Madonna, which, when opened up, revealed the iron spikes of an 'Iron Maiden'. These closed in on victims of the Spanish Inquisition, mutilating them before releasing their living bodies to be finally torn apart on bladed wheels below. Both text and dramatic woodcuts dwelt lingeringly on the details (see **Fig. 5**). Here is a brief extract:

> [T]he thrilling notes of her mortal anguish penetrated more clearly through the wooden trap-door over which the colossal effigy stood. For the spikes had pierced her eyes and the sharp blades had inflicted a thousand ghastly gashes upon her palpitating flesh,—and still she lived! [...] Blinded—wounded all over—and covered with blood she fell between the two uppermost cylinders, while the dreadful bell went clanging on.[36]

Was this fiction designed to exploit the 'basest passions' of Reynolds's readers? It is clear that Reynolds knew the power of shock and horror to sell his journals and it is impossible to justify his sadistic anti-Catholicism. But he was also attacking the cosy domesticity of journals like *Chambers's* and the *Family Herald*, creating a journal that could include the more brutal issues confronting life in the mid-century. In a *Miscellany* article, he asserted that the horrors of the Spanish Inquisition were historically true, foreshadowing the reactionary forces repressing liberation movements in contemporary Europe, and that Jesuits were still active in Victorian Britain.[37]

If Reynolds's fiction did not avoid issues of human cruelty, his equally controversial portraits of women in his fiction directly confronted middle-

---

[35] 'The Bronze Statue' ran in *Reynolds's Miscellany* from 31 March 1849 to 14 March 1850.

[36] G. W. M. Reynolds, 'The Bronze Statue', *Reynolds's Miscellany*, n.s. Vol. III (22 December 1849), chapter lxxxv, p. 339.

[37] G. W. M. Reynolds, 'The Jesuits and the Inquisition', *Reynolds's Miscellany*, n.s. Vol. III (25 August 1849), 69-70.

class stereotypes of the passive, sexless heroine, as well as investment in single women's virginity. Nisida, the masculine-hearted heroine of Reynolds's serial, 'Wagner the Wehr-Wolf' (1846-47), is feisty, independent and uninhibited in displaying her sexual attractions:

> She was attired in deep black: her luxuriant raven hair, no longer depending in shiny curls, was gathered in massy bands at the sides, and in a knot behind, whence hung a rich veil that *meandered over her body's splendidly symmetrical length of limb in such a manner as to aid her attire in shaping rather than hiding the contours of that matchless form.* The voluptuous development of her breast was shrouded, not concealed, by the stomacher of black velvet which she wore, and which set off in strong relief the dazzling whiteness of her neck.[38]

Later Nisida enjoys a passionate relationship with Wagner on an idyllic Mediterranean island. As he gazes on her sleeping,

> Wagner fancied that his companion had never appeared as magnificently beautiful as now, while she lay half reclining in his arms, the rays of the setting sun faintly illuminating her aquiline countenance, and giving a glossy richness to the luxuriant black hair which floated negligently over her naked shoulders.[39]

Dickens would undoubtedly have seen this as exploiting his readers' 'basest passions', but such scenes are genuinely tender and it is only in the later instalments of his penny weekly *Mysteries of the Court of London* (1848-55) that Reynolds verges towards pornography. As Margaret Dalziel pointed out, Reynolds's treatment of sex is unique for popular magazine fiction of the 1840s:

> His lovers, the women as well as the men, *enjoy* themselves. They may not escape punishment (though they often do) but neither do they drag out a miserable existence tormented by the reproaches of

---

[38] G. W. M. Reynolds, 'Wagner the Wehr-Wolf', *Reynolds's Miscellany* (26 November 1846), chapter x, p. 53 (Reynolds's emphasis).
[39] G. W. M. Reynolds, 'Wagner the Wehr-Wolf', *Reynolds's Miscellany* (10 April 1847), chapter liv, p. 355.

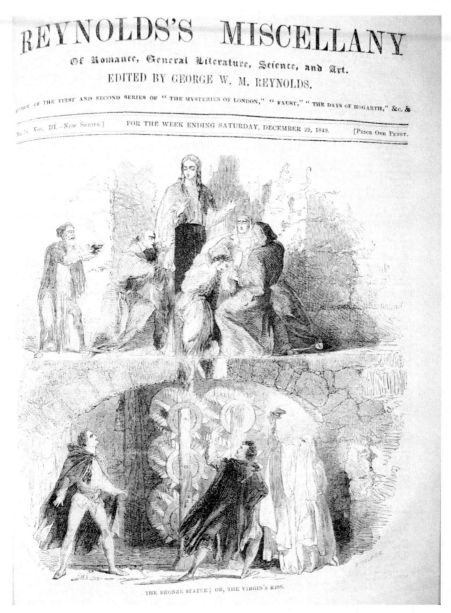

Fig. 5. Masthead of *Reynolds's Miscellany* 22 December 1849. Reproduced with permission from the Canterbury Cathedral Library (Catalogue reference K9-14).

conscience and each other, cut off from family and friends, and at length, the females anyway, sinking into an early grave.[40]

Yet if a case might just be made for his direct treatment of violence and female sexuality, Reynolds makes little attempt to address, in the way Dickens does, the common experience of common readers. Dickens placed Elizabeth Gaskell's tale of Manchester life, 'Lizzie Leigh', in the first issues of *Household Words*.[41] Stories of working-class life by others occur in *Reynolds's Miscellany*.[42] When Reynolds himself deals with labour issues in *The Seamstress: A Domestic Tale* (23 March-10 August 1850), the suffering of the impoverished needlewoman is there as a nail on which to hang a moral fable, in which the long-suffering heroine is finally rewarded by the discovery of her noble birth.

But the difference between the fiction in *Household Words and Reynolds's Miscellany* lay not so much between responsible and irresponsible journalism, as between the ways literature functioned in two different cultural worlds. There was a gulf between 'the view from Brick Lane', the perspective of Reynolds's working- and lower-middle-class readers, and the outlook of families living in the comfort of areas like Bloomsbury.[43] Dickens declared his aim in *Household Words* was 'To show to all, that in all familiar things, even in those which are repellent on the surface, there is Romance enough, if we find it out'.[44] Reynolds—who in his dark years, struggling to survive in a Bethnal Green tenement, would almost certainly have seen his children go without food—took a less Romantic view.

Reynolds wrote for those who read fiction to escape from their immediate reality. This does not mean such reading was necessarily disconnected from a social consciousness. Today the characters and situations common to melodrama have set into comic clichés, but cultural analysts such as Anna Clark have demonstrated the ways in which, over a

[40] Margaret Dalziel, *Popular Fiction 100 Years Ago: An Unexplored Tract of Literary History* (London: Cohen and West, 1957), pp. 38-39 (original emphasis).
[41] [Elizabeth Gaskell], 'Lizzie Leigh [i]', *Household Words*, Vol. I, No. 1 (30 March 1850), 2-6; 'Lizzie Leigh [ii]', *Household Words*, Vol. I, No. 2 (6 April 1850), 32-35; 'Lizzie Leigh', *Household Words*, Vol. I, No. 3 (13 April 1850), 60-65.
[42] See, for example, 'The Factory Girl' by the pseudonymous 'Paul Pimlico', *Reynolds's Miscellany*, n.s. Vol. I (20 October-24 November 1849).
[43] Louis James, 'The View from Brick Lane', *Yearbook of English Studies*, 11 (1981), 87-101.
[44] [Dickens], 'A Preliminary Word', p. 1.

century of social change, sensational stories of crime and seduction became forged into the melodramatic iconography of the class struggle.[45] One example is 'the murder in the Red Barn'. In 1827, Maria Marten, a twenty-five-year-old woman with two children from earlier liaisons, living in Polstead, Suffolk, had an affair with William Corder, the philandering son of a local farmer. When Maria became pregnant, Corder murdered her to avoid his responsibilities and buried the body in a farm outbuilding. A year later, Maria's step-mother recounted dreaming of the murder, a vision that brought Corder to the gallows. The dream was almost certainly fabricated, but the story caught the public imagination and became a parable of Heaven defending the virtuous poor against the wicked rich. So, in countless melodramas, Maria was portrayed as an innocent virgin and Corder as the wealthy seducer, in a crime Heaven avenged by a vision given to Maria's aged mother.

Such popular myth-making was central to the melodramas that emerged on the streets of post-Revolutionary Paris, where René Charles Guilbert de Pixérécourt (1773-1844) created his sensational theatre to entertain those who couldn't read—the newly-liberated populace—using traditional mime, thrilling physical action and startling spectacle. The plots were designed to evoke powerful emotions, giving them an appeal that cut across barriers of class and genre. These feelings were intensified by the music, or 'melos', that accentuated the actions and identified the moral character of each actor, giving 'melodrama' its name. If Pixérécourt wished to entertain his popular audience, he also wished to educate them as moral members of the new democratic republic, dramatising simple tales in which goodness always overcomes the wiles of the evil rich and the common good is restored. It has been estimated that his plays enjoyed some 30,000 performances, making Pixérécourt 'the most successful dramatist of the first decades of the century'.[46] As fast as his plays were produced in France they were translated and acted in England, often without acknowledgement. Dickens may have had Pixérécourt in mind when describing Vincent Crummles instructing Nicholas Nickleby in the art of play-writing. Crummles thrusts a French manuscript into Nicholas's hands declaiming, "'Invention! What the devil's

---

[45] Anna Clark, 'The Politics of Seduction in English Popular Culture', in *The Progress of Romance*, ed. by Jean Radford (London: Routledge and Kegan Paul, 1986), pp. 47-70.

[46] René Charles Guilbert de Pixérécourt, *Four Melodramas*, translated and introduced by Daniel Gerould and Marvin Carlson (New York: Martin E. Segal, 2002), p. ix.

that got to do with it! [...] There, just turn that into English, and put your name on the title-page.'"[47]

Although no stage performances of Reynolds's fiction have been identified, his fiction is much indebted to the myth-making modality of melodrama. Because of its title and urban descriptions, his best-known work *The Mysteries of London* is usually seen as a novel of city life. But Reynolds's London is significantly different to that in Dickens's fiction. Rather than reflecting actual London life in all its diversity, Reynolds's city is there to dramatically represent the timeless conflict between 'WEALTH/POVERTY'.[48] It is a struggle in which a spectrum of privileged classes victimise the poor and the good, while both are threatened by the anarchic underworld of the criminal classes. Reynolds's Miscellany serials characteristically rest on a basis of socialist parable. So his *Faust* rewrites the traditional legend as a fable of the social evils of questing for wealth and power. *The Coral Island* (1848-49) relates social oppression to a disease that can only be cured by a plant from a primitive, innocent garden island. For all its horror, the metal Madonna of *The Bronze Statue* is an effective image representing Reynolds's view of established religion as externally attractive, but cruelly destroying the lives of those trapped within it. In the story as a whole, it provides a counter to a narrative of revolutionary struggles and ends with Zitzka, a Bohemian freedom fighter, caught up on his death-bed in an ecstatic vision of revolutionary change:

> I am hurried over the barriers of Time—into the middle of the Nineteenth Century—and O joy! I behold crowns falling—thrones crumbling to pieces—sceptres snapping in twain—and the PEOPLE agitating throughout Christendom! Yes—I see it all—the nations have risen—the proletarians have broken their chains—the day of retribution has come—and the slaves and the serfs of the World are asserting their rights to its mastership![49]

Stage censorship by the Lord Chamberlain's office in the period would have made it impossible to stage such a speech at the Britannia; but, if it had been, I think Mr Whelks would have cheered.

---

[47] Charles Dickens, *Nicholas Nickleby* [1838-39], ed. by Mark Ford (London: Penguin, 2003), pp. 287-88.
[48] Reynolds, *The Mysteries of London*, Vol. I, p. 416.
[49] G. W. M. Reynolds, 'The Bronze Statue', *Reynolds's Miscellany* (14 March 1850), chapter cvi, pp.114-15.

If both Reynolds and Dickens used elements from melodrama to reach out to their popular audience, Dickens came to the task from a very different perspective. I return to the quotation, with which I began, from 'The Amusements of the People', where Dickens writes of watching a performance at the Britannia Theatre:

> It is but fair to MR WHELKS to remark on one curious fact in this entertainment. When the situations were very strong indeed, they were very like what some favourite situations in the Italian opera would be to a profoundly deaf spectator. The despair and madness at the end of the first act, the business of the long hair, and the struggle in the bridal chamber, were as like the conventional passion of the Italian singers, as the orchestra was unlike the opera band, or its 'hurries' unlike the music of the great composers. So do extremes meet; and so there is some hopeful congeniality between what will excite MR WHELKS, and what will rouse a Duchess.[50]

In opera, Dickens introduces an objective correlative for upper-class tastes— 'what will rouse a Duchess'—to place against a popular melodrama. Italian opera, 'drama by means of music', has a classical genealogy going back at least as far as Monteverdi's *Orpheus*, first produced in Mantua in 1602. Popular melodrama emerged, as we have seen, from the social turmoil produced by the French Revolution. Yet 'Grand Opera' and melodrama shared some common roots. They both attach meanings to specific gestures and facial expressions in drama and the visual arts, in conventions going back to the seventeenth century. Both were affected from the latter part of the eighteenth century by the European Romantic Movement. In 1770, some years before Pixérécourt began producing his populist melodramas for the Parisian (later nicknamed the 'Boulevard du crime' because of the many crime melodramas shown there), Jean-Jacques Rousseau composed the first scene specifically designated a 'mélodrame'. This was *Pygmalion* (written around 1762, first performed 1770), written to demonstrate the primacy of the emotions inspired by music and movement over the socially learnt medium of words. Here, the sculptor's short monologues alternated with music, building up to a climax of passion so intense that it brought the statue Galatea to life. Music's power to evoke dramatic emotion became central, too, to operatic performance. By the 1840s the Romantic operas of Rossini

---

[50] [Dickens], 'The Amusements of the People [ii]', p. 60.

and Donizetti were being enthusiastically received in London and Covent Garden was renamed the Royal Italian Opera in 1847.

On 26 April 1849 Dickens invited John Leech to join him there to hear Catherine Hayes as Lucia at the first night of Donizetti's *Lucia di Lammermoor*.[51] This performance may well have been in his mind when he attended the Britannia Saloon a year later. The script for *Eva the Betrayed*, the second play on the bill at the Britannia, appears to have been lost. But Dickens describes the climax, in which Eva, having been betrayed into marriage by the villain Thornley, emerges from her wedding ceremony to find her true love Walter alive. She falls into 'despair and madness' and, after a violent scene, is carried away. This directly parallels the climax to Donizetti's opera, where the betrayed Lucia goes mad on seeing Edgardo.

In 'A Preliminary Word' to *Household Words*, Dickens wrote that his aim was to 'cherish that light of Fancy which is inherent in the human breast', significantly locating the light of the imagination not in the head but the heart.[52] This sentiment has a profound affinity with Keats's declaration to Benjamin Bailey, 'I am certain of nothing but of the holiness of the Heart's affections and the truth of Imagination'[53] Both fancy and the heart share in Dickens's intimation, sensed in a working-class playhouse, of a 'hopeful congeniality' between cultures. For this emerged in moments in which audiences, whether at the Royal Italian Opera House or the Britannia Saloon, became united by the intense feelings evoked by imagined events represented on the stage.

Dickens illustrated this 'congeniality' in *Household Words* nowhere better than in the seventeenth instalment of *Hard Times* (1854), the novel he wrote specifically for the periodical. Here, the middle-class Louisa Gradgrind, destroyed by a passionless Utilitarian education and her loveless marriage to Bounderby, seeks solace from the 'stroller's child', Sissy Jupe. Uniting action and words, Louisa falls on her knees at the feet of Sissy, crying,

> "'Forgive me, pity me, help me! Have compassion on my great need, and let me lay this head of mine upon a loving heart.'"
>
> "'O lay it here!' cried Sissy. 'Lay it here, my dear.'"[54]

---

[51] To John Leech, [?26 April 1849], *The Letters of Charles Dickens*, Vol. V, p. 528.

[52] [Dickens], 'A Preliminary Word', p. 1.

[53] To Benjamin Bailey, 22 November 1817.

[54] Charles Dickens, 'Hard Times [xvii]', *Household Words*, Vol. IX, No. 226 (22 July 1854), 525-31 (p. 527).

'Serviceable Friends': The Two Supplements to *Household Words*

Koenraad Claes

DURING the ongoing Dickens bicentenary, a lot of attention has been paid to the importance of periodical publications in the career of the celebrated author. This should not come as a surprise. Long before Victorianists began to fully appreciate the historical relevance of journalism in the second half of the twentieth century, biographies and critical studies had pointed out the exceptionally central role Dickens assumed as editor of his magazines, or, as he preferred to style himself, their 'Conductor'. Much in the same way as Dickens was firmly in control of the novels he published, he also famously micromanaged his periodicals. It is common knowledge that although most articles in *Household Words* (as later in *All the Year Round*) were supplied by other authors, he often thoroughly edited these before they went to the printers. A certain uniformity could thereby be achieved that enabled the magazine to convey a coherent message in a tone and register that its dedicated Conductor agreed with. Percy Fitzgerald, who as a young man had written for *Household Words*, stated in his 1913 *Memories of Charles Dickens* that:

> The notion of a magazine thus inspired and directed, not merely edited in the popular phrase, would be impossible in our day, for the reason that there is no one either to inspire, or whose 'inspiration' people would care for. Homogeneousness is not asked for nowadays; the popular magazine is a sort of hotch-pot.[1]

Scholarship has since revealed that the posited harmony among *Household Words* contributors was often less than self-evident; yet the fact remains that the magazine has to be studied intently, and with much recourse to elusive secondary sources, before the small yet significant ruptures in this apparent

---

[1] Percy Fitzgerald, *Memories of Charles Dickens: With an Account of Household Words and All the Year Round, and of the Contributors Thereto* (London: Simpkin, 1913), p. 105.

monolithic unity can be traced. Strangely, all the while, two more obvious, structural ruptures have been all but disregarded. I am referring to two regular feature supplements that are usually not distinguished from *Household Words* proper, even though they were published alongside the magazine rather than incorporated into it: namely, the *Household Narrative of Current Events* and the *Household Words Almanac*. I will argue that these can be read as extending the range of their homogeneous parent publication, without unsettling its hallowed intrinsic balance. To understand how this works, it is necessary for us to look into the functional links between these two supplements and *Household Words* proper.

The functional diversity of the various kinds of addenda that are referred to as supplements prohibits us from drawing up an exhaustive checklist for the entire genre, but we may suggest here a primary working definition. A periodical supplement should minimally comply with the following three broad but vital aspects: (1) be issued in some form of conspicuous association with a periodical—referred to as the 'parent publication'; (2) depend on the association with this parent for full signification; (3) at the same time show some form of demarcation from it. The presence of a supplement paradoxically implies an inherent completeness in the parent publication that it is supplementing, but, also, a need for this extraneous body of text. This paradox is the key to understanding supplements, as it is exploited by their publishers for commercial and ideological reasons, allowing them to expand towards territories that for practical or legal reasons would be risky for the parent publication itself to enter.[2] The very presence of supplements therefore begs the question: what function do they fulfil? What kind of lacuna in the parent publication are they indirectly filling up, and why was their content not deemed appropriate to be included there in the first place? Popular weeklies such as *Household Words* were above all business ventures, and their supplements fitted into well-considered strategies for market positioning. Both supplements under consideration here arguably cater to an additional market niche, but also craftily aid the magazine's ideological mission.

The first supplement under scrutiny is the monthly *Household Narrative of Current Events*.

---

[2] For a more thorough discussion of the supplement genre, see Koenraad Claes, 'Supplements and Paratext: The Rhetoric of Space', *Victorian Periodicals Review*, 43:2 (Summer 2010), 196-210, as well as the other articles in this special issue.

Monthly Supplement to "*HOUSEHOLD WORDS*," *Conducted by* CHARLES DICKENS.

THE

HOUSEHOLD NARRATIVE

OF CURRENT EVENTS.

1850.]   FROM THE 1ST TO THE 30TH JANUARY.   [PRICE 2*d.*

THE THREE KINGDOMS.

THE NEW YEAR has opened with a discussion which would seem to exhibit the world getting suddenly too old to remember rightly its own age. Whether or not the first half of the century is completed, or must wait another year, has been the subject of this eager dispute; and it is not yet by any means settled. One set of disputants maintain that the year One is completed before it begins, the other would more reasonably suggest that it must begin before it is completed. But then, retorts the logical dealer in subtleties, there is a zero year before the absolute year can count, which explains the apparent discrepancy; just as there is a zero pound while the shillings that compose it are being counted, and not till the twentieth shilling is flung down does the pound absolute make its appearance. Whereto the practical man replies, that whether the year One is to be counted at the end or beginning of its months, is all the same to him; but that he clearly declines to count number Two till he has had the full value of it, and that no conceivable number of unsubstantial shillings could ever produce to his satisfaction any one substantial pound. Supposing a baby born on the first year of a century, he may have been clearly a nothing baby for nine months preceding; but would anybody therefore call him nine months old at his birth? The logician again responding not less learnedly, the question is left a profound puzzle, and as such must probably remain; but we are decidedly of opinion that for common-life purposes the practical view is the more convenient one, and that if we bargained to subscribe for fifty copies of *Household Words* we would by no means be content with forty-nine plus nothing.

Though the memory of the century is thus decrepit, however, let it not be supposed that it has not vigour of life notwithstanding. There is nothing so common now-a-days as all kinds of professed ailments in midst of the sturdiest evidences of health and strength. Nothing can equal the energy and vitality, for example, with which the protectionists have been proclaiming all over England the entire collapse and absolute decease of agricultural prosperity. In Worcester, Nottinghamshire, Edenbridge, Ross, Devonshire, York, Kent, Waltham, and Northampton; in Bucks, Leicester, Horsham, Ely, and Stafford; they have daily, within the past month, exhibited the activity and energy of a more than mortal despair. But it is plainly a case of Killing No Murder, and the public look on enjoying the joke, as much as ever they enjoyed the venerable farce of that name. No year has opened during the present century with more unequivocal indications on every side of extraordinary commercial prosperity. In spite of such adverse events as the war in India, the Danish blockade, and the cholera, trade has made unequalled progress during the year past, and the condition of the bulk of the people has been proportionately improved. Shipping, too, has increased, as a matter of course, with the increase of imports and exports; the building yards are at present as full as the mills and factories; and the first year of the repeal of the navigation laws sees apparently firmer than ever the wooden walls of Old England. Let the wooden heads take comfort, therefore; and listen, with what patience they may, to the admissions which Mr. Disraeli has again during the past month more than once emphatically repeated, as to the utter impossibility of a present or speedy restoration of protection. Is it not strange, by the way, that so clever a person as the protectionist orator cannot perceive, that in proportion as his own hopes of seeing protection restored have been declining (and less and less hopeful, from year to year, has his language gradually become), there must be a reason in the growing satisfaction of the people with the system that displaced it? Would it be possible to maintain free trade for a day beyond the time that the really preponderating interests of the country demanded a re-imposition of protection? The real truth is, that the instinct of the difficulty of returning to the old system possessed by all men out of top-boots and leathers, or in the least degree above the lowest range of the bucolic intellect, is substantially a confession of the abuse which free trade had thrown down. If the new arrangement were not just, or if the old one had not involved what was the reverse of just, change would not now be so difficult or distant as it is confessed by Mr. Disraeli and the most ardent protectionists to be. In a few more years, it is to be hoped, this instinct will ripen into the sensible resolve of not desiring to resume swaddling-clothes at all; in which case we shall have a manly effort to dispense altogether with petting and coddling, and, after the fashion of Mr. Cobden at his farm in Sussex, shall see rents reduced, game surrendered, land drained, trees cleared, fences moved, and, amidst all this, not only both farmers and labourers employed and contented, but landlords cheerful and hopeful. Mr. Cobden went the other day to Aylesbury, to give the farmers the benefit of that quite unprecedented strange agricultural experience; whereat the honest farmers at first began to hiss, then to laugh, and then to cheer. It is clear that even their's is not a case for despair. Even by them the signs of the times do not pass utterly disregarded; and such signs, adverse to their wishes, have lately been more than usually abundant. Protection has been within these few days defeated in what was supposed to be its metropolitan stronghold, among the weavers of Stepney; at a meeting invoked against "the present unfair and ruinous system of competition," backed by all the pretences most likely to gull the well-meaning but half-informed artisan, and presided over by the great guns of the "great central protection society itself." Against all these influences the working men stood firm; supported their own views; flung plentiful cold water over a notorious oratorical firebrand, Mr. Oastler; carried a series of sensible resolutions, to the effect that the best protection they desired to

b

Fig 1. Household Narrative of Current Events.

It was announced in the third number of *Household Words* as 'a design closely associated with our Household Words [...] a supplementary number'.[3] The price of the monthly instalment was the same as that of the parent publication, being two pence. It is not at all rare for such items to come at an additional price, though that may be counter-intuitive for a supplementary publication. The acclaimed 'Extra Christmas Numbers' of *Household Words* and *All the Year Round* were also consistently sold separately and, half a century later, the iconic *Times Literary Supplement* sold for a penny during a period when it was still published in closer association with *The Times* than is the case now.[4]

The announcement of the *Narrative* in *Household Words* proper suggests that it suits our working definition:

> It is scarcely necessary to explain that it is not proposed to render the purchase of THE HOUSEHOLD NARRATIVE compulsory on the purchasers of Household Words; and that the supplementary number, though always published at the same time as our monthly part, will therefore be detached from it, and published separately.[5]

With the last number of every year an index was included, as well as a title page for readers who might wish to have their self-assembled yearly sets bound. Again according to this introductory piece, the *Narrative* would constitute

> [A] comprehensive Abstract or History of all the occurrences of that month, native or foreign [...] a complete Chronicle of all that year's events, carefully compiled, thoroughly digested, and systematically arranged for easy reference; presenting a vast mass of information that must be interesting to all, at a price that will render it accessible to the humblest purchasers of books.[6]

In the same way as serialised novels in the mid-nineteenth century drew a vast readership that would normally not have access to quality fiction due to limited funds, the *Narrative* could delve into an audience eager for information that could not afford more expensive publications, let alone

---

[3] [Charles Dickens] 'The Household Narrative', *Household Words*, Vol. I, No. 3 (13 April 1850), p. 49.
[4] Derwent May, *Critical Times: The History of the Times Literary Supplement* (London: Harper Collins, 2001), p. 93.
[5] [Charles Dickens 'The Household Narrative', p. 49.
[6] [Charles Dickens], 'The Household Narrative', p. 49.

afford to freely purchase books. The tantalising 'comprehensive Abstract or History' was assembled one instalment at a time, and could be collected and looked out for every month. This is no doubt also why the binding of the individual *Narrative*s was encouraged by the issue of that useful paratextual front matter at the end of each year.

There is however another reason why this content could not simply be included within *Household Words* proper. Dickens, and his *Narrative* in particular, played a prominent though ambiguous role in the abolishment of the Stamp Duty, as has been thoroughly documented by John Drew.[7] Any periodical that was deemed to offer 'news' had to be 'stamped', and was thereby subject to a so-called 'Tax on Knowledge'. This was a problem that the parent publication was not faced with, because though it contained essays that took their cue from topical events, these were seldom direct reactions to recent developments in politics. Therefore the magazine did not belong to the awkwardly vague class of 'newspapers' that the Stamp Duty was mainly meant to tax and to indirectly keep in check. On the other hand, the *Narrative*, also unstamped, could easily be considered a 'news' publication, and soon after its first appearance in 1850 the supplement was thus forbidden by the Court of the Exchequer. This ban was legally contested by publishers Bradbury and Evans and was ignored throughout the ensuing court case, which lasted a year and a half and fortunately ended in an acquittal.

The first point that saved the *Narrative* was that its publication interval was greater than twenty-six days, soon to be the legal definition for 'monthly' frequency, and thus it wasn't classed among the daily or, at most, weekly newspapers.[8] Secondly, the *Narrative* had, as we have seen, always cunningly averred that it merely chronicled the past month. It was therefore not topical enough to be classed as 'news', being instead 'historical' in focus. The recurrent mention of the fact that the *Narrative* was meant to constitute a 'chronicle' is very important. Mark Turner has demonstrated that the title of the earlier supplement *The Retrospective Chronicle of Events*, issued with Charles Knight's *Companion to the Newspaper* (1834-37), which was linked to the Society for the Diffusion of Useful Knowledge, was meant to class it among publications meant for future reference rather than for topical commentary. The 'Tax On Knowledge', which was then levied on periodicals covering ongoing events, could thus be avoided by cleverly positing this as the

---

[7] John M. L. Drew, *Dickens the Journalist* (Houndmills: Palgrave Macmillan, 2003), pp. 183-87.

[8] Drew, pp. 185-86.

defining feature of the ever slippery concept 'news', which never had a conclusive legal definition.[9] In the case of the *Narrative*, the matter is even more ambiguous because its full title specifically mentions 'Current Events'. It is safe to assume that this was intentional, an attempt to push the boundaries of what was legally possible at the time and exploit the relative security that the supplement could offer. If nothing else, the self-contradictory verdict of the Court serves to demonstrate how arbitrarily Stamp Duty was enforced in its final stage. The *Narrative* commented triumphantly that

> What the Court of Exchequer has declared by that judgment, is, that the 'HOUSEHOLD NARRATIVE' belongs to the class of history rather than of news; and this exactly is the view in which it originated, and with which, in future Numbers, it will be more carefully and completely worked out. We desire it to be, in future, a perfectly impartial digest and record, that shall from month to month as faithfully keep note of the changing opinions, as it records the unchanging facts, which constitute the History of the time. Not subserving party politics, yet not excluding anything that claims to be a part of the actual interests of the day, our hope is to make it ultimately a not unwelcome or unuseful companion to the publication out of which it arose.[10]

It is not clear precisely what kind of future emendations are hinted at here, as the *Narrative* does not seem to change that much throughout the three remaining years of publication. Perhaps the editors were simply taking care that they would not get into trouble again, as Stamp Duty for monthly publications was only completely abolished more than a year later in August 1853.

To assess how impartial this purported 'perfectly impartial digest' in effect was, a closer look at its contents is needed. The *Narrative*, each issue containing twenty-four pages of text and no advertisements, is divided into recurrent sections of varying length. The first and longest are the 'Narrative of Parliament and Politics', the 'Narrative of Law and Crime' and the 'Narrative of Accident and Disaster'. These give detailed chronicled information of recent occurrences in these specific categories, and are indeed

---

[9] Mark W. Turner, 'Companions, Supplements, and the Proliferation of Print in the 1830s', *Victorian Periodicals Review*, 43:2 (Summer 2010), 119-32.

[10] [?John Forster], 'The Three Kingdoms [xxiv]', *The Household Narrative of Current Events*, Vol. II, No. 12 (27 November 1851), 265-67 (p. 265).

quite unbiased in tone, though it should be noted that the selection of events on which to report will already have involved a conscious choice on the part of the unidentified contributors. The following 'Personal Narrative' provides gossip in the nineteenth-century sense of the term, i.e., short paragraphs on public figures ranging from royalty and the peerage to high-ranking civil servants and singers, whose untimely demise is recorded in the subsequent 'Obituaries of Notable Persons'. 'Colonies and Dependencies' and the 'Narrative of Literature and Art' similarly cover those specific categories of news, and the closing section is always a 'Commercial Record', which provides figures relating to exchange rates and sale prices for raw materials. In most issues a section on 'Social, Sanitary and Municipal Progress' is also included. The latter is obviously a prominent cause in the journalistic campaigning of Dickens and his associates within *Household Words* proper, and scholars studying how this topic is treated broadly in the parent publication will surely be interested in which specific instances are discussed here. Another regular section, the 'Narrative of Foreign Events', shows a characteristically democratic stance, for instance, in its recurrent focus on the tumultuous republican struggles that were then taking place in France.

If the brief reports in these individual 'narratives' are usually self-effacing, they do clearly 'supplement' the subject matter dealt with in the parent publication. The *Narrative* is explicitly presented as a 'companion' to *Household Words* proper and primarily serves to emphasise

> [T]he intimate connexion between the facts and realities of the time, and the means by which we aim, in Household Words, to soften what is hard in them, to exalt what is held in little consideration, and to show the latent hope there is in what may seem unpromising [...]. All that we sought to express in our Preliminary Word, in reference to this work, applies, we think, to its proposed companion.[11]

The above-mentioned 'A Preliminary Word' is the mission statement that opened the very first number of *Household Words* proper. In this editorial Dickens said that the magazine would strive to be 'the comrade and friend of many thousands of people, of both sexes, and of all ages and conditions', but he also made it clear that *Household Words*, though aimed at a nonpartisan readership, was to be a publication with certain ideological aspirations. At the end of this editorial he even declares that the magazine is also to be an alternative to those competitors who defend positions 'whose existence is a

---

[11] [Charles Dickens], 'The Household Narrative', *Household Words*, Vol. I, No. 3 (13 April 1850), p. 49.

national reproach. And these, we should consider it our highest service to displace'.[12] Apparently to this end, the earliest instalments of the *Narrative* open with a seemingly out-of-place column called 'The Three Kingdoms', which delivers remarkably pronounced opinions. They are unsigned, but have been tentatively ascribed to John Forster, and the pieces do indeed fit the image of that combative journalist, who was editor of *The Examiner* throughout the period of the *Narrative*'s publication and well used to imposing editorial weight.[13] More than simply corresponding to Forster's comparatively heated style, we also see his pet peeves appearing in these articles. 'The Three Kingdoms', for instance, repeatedly attacks protectionist tendencies in Parliament, unsurprisingly with recurrent contempt for the Conservative Party of the post-Peel era. *Household Words'* typical distrust of radical reformists is amplified when in the same breath Chartism is decried as representing the 'renewed hopes of Protection', with Chartist leaders being dubbed 'selfish and sordid braggarts'.[14] A vehement reply appeared in the radical *Reynolds's Newspaper* (1851-1967) that held Dickens the author of the piece, an inevitable and frequent side effect of him being the only staff member named in *Household Words* or its supplements.[15] The page-long rebuttal accuses him of wilfully misrepresenting the Chartist cause and 'dangl[ing] at the heels of Lord John Russell'.[16] Luckily for the Conductor, this skirmish did not develop into a full-fledged polemic, but it is a good example of how Forster could make enemies on the left and right of the political spectrum.

The December 1852 *Narrative* has the last 'Three Kingdoms', stating that the 'introductory article' has been discontinued 'in consideration of the advisability of separating the expression of opinion from a faithful record of events; and in consideration of that record requiring all the space we can

---

[12] [Charles Dickens], 'A Preliminary Word', *Household Words*, Vol. I, No. 1 (30 March 1850), 1-2 (p. 2).

[13] Drew, p. 129.

[14] [?John Forster], 'The Three Kingdoms [xvi]', *The Household Narrative of Current Events*, Vol. II, No. 4 (27 March 1851), 73-75 (p. 73).

[15] Conversely, American and Continental pirated editions of fiction by Elizabeth Gaskell, Wilkie Collins and G. A. Sala that were originally anonymously serialised in *Household Words* would often read 'by Charles Dickens' on the cover. See Lillian Nayder, *Unequal Partners: Charles Dickens, Wilkie Collins, and Victorian Authorship* (Ithaca, NY: Cornell University Press, 2002), pp. 19-20.

[16] [Anon.] 'Charles Dickens and the Democratic Movement', *Reynolds's Newspaper*, 8 June 1851, p. 7

allot to it'.[17] The implication is that *Household Words* proper is where we would have to look for (explicit) assessments of topical events, whereas the *Narrative* would limit itself to the bare facts. What exactly caused the termination of the opinion pieces is unclear, but it does happen in what for Forster was a period of generally decreasing contribution to the entire *Household Words* enterprise. Similarly, no reason is given for the eventual folding of the *Narrative* in December 1855, but John Drew speculates that it had something to do with the end of Forster's involvement in *Household Words* due to his retirement from full-time journalism.[18]

What is perhaps significant is that it was during the final month of the *Narrative* that a new project was announced, in the form of *Household Words'* second supplement. This was the *Household Words Almanac* (1856-57), edited by Henry Morley, which lasted for only two annual issues, priced at four pence.[19] This was rather steep for a mere twenty-eight pages of text, one of which was taken up by advertisements, especially in comparison to the parent publication and the previous supplement, which offered more value for money. Although of all types of annual publications the almanac is maybe the most ephemeral, the *Household Words Almanac* goes to some trouble to claim a lasting relevance for itself:

> With all humility and simplicity, we shall endeavour, in successive numbers of this Almanac, to pass from truth to truth, and so to add, year after year, line upon line, as to make out the whole series, even though it should last for a century, a single Year Book.[20]

It is worthy of note that the Narrative too was said to appeal to the 'most humble purchasers of books', whose hoarding instincts the publishers were seeking to stimulate. The idea of a continuous series of general interest, rather than a disposable publication of passing relevance, requires the avoidance of direct references to facts that would only be pertinent to the present year, although it is of course questionable whether any kind of almanac would be actually consulted after its year of issue. A new selling point was introduced for this publication in the form of decorative woodcuts, which makes the *Almanac* at least stand out from *Household Words* proper and the *Narrative* with their lack of illustration.

---

[17] [Anon.], 'Notice', *The Household Narrative of Current Events*, Vol. IV, No. 1 (27 December 1852), p. 73.

[18] Drew, p. 130.

[19] J. W. T. Ley, *The Dickens Circle* (London: Chapman & Hall, 1919), p. 307.

[20] [Henry Morley], 'January—The Quarter', *Household Almanac*, Vol. II (1857), p. 2.

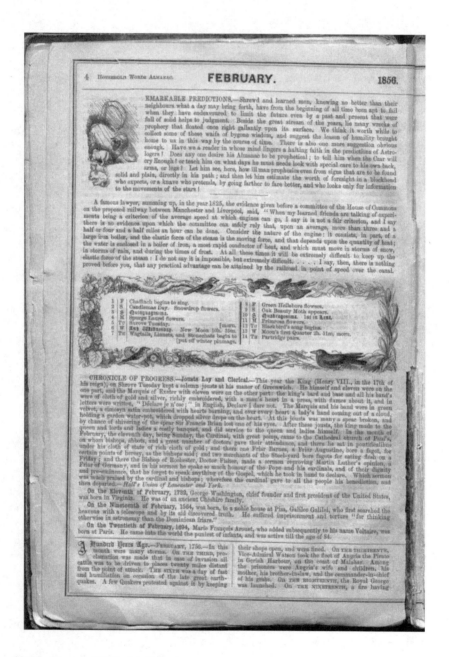

Fig 2. *Household Words Almanac*

These illustrations are however limited to decorative initials for the opening article of each month and the occasional decorated frame.

All this was however not rare in the middle of the nineteenth century, when the old-fashioned almanacs with their stock images, astrology and folk meteorology were increasingly rejected as insubstantial cant. A market arose for ironic versions like the *Comic Almanack* (1835-53) and the enormously successful *Punch's Almanack* (1841-1935), and other comic annuals in which the superstition of the traditional almanacs was lampooned. These had incorporated stylistic features from the annual keepsakes that had been especially popular in the early nineteenth century, and had appealing illustrations to offer, often in the form of caricatures. Almanacs, just like annual keepsakes, were published around early December to catch the shopping spree of the coming holidays, and were (implicitly) marketed as desirable presents. *Household Words Almanac* was no exception, as it was issued in the last week of November, but its frugal decorations could not compete with those of its more playful counterparts. Its illustrations were always based on scenes from nature, and thereby always linked to the traditional cyclical organisation of the almanac genre.

As he had done with the *Narrative* it, the Conductor announced in *Household Words* proper that the *Almanac* would be edited along the same lines as its parent, so as to form a 'a serviceable friend', not only to the reader, but also to the parent publication.[21] We can infer from this that like the *Narrative*, the *Almanac* was meant to expand the larger *Household Words* project into territories that were deemed unsuitable for the parent publication itself to enter. While the *Narrative* was characterised by a crusading zeal in the form of editorials that were harsher than anything appearing in the parent publication, Dickens and Morley were overambitious for their *Almanac* as well:

> In the contemplation of the beautiful harmonies by which Man is surrounded, and of the adorable beneficence by which all things are made to tend to his advantage, and conduce to his happiness, we hope we may have necessarily infused into our work, a humble spirit of veneration for the great Creator of the wonderful Universe, and of peace and good-will among mankind.[22]

---

[21] [Charles Dickens] 'Our Almanac', *Household Words*, Vol. XII, No. 296 (24 November 1855), p. 385.

[22] [Charles Dickens] 'Our Almanac', p. 385.

In reality the *Household Words Almanac* turned out to be unimpressive, mostly delivering the little fun facts that were the traditional fare of almanacs. Dickens realised this and is on record as having remarked that 'the Almanac ought to have done more'.[23]

Apart from the obligatory calendars of Christian holidays and other important dates, there are arguably two types of contributions. First there are seasonal contributions that remind us of the influence the natural cycles have on our constitution, gathered by former physician Morley in a section called 'Serviceable Information'. For instance, in January 1856 we get the sound advice that

> The young lady after a ball, or anyone after attendance at a crowded meeting, had better *not* stand still to cool in the draughts of the entrance-hall, but walk briskly home, well shod and well wrapped up; or, next best, slip at once, warmly cloaked, into a carriage, and make haste to bed.[24]

There is also general information about the cyclical changes in nature in the respective seasons, mostly botanical, in a section called 'The Quarter', which opens the page for every month in which a new season starts.

The second focus of the *Almanac* is more interesting, because it demonstrates a deeper ideological programme:

> We have attached to the Calendar of every month, a Chronicle of Progress, enabling the reader to compare the times in which he lives, with the times of a hundred years ago. We have accumulated a number of remarkable Predictions, all falsified by the result, inculcating the wisdom of not too venturously binding down the Future.[25]

There is an element of humour in these 'Chronicles of Progress', demonstrating bizarre superstitions adhered to in bygone ages. They are not always pleasant because the satire is often downright condescending, rather than teasing in the Dickensian vein, and ideologically quite commonplace as belief in linear historical progress was arguably part and parcel of mid-Victorian public ideology. The 'Remarkable Predictions' too are used to highlight the ignorance of past ages, but as can be guessed from the name,

---

[23] From a letter quoted in Drew, p. 131.

[24] [Henry Morley], 'January—Serviceable Information: Care of the Health in Cold Water', *Household Words Almanac*, Vol. I (1856), p. 3.

[25] [Charles Dickens] 'Our Almanac', p. 385.

these are specifically aimed at past anti-reformers of diverse plumage, who with the aid of hindsight are dismissed as reactionary naysayers. In May 1856 there is, for example, mention of an opponent of vaccination who had proclaimed that Britain would be doomed if this measure, afterwards proven beneficial, were introduced.[26] In a supplement to a periodical known for its activism in the field of sanitation, written by its greatest advocate Morley, the rhetorical strategy is crystal-clear. Another concern that the *Almanac* shares with both its parent and the *Narrative* is shown in the following quote:

> A noble Earl, in the year 1846, opposing with an amendment in the Lords, the motion for Free Trade in Corn, said: 'He knew what the result would be. He knew that the effect would be, an immediate and sudden reaction, which would drive like chaff before the wind the advocates of Free Trade—which would render the very name odious to all classes in the country—and which would restore, in all their force, the prohibitory and protective system of their ancestors'.[27]

The predictions in the *Almanac* are therefore used to ridicule opponents of the political aims of *Household Words* and thus, as in the *Narrative*, an otherwise neutral genre is subtly reclaimed for political purposes, supplementing the ideological and commercial aspirations of the parent publication.

Due to the irregular quality of the content, and the troublesome market positioning they encountered, the two regular feature supplements to *Household Words* may be said to have been failures and they certainly never enjoyed the great success of the far more widely read 'Extra Christmas Numbers'. The *Narrative* and the *Almanac* are nevertheless highly relevant when considered as extensions to the parent publication and the *Dickens Journals Online* project has done the scholarly community a great service by making their entire run available, free of charge.

---

[26] [Henry Morley 'May—Remarkable Predictions', *Household Words Almanac*, Vol. I (1856), p. 10.

[27] [Henry Morley], 'August—Remarkable Predictions', *Household Words Almanac*, Vol. I (1856), p. 16.

SECTION 2

Laura Foster

PERHAPS the most enduring representation of the nineteenth-century workhouse is that created by Charles Dickens in *Oliver Twist* (1837-39). As one of the most famous attacks upon the 1834 New Poor Law, Dickens's novel draws attention to the corruption and inhumanity of the workhouse regime. However, Dickens's most prolific anti-Poor Law writings take the form of factual accounts. As well as authoring articles, Dickens also edited and published numerous pieces about the New Poor Law in *Household Words* and *All the Year Round*. By contrast to *Household Words*, *All the Year Round* prioritised serialised fiction over factual examinations of society; nevertheless, the New Poor Law remained a recurrent topic of debate in *All the Year Round*, with articles that drew attention to the unsuitability of workhouses for the very old, the young and the sick.[1] These politicised texts provided a platform for contemporary discussion of the social debates surrounding these institutions and agitated for workhouse reform.

The intense anti-Poor Law debates of the 1830s and 1840s were reignited in the 1860s by a series of workhouse scandals reported by the press.[2] In 1867, Dickens sent an angry letter to Joseph Charles Parkinson, a

---

[1] John M. L. Drew, *Dickens the Journalist* (Houndmills: Palgrave Macmillan, 2003), p. 138.

[2] The deaths of Timothy Daly in 1864 and Richard Gibson in 1865 as a result of their care in workhouse infirmaries were reported by newspapers, such as *The Times*. Following the deaths of these paupers, the *Lancet* Sanitary Commission was set up in 1865 to investigate the state of workhouse infirmaries and published numerous reports exposing the dirty and crowded conditions of the wards in metropolitan and country workhouses. See the announcement '"The Lancet" Commission to Inquire into the State of Workhouse Hospitals', *Lancet*, Vol. LXXXV, No. 2172, 15 April 1865, 410 (p. 410). More dramatically, James Greenwood disguised himself as an impoverished engraver and went undercover in the casual ward of the Lambeth

contributor to *All the Year Round*, asking him to write an article entitled 'What is Sensational?'[3] The letter opens with Dickens's instruction that '[u]nder this title I want the most ferocious and bitter attack made upon Mr Hardy of the Poor Law Board, that can possibly be made by a writer who respects himself and his vocation'.[4] These passionate words were written in response to a speech made by Gathorne Hardy, the president of the Poor Law Board. Hardy had accused journalists of writing sensationally about workhouses and had referred, as an example of this sensationalism, to press coverage about the neglectful treatment of paupers in workhouse infirmaries.[5] Incensed by what he interpreted as Hardy's attempt to downplay the scandalous lack of care for sick paupers, Dickens continued in his instructional letter to Parkinson:

> What does he mean by Sensational? Is it Sensational to tell the Truth? Is it Sensational to call the public attention to a noteworthy example of a costly Board existing under false pretences and showing mankind How not to do it? Is it sensational to be poor, abject, wretched, dying?[6]

Parkinson's article was published on 2 March 1867 and, as requested by Dickens, was a scathing attack upon the Poor Law Board.

The three articles that I will focus upon here are 'A Workhouse Probe', 'Another Workhouse Probe' and 'A Country Workhouse', which were published in consecutive issues in *All the Year Round* between 30 November and 14 December 1867.[7] Attributed to Joseph Charles Parkinson, the articles

---

workhouse. His sensational three-part narrative, 'A Night in a Workhouse', was published in the *Pall Mall Gazette* from 12-15 January 1866 and made the foetid conditions of the casual ward the focus of a public scandal.

[3] To J. C. Parkinson, ?Mid-February 1867, headed 'What is Sensational', *The Letters of Charles Dickens*, ed. by Kathleen Tillotson, Graham Storey and others, Pilgrim Edition, 12 vols (Oxford: Clarendon Press, 1965-2002), Vol. XI, pp. 314-15 (p. 314).

[4] *The Letters of Charles Dickens*, Vol. XI, p. 314.

[5] Hardy's speech was reported in 'Imperial Parliament', *Daily News*, 9 February 1867, p. 2. A portion of the speech is referred to in the editorial notes to Dickens's letter, as well as the circumstances of the deaths of Timothy Daly and Richard Gibson, whom Hardy also mentioned in his speech. See notes for To J. C. Parkinson, *The Letters of Charles Dickens*, Vol. XI, p. 315.

[6] *The Letters of Charles Dickens*, Vol. XI, p. 315. Here, 'How not to do it' is an implicit reference to Dickens's *Little Dorrit* (1855-57).

[7] [Joseph Charles Parkinson], 'A Workhouse Probe', *All the Year Round*, Vol. XVIII, No. 449 (30 November 1867), 541-45; 'Another Workhouse Probe', *All the Year*

extend the magazine's attack upon the workhouse system.[8] In these three first-person investigative articles, each of which explore a different workhouse, the narrator pokes and pries into the hidden corners of the buildings and attempts objectively to represent the workhouse space to readers. By dramatising the human suffering within the workhouses, these articles ostensibly seek to demonstrate what Dickens had angrily stated in his letter months earlier—that the truth is inherently sensational. The regular weekly appearance of these texts reflects the magazine's sustained commentary upon the New Poor Law and the part played by the media in opening up the workhouses to public dissemination.

The articles both respond to, and provoke, a climate of increasing public concern about the treatment of paupers and can be situated within a wider discourse of anti-workhouse writing in the autumn of 1867. Having investigated metropolitan workhouse infirmaries, the *Lancet* turned its attention to the condition of country workhouses and began to publish reports on these from September 1867. Of the reports on country workhouses, the most memorable is the article on the Farnham workhouse, published in October, which draws readers' attention to the case of an epileptic pauper who had died after falling into the cesspool that he had been ordered to clean out. The *Lancet* report provoked a reaction from both the press and the Poor Law Board. When *All the Year Round* published the first workhouse article, the newspapers were still providing the public with frequent updates about the subsequent investigation into Farnham. In addition to the circulation of factual workhouse narratives, the first instalment of Anne Thackeray Ritchie's novella, *Jack the Giant-Killer* (1867-68), was published in the *Cornhill Magazine* in November. The bleak description of the workhouse in the story, in which the paupers drink water that is channelled through the cesspool, resonates with the *Lancet*'s report on Farnham. It was in this context of workhouse debate that the articles in *All the Year Round* appeared.

The first article, 'A Workhouse Probe', informs readers that the narrator is accompanying the *Lancet* Sanitary Commissioners on their investigations into country workhouse infirmaries. This medical association, together with the title word 'probe' of the first two articles, implies the objective and quasi-

---

Round, Vol. XVIII, No. 450 (7 December 1867), 558-64; 'A Country Workhouse', *All the Year Round*, Vol. XIX, No. 451 (14 December 1867), 16-20. All subsequent references to these works will be made in the text.
[8] Ella Ann Oppenlander, *Dickens' All the Year Round: Descriptive Index and Contributor List* (Troy, NY: Whitson, 1984), pp. 195-96.

scientific analysis of the workhouse by the magazine. In contrast to the reports in the *Lancet*, however, which name the workhouses that were investigated, the articles in *All the Year Round* withhold the names and the exact locations of the workhouses described. This lack of factual detail detracts from the empiric nature of the reports. The seeming factuality of the articles is also compromised by veiled allusions to fiction, in the form of novels. In 'A Workhouse Probe', the workhouse is described as being akin to 'Mr. Wemmick's Walworth fortress', which is a reference to *Great Expectations* (1860-61) ('A Workhouse Probe', p. 451). A pauper nurse is likened to 'Smike' from *Nicholas Nickleby* (1838-39) and a baker to 'Mr. Tulliver' in *The Mill on the Floss* (1860) ('Another Workhouse Probe', pp. 560, 563). The paid nurse in 'A Country Workhouse' reminds the narrator of 'Miss Miggs', a character who appears in *Barnaby Rudge* (1841) ('A Country Workhouse', p. 20). The articles' analyses of the workhouses thus rely upon a novelistic vocabulary that is assumed to be shared by readers. This entanglement of fiction and fact blurs the boundaries between the two and so implicitly suggests a sensationalising of the facts, as Hardy had argued.

The representation of the workhouse in 'A Workhouse Probe' is contradictory. A cesspool lies beneath the infirmary windows and the privies are reported to be 'disgustingly unfit for human use' ('A Workhouse Probe', p. 541). But the narrator also acknowledges the cleanliness and contentment of the paupers and observes the matron's kindness to the children. When the visitors 'peer' into the kitchen soup coppers at the 'deliciously appetising' meal being prepared for the inmates, the narrator declares that they are 'hungry enough to envy the paupers' ('A Workhouse Probe', p. 542).

Then the second half of the article moves into a direct attack upon the workhouse system and disrupts any positive impressions that readers may have received about this individual workhouse. The text's criticisms centre upon the fact that the guardians, who should be disinterested, are tradesmen who benefit financially from the workhouse contracts, suggesting the potential for corruption inherent in the head guardian doubling as workhouse landlord.[9] Yet it is the district inspector, as the representative of the Poor Law Board, who the article sets out to lampoon. As evidence of the inspector's failure to report abuses, the narrator says:

> Let us turn, then, to the visiting-book, and see how the official
> visitor, who is already celebrated for his discharge of duty at

---

[9] Each workhouse had a board of guardians who oversaw the running of the institution.

Farnham, has performed his duty. His inspections have been made with great regularity twice a year, and 'Wards in good order,' 'Satisfactory,' 'Very Satisfactory,' form the staple of his monotonous remarks. Not a syllable concerning sanitary arrangements, closets, cesspools, classification, or the ownership of the house ('A Workhouse Probe', p. 544).

The inspector is identified in 'A Workhouse Probe' as the same person responsible for the atrocities of Farnham workhouse. The *Lancet* report on Farnham similarly attributes blame to this individual and points out that '[t]here is little trace in the inspector's work at Farnham of the seeing eye, the hearing ear, or the smelling nose'.[10] The inspector is constructed as a figure of public ridicule by *Punch*. Commenting upon the failure of the inspector to actually inspect the workhouse, *Punch* suggests that he should instead be called a 'Poor-Law Neglecter'.[11] By contrast to the Poor Law Inspector's wilful blindness, the visiting party in 'A Workhouse Probe' peer into the nooks and crannies of the workhouse, sniff out the smells and converse with the inmates.

'A Workhouse Probe' concludes that the power of inspection should be shifted from the Poor Law authorities to the public; as the narrator points out, '[o]ur workhouses must no longer be close boroughs, jobbed and managed, or mismanaged, by a clique or coterie. Inspection must be in the hands of the ratepayers' ('A Workhouse Probe', p. 544). The article suggests that the only restraint on the abuses of the workhouse system is the use of '[p]ublicity' to shed light, literally and metaphorically, into the hidden corners of these institutions ('A Workhouse Probe', p. 544). This belief in the reforming power of 'publicity' suggests the political importance of the press and the social and moral onus placed upon the readers of *All the Year Round* to turn their attention to the state of workhouses.

By contrast to the first article, 'Another Workhouse Probe' is an unrelenting attack. The text opens with a grimly satirical account of the workhouse master's delight with a new funeral hearse. The master proudly explains to the visitors that the hearse was provided after a guardian witnessed a group of paupers struggling to carry a heavy body to the

---

[10] [Anon.], 'The Lancet Sanitary Commission for Investigating the State of the Infirmaries of Workhouses; Country Workhouse Infirmaries. No. III. Farnham (Near Aldershot.)', *Lancet*, Vol. XC, No. 2303, 19 October 1867, 496-98 (p. 498).
[11] [Anon.], 'A Probe in the Poorhouse', *Punch*, Vol. LIII, No. 1373 (2 November 1867), 178-81 (p. 178).

cemetery and that, as a consequence of the hearse, the paupers now look forward to funerals. The extravagance of the hearse contrasts with the stark conditions in which the paupers live, with only a shambling pauper nurse to attend the sick at night; the article implies that the guardians are far more concerned with the public show of a funeral procession than with the welfare of the living paupers. Later in the article, the text draws attention to the 'black harness' of the hearse that hangs temporarily in the guardians' boardroom ('Another Workhouse Probe', p. 563). The macabre reminder of the hearse implicitly invites readers to make connections between the administrative powers of the workhouse and the inevitable fate of the paupers who reside there.

The exploration of the workhouses in *All the Year Round* is an attempt to familiarise readers with these closed institutions and, by implication, gain control over the pauper space. As the narrator points out in 'Another Workhouse Probe':

> We want to master details of their daily lives, to know the lying down and getting up of people to whom a funeral of one of their number is a treat, and who take a pride in following the ghastly hearse which they themselves are soon to fill ('Another Workhouse Probe', p. 561).

The desire to 'master' the intricacies of the paupers' lives suggests that these investigative articles are about making sense of the workhouse and understanding what a pauperised existence means. At the same time as they attempt to 'know' the workhouse, however, the articles also suggest an inherent otherness of the space that eludes understanding. A macabre vocabulary is inscribed upon the building in this article: the sleeping ward for the old men is compared to a 'living tomb' that shows as little evidence of human life as 'would be found in a row of trestles upon which corpses were to rest' ('Another Workhouse Probe', p. 563). Even the most mundane rooms of the workhouse hold sights that the visitors find strange and disturbing. In the laundry, for example, the visiting party encounters 'an imbecile female dwarf of sixty' who is described as giving the visitors 'the most grotesquely hideous grimace it has been our fortune to see save in a gurgoyle [*sic*] or a pantomime' ('Another Workhouse Probe', p. 563). The text positions readers of this article alongside the visiting party as the voyeurs of eerie workhouse spectacles. The deliberate selection of these sights suggests the inability of the narrative to escape a sensationalised reporting of the facts.

Of particular concern in 'Another Workhouse Probe' is the harshness of the disciplinary treatment that is meted out to the aged. Though the workhouses were originally designed to discipline the lazy and workshy able-bodied, the actual pauper population of the workhouses in the mid-nineteenth century consisted mainly of the sick and elderly. The text describes the pitiful sight of haggard old men scraping potatoes in a cold outbuilding and points out that it is comfort that these men are in need of, not punishment. The comment that 'to leave them neglected in an open outhouse, is simply shortening their lives' incriminates the workhouse system, by placing on it the responsibility for their deaths' ('Another Workhouse Probe', p. 561). The incongruity between the intended function of the workhouses and their actual purpose is emphasised by the article's description of the sleeping wards of these feeble old men—though the room would 'be excellent for healthy vigorous lads', it is 'desolately penal for the decrepit wretches sleeping in it' ('Another Workhouse Probe', p. 561). The article reveals that, at night, these men are left wholly unattended and have no method of contacting the master in case of illness.

Later, the text draws attention to the consequences of this neglectful practice of locking up the paupers overnight. The article refers to the 'ugly circumstance' of an old man who had fallen out of bed and died in the Bethnal Green workhouse ('Another Workhouse Probe', p. 561). The man's body was left there until the next morning because the pauper wardsman chose not to shout for the master. The article explains that, as a result of the public outcry, an investigation was launched that ended in the exoneration of all the officials involved and the announcement that there were bells in the workhouse that could have been rung to summon help. However, the text informs readers that 'the present writer [felt] doubtful concerning this pauper's death, and the circumstances surrounding it' and conducted a private investigation of the ward in advance of the official one ('Another Workhouse Probe', p. 562). The revelation that the bells were put up after the man's death draws attention to the workhouse officials' corrupt attempt to conceal their neglect of the paupers.

As well as referring to the Bethnal Green case, 'Another Workhouse Probe' also refers directly to the scandalous deaths of the paupers Timothy Daly and Richard Gibson, as a result of their care in other workhouse infirmaries.[12] The text states that

---

[12] The deaths of Daly and Gibson were attributed to neglectful treatment in the Holborn and St Giles's workhouses respectively. Daly, in particular, is described in reports in *The Times* as being 'a strong man when he went into the workhouse'

It was a pauper nurse at the Holborn Union workhouse who, on her own responsibility, plunged the dying Timothy Daly into a warm bath on an inclement day in December; and a pauper nurse who improperly applied fuller's-earth to his sores. It was a pauper nurse who, at last, mercifully killed off Richard Gibson, at the St Giles's Union, by giving him gin ('Another Workhouse Probe', p. 562).

In this text, blame is placed upon the inadequacies of workhouse infirmaries and the neglect that inevitably results from using pauper inmates to nurse the sick.[13] By referring to incidents that were widely condemned in the newspapers, the text situates itself within a factual reality and lends weight to its campaign for reform.

Of the three articles, 'A Country Workhouse' offers the most damning representation of all. The opening lines of the article inform readers that the visiting party are '[s]till on the track of shameful, flagrant abuses; still fighting the drearily, uphill fight against highly sanctioned cruelties and legally committed wrong' ('A Country Workhouse', p. 16). The visitors are constructed in these lines as detectives of workhouse abuses, seeking to expose the hidden cruelties of the workhouse system. The emphasis on the 'legal' and 'sanctioned' nature of the 'cruelties' and 'wrong' suggests the inherent criminality of the ruling authorities and depicts the visitors as subversive crusaders against the state-approved inhumanities of the Poor Law Board.

As in the previous two articles, 'A Country Workhouse' calls attention to the inadequacies of the workhouse and the officials who manage it. In particular, this article subverts the authority of the workhouse master when the visiting party assume that he is the gardener. The master's lower-class status is confirmed by the revelation that he used to be the porter and that

---

suffering from rheumatic fever. The inattention of the infirmary nurses resulted in him developing large bedsores which caused his death. See 'The Holborn Union', *The Times*, 28 December 1864, p. 10. Similarly, *The Times* reported that Richard Gibson's death in the St Giles's infirmary was 'greatly accelerated by the neglect [he] received at the hands of the whole of the officials connected with the St. Giles's Workhouse'. See 'The Sick Pauper in St. Giles's Workhouse', *The Times*, 31 March 1865, p. 11.

[13] The articles of the *Lancet* Sanitary Commissioners similarly exposed the horrors that resulted from using paupers instead of paid nurses. See for example the description of the St Leonard's workhouse infirmary in 'Reports of the Commissioners. No. III. Metropolitan Infirmaries. St. Leonard's, Shoreditch', *Lancet*, Vol. LXXXVI, No. 2187, 29 July 1865, 131-34 (pp. 132-33).

he is now looking forward to being 'superannuasiated' ('A Country Workhouse', p. 17). By quoting the master's mispronunciation, the text pokes fun at the ignorance of this man and draws attention to the lower-class associations of this poorly paid job. The master, who is said to be more suited to a career in the army, is incompatible with a role caring for the sick and elderly, who form the vast majority of the workhouse population. In this text, the disciplinary function of the house and its management is reflected in the architectural design; the workhouse has a 'barrack-prison-penitentiary air' and the windows are so high up that the paupers in the wards cannot look out of them ('A Country Workhouse', p. 17).

At the same time as the article seeks to make the workhouse interior known, 'A Country Workhouse' simultaneously points to the limits of what the visiting party and the readers of the magazine can truly understand about these institutions. As a pauper in one of the sick wards tells the visitors, '[l]ie here on yer back for three weeks—lie here on yer back, and then ye'll know more than yer'll get by poking about with a pencil and a little book, and asking questions about winders' ('A Country Workhouse', p. 19). The pauper's words strip these social investigators of any grandiose pretensions to being humanitarian crusaders and turn the visitors' scrutiny of the workhouse back upon them; rather than 'probing' the workhouse, they are, in fact, seen by the paupers to be pointlessly 'poking about'.

Even as this text ostensibly sheds light onto the workhouse, the narrator, when describing one of the sick wards, suggests that '[i]t would be improper to detail in these columns the worst of the evils rampant here' ('A Country Workhouse', p. 19). This reticence to 'detail' abuses in *All the Year Round* is at odds with the apparent intention to open up the workhouses to the public eye. The implication that the sights witnessed are too disturbing to be committed to print and read by even the socially-aware readers of *All the Year Round* is a classic trope of sensationalism and reminds readers of a selective narrator whose representation of the workhouse is a textual construct. In contradiction of the aim to 'probe' the workhouse, the narrative unintentionally suggests that any scrutiny of the workhouse is obscured by the narrator's own agenda. Although the texts attempt to provide an objective exploration of the workhouses, they seem unable to escape the techniques of sensation writing and inadvertently sensationalise the already sensational facts.

Collectively, these articles seek to open up the workhouses to public debate and deliberation. By directing the gaze of readers into the shadowy inner corners of the workhouse space, the articles aim to provoke public outrage at the treatment meted out to the sick and the old. Dramatising the human suffering in Poor Law workhouses, the articles advocate for the power of inspection to be placed instead in the hands of the public, a public that is, implicitly, the readers of *All the Year Round*.

Organicism and Francomania in *Houshold Words*[1]

Ignacio Ramos Gay

FRANCE was undoubtedly Dickens's other country. It was the mythical ground that used to greet him with 'the three charming words, Liberty, Equality, Fraternity, painted up (in letters a little too thin for their height) on the Custom House Wall', his novels, travelogues and stories are rife with references to French characters, cities and French history, which provide colourful explorations of his personal attachment to France.[2] A forerunner of Oscar Wilde's cultural and linguistic Francophilia, Dickens's command of French anticipated the Irishman's desire to explore a new instrument to which Wilde 'had listened all [his] life, and [he] wanted once to touch [...] to see whether [he] could make any beautiful thing'.[3] In Dickens's letters, he recurrently incorporated French phrases, revealing his Francophile inclination: 'La difficulté d'écrire l'Anglais m'est extrêmement ennuyeuse. Ah, mon Dieu! Si l'on pourrait [*sic*] toujours écrire cette belle langue de France!'.[4] Dickens felt at home in France, where he took up residence for

---

[1] I am grateful to John Drew for pointing out the publication of E. S. Dixon's article 'A Sensible Town' (*Household Words*, Vol. VIII, No. 192 [26 November 1853], 302-305) around which this chapter partially revolves. All subsequent references to this article will appear in the text. Dixon (1809-93) was a regular contributor to *Household Words,* authoring 145 articles, 20 of which featured as leaders.

[2] [Charles Dickens], 'A Flight', *Household Words*, Vol. III, No. 75 (30 August 1851), 529-533 (p. 531).

[3] *Oscar Wilde, Interviews and Recollections*, ed. by E. H. Mikhail, 2 vols (London: Macmillan, 1979), Vol. I, p. 188.

[4] To John Forster, 7 May 1850, *The Letters of Charles Dickens*, ed. by Kathleen Tillotson, Graham Storey and others, Pilgrim Edition, 12 vols (Oxford: Clarendon Press, 1965-2002), Vol. VI, pp. 94-95. Adjusting for Dickens's mistake in writing 'pourrait' instead of 'pouvait,' this translates as, 'The difficulty of writing English is

extensive periods of time, and his vision of the country stands as a complex synecdoche for the Modern World.

This is particularly noticeable when attempting to redefine national identity in terms of urban sanitation and the management of nature. In a myriad of articles published in *Household Words* and *All the Year Round*, the recreation of France departs from strict journalistic discourse and at times borders on travel fiction. Based on personal trips and experiences in French cities and towns, the articles are frequently permeated with colourful references and comments that connote personal affection. Commentators have contended that more than a specific location, France represented in Dickens's work an idealistic aspiration, the aim of which was to attack his compatriots' insularity, or, in John Edmondson's words, 'to highlight what is wrong with the British system' and to ridicule 'the dismissive and xenophobic assumption of British superiority'.[5] Although it is necessary to admit that Dickens was far from a blind, Francophile venerator—as shown by his harsh criticism of animal welfare policies and the lack of empathy shown towards non-human others in French abattoirs, despite the passing of the Loi Grammont in 1851—the literary concoction of France in *Household Words* follows subjective, if not mythical, representations of the country's nineteenth-century grandeur, following the path of many British, Irish and American travellers who regarded it as a social and cultural inspiration.[6]

Despite being grounded in factual information, the literary incarnations of French towns in Dickens's journal unveil a visionary system of nature management that echoes classic utopian societies. In a number of articles illustrating personal experiences in Picardie and the Paris region in the early 1850s, the journal describes the integration and exploitation of natural resources within French civil society as a teleological instance of political and social perfection. Reflections on the abattoirs of Montmartre and Grenelle, and on the urban physical arrangement of the city of Amiens, portray the incorporation of the natural world within urban design in an idealist manner that takes after and updates classic organicist constructions of the city.

---

most tiresome to me. My God! If only we could write this beautiful language of France at all times'.

[5] *Dickens on France: Fiction, Journalism, and Travel Writing*, ed. by John Edmonson (Northampton, MA: Interlink Books, 2007), p. 268.

[6] The Loi Grammont was a law passed by the French National Legislative Assembly outlawing cruelty towards domestic animals. It punished 'persons who publicly inflicted abuse on pets' with a fine of up to fifteen francs and a sentence of up to five days in jail.

Carolyn Merchant defines Renaissance organicism as the retrieval of Platonic postulates based upon the organism metaphor, resulting in a 'living chain of being, each member a step in a stable, ordered, spherically-enclosed world', by which humanity 'was linked to the animal world below, with which he shared sensation, and to the angels above, with whom he shared rationality'.[7] I will particularly concentrate on the metaphoric description of French abattoirs and towns as organic bodies in two articles focusing on French recollections: 'A Monument of French Folly' and 'A Sensible Town'.[8] In both cases, the literary reflection of urban, material constructions provides these spaces with the organic attributes of living beings, thus infusing them with an animistic essence that can be linked to a post-Romantic reading of nature.

Ventilation and Organicism in 'A Monument of French Folly'

In 'A Monument of French Folly', Dickens renders French slaughterhouses and markets as salubrious places, particularly in comparison with their English counterparts, and most notably in contrast with Smithfield, the largest wholesale market in the United Kingdom. Based in the City since the Middle Ages, the market had been originally built on the outskirts of London, yet the massive growth of the city's population steadily modified its original location until it eventually came to occupy a nuclear position in the capital. As a result, the animals were brutally driven through narrow and heaving streets crammed with local trades and industries associated with the market, and became a hazard to public health and security. Intended as a harsh attack on the City of London Corporation's refusal to relocate the Smithfield market from the centre to a faraway area on the city limits, 'A Monument of French Folly' praises the geometric regularity, supervised organisation, cleanliness and ventilation of French abattoirs. The conclusion is that, in France,

> of a great Institution like Smithfield, they are unable to form the least conception. A Beast Market in the heart of Paris would be regarded as an impossible nuisance. Nor have they any notion of slaughter-houses in the midst of a city ('A Monument', p. 553).

---

[7] Carolyn Merchant, *The Death of Nature: Women, Ecology and the Scientific Revolution* (New York: Harper Collins, 1980), p. 100.

[8] [Charles Dickens], 'A Monument of French Folly', *Household Words*, Vol. II, No. 50 (8 March 1851), 553-58. All subsequent references will appear in the text.

One of the most original aspects of Dickens's advocacy for the adoption of French hygienic measures on the part of the English administration of public cattle-markets was his literary depiction of the French slaughterhouses of Montmartre and Grenelle as ventilated, 'breathing bodies'. Dickens's views on improving markets' and slaughterhouses' sanitary conditions revealed a deep belief in air circulation and oxygenation much in the line of classic Darwinian ideas of substance re-use and state regeneration, or what Joe Amato terms 'the popular mid-century belief in the cyclical quality of all natural things'.[9] In *Our Mutual Friend* (1864-65), Mr Venus's taxidermist skills lie in 'creating an integrity for that which has been disintegrated, and in procuring value from that which has been used'.[10] In 'A Monument of French Folly', Dickens enthusiastically endorses a similar argument when encouraging an understanding of ventilation and air renewal as a healthy source of life and urban progression. As Robert Macfarlane observes, Dickens was mostly influenced by contemporary 'medical science's miasmic theories of infection, which attributed not just the spread but also the generation of disease to the accumulation of waste matter', a practice which had come to be perceived 'as a symptom of societal disorganization and ill-health'.[11]

Much has been written about Dickens's involvement in the mid-Victorian sanitation movement, as shown by his early interest in the Metropolitan Improvement Society and the Metropolitan Sanitary Association. Furthermore, Dickens's brother-in-law, Henry Austin, was a chief inspector of the General Board of Health, and was 'influential in forming the novelist's interest in these issues'.[12] An *avant-la-lettre* advocate of air purification against corruption, Dickens contended that ventilation problems, both within over-populated markets and inside the slaughterhouses, caused disease:

> [I]nto the imperfect sewers of this overgrown city, you shall have the immense mass of corruption, engendered by these practices, lazily thrown out of sight, to rise, in poisonous gases, into your house at night, when your sleeping children will most readily absorb them,

---

[9] Joe Amato, 'No Wasted Words', *Nineteenth-Century Studies*, 12 (1998), 37-63 (p. 50).
[10] Robert Macfarlane, *Original Copy: Plagiarism and Originality in Nineteenth-Century Literature* (Oxford: Oxford University Press, 2007), p. 50.
[11] Macfarlane, p. 52.
[12] Karl Ashley Smith, *Dickens and the Unreal City: Searching for Spiritual Significance in Nineteenth-Century London* (Houndmills: Palgrave Macmillan, 2008), p. 63.

and to find its languid way, at last, into the river that you drink ('A Monument', p. 554).

The domestic threat that the author addresses derives from the inexorable cycle of decomposition and composition, the menace of metamorphosing diseases which engenders a discourse of urban hazard in which clean and fresh air acts as a revitalising element. From a metaphoric perspective, Macfarlane argues that in Dickens's work, 'circulation plainly emerges as a desideratum' while 'circulation's obverse, "blockage", is figured as hateful: the images of grease, fat, ooze, and miasma [...] are the physical consequences of congestion, all designate moral or metaphysical stagnancy or some sort'.[13] Unopened spaces such as English markets and slaughterhouses are, therefore, 'victims of their own stasis'.[14] They emerge as places where concentrated gases saturate the regeneration process:

> [S]laughter-houses, in the large towns of England, are always [...] most numerous in the most densely crowded places, where there is least circulation of air. They are often underground, in cellars; they are sometimes in close back yards; sometimes (as in Spitalfields) in the very shops where the meat is sold. Occasionally, under good private management, they are ventilated and clean' ('A Monument', p. 553).

Clean air and the recycling of oxygen is one of Dickens's foremost obsessions in this article, to the extent that the whole narrative on English hermetic markets and slaughterhouses tends to penetrate his actual writing style, which becomes spirally asphyxiating as it condenses images and ideas within its insulating syntax: 'The busiest slaughter-houses in London are in the neighbourhood of Smithfield, in Newgate Market, in Whitechapel, in Newport Market, in Leadenhall Market, in Clare Market. All these places are surrounded by houses of a poor description, swarming with inhabitants' ('A Monument', p. 553). His claustrophobic account of an area densely infested with dwellings, inhabitants and slaughterhouses becomes as circular, accumulative and suffocating as the locations appearing in it. Verb tenses and the syntactic profusion of nouns, adjectives and compounds act as intensifying vehicles of a sweltering condensation:

> Prosperity to cattle-driving, cattle-slaughtering, bone-crushing, blood-boiling, trotter-scraping, tripe-dressing, paunch-cleaning, gut-

---

[13] Macfarlane, p. 55.
[14] Macfarlane, p. 61.

spinning, hide-preparing, tallow-melting, and other salubrious proceedings, in the midst of hospitals, churchyards, workhouses, schools, infirmaries, refuges, dwellings, provision-shops, nurseries, sick-beds, every stage and baiting place in the journey from birth to death ('A Monument', p. 554).

This nauseating piling of people, live animals and pestiferous animal corpses and remains in a deplorable state suggests a significant correlation between humans and non-human others. Humans are portrayed as if being incarcerated within the walls of oppressive areas, thus recreating an incestuous atmosphere of a deterministic nature. Within the limits of such specific urban arrangements, man's death sentence is comparable to that of beasts about to be slaughtered in the abattoir, and the link to human death is made even more explicit by Dickens when disclosing that some of these slaughterhouses are 'close to the worst burial-grounds in London' ('A Monument', p. 553).

According to Dickens's personal experience, French abattoirs proved to be the exact opposite of their English counterparts. Despite being built within the city walls, they stood on the borders: the Abattoir of Montmartre was located 'in a sufficiently dismantled space', which covered 'nearly nine acres of ground' ('A Monument', pp. 556-57). Full ventilation was then assured for buildings of magnificent proportions standing 'in open places in the suburbs, removed from the press and bustle of the city' ('A Monument', p. 556). Contrary to the 'unventilated and dirty' London slaughterhouses with 'reeking walls, putrid fat and other offensive animal matter clings with a tenacious hold' ('A Monument', p. 553), the interior design of the French abattoir, made up of a number of opposing doors and windows, facilitated air circulation, preventing aerial corruption: 'there may be a thorough current of air from opposite windows in the side walls, and from doors to the slaughter-houses' ('A Monument', p. 557).

Echoing his animalisation of humans in his novels, here Dickens casts the French abattoir's airing system in imitation of a human organism. Dickens's personification of the slaughterhouse shows it as a breathing space, a physical location endowed with autonomous respiration and therefore with life. Unlike English abattoirs and markets, defined by their insulation and claustrophobic closed-mindedness, their French counterparts were breathing edifices 'open on all sides', inhaling new fresh air and exhaling corrupted winds ('A Monument', p. 555). Dickens's organicist metaphor of markets and slaughterhouses as fully ventilated, 'lunged' bodies preventing aerial corruption and putrefaction may have been ignited by the reading of Poor Law Commissioner Edwin Chadwick's 1842 *Report on the Sanitary Condition of the Labouring Population of Great Britain*, and by 'exposure to the socio-political discourse of circularity and circulation' prominent during the 1840s.[15] Slow as political action was to follow, the politics of public health inevitably 'began to shape his imagining of the disposition and regulation of society', and 'A Monument of French Folly' credits this cycle of motion and change as the process of natural life renewal in which circularity is infused both with biological and animistic connotations.[16]

Haematological Metaphors in 'A Sensible Town'

A similar reference to French abattoirs can be found in E. S. Dixon's article on the 'sensible town' of Amiens. Dickens himself was well acquainted with the town, as he visited it on many occasions travelling to and from England and Paris. John Forster recalls numerous trips with Dickens's friends in his chapter 'Three Summers at Boulogne 1853, 1854, 1856', and emphasises the fact that the excursions to Amiens and Beauvais 'relieved' his work on his novels.[17] Dickens's most recent visit had come at the end of July 1853, after which he had commented to a friend that he had taken 'a trip to Amiens the other day, where there is a great deal done for the health and comfort of the working people which we might copy to advantage' – indicating that 'A Sensible Town' may have been written at his direct suggestion.[18]

Located in the valley of the Somme, and built around the river of the same name, the geographic distribution of the town of Amiens according to the land's orography revealed, in Dixon's eye, a sensible exploitation of natural resources. Marketplaces, abattoirs and public amenities were erected in harmony with the alternating upward/downward physical effects of the valley, guided by the natural path of the river and the mountain. City baths

---

[15] Edwin Chadwick, *Report on the Sanitary Condition of the Labouring Population of Great Britain* (London: Printed by W. Clowes and Sons for H.M.S.O, 1842); Macfarlane, p. 54.

[16] David Trotter, *Circulation: Defoe, Dickens, and the Economies of the Novel* (Houndmills: Macmillan, 1988), p. 104.

[17] John Forster, *Life of Charles Dickens* [1872-74] (London: Diderot Publishing, 2005), p. 430.

[18] To Dr William Brown, 1 August 1853, *The Letters of Charles Dickens The Letters of Charles Dickens*, ed. by Kathleen Tillotson, Graham Storey and others, Pilgrim Edition, 12 vols (Oxford: Clarendon Press, 1965-2002), Vol. VII, p. 123; there are no further references to the article in Dickens's correspondence.

and public services were placed above the town, thus accessing 'the freshest waters' ('A Sensible Town', p. 303). Correspondingly, 'the outscorings of the abattoirs, and also the gas-oozings from the opposite side, as well as the foul brooks which have served the uses of the dyer and the tanner' entered 'the stream below' ('A Sensible Town', p. 303). In Dixon's portrayal of Amiens, the cleansing function of air ventilation displayed in the abattoirs of Grenelle and Montmartre is replaced by the purifying virtues and restorative powers of the water naturally flowing down the mountain's surface. The natural hydrological ecosystem of the valley secures a perpetual stream circulation that maintained the cleanliness of freshwater in the town.

In Dixon's appreciation of the town, air renewal equates water renewal, and the U-shaped geomorphology of the valley guarantees the 'inhaling' absorption of fresh water just as much as the 'exhaling' secretion of refuse liquid. Water distribution, together with a sensible structuring of the settlement in compliance with the mountainous environment's ecosystem, secures the water's powers as an active source of wealth and a depurating agent. 'The Somme at Amiens is the best used river in the world', the author declares ('A Sensible Town', p. 303). Not surprisingly, such a position invites comparison with an ironic, yet likely, absurd British exploitation of the natural environment, as it would be

> quite possible, however, to imagine a congregation of human beings, say even a Body Corporate, who shall, through chance, want of forethought, or obstinate individual selfishness, place the slaughter-house, the gas-works, and the dyeing-offices at the inlet, and the baths at the outlet of a stream passing through the midst of their camp' ('A Sensible Town', p. 303).

Again, natural resource management in France acquires its magnificence and efficiency in the light of the sharp contrast it presents against its British duplicate.

As stated above, organicist metaphors in 'A Monument of French Folly' had led Dickens to picture Paris abattoirs as 'lunged' edifices endowed with breathing capabilities and therefore with self-autonomous life. His personifications followed an anatomical construction of the buildings as if supplied with vital attributions. With a clinical eye, Dickens penetrated and surgically dissected the French slaughterhouses in order to unearth the principles governing their organicist construction. Such a microscopic analysis is continued in Dixon's description of the function of the river in Amiens. If Montmartre's slaughterhouse resorted to oxygenation and respiration as a means of healthy energy production enlivening the larger metabolism, in Amiens, this idea of the aerobic organism is substituted by that of a cardiovascular system. As will be shown, the literary portrayal of the river Somme is intended to mirror the circulatory system by means of recreating the animating function associated with a blood distribution network.

Beginning with analogies based on liquid substances and natural flow, Dixon's parallelism between water and blood is furthered on the grounds of their properties as inherent, life-invigorating energies. In Amiens, water equates life, which is why, Dixon notes, in the town's cemetery, 'the beds of the sleepers may be dry' ('A Sensible Town', p. 305). The bodily fluid's function of transport and delivery of nutrients and oxygen to the cells, as well as its role in washing away metabolic waste, is visibly paralleled by the stream running through the village and providing its inhabitants with fresh water. Just as the circulatory system secures life within a living organism, water guarantees splendorous vegetation as well as a number of quality services for humans. Beyond a stance of mere utilitarianism where water is regarded as simply and primitively carrying substances, Amien's water flow is viewed as as accommodating human needs. Its use transcends a mere mechanic distribution of liquid. In an anticipation of what could be termed sustainable 'natural economy' and 'social ecology', the river is meant to support humankind by providing it with its natural 'wealth'. As Dixon observes, 'the Picard rivulets work with intelligence, earn money by their active power, put out for the benefit of their masters skilfully' ('A Sensible Town', p. 303). Far from the animalistically-portrayed 'Venetian waters', those 'beasts of burden', the aim of which is merely to carry 'what is upon them' ('A Sensible Town', p. 303), the canals in Amiens are designed according to a teleological plan to improve the living condition of society. Water management enforces and guarantees its productivity, and hence Amiens's sophisticated 'blood vessels' emerge as a source of economic advantage and service for the population. Aside from the 'Chinese baths' Dixon comes across at the town entrance, the river banks enable the development and subsistence of several city gardens, a swimming pool and other public services, the most important being the supply of 'pure water' for the population ('A Sensible Town', p. 303).

Moreover, the river's urban design imitates the metabolic arrangement of veins and arteries within a living organism. Dixon resorts to an organicist allegory to describe and justify the municipal division of the main stream into a myriad of interconnected rivulets and channels. He narrates how the men of Amiens allotted and subdivided the river, so that 'the integral stream is split into twelve fractions or streamlets, each of which has at least a score of duties to perform' ('A Sensible Town', p. 303). The principal, muscular 'artery' is thus segmented into multiple 'veins' securing a correct 'blood distribution' all along the whole 'city body' and the proper functioning of its appendixes. The conceptualisation of the river as a mechanism labouring for human benefit is reinforced by the onomatopoeic portrayal of the streamlets at work: 'they are all torn and broken upon wheels, among which they rush, and roar, and splutter, some become stained, as with ink; others escaping from the work with a strong smell of hides upon them' ('A Sensible Town', p. 303).

Veins or streamlets are activated by a number of valves assuring the coronary flow and the administration of blood to every part of the body. This function is reproduced in Amiens by a democratic principle articulating water dispersal that guarantees its public, shared consumption by means of 'a hundred and twelve public fountains, or rather taps' that 'within the town distribute water to the population at large' ('A Sensible Town', p. 304). Fountains act as 'pumps', adding to the cadence, alternatively opening and closing, and providing 'pure and plentiful' water ('A Sensible Town', p. 303). The heart-like main valve is to be found in the shape of a 'square solid building, known as the hydraulic machine' ('A Sensible Town', p. 303). The heart's repeated, rhythmic contractions that pump blood through the vessels are imitated by civil engineering technology. Enthused as he was about Amiens's self-sustainable natural resource management, Dixon conveys that the process, however, is ultimately incomplete. In an allusion to blood pressure, the author points out that water pressure is also a necessary condition for an efficient absorption of all the natural qualities the resource has to offer. He suggests that further advancements and technological innovations still need to be applied, for 'constant high pressure water supply to every house is one of the good things yet to come in Amiens' ('A Sensible Town', p. 304).

The metaphoric coronary circulation is finally perfected through the image of the systemic, pendular movement of the waters as they are segregated into multiple streams and later on reunited into main arteries, following their course through the streets and thus assuring a biological circuit:

> I determined that though union makes strength, division may sometimes beget activity. This separation of the waters of the Somme is but of short continuance. With the exception of two or

three canals [...] the streams are again united at the Bridge of St. Michael just below the town. The river, restored to its natural dimensions, forms the Port which is called d'Aval, or of the west ('A Sensible Town', p. 303).

According to the author, 'there is more real life in one Amiens canal than in all the Venetian waters put together'('A Sensible Town', p. 303). Life comes as the result of a wise and sensible distribution and management of water supplies, as society models its urban infrastructure on an organism able to satisfy each of its interconnected and interdependent parts.

The haematological allegory demands a conclusive note on the analogy between water and blood as precious elements. Although naturally and automatically regenerated, both fluids conduct life and therefore are to be carefully preserved. Metaphors of receptacles and chambers for holding water abound in the text. 'The canals cut the land up into little islands' ('A Sensible Town', p. 303), and water is transferred from the main stream to reservoirs in 'covered aqueducts' that resemble the above-mentioned veins and arteries ('A Sensible Town', p. 304). Like a human body, the principal reservoir 'is roofed with brickwork, vaulted like a cellar, and supported internally by columns, so that the water is completely sheltered-against soot and dust, and all defilement' ('A Sensible Town', p. 304). Solid materials protect it from external menaces, and the parallelism with the physical structure and material substance of an organism is easily recognised.

Moreover, blood and water being vital substances, they are not to be wasted. Contrary to the neglectful use of water in Great Britain, where a 'refreshing current [...] passes down Trumpington Street, from Hobson's Conduit at Cambridge', Dixon observes that 'no street with a small stream of clear water constantly flowing through it' can be found in Amiens ('A Sensible Town', p. 304). Unlike in Britain, water is not employed uselessly or recklessly. To avoid careless misuse and to protect the town from a flood, 'the principal streets [...] have been lately repaved, with underground drains, foot-pavements, and a surface which is highest in the centre; in others the gutter runs down the middle, with no footpath, in old fashioned style' ('A Sensible Town', p. 304).

Amiens as an Anatomic Body

The cardiovascular representation of Amiens in *Household Words* reflects a city conceived as an organic, living body. Yet such a biological description is not limited to the inner collection of tissues joined in a structural unit and performing a specific function. The focus is shifted from the interior workings of living matter to the city as an external, physical body, defined by the articulation of its different constituents, its geometric regularity and its defence and preservation against the penetration of alien agents.

The union of the different organs is reflected by the fact that, in Dixon's words, the whole town is divided by canals that 'cut the land up into little islands' ('A Sensible Town', p. 303). In a clear attempt to draw on the resemblance between maps and anatomical charts, the author resorts to a bird's eye view typical of the journal's adoption of unusual perspective, to discursively depict the structural distribution of the city in portions or shares reminiscent of the limbs and muscles of a body and the canals and rivulets as ligaments and veins. Moreover, the entire river that traverses Amiens conjoins the town in the form of a spinal column. During his wandering, Dixon decides to follow its course so as to study the animating, natural structure that sustains the town and connects the main muscles of the city. Conceived of as a vertebrate mechanism, the Somme supports the city's skeletal frame and assures the articulate motion of the limbs of Amiens. Dixon thus dissects the city both in terms of its function and geography, and establishes an essential—even biological—conceptualisation of its arrangement that emphasises the location and construction of the town, not as a result of a capricious urban partition, but as a societal endeavour to physically empower the body.

Further anatomic analogies are to be noted in the geometric construction of the city body. The author observes that cross-roads run 'like vaults under the trees, conduct from the centre of this park to lateral avenues, which had branched, right and left, from the main trunk promenade at its entrance' ('A Sensible Town', p. 304), and that those pavements, or rides, 'after making a slight bend, run boldly out into the distant perspective', the end of which 'is an exactly circular lake, containing two exactly circular islands and a pair of milk-white swans. Round the lake is a circular drive—the ring of Amiens under a zone of trees' ('A Sensible Town', p. 304). Here the article plays on Platonic ideas of radial and spherical anatomic symmetries that mirrored cosmological planning and the construction of the world—an idea essential to ancient understandings of geometry. 'The plan of the Hotoie demanded regularity' ('A Sensible Town', p. 304), he remarks before he proceeds to describe Amiens as a 'well-ordered town' ('A Sensible Town', p. 305). The Somme guarantees a further bilateral symmetry by which inhabitants come regularly in pairs:

They have placed the baths up-stream, the slaughterhouse down-stream; the theatre half-way up the principal Street (in the middle); the fruit-market in the town, the brute-market out of it; in which the dyers and fell-mongers have canals to themselves; and every body has green walks and parks in addition to his own private and domestic garden' ('A Sensible Town', p. 305).

The interdependence of and reliance on orderly, proportional, regular and measured forms binds geometric urban anatomy to mathematical principles, and thus, according to Galileo, for whom the book of nature was written in the language of mathematics, to the secret of nature itself.

The journal's reading of the integration of nature within the city is quite far removed from baroque depictions of nature as a chaotic, bizarre and anarchistic entity. Rather, the vision is impregnated with neo-classic teleology and entelechy, and its essence is deeply connected with human destiny and biological self-preservation. More of an animated ally than an untameable and free-roaming entity impervious to human will and reason, the nature of Amiens as written by this contributor to *Household Words* is one that works in symbiosis with humanity for both self-defence and protection. Ultimately, this nature visibly operates as the membrane and the external integument of the live organism—the skin. This is why, Dixon notes, green pastures replace the old city ramparts as a far more efficient means of protection of the symbolic city-body: 'on the site of the old ramparts are now planted the Boulevards, defending against a thousand enemies to health with a stout wall of living Green [...] rows of trees and sloping gardens form the outworks of this peaceful fortress' ('A Sensible Town', p. 304). Such vegetation acts as a form of immune system, defending the town from micro-organisms such as bacteria, viruses, fungi and hydraulic refuse. By resorting to the war metaphor, Dixon acknowledges the constant struggle for survival as he extends his thoughts to the most deadly of modern enemies, environmental degradation, in premonition of what would in time come to be known as ecocide.

Conclusion: Environmental Poetic Justice and Gardens of Knowledge

The organicist metaphors favoured by *Household Words* in these articles unearth a conceptualisation of urban planning as the fundamental basis for the integration of natural resources. French markets, slaughterhouses and cities stand for the measured imbrication of human stewardship and nature's potentialities. Even though there is an evident utilitarian objective, the journal resists an exclusively anthropocentric stance by proposing a utopian, Edenic garden-like understanding of nature that challenges man's superiority over non-human organisms. Such biblical connotations can be gathered from Dickens's reading of the natural world in 'A Monument of French Folly' as an entity bestowed with a sense of environmental poetic justice, 'aveng[ing] infractions of her beneficent laws' on those who 'determined to warp her blessings into curses' ('A Monument', p. 554). The effects of human corruption cyclically reach humanity itself; nature is construed as an anointed force capable of chastising those contravening its original godsends and its main role is to impose divine order on the earth. The natural cycle loses its original Rousseaunian benignity to embrace personification as an ominous presence menacing mankind and foreshadowing a catastrophe.

In this sense, it would be logical to conclude that the journal's complex reading of nature combines biblical discourse with contemporary environmental axioms. Dickens's natural world is one that helps preserve humankind and therefore, one from which knowledge of humankind itself can be drawn. Far from the Romantic iconography of violent natural landscapes, the description of gardens and vegetation in Amiens is reminiscent of the Enlightenment's rational views. Voltaire brought to a close his short story *Candide* (1759) by stating 'il faut cultiver notre jardin'.[19] A similar view could be perceived in *Household Words*'s interpretation of the gardens of Amiens, which are also meant to be cultivated by humankind so as to preserve itself.

---

[19] This translates as 'We must cultivate our own garden'.

Detecting Disease in London's Underworld: *Household Words* and the Campaign for Sanitary Reform

Clare Horrocks

ACCORDING to the economic historian George Southgate, in order to maintain the working of the Victorian city 'one of the essentials of power was the maintenance of a large and healthy generation'.[1] A healthy and able-bodied population was needed to contribute to the national economy through labour and consumption. How this was to be achieved was at the heart of debates surrounding public health reform in the mid-nineteenth century and is evident from changes in the style and content of articles that appeared in the mid-Victorian periodical press from 1849. A variety of reports on London's population in the 1840s had revealed a malnourished nation, unfit for labour and the future growth of the economy. The press advocated a humanitarian response to reform, united in their belief that one of the principle methods for accomplishing change must be a civic one, achieved through the systematic regulation and policing of the city. Such concerns for the future of the country resulted in calls for reform emerging in many novels and magazines of the period following 1849, as this article will consider through an examination of one particular magazine: *Household Words*.

In March 1850 Dickens advertised his new magazine *Household Words* as a journal that 'was to help in the discussion of the most important social questions of the time'.[2] One of the fundamental 'social questions' that the magazine can be seen to have engaged with was the necessity for sanitary

---

[1] George W. Southgate, *English Economic History* (London: J. M. Dent & Sons, 1934; repr. 1960), p. 69.
[2] Anne Lohrli, *Household Words: A Weekly Journal 1850-1859, Conducted by Charles Dickens. Table of Contents and List of Contributors and their Contributions* (Toronto: University of Toronto Press, 1973), p. 4.

reform and how disease could be 'detected', controlled and essentially eradicated. The importance of using the magazine as a platform for discussing issues of public health can be found in his decision to hire two medical writers for the magazine, Henry Morley and Frederick Knight Hunt. Morley's output in particular was prolific, clearly influenced by his work for the *Journal of Public Health* and the knowledge he had gained from practising medicine from 1844 to 1848.[3] Many of the lead articles for the magazine were written by Dickens, however, and demonstrate his continued interest in 'policing' the sanitary condition of the Metropolis. Dickens sought to make 'important social questions of the time' more accessible by combining methods of 'Instruction AND Entertainment'—the blend of 'fancy' with 'fact' that characterised the success of the magazine—for 'an imaginative or "fanciful" mode of address for Dickens was key to inter-class communication, cultural inclusivity and social cohesion'.[4] It is the purpose of this essay to examine this style of approach, alongside Dickens's fascination with the Metropolitan police force, and situate it within a discursive matrix constructed around the numerous discourses debating the necessity of social and particularly sanitary reform at this time.

One timely article which demonstrates this is 'To Working Men', published on 7 October 1854.[5] The summer of 1854 had witnessed another cholera epidemic across England and Wales and by the end of September more than 20,000 were dying or dead, and the nation trembled in fear and grief. Dickens, summering in Boulogne, received on 25 September, Numbers 237 and 238 of *Household Words* and immediately wrote to Wills:

> I really am quite shocked and ashamed on looking at the New No. to find nothing in it appropriate to the memorable time. I have written

---

[3] Lohrli, pp. 370-80. Key pieces include 'A Foe Under Foot', *Household Words*, Vol. VI, No. 142 (11 December 1852), 289-92; 'The Quiet Poor', *Household Words*, Vol. IX, No. 212 (15 April 1854), 201-06; 'Conversion of a Heathen Court', *Household Words*, Vol. X, No. 247 (16 December 1854), 409-13.

[4] Juliet John, *Dickens and Mass Culture* (Oxford: Oxford University Press, 2010), p. 121.

[5] [Charles Dickens], 'To Working Men', *Household Words*, Vol. X, No. 237 (7 October 1854), 169-70. Further references to this article will appear in the text.

a little paper 'To Working Men' which I hope may do good, and I send it to you enclosed.[6]

The weekly production of the magazine and the continuous editing Dickens and Wills undertook meant that they were able to 'turn around' the content of the paper in accordance with immediate topics of interest at short notice, maintaining a vigilant watch over the health of the city, as in October 1854 with 'To Working Men'. Dickens's hope that the article 'may do good' and his conviction that it was his duty to inform people of the necessity for sanitary improvement can be seen in the opening lines of the same article:

> It behoves every journalist, at this time when the memory of an awful pestilence is fresh among us, and its traces are visible at every turn in various affecting aspects of poverty and desolation, which any of us can see who are not purposely blind, to warn his readers, whatsoever be their ranks and conditions, that unless they set themselves in earnest to improve the towns in which they live, and to amend the dwellings of the poor, they are guilty, before GOD, of wholesale murder ('To Working Men', p. 169).

It is ironic that the article is addressed to 'working men' for it is clearly aimed at a much wider audience 'whatsoever be their ranks and conditions'. As with many of his articles, Dickens is keen to assert that the problems of sanitation do not affect the lower orders alone. Another cholera epidemic provided him with the material to satirise complacency and 'To Working Men' suggests that the middle classes can no longer shy away from the reality, and indeed proximity, of the problem for 'The whole powerful middle-class of this country, newly smitten with a sense of self-reproach—far more potent with it, we fully believe, than the lower motives of self-defence and fear—is ready to join them' ('To Working Men', p. 170). Dickens goes on to highlight the need for a 'better understanding between the two great divisions of society' in order to mount a collaborative effort to improve and regulate the sanitary condition of the city ('To Working Men', p. 170). His closing remarks in 'To Working Men' echo those of other writers working for sanitary reform, such as Charles Kingsley:

> [A] habit of kinder and nearer approach, an increased respect and trustfulness on both sides, a gently corrected method in each of

---

[6] To W. H. Wills, 25 September 1854, *The Letters of Charles Dickens*, ed. by Kathleen Tillotson, Graham Storey and others, Pilgrim Edition, 12 vols (Oxford: Clarendon Press, 1965-2002), Vol. VII, p. 241.

considering the views of the other, would lead to such blessed improvements and inter-changes among us, that even our narrow wisdom might within the compass of a short time learn to bless the sickly year in which so much good blossomed out of evil ('To Working Men', p. 170).

Kingsley had echoed exactly the same sentiment following the cholera epidemics in a series of Cholera Sermons, later published as a pamphlet entitled 'Who Causes Pestilence?' in the summer of 1854.[7] Like Kingsley, Dickens believed that sanitary reform must precede all other reform, for until the populace was housed and fed adequately, all other types of reform were futile. The responsibility for improvement cannot solely lie with the slow grind of legislation and parliamentary papers, 'To Working Men' argues, but with individuals and groups across the community.

Patrick Carroll claims that there was a 'culture of medical police' within mid-Victorian society that was obviously influenced by the models outlined at the beginning of the century by reformers like Johann Frank.[8] At the core of that culture was the development of the periodical press and fiction, educating and motivating different social groups, as well as the medical profession, to acknowledge the city's sanitary problems. The difficulty with implementing a system of inspection and policing, as Alexander Welsh notes in *The City of Dickens* (1971), was that 'in Victorian England the spirit of reform contended with the doctrine of non-interference'.[9] Many feared that the police, in the fulfillment of their duties, would challenge individuals' civil rights and liberty—a fear that frequently impeded social reform and the establishment of a systematic approach to administration. Chadwick contributed to the 1839 Report of the Royal Commission on a Constabulary

---

[7] Charles Kingsley, *Who Causes Pestilence? Four Sermons, with a Preface* (London: Griffin and Co., 1854).

[8] Patrick E. Carroll, 'Medical Police and the History of Public Health', *Medical History*, 46:4 (2002), p. 464. Though Johann Frank's five-volume work on the Prussian states, *A System of Complete Medical Police*, published between 1779 and 1827 was specific to the ideological and administrative structure of Germany, it was its basic principles of health education and jurisprudence that found support across Europe and particularly in the practice of medicine at the University of Edinburgh. Underpinning these principles was a firm belief that this education could be both formal and informal and in the arena of popular culture, periodicals and newspapers can certainly be seen to have fulfilled this purpose.

[9] Alexander Welsh, *The City of Dickens* (Oxford: Clarendon Press, 1971), p. 35.

Force where he sought to encourage a more 'social' form of policing.[10] Meeting with little success, Chadwick went on to work in other areas of social reform, including the Commission that contributed to the 1842 Report on the Labouring Population. His proposals for the introduction of Medical Officers of Health to assist in the detection and prevention of disease sought to achieve an alternative method of policing for Victorian London, one which Dickens was keen to explore in *Household Words*.

'On Duty with Inspector Field' was written in June 1851 and concluded a series that Dickens had been running looking into the organisation of the Detective Department, established in 1842.[11] Other stories included 'The Metropolitan Protectives', 'A Detective Police Party', 'Three "Detective" Anecdotes' and 'Down With the Tide'.[12] 1851 was also the year of the Great Exhibition and it is ironic that while Britain was celebrating its industrial superiority the poor were experiencing some of the worst conditions ever. As Donald Thomas notes in *The Victorian Underworld*:

> In 1851, while London was trumpeted by the catalogue of the Great Exhibition as the showplace of 'the industrial triumphs of the whole world', Henry Mayhew concluded his Preface of *London Labour and the London Poor* by remarking that the extent of 'misery, ignorance and vice, amidst all the wealth and great knowledge of "the first city in the world" is to say the least, a national disgrace to us'.[13]

A similar sentiment can be traced through a number of the articles in *Household Words* at this time, not just the detective series. However, 'On Duty with Inspector Field' was an important article for demonstrating the need for

---

[10] Royal Commission on a Constabulary Force in the Counties of England and Wales, *First Report of the Commissioners Appointed to Inquire as to the Best Means of Establishing an Efficient Constabulary Force in the Counties of England and Wales* (London: W. Clowes for H.M.S.O., 1839).

[11] [Charles Dickens], 'On Duty with Inspector Field', *Household Words*, Vol. III, No. 64 (14 June 1851), 265-70. Further references to this article will be made in the text.

[12] [Charles Dickens and W. H. Wills], 'The Metropolitan Protectives', *Household Words*, Vol. III, No. 57 (26 April 1851), 97-105; [Charles Dickens], 'A Detective Police Party [i]', *Household Words*, Vol. I, No. 18 (27 July 1850), 409-14; [Charles Dickens], 'A Detective Police Party [ii]', *Household Words*, Vol. I, No. 20 (10 August 1850), 457-60; [Charles Dickens], 'Three "Detective" Anecdotes', *Household Words*, Vol. I, No. 25 (14 September 1850), 577-80; [Charles Dickens], 'Down With the Tide', *Household Words*, Vol. VI, No. 150 (5 February 1853), 481-85.

[13] Donald Thomas, *The Victorian Underworld* (London: John Murray Ltd., 1998), p. 11.

a collective response to reform, which was becoming recognised as a necessary approach to discussing, and indeed identifying, the social problems of the city. From 1849, publications like *Punch* had been at the forefront of a range of popular periodicals that sought to generate public awareness of the need for sanitary reform. This collective response helped to pave the way for a new era of social reform that was characterised by the rhetoric of social responsibility and policing that Dickens can also be seen to have adopted in *Household Words*. Underpinning the methods for visualising change was a narrative of inspection, each magazine presenting itself as an Inspector of Nuisances who was to monitor the health of the city and raise its readers' awareness. This narrative was fuelled by the 1848 Public Health Act and the appointment of John Simon as the first Medical Officer of Health for the City of London in 1848. However, the discourse was only practically realised following the Metropolis Management Act of 1855, when the appointment of Medical Officers of Health was made mandatory.

One associated social problem of sanitary reform was the issue of criminality. Philip Collins, in the seminal text *Dickens and Crime* (1964), identifies three key Victorian debates around the very nature of what was meant by 'crime'.[14] First, education—if crime was about ignorance, then education needed to be improved. Second, a field of study that came to be known as 'criminal ecology', which posits crime as a social phenomenon influenced by geographical location—social responsibility could be most positively encouraged by improving housing and living conditions and destroying the rookeries. Third, Collins identifies a further supposition that the true 'causes' of crime were drunkenness, vagrancy and over-population. These three debates were inextricably linked and it would be arbitrary to attempt to separate them, especially when studying a magazine such as *Household Words*, which clearly engages with one or all of these issues in each instalment.

The content of 'On Duty with Inspector Field' reveals Dickens's personal interest in geographical location and the poverty and squalor prevalent in areas like St Giles and Bermondsey, maintaining a continued thematic concern about poor sanitary conditions that can be linked back to the publication of *Oliver Twist* (1837-39). In the 1850 preface to that novel Dickens declared:

> I was as well convinced then, as I am now, that nothing effectual can
> be done for the elevation of the poor in England, until their

---

[14] Philip Collins, *Dickens and Crime* (London: Macmillan, 1964; repr. 1968), p. 9.

dwelling-places are made decent and wholesome. I have always been convinced that this Reform must precede all other Social Reforms […] and that, without it, those classes of the people which increase the fastest, must become so desperate and be made so miserable, as to bear within themselves the certain seeds of ruin to the whole country.[15]

Dickens's reference to 'the people which increase the fastest' correlates with Collins's final point that over-population is frequently identified as a source of crime. Yet if their accommodation were more adequate, would this problem be as prominent? There is an obvious concern running through Dickens's narratives and much of *Household Words* regarding the reorganisation of the dwelling houses of the poor, as a series of commissioned articles by Henry Morley demonstrates (among a plethora of other articles about model lodging and dwelling houses that focus on the positive outcome, across communities, which could be achieved from adopting this model of living).[16]

As Harry Stone notes,

[Dickens] felt that every number should amuse, teach, improve, arouse and delight. A typical issue might contain a social or political piece, a poem, a story or a historical or biographical piece, an article of 'useful' knowledge and an article of exotic or sensational or amusing information.[17]

The very art of writing about issues of contemporary significance, empirical research and fiction, was in itself a method of educating the Victorian reading public as to the need for social reform. As Juliet John suggests, it was Dickens's understanding 'of the matrix of forces affecting questions of social justice that helped [him] to his unrivalled, if not unique position as a commercially successful and artistically respected journalist who espoused popular and radical causes'.[18] One may criticise the article 'On Duty with Inspector Field' for what Collins terms the 'almost hyperbolic language' that Dickens used when discussing the subject of the police. However, within the magazine's remit this criticism would seem unfounded, for Dickens deliberately sought to present 'evidence of an imagination at work; for

---

[15] Charles Dickens, *Oliver Twist* [1837-39] (London: Penguin Classics, 2003), p. 461.
[16] For a full list of attributed articles, see Lohrli, pp. 373-80.
[17] Stone, Vol. I, p. 19.
[18] John, p. 119.

though he felt acutely the responsibility of the journalist to give some account of the fact of this continuing process, he knew he could only achieve it through fancy'.[19]

In this way the prose of such lead articles as 'On Duty with Inspector Field' can be seen as a conscious construct aimed at appealing to as wide an audience as possible, as opposed to being a structural deficiency. This is clear from the opening of the story:

> Inspector Field comes in, wiping his forehand, for he is of a burly figure, and has come fast from the ores and metals of the deep mines of the Earth, and from the birds and beetles of the tropics, and from the Arts of Greece and Rome, and from the Sculptures of Nineveh, and from the traces of an elder world, when these were not. Is Rogers ready? Rogers is ready, strapped and great-coated, with a flaming eye in the middle of his waist, like a deformed Cyclops. Lead on, Rogers, to Rats' Castle ('On Duty', p. 265).

This circumlocution refers to the fact that Inspector Field has just finished duty at the British Museum. The tone is reminiscent of a boy's adventure story and one may find it hard to remember that the material Dickens is dealing with is actually based on reality. However, if we turn this criticism of his 'boyish hero worship' of the police around, we see a distinctive response to mid-century philanthropy. John Carey in *The Violent Effigy* (1973) notes that:

> Dickens was partial to nights out with the police. Under the protection of several officers he would visit slums or thieves' dens or houses of ill repute regularly entranced by the firm, knowing air with which his uniformed escort handled the various shifty or impertinent characters they came across.[20]

The key word here is 'protection', for the presence of the police facilitated Dickens's access to a number of areas that would have been closed to other philanthropists, thus adding a distinct perspective to Dickens's contributions to the collective call for reform in which he was participating. It becomes apparent through reading Dickens's work that there was more than one way

---

[19] Charles Dickens: *Selected Journalism 1850-1870*, ed. by David Pascoe (London: Penguin, 1997), p. xi.

[20] John Carey, *The Violent Effigy: A Study of Dickens' Imagination* (London: Faber and Faber, 1973), p. 39.

to respond to the 'problem of the city'. As Welsh suggests, what becomes clear is that:

> Next to the sheer size of London, and the strains and dislocations of its rapid growth, the foremost factor distinguishing mid-century attitudes toward the metropolis from those of earlier generations, was the increasing conviction that the well-being or lack of well-being, and even the moral condition of the city dweller, were being caused by forces beyond their control.[21]

This 'conviction' is personified through the character of Inspector Field who exemplified the very range of implications embodied in the term 'policing' the city. Indeed, personification was just one of the devices that Dickens deployed in order to blend the factual and informative with the fanciful and imaginative. As Anne Lohrli observes, 'as one means to this end, writers resorted to such devices as personification, fantasy, vision, fable, fairy-tale, imaginary travels, contrived conversations, and the use of fictitious characters to serve as mouthpieces of information and opinion'.[22] This is how Dickens uses Inspector Field, as a spokesperson for his own personal message:

> Inspector Field is the bustling speaker. Inspector Field's eye is the roving eye that searches every corner of the cellar as he talks. Inspector Field's hand is the well-known hand that has collared half of the people here, and motioned their brothers, sister, fathers, mothers, male and female friends, inexorably, to New South Wales. Yet Inspector Field stands in this den, the Sultan of the place. Every thief here, cowers before him, like a schoolboy before his schoolmaster ('On Duty', p. 266).

This conveys the breadth of the work of 'policing' a community only acknowledged in works like the reports of Medical Officers of Health where there is a repetition of the necessity for constant surveillance. Inspector Field is the 'roving eye', the man who commands respect both for his fairness and his philanthropic work, as well as his abilities at upholding criminal justice.

Within all such pieces, Dickens maintains an insistence on acknowledging 'truth', though encased within an imaginative form. The role of the narrator is of vital importance for interjecting and reinforcing 'fact' and 'truth', in case the reader may have missed the subtlety of one of Field's

---

[21] Welsh, p. 23.
[22] Lohrli, p. 9.

anecdotes or experiences. The acerbity and condemnatory tone is immediately evident from the opening page of both the story and the magazine itself.

> How many people may there be in London, who, if we brought them deviously and blindfold, to this street, fifty paces from the Station House, and within call of Saint Giles's church, would know it for a not remote part of the city in which their lives are passed? How many, who amidst this compound of sickening smells, these heaps of filth, these tumbling houses, with all their vile contents, animate and inanimate, slimily overflowing into the black road, would believe, that they breathe this air? ('On Duty', p. 265).

The volley of rhetorical questions hammers on the ears of the readers as though the narrator individually addresses each and every one. The 'sickening' smells that pollute the air, the same air inhaled by the whole metropolis, regardless of class, engages with anti-contagionist debates that infection is passed on by inhaling the same miasmatic vapours that arise from the effluvia of such districts as St Giles. The 'heaps of filth' anticipate the dust heaps found in *Our Mutual Friend* (1864-65). Dickens is not shy in attacking procrastination, prevarication and the endless red tape that he saw as the source of the piecemeal and ineffective attempts at sanitary reform. As Dickens had commented in an earlier article, aptly named, 'Red Tape':

> All human creatures bred in darkness droop, and become degenerate. Among the diseases distinctly known to be engendered and propagated by the want of Light, and by its necessary concomitant, the want of free Air, those dreadful maladies, Scrofula and Consumption, occupy the foremost place. At this time of day, and when the labours of Sanitary Reformers and Boards of Health have educated the general mind in the knowledge of such truths, we almost hesitate to recapitulate these simple facts: [...] within a few years, even these truths were imperfectly and narrowly known. Red Tape, as a great institution quite superior to Nature, positively refused to receive them—strangled them, out of hand—labelled them Impositions, and shelved them with great resentment.[23]

The 'truths' of the necessity for Light and Air are indeed continually affirmed in *Household Words*, as Morley's comparatively scientific article entitled 'Light

---

[23] 'Red Tape', *Household Words*, Vol. II, No. 47 (15 February 1851), 481-484 (p. 482).

and Air', published in September 1851, also confirms.[24] The intention is to alert readers, to motivate them to initiate change. In this way the periodical press served its duty as Inspector for the People, policing the sources of resolution and change.

Just before the single volume publication of *Little Dorrit* in 1857 in a letter to Henry Austin Layard, Dickens wrote:

> There is nothing in the present time at once so galling and so alarming to me as the alienation of the people from their own public affairs [...]. So, every day, the disgusted millions with this unnatural gloom and calm upon them are confirmed and hardened in the very worst of moods [...]. And until the people can be got up from the lethargy which is an awful symptom of the advanced state of their disease, I know of nothing that can be done beyond keeping their wrongs continually before them.[25]

Clearly writers chose to respond to this 'alienation of the people' by raising awareness as to the true 'Condition of England', identifying where the solution and reform could most effectively be started—with the readers of their periodicals and fiction. What this article has sought to demonstrate is the necessity of re-evaluating the role of *Household Words* in the mid-Victorian campaign for sanitary and social reform. The interconnectedness of health reform received increased acknowledgement in a range of sources from 1848 and the first major Public Health Act that advocated the need for policing the City. The mid-Victorian press's role as inspector, educator and entertainer, in which *Household Words* played so formative a role, was fully vindicated by the introduction of the 1855 Metropolis Management Act and the mandatory appointment of Medical Officers of Health. It is clear that as the interrelated parts of the campaign for sanitary and social reform came together the need for social responsibility and inspection was intensified. In this way, *Household Words'* attention to important social questions demonstrated an increased commitment to proselytise reform, which in itself functioned as a method for public inspection through the vehicle of the periodical press. Developing a distinct style of blending 'fact' with 'fancy', Dickens and his fellow journalists and editors created pieces of work that both informed and entertained. Read alongside the Blue Books, and other contemporary investigative journalism, fiction and medical reports, they

---

[24] 'Light and Air', *Household Words*, Vol. III, No. 78 (20 September 1851), 97-99.
[25] Charles Dickens cited in Sylvia Bank Manning, *Dickens as Satirist* (London: Yale University Press, 1971), p. 28.

provide an insight into the complexity of the mid-Victorian campaign for sanitary reform and the ways in which disease could be 'detected'.

The Perils of Sociability: Dickens, Victorian Journalism and the Detective Police

John Tulloch

[I]t is my habit to regard my walk as my beat, and myself as a higher sort of police-constable doing duty as the same.[1]

THE Leveson Inquiry, and the scandals that gave rise to it, raises an old question—what is the appropriate relationship between journalists and the police? This remains, also, an old question in the study of Charles Dickens and many scholars have felt it to be problematic. 'Nowhere else in his work', says Philip Collins, 'does Dickens indulge this vein of boyish hero-worship'.[2] What do Dickens's difficult relations with the police have to tell us about our contemporary crisis?

By late March 2012 the Metropolitan police had made a total of forty-eight arrests of forty-one individuals in the phone-hacking/bribery scandal as a result of the imaginatively entitled Operations Weeting, Elveden and Tuleta. Operation Elveden, which is concerned with the payment of police by journalists, and whose terms of reference have been extended to include public officials, has so far arrested and bailed twenty-three people, including sixteen journalists.[3]

---

[1] [Charles Dickens], 'New Uncommercial Samples: On an Amateur Beat', *All the Year Round*, New Series, Vol. I, No. 13 (27 February 1869), 300-03 (p. 300). This piece was the thirty-fourth of Dickens's thirty-six 'Uncommercial Traveller' articles, written in 1860, 1863 and 1868-69.

[2] Philip Collins, *Dickens and Crime*, 2nd edn (London: Macmillan, 1965), p. 206.

[3] Sue Akers, 'Statement made on behalf of the Commissioner of Police of the Metropolis to the Leveson Inquiry, 24 February 2012', *The Levenson Inquiry* <http://www.levesoninquiry.org.uk/wp-content/uploads/2012/02/Second-Witness-Statement-of-DAC-Sue-Akers.pdf> [accessed 26 March 2012]; David

For Britain, the number of journalists arrested is unprecedented and one fall-out is that, subject to court proceedings, we may need to revise the essentially comforting proposition in academic literature on crime and the media that payments to police for information by the press have been comparatively rare.

To take one major example: Steve Chibnall's classic book *Law-and-Order News*, published in 1977, has been highly influential for a generation in setting a frame within which British police-press relations could be viewed.[4] Crudely summarised, Chibnall argues that instances of the payment of police sources are relatively minor and that payment is only a part, and a small part, of the rich spectrum of police-press relations—and one mainly used by less experienced reporters, 'on the fringe of a specialization', without the right contacts. Chibnall says:

> I was told of one such journalist who was obliged to take a bottle of whisky with him every time he visited a policeman [...]. A second complained 'I'm in a moral dilemma—I will not pay policemen for information (although I'm prepared to buy them a beer or a meal) and I do not have the regular contacts which most crime reporters have. So what do you do when you want information? Well, the best

---

Leigh, 'Police chief tells Leveson the Sun had 'culture of illegal payments' to sources', *The Guardian*, 27 February 2012 <http://www.guardian.co.uk/media/2012/feb/27/sun-culture-illegal-payments-leveson> [accessed 26 March 2012]; Lisa O'Carroll, 'Phone hacking: ex-News of the World US editor faces "no further action"', *The Guardian*, 27 March 2012 <http://www.guardian.co.uk/media/2012/mar/27/phone-hacking-news-of-the-world?INTCMP=SRCH>[accessed 27 March 2012].

[4] Steve Chibnall, *Law-and-Order News: An Analysis of Crime Reporting in the British Press* 1(London: Tavistock Publications, 977). See also Steve Chibnall, 'The Crime Reporter: A Study in the Production of Commercial Knowledge', *Sociology*, 9:1 (January 1975), 49-66; Steve Chibnall, 'The Police and the Press', in *The Police and the Community*, ed. by John Brown and Graham Howes (Lexington, MA: Lexington Books, 1975), pp. 67-82; Steve Chibnall and Peter Saunders, 'Worlds Apart: Notes on the Social Reality of Corruption', *British Journal of Sociology*, 28:2 (June 1977), 138-54; Steve Chibnall, 'Chronicles of the Gallows: A Social History of Crime Reporting', in *The Sociology of the News Media*, ed. by H. Christian, Sociological Review Monograph, 29 (1980), pp. 179-217; Steve Chibnall, 'The Production of Knowledge by Crime Reporters', in *The Manufacture of News: Mass Media and Social Problems*, ed. by Stanley Cohen and Jock Young, 2nd edn (London: Constable, 1981), pp. 75-97.

sources are either bent policemen who want money for stories, or disgruntled policemen who don't usually want payment'.[5]

In a brilliantly suggestive scenario, Chibnall describes a pattern in which friendship and trust between journalists and police officers are 'characterized by exchange'.[6] In this analysis, journalists and police are in a trading relationship in which intangible, invisible goods such as friendship, sociability, information, gossip and the reinforcement of mutual esteem count for more than cash:

> The most obvious exchange resource the journalist has at his disposal is money. But, although direct payment of certain types of sources is recognized as legitimate, it is generally considered an inappropriate (although not unknown) method of getting information from the police. It is far too crass and unsubtle and defines the reporter/source relationship as one of business rather than friendship. The offer of food and drink, on the other hand, carries connotations of sociability rather than commerce or corruption [...] other, more powerful exchange resources [...] derive from [the reporter's] position within an organization offering the possibility of instant communication with the public [...] the crime reporter is able to act as intermediary between the press and the police [...] can facilitate the launching of formal public appeals about crimes but he can also help the police to communicate with specific individuals or minority groups [and make] favourable comment on police activities.[7]

Over time, Chibnall argues, this leads to a process of 'assimilation'—and police officer and journalist bond and begin to reflect each other. One example is my subject, Charles Dickens, who became so enthusiastic an advocate of policing that he musingly sees himself in one article as 'a higher sort of police-constable doing duty as the same'.[8] More notably, he became a friend of the most celebrated detective of his day, and helped create his reputation.

Overall this is a comforting picture of human sociability, as a sort of self-regulating process of mutual support and solidarity. 'Sociability', of course, is

---

[5] Chibnall, 'Worlds Apart', pp. 149-50.
[6] Chibnall, 'Worlds Apart', p. 152.
[7] Chibnall, 'Worlds Apart', pp. 153-54.
[8] [Dickens], 'Amateur Beat', p. 300.

a flexible friend—we might extend it and update it to include what appears to have been a deal, revealed at the Leveson Inquiry, in which Scotland Yard's Press Chief, Dick Fedorcio, facilitated the loan of a police horse to Rebekah Brooks just a few days before his son was given work experience at her newspaper. We may recall that Mr Fedorcio told the Leveson Inquiry that he merely introduced Mrs Brooks to a Metropolitan Police mounted branch inspector because 'I felt this could possibly lead to some positive coverage about the care of retired police horses'.[9]

We are predisposed to suspect such professionally cosy relationships as a conspiracy in some form against the public. But it confirms a human side of the police and of the journalist, where mutual manipulation is softened by friendship and the two parties to the relationship are provided with a narrative that enables them to regard their links as unproblematic. However, this essentially sentimental picture is called into question by the industrial scale of the *News of the World* and the *Sun* revelations, which paint it as another one of journalism's sustaining myths.

Two conclusions might be drawn. The first is that the comforting myth is in part true, and there has simply been a major change in the relationship between the media and the police in the last thirty years. Specifically, we might point to the rise of the modern private investigation industry, worth £250 million a year and staffed in many cases by ex-police officers, acting as an intermediary by means of which this relationship, like many others under capitalism, can be outsourced.[10]

We might also note the escalating expenditure on police public relations—for example, recent figures indicating that the police spent £30 million on public relations—enough to pay for an additional 1,000 officers—with budgets increasing by 40% in the last five years.[11] Policing now appears

---

[9] Dick Fedorcio, 'Witness Statement made by Dick Fedorcio to the Leveson Inquiry, 13 March 2012', *The Leveson Inquiry* <http://www.levesoninquiry.org.uk/wp-content/uploads/2012/03/Witness-Statement-of-Dick-Fedorcio.pdf> [accessed 26 March 2012], p. 14.

[10] Cahal Milmo, Jonathan Brown and Matt Blake, 'Beyond the Law: Private Eyes Who Do the Dirty Work for Journalists', *Independent*, 13 July 2011 <http://www.independent.co.uk/news/media/press/beyond-the-law-private-eyes-who-do-the-dirty-work-for-journalists-2312702.html> [accessed 27 October 2011].

[11] [Anon.], 'Police spend £30m on PR', *Daily Telegraph*, 25 March 2010 <http://www.telegraph.co.uk/news/uknews/law-and-order/7523223/Police-spend-30m-on-PR.html> [accessed 23 March 2012].

to depend more than ever on a promotional culture in which public opinion is continuously managed, and messages to the media are heavily controlled.

We might add some observations about extraordinarily rich or desperate newspapers in ferocious competition. This is broadly the conclusion of Nick Davies, who argues that 'there has always been a little dirty place, a little illegal stuff going on in the shadows of Fleet Street'.[12]

However, one might draw a second, contrary conclusion: that something has been missed, and/or not much talked about, in descriptions of the history of crime journalism. 'Assimilation' was often on the basis of a mutually profitable relationship between police and journalists, one that frequently had to be reined back, due to the public interest or more venal fears of the political class.

Few things are more tedious than the historian's reflex of 'nothing new'. But it can be argued that the issue of corrupt or suspect relationships between press and police goes back to the birth of the popular press and that we simply have no reliable evidence to assess its scale. What can be inferred is that crime news was one of the basic staples in the rise of the press in the early nineteenth century, along with gambling, sexual scandal and sport. Along with sport and scandal, crime was commodified. The *Newgate Calendars* of the late eighteenth century, full of bloody murders and last dying speeches on the scaffold, blazed the way, and were the most popular and profitable publications of their day. Newspapers created a rough and ready form of 'soft' social regulation while the early police played the 'hard' role.

A fascinating feature in the Victorian development of crime news is of course the pre-eminent role of the century's greatest novelist, and perhaps its greatest journalist, Charles Dickens, in its coverage. And to the extraordinary merits of his reporting, and his great influence as a public figure, can be added the fact that Dickens flourished as a writer just at the point where the old regime of policing gave way to the new. Indeed Dickens refers disparagingly to the 'Old Bow-Street Police' and their propensity to hang around with Grub Street denizens and collude in the creation of thief-taking myths:

[W]e think there was a vast amount of humbug about these worthies. Apart from many of them being men of indifferent character, and far too much in the habit of consorting with thieves and the like, they never lost a public occasion of jobbing and trading in mystery and making the most of themselves. Continually puffed besides by

---

[12] Nick Davies, *Flat Earth News* (London: Chatto and Windus, 2008), p. 266.

incompetent magistrates anxious to conceal their own deficiencies, and *hand-in-glove with the penny-a-liners of that time*, they became a sort of superstition.[13]

Note that Dickens's contempt for the Runners is in part based on their closeness to inferior journalists—'penny-a-liners'. The Bow Street office was finally disbanded in 1838. Dickens himself played a significant role in the rise of the modern British police and his enthusiastic promotion of the Metropolitan Police, founded in 1829, and the creation of the Detective Department in 1842, directly parallels the creation of the modern popular press. Along the way, he helped to create another superstition—that of the omniscient Scotland Yard detective.[14]

The prime exponent of this popular press was to become the *News of the World*, from its start in 1843, but it joined a host of weekly popular newspapers, such as Robert Bell's *Penny Dispatch* (1841) and Edward Lloyd's *Penny Sunday Times and People's Police Gazette* (1840), in shocking crime news and a diet specialising in 'seductions, rapes, murders and any other sort of horror'.[15] Until the advent of Alfred Harmsworth and the rise of the popular daily newspaper of the 1890s, this was the largest and economically most buoyant part of the British press, organised on a prototype of the factory lines that fifty years later would become commonplace.

Given its size and profitability, it is at least plausible that paying, as well as wining and dining, police officers and detectives for tips, was fundamental to this culture of Victorian popular journalism. However, these papers—particularly Robert Bell's—were also frequently prepared to attack the newly-established police as well as the church 'and anything else established'.[16]

This was not just a working-class market. The middle-class magazine *Household Words*, which Dickens started in March 1850, fished in the same waters with somewhat different motives and featured a substantial number

---

[13] [Charles Dickens], 'A Detective Police Party [i]', *Household Words*, Vol. I, No. 18 (27 July 1850), 409-14 (p. 409, my emphasis).

[14] See 'History of the Metropolitan Police—Timeline', *Metropolitan Police*, <http://www.met.police.uk/history/timeline_index.htm> [accessed 27 October 2011]; Collins, *Dickens and Crime*; Haia Shpayer-Makov, 'From Menace to Celebrity: The English Police Detective and the Press, c.1842-1914', *Journal of Historical Research*, 83:222 (2010), 672–92.

[15] Stanley Morison, *The English Newspaper: Some Account of the Physical Development of Journals Printed in London between 1622 and the Present Day* (Cambridge: Cambridge University Press, 1932), p. 242.

[16] Morison, p. 242.

of articles on the police, many concentrated in the first issues and focusing on the work of detectives. While the popular press was alert to the oppressive character of the new regime of policing, and its servicing of middle-class interests, Dickens ensured that *Household Words* was, from the outset, an enthusiastic supporter. Although the evidence is slight, it is possible that Dickens made payments to favourite police officers, as well as hosting what he claimed to be only modestly convivial parties for detectives in his offices. These parties form an integral part of some of his articles.[17] He wrote stories for his magazines based on the extensive use of his police contacts, edited and rewrote police articles by his contributors, and accompanied police raids into the East End. In an age that was very suspicious of the organised state, he functioned as a one-man propagandist for the new police force. As Philip Collins reminds us, his colleague George Augustus Sala observed in him 'a curious and almost morbid partiality for communing with and entertaining police officers'.[18]

This campaign involved a high degree of selective perception and contemporaries criticised what appeared to be a hero-worshipping tendency—most unlike Dickens—that seemed to take him over when he got near a detective or an 'imperturbable' man in blue. Other critics, such as Humphry House in his classic book *The Dickens World* (1942), put it down to his authoritarian tendencies and his obsession with neatness and precision, and—House was writing in the Freudian-ravaged 1930s—his anality. Untidy criminality needed to be sorted out and his articles about night tours with the police and the detective parties in his office, House says, 'show a kind of clerical satisfaction in the functioning of a well-run organization'.[19]

This account has considerable explanatory power, although 'clerical' is not the most appropriate term to describe the wild poetry of Dickens's night-time forays, and it ignores a fundamental source of the detective-author love-in—for Dickens and for other journalists. This is the fundamental congruence of their respective crafts, well-summarised by Haia Shpayer-Makov:

The essence of their work relied on investigation—on the act of

---

[17] See [Dickens] 'A Detective Police Party [i]' and also [Charles Dickens], 'A Detective Police Party [ii]', *Household Words*, Vol. I, No. 20 (10 August 1850), 457-60.
[18] Collins, p. 196; John Carey, *The Violent Effigy: A Study of Dickens' Imagination* (London: Faber and Faber, 1973), p. 39.
[19] Humphrey House, *The Dickens World,* 2nd Edition (Oxford: Oxford University Press, 1942; repr. 1965), p. 202.

probing and exposing [...] both developed the skills of taking evidence, interviewing witnesses and, on the basis of scattered pieces of information, constructing a narrative, often explaining a burning or puzzling issue. Their professional status depended on their ability to perform these tasks repeatedly and successfully.[20]

Any payment of course would be, by its nature, covert. One of the most celebrated policemen of the Victorian age, Inspector Charles Frederick Field (1805-74), Chief of the Detective Branch from 1846, owed his prominence to Dickens. After Field retired in December 1852 and opened a private inquiry bureau, Dickens is reported to have subscribed £300 to a testimonial (a sizeable sum equivalent to about £25,000 today), although there is some dispute about this. Dickens denied in *The Times* a press rumour that he might be writing Field's biography, but the fact that this was seen as conceivable is perhaps significant in itself. Certainly Field's ability to mount a successful career in the private sector depended to a large extent on the lavish publicity conferred on him by his inimitable mentor.

Other evidence of payments is a bit scarce. As an editor Dickens was tight with money in his payment of contributors to *Household Words*.[21] However, in a letter to his chief subeditor W. H. Wills in April 1851, setting out his plan for another police article that became 'The Metropolitan Protectives', he wrote:

[A]ny of the Scotland Yard people will do it, I should think; if our friend by any accident should not be there, I will go into it. If they should recommend any other station house as better for the purpose, or would think it better for us to go to more than one under the guidance of some trustworthy man, *of course we will pay any man and do as they recommend*. But I think one topping station-house would be best.[22]

---

[20] Haia Shpayer-Makov, 'Journalists and Police Detectives in Victorian and Edwardian England: An Uneasy Reciprocal Relationship', *Journal of Social History*, 42:4 (2009), 963-87 (p. 963).
[21]William E. Buckler, 'Dickens the Paymaster', *PMLA*, 66:6 (December 1951), 1177-80 (p. 1180).
[22] [Charles Dickens], 'The Metropolitan Protectives', *Household Words*, Vol. III, No. 57 (26 April 1851), 97-105; Harry Stone, *The Uncollected Writing of Charles Dickens, Household Words 1850-1859*, 2 vols (London: Allen Lane, 1969), Vol. I, pp. 253-54 (my emphasis).

Over this period, and despite Dickens's best efforts, the Metropolitan Police began to acquire an unsavoury reputation for corruption and incompetence, and there were some big scandals in the 1870s after Dickens's death. Philip Collins very reasonably states that there was 'a striking absence of important allegations of corruption' before this date.[23] From its origins, the question of 'perks' was a live issue, although four out of five of the men dismissed were sacked for drink-related offences.[24] Recurrent efforts were made to control the use of perks at various points in the nineteenth century. Indeed, ferocious attacks by the press on police venality and incompetence were a feature of the late Victorian scene—particularly marked during the outbreak of murders in the East End in the 1880s attributed to 'Jack the Ripper'.[25] Conan Doyle's limited Inspector Lestrade, 'one little sallow rat-faced, dark-eyed fellow', sprang from the fertile ground of a stack of press cuttings.[26] Payments to policemen only in fact became comprehensively illegal with the passing of the Prevention of Corruption Act in 1901, and it was made an offence for a police officer to receive payment and for someone to make one in the context of recent increases in police pay and allowances.[27] A major reason for the reluctant establishment of the Scotland Yard Press Office in 1919 was 'fears about unauthorized leaks produced by reporters bribing officers'.[28]

By that time a cosy and, to some extent, self-regulating culture had arisen between a corps of Fleet Street crime correspondents and the police in which each side needed the other. The police used the press for publicity, to get a result, to fight for better resources and to advance their careers; journalists relied on police tip-offs to get the latest information, access to victims and lurid details to dress up stories. Copious amounts of alcohol in a number of well-established London watering holes oiled the relationship.

---

[23] Collins, p. 200.

[24] Clive Emsley, *The English Police: A Political and Social History* (London: Harvester Wheatsheaf, 1991), p. 221.

[25] Geoffrey Belton Cobb, *Critical Years at the Yard: The Career of Frederick Williamson of the Detective Department and the C.I.D.* (London: Faber and Faber, 1956), pp. 225-39.

[26] Arthur Conan Doyle, *A Study in Scarlet* (London: Ward, Lock and Co., 1887; repr. 1893), p. 21.

[27] Geoffrey Robertson, 'News of the World: A newspaper is gone, but an inquiry is as urgent as ever', *The Guardian*, 8 July 2011 <http://www.guardian.co.uk/profile /geoffreyrobertson> [accessed 25 October 2011].

[28] Steve Chibnall, 'The Wooing of the Fourth Estate: The Metropolitan Police and the News Media 1970-1976', in *British Police*, ed. by Simon Holdaway (London: Edward Arnold, 1979).

But references to money payments in journalists' memoirs are sparse. Hints remain. Consider the guarded references of Frederick Higginbottom—a noted *Pall Mall Gazette* journalist—in his memoirs:

> Go back to notorious murder mysteries of the eighties of last century […]. Every one was written up by expert reporters in touch with the police, and each of them provided sensations for months. The police used the Press then, as they do now, and they gave away information *freely* if it helped them to trace a missing suspect.[29]

Now a host of accounts have begun appearing in the press testifying to the ubiquity of this culture. For example, Duncan Campbell observes:

> It has *always* been known, by both police and the press, that some officers will trade information for money. Victims of crime or tragedy are often amazed at the speed with which the media arrive in the wake of the emergency services. Now they know why.[30]

A 'veteran journalist' in the *Camden New Journal* claims:

> I CANNOT see why such unforgiving looks were given to Rebecca Brooks, chief executive of News International, for telling a Commons committee that journalists paid police officers for stories—or words to that effect.
>
> Journalists of another generation would know that it was *common practice* to pay policemen for stories.
>
> When I worked on a west London weekly, too far back in time to date in this column, I would drop in to the local cop shop and if a story given by an officer was sold on to a national or London evening, the proceeds would be shared.
>
> Today, this would be considered a corrupt practice, I suppose, but it shades into insignificance compared with what is fundamentally wrong with many journalists.[31]

---

[29] Frederick J. Higginbottom, *The Vivid Life: A Journalist's Career* (London: Simpkin Marshall, 1934), p. 15 (my emphasis).

[30] Duncan Campbell, 'The Man in the Mac: A Life in Crime Reporting', *The Guardian*, 5 September 2009 <http://www.guardian.co.uk/uk/2009/sep/05/crime-reporting-duncan-campbell> [accessed 17 October 2011] (my emphasis).

[31] [Anon.], 'Paying Police for News Stories isn't the Malaise of Modern Journalism', *Camden New Journal*, 26 May 2011 <http://www.camdennewjournal.com/paying-

As the *Daily Telegraph* observes:

> Payments by journalists to police officers have a long history. One long-retired crime correspondent recalls having a list of officers to whom he would regularly send a £5 note 'wrapped in a plain WH Smith envelope'.

> 'I'd never use office stationery and I'd use a different typewriter each week so it couldn't be traced,' he said.

> 'I never felt I was bribing them but of course I was'.[32]

In contrast, the researcher of Victorian journalistic morals finds real difficulties in uncovering a covert culture whose basis was cash—the beauty of cash being of course its untraceability. Modern prosecutors, with many more tools at their command, still face great difficulties.

Sociability and Stridency

Cash may have played a small role in Dickens's links to the detective police. What is striking is the combination of sociability and stridency in the relationship. Indeed, his attitude to the police has generally been regarded as displaying his most questionable features: a tendency to exaggeration, an instinctive authoritarianism, and a contempt and revulsion for the lower orders that can border on the hysterical.[33] This was manifest within the context of a set of attitudes to law and order that became strikingly illiberal as he aged. As a pioneer of the various voices of popular journalism,[34] one of his most dubious achievements is the creation of a version of the hectoring, button-holing, columnist manner manifested, for example, in his assault on 'ruffians' in a late article in *All the Year Round*:

---

police-news-stories-isn't-malaise-modern-journalism> [accessed 17 October 2011] (my emphasis).

[32] Matthew Born, 'Paying the Police: Newspapers have a Lot of Form', *Daily Telegraph*, 14 March 2003 <http://www.telegraph.co.uk/news/uknews/1424573/Paying-the-police-newspapers-have-a-lot-of-form.html> [accessed 17 October 2011].

[33] Alexander Welsh, *The City of Dickens* (Cambridge, MA: Harvard University Press, 1986), pp. 47-53.

[34] John Tulloch, 'Charles Dickens and the Voices of Journalism', in *The Journalistic Imagination: Literary Journalists from Defoe to Capote and Carter*, ed. by Richard Keeble and Sharon Wheeler (London: Routledge, 2007), pp. 58-73.

It is to the saving up of the Ruffian class by the Magistracy and the Police—to the conventional preserving of them, as if they were Partridges—that their number and audacity must in great part be referred. Why is a notorious Thief and Ruffian ever left at large? He never turns his liberty to any account but violence and plunder, he never did a day's work out of gaol, he never will do a day's work out of gaol. As a proved notorious Thief he is always consignable to prison for three months. When he comes out, he is surely as notorious as he was when he went in. Then send him back again. 'Just Heaven!' cries the Society for the protection of remonstrant ruffians. 'This is equivalent to a sentence of perpetual imprisonment!' Precisely for that reason it has my advocacy. I demand to have the Ruffian kept out of my way, and out of the way of all decent people. I demand to have the Ruffian employed, perforce, in hewing wood and drawing water somewhere for the general service, instead of hewing at her Majesty's subjects and drawing their watches out of their pockets'.[35]

This is extracted from Dickens's celebrated article in which he explains his insistence on pursuing a girl for using bad language in the street and ensuring her persecution. It is Swiftian in its coruscating nastiness, without Swift's irony and lightness of touch, and it is a model of what we might term the mature Littlejohn saloon-bar manner: jeering, contemptuous of liberal opinion and heavy-handedly sarcastic.

The sociable note with the police is hit early on in Dickens's mature journalism. The first police article in *Household Words* is the relatively mundane 'The Modern Science of Thief-Taking', authored by W. H. Wills, but closely supervised by Dickens. But this was shortly followed by a striking article authored by Dickens, 'A Detective Police Party', printed in two consecutive issues of *Household Words*, already quoted from above.[36]

The 'party' to which we are invited is presented as being conducted within the offices of the magazine in Wellington Street off the Strand. Dickens repeatedly stresses the factuality and accuracy of his account 'as

[35] [Charles Dickens], 'The Ruffian by The Uncommercial Traveller', *All the Year Round*, Vol. XX, No. 494 (10 October 1868), 421-24 (p. 421). This piece was number twenty-nine in Dickens's 'Uncommercial Traveller' series and the first of the final group of eight, written in 1868-69.

[36] [W. H. Wills], 'The Modern Science of Thief-Taking', *Household Words*, Vol. I, No. 16 (13 July 1850), 368-72; [Dickens], 'A Detective Police Party [i]' and 'A Detective Police Party [ii]'.

exact as we can make it', 'perfectly reliable' and 'a piece of plain truth'. Does he protest too much? The scene is carefully set as 'a sultry evening at dusk' with the racket from the 'Fairy-land' of central London coming through the open windows and 'glasses and cigars' set 'upon a round table'. In short, we are in a convivial setting for the telling of yarns over the after-dinner brandy (although Dickens reminds us that the glasses are used 'very temperately') of innumerable detective tales, and Conrad's great story 'Heart of Darkness'.[37]

Disguised with light pseudonyms, Inspectors 'Wield' and 'Stalker' are introduced and described, then five sergeants—so that Dickens can claim 'we have the whole detective force of Scotland Yard with one exception'.[38] They share certain common features: they are all,

> respectable looking men, of perfectly good deportment and unusual intelligence; with nothing lounging or slinking in their manners; with an air of keen observation, and quick perception when addressed; and generally presenting in their faces, traces more or less marked of habitually leading lives of strong mental excitement.

Dickens notes that they speak modestly, take turns, do not contradict each other, and 'only come to the assistance of each other—not to the contradiction'.[39] The yarns they relate demonstrate quick-wittedness, the adroit use of disguise and close observation.

The opposite to this somewhat implausibly positive vision of vigilant sociability is posed in Dickens's extraordinary essay, 'On Duty with Inspector Field', which succeeds in being both one of his most brilliant pieces of journalism and also one of his most repellent. In it he demonstrates poetically Field's mastery of the dangerous areas of London, a 'bustling speaker' keeping the dangerous classes in order.[40] Against the amiable, alert affability of the off-duty detective is juxtaposed a managing, bullying, threatening impresario of the lower orders, constructed through a series of small poems of social threat. Although the narrative is organised around the striking clocks of night-time London, with a precise sense of place, the style is very far from documentary realism. We are in the dangerous landscape of night, in which the sociability of the off-duty detectives is transformed, while

---

[37] [Dickens], 'A Detective Police Party [i]', pp. 409-10.
[38] [Dickens], 'A Detective Police Party [i]', p. 409.
[39] [Dickens], 'A Detective Police Party [i]', p. 410.
[40] [Charles Dickens], 'On Duty with Inspector Field', *Household Words*, Vol. III, No. 64 (14 June 1851), 265-70 (p. 266).

the dangerous others that the police are presented with are depicted as devoid of individuality as worms:

> Ten, twenty, thirty—who can count them! Men, women, children, for the most part naked, heaped upon the floor like maggots in a cheese! Ho! In that dark corner yonder! Does any body lie there? Me Sir, Irish me, a widder, with six children. And yonder? Me Sir, Irish me, with me wife and eight poor babes. [...] Thus, we make our New Oxford Streets, and our other new streets, never heeding, never asking, where the wretches whom we clear out, crowd.[41]

Dickens contemptuously ventriloquises the voices of his subjects as he moves towards that extraordinary final sentence, with its crashing final verb—'crowd'—a breathless declaration of the incompetence of middle-class urban planning. Field and his colleagues are presented as the guardians, the competent few, who rule their colonial subject people by moral authority and superior intelligence, rather than numbers, so the subjects 'know that [they are] no match for this individual energy and keenness, or this organized and steady system'.[42]

Dickens's characteristic ebullience here becomes distinctly sinister, embodying a 'triumph of discipline and uniform which enabled one human being simply to ignore the misery of another'.[43] At times this extraordinary piece breaks into iambic pentameters—'to show the houses where the sailors dance'—and makes of Field a poetic construct rather than a flesh and blood policeman:

> I should like to know where Inspector Field was born. In Ratcliffe Highway, I would have answered with confidence, but for his being equally at home wherever we go. *He* does not trouble his head as I do, about the river at night. *He* does not care for its creeping, black and silent, on our right there, rushing through sluice gates, lapping at piles and posts and iron rings, hiding strange things in the mud, running away with suicides and accidentally drowned bodies faster than a midnight funeral should, and acquiring such various experience between its cradle and its grave. It has no mystery for *him*.[44]

---

[41] [Dickens], 'On Duty', pp. 266-67.
[42] [Dickens], 'On Duty', p. 268.
[43] Carey, p. 40.
[44] [Dickens], 'On Duty', p. 269 (original emphases).

The hectic pace of the description refuses to slacken, as Field zigzags across London on his slumming expedition, safely shepherding his middle-class patrons, and hauling people out of bed with threats, such as the surly lodging house keeper 'Bark':

> Bark sleeps in an inner wooden hutch, near his street-door. As we parley on the step with Bark's Deputy, Bark growls in his bed. We enter, and Bark flies out of his bed. Bark is a red villain and a wrathful, with a sanguine throat that looks very much as if it were expressly made for hanging, as he stretches it out, in pale defiance, over the half-door of his hutch. Bark's parts of speech are of an awful sort—principally adjectives. I won't, says Bark, have no adjective police and adjective strangers in my adjective premises! I won't, by adjective and substantive!'[45]

Here is energy of a repellent kind, as Bark's language is over-mastered by the contemptuous journalist, ostensibly protecting the sensibilities of his readers while administering an insouciant lesson in colonial control.

> We are shut up, half a dozen of us, in Bark's house, in the innermost recesses of the worst part of London, in the dead of the night—the house is crammed with notorious robbers and ruffians—and not a man stirs. No, Bark. They know the weight of the law, and they know Inspector Field and Co. too well.[46]

Bark's forces are kept at bay by the moral authority of a thin blue line and the power of authoritative language.

Conclusion

The current crisis in relations between the media and the police is distinctive in the scale of arrests and the political fall-out. However, in many ways it represents nothing strange. Police-media relations are characterised by a set of shared needs for publicity and law-and-order stories, the management of public opinion and the protection of a set of social and economic interests which remain permanent.[47] In many cases this has led in crime reporting to a mutual process of source capture in which journalists and police connive to

---

[45] [Dickens], 'On Duty', pp. 269-70.
[46] [Dickens], 'On Duty', p. 270.
[47] See Shpayer-Makov, 'From Menace to Celebrity' and 'An Uneasy Reciprocal Relationship'.

construct law and order propaganda that idealises the police and allows the press to perform the function of, in Dickens's words, 'a higher sort of Police Constable', amateur soft cops, regulating society with words.[48] A recurring feature of this process is something akin to a bargain between the police, the political class and the media that excludes the public. The current crisis has arisen because this equilibrium has been disturbed, by what appears to have been an industrial-scale network of corruption.

Dickens's relations with the police are an early example of this close relationship in which the forces of law and order are idealised and the journalist receives exceptional access. The worst result here is class propaganda of a repellent kind, rather than systemic corruption, although it can be argued that hero-worship of this kind creates the conditions for corruption to breed. On the other hand, in Dickens's exceptional case, it results in some wonderful journalism.

---

[48] [Dickens], 'Amateur Beat', p. 300.

From 'The Great Exhibition to the Little One' to 'China with a Flaw in It': China, Commodities and Conflict in *Household Words*

Hannah Lewis-Bill

FOR some time the relationship between Britain and China in Dickens Studies has, with regard to objects and their role in developing transnational parlance, been overlooked. This work addresses the ways in which, through complex textual layering, Dickens inserts China into the British psyche in *Household Words* (1850-1859) and looks at the role the journal played in making 'familiar in their mouths' the relationship between China and Britain.[1] Focusing on 'The Great Exhibition and the Little One', published on 5 July 1851 by Dickens and Richard Horne, and 'China with a Flaw in It' by Henry Morley, published on 3 July 1852, this essay will examine how the authors legitimise negative cultural and social representations of China, while exhibiting a fascination with the very aspects of Chinese culture that render it potentially threatening. While Dickens and Horne are keen to demonstrate Chinese failings in trade, production and development, playing on the term 'little' throughout, ultimately, their article serves to contextualise where and how these objects and this locale relate to Britain in the public consciousness and to open up an exciting discourse regarding China and Britain. Similarly, 'China with a Flaw in It' uses a statistical or governmental cataloguing framework and, through a combination of opinion and quantitative analysis, propagates a negative image of China in terms of trade and commerce while at the same time acknowledging the desirability of Chinese products. The pun of a flaw in the 'china' is used as a marker of a crucial flaw in the country's outlook—and by extension its trade—yet it also highlights a commodity that was very valuable to the Chinese in trading terms with Britain and equally desirable to the British consumer.

---

[1] This forms part of *Household Words'* full title and is taken from William Shakespeare, *Henry V*, Act IV, Scene III, line 52.

Both 'The Great Exhibition and the Little One' and 'China with a Flaw in It' were published after the Opium War of 1839-42 and use this as an important frame of reference. Horne and Dickens begin the 'The Great Exhibition and the Little One' by outlining the values of the Great Exhibition: the ideas of progress, population and commerce. This swiftly moves into an article of two parts contrasting Britain's superiority with China's insignificance. Initially, the article does not explicitly name China:

> There may be an odd, barbarous, or eccentric nation, here and there, upon the face of the globe, who may see fit to exercise its free will, in the negative form of will-not, and who may seclude itself from the rest of the world, resolved not to move on with it.[2]

The circular image of the globe suggests an interest in a notion of circularity. That the globe is one continuous circle, unbroken and unending in many ways mirrors the trading battles that were occurring between the two nations. The article then moves on to state that:

> As it is impossible in any allowable space to 'go through' the whole Exhibition, or touch upon a tithe of its Catalogue, let us suggest as curious subjects of comparison, these two countries which display (on the whole) the greatest degree of progress and the least—say England and China. England, maintaining commercial intercourse with the whole world; China, shutting itself up, as far as possible, within itself ('The Great Exhibition', p. 357).

This notion of shutting itself up and sequestering itself deliberately from the rest of the globe articulates a key British concern. 'England, maintaining commercial intercourse with the whole world' has a 'go through' mentality that is frustrated both by the structure of the Great Exhibition and by China's insularity. This is the foundation of the article's discomfort with China—a lack of information and knowledge. The perceived isolation of China renders it unknowable, leading to a sense of cultural alienation.

Sabine Clemm notes that 'the Chinese collection at the Crystal Palace had not in fact been assembled by the Chinese but by the East India Company and thus represented a British construction of China'.[3] Clemm

---

[2] [Charles Dickens and Richard H. Horne], 'The Great Exhibition and the Little One', *Household Words*, Vol. III, No. 67 (5 July 1851), 356-60 (p. 356). All subsequent page references will appear in the text.

[3] Sabine Clemm, Dickens, *Journalism, and Nationhood: Mapping the World in Household Words* (New York and London: Routledge, 2010), p. 25. From Jeffrey A. Auerbach,

suggests that 'The Great Exhibition and the Little One' portrays Chinese progress as reliant upon Western influence. However I would suggest an alternative reading that while the article forwards the idea that China is dependent on cooperation with the West, this is a veneer covering a deeper fear of the potential threat and heightened influence that China itself exerts and a need to culturally control the perception of China. This current of fear is detectable in the argument the article sets out, as well as in the statistics, wordplay and imagery it employs to construct its argument.

Dickens and Horne use statistics as a means of compartmentalising the world and ordering locales. By sectioning off the globe in this way Dickens and Horne create a regressive picture of other transnational spaces while simultaneously elevating Britain and its sense of progress. They use statistics to organise the world's spaces in terms of Empire and the ways in which Britain is:

> [M]oving in a right direction towards some superior condition of society [...]. It appears that England doubles its population in fifty-two years; France in one hundred and twenty-five years; Russia, in forty-two years; the United States of America in twenty-two and a-half years; Sweden doubles its population in one hundred years; and all Europe in fifty-seven years. What are we to say of China? We believe the figures are not known; and, even if they were, the practice of infanticide would in a great measure perplex, if not defeat, our judgment and deductions ('The Great Exhibition', pp. 356-57).

Both Dickens and Horne are at pains to appear precise throughout this statistical privileging; it is interesting, then, that this precision is biased. The cataloguing of population growth is evidently seen as significant in expounding the value of progress. Britain, Russia and the United States of America are, through this method, clearly situated as three hubs of world power. However, if we look at the figures with reference to China, this is not the case. The authors use words such as 'believe' and 'even if they were'. This focused absence of facts is important. China in 1851 had a population of 450 million, dwarfing the 'little' population of England with the 'great' population of China. That Dickens and Horne neglect to provide any precise details about the population suggests a disingenuously swift dismissal on their part, or an inability to locate the appropriate facts, rather than a real absence. That, at this juncture, only a few Chinese ports were open to trade

---

The Great Exhibition of 1851: A Nation on Display (New Haven: Yale University Press, 1999), p. 176.

is also highlighted here but is referred to in greater detail in 'China with a Flaw in It'.

There is also, excitingly, a clear interest in this article in commodities and materiality. Dickens and Horne set about cataloguing British raw materials, positioning them as obviously superior. However, what is intriguing in the prose here is the textual layering process: first, Dickens and Horne ask the reader to 'Consider our English raw materials'; next they ask the reader to 'Consider the materials employed at the great Teacup Works of Kiang-tiht-Chin (or Tight Chin)'; and finally, the article asks the reader to consider in tandem 'the greatness of the English results, and the extraordinary littleness of the Chinese' ('The Great Exhibition', pp. 357-58). The emphasis this places on comparing and contrasting China and Britain encourages the reader to reflect on the ways in which China and Britain interact. A similar cumulative effect is employed in the article's discussion of teapots. It begins with 'cabinets, and richly painted lanthorns, and teapots, and tea cups', followed by 'we have more teapots; and a revolving lanthorn' and then concludes with 'more teapots' ('The Great Exhibition', p. 359). This repositioning of the language, the slight modification and alterations of word order underscores the ways in which certain key themes are inserted within the narrative to construct a transnational dialogue.

Commodities as well as raw materials are catalogued by Dickens and Horne,[4] resulting in the creation of a global shopping list, one that reveals Britain's increasing reliance on foreign produce: 'medicine roots, hemp-seed, vegetable paints, varnishes, dyes, raw silk, oils, white and yellow arsenic, saffron, camphor, green tea dyes, &c.' ('The Great Exhibition', p. 358). The circular motif resurfaces at this juncture, connecting this list with notions of the globe, circularity and China's lack of progress. Further connections are also forged between silk and the popular ivory balls that British consumers desired:

> Go from the silk-weaving and cotton-spinning of us outer barbarians, to the laboriously-carved ivory balls of the flowery Empire, ball within ball and circle within circle, which have made no

---

[4] Much important work has been undertaken on commodity culture in *Household Words*. Please see Catherine Waters, *Commodity Culture in Dickens's Household Words: The Social Life of Goods* (Aldershot, Ashgate, 2008). See also: Juliet John, *Dickens and Mass Culture* (Oxford: Oxford University Press, 2010). For further work on Victorian 'Things' please see: Elaine Freedgood, *The Ideas in Things: Fugitive Meaning in the Victorian Novel* (Chicago: Chicago University Press, 2006).

advance and been of no earthly use for thousands of years ('The Great Exhibition', p. 358).

Yet these are commodities that the British purchased, and which, for all the ridicule, became, along with tea and tea-making paraphernalia, fetishised objects in the British home. Dickens and Horne's shopping list emphasises the ubiquity of foreign commodities in British shops and homes.

Dickens and Horne then reflect on the 'Chinese Junk', which is introduced to the reader as another example of Chinese inefficiency:

> Compare these with the models of junks and boats in the Chinese Exhibition. Compare these with the Junk itself, lying in the Thames hard by the Temple-Stairs. As a bamboo palanquin is, beside a Railway–train, so is an English or American ship, besides this ridiculous abortion ('The Great Exhibition', p. 358).

Here Dickens and Horne are referring to a popular attraction where a boat came from China with a mixed crew of Chinese and British sailors and was moored on the Thames. Dickens wrote an article about this for *The Examiner* in 1848 called 'The Chinese Junk' (the title possessing a strong double sense of meaning). In the process of writing this article, Dickens made two visits to the boat. He was at once both dismissive and intrigued by the sights while recommending it as one 'which all who can, should see'. While the overwhelming sense of derision is unavoidable it is important, I argue, to reflect on exactly why he felt it worthy of a second visit. Dickens's description of the Chinese Junk as more 'like a china pen tray' and a 'floating toyshop' draws on connections between China and objects and further cements that union in the British psyche.[5] As John Drew argues, Dickens is 'building on the exaggerated contrast between East and West [...] and reproducing both factual details and stereotyped attitudes towards Chinese culture'.[6] It is also of note that there was a small Chinese settlement located in Limehouse, East London and it is intriguing to reflect on how—in this sense—on British soil the two cultures interacted. The article states that, 'One of the indications of the progress of a nation is "interchange," including internal communication and trade, and external communication and commerce, currency, and wages' ('The Great Exhibition', p. 360). That

---

[5] Charles Dickens, 'The Chinese Junk', *The Examiner* (24 June 1848) p. iii.

[6] John M. L. Drew, *Dickens the Journalist* (Houndmills: Palgrave Macmillan, 2003), p. 98.

Britain actively stifled this interchange with excessive taxation is dealt with, though not critiqued, by Morley in 'China with a Flaw in It'.

As Catherine Waters suggests, 'By the middle of the nineteenth century ordinary men and women were experiencing the pleasures and pains of consumer choice on a scale hitherto unknown'.[7] The consumer pain that Waters identifies here was closely tied up with an awareness that this level of choice brought a greater transnational interconnectedness and, with that, a potential cultural uncertainty. Clearly China was making up part of this consumer choice; the influence of *Chinoiserie* and products from China such as silk, rice, tea and chinaware meant that while British produce lacked exoticism, Chinese products had it in abundance. In competition with Western products, it is noted that the Little Exhibition presented '"a very curious porcelain box in the form of a crab, with moveable eyes and feet"' ('The Great Exhibition', p. 359). If one questions whether the items are useful then clearly the answer is no. However, with a burgeoning middle class that was increasingly interested in foreign commodities, the use value was perhaps of little significance. For Dickens and Horne, this casual adoption of global commodities and the growing reliance by the British on transnational locales while China maintained its unwillingness to move away from its own culture marked a dangerous shift.

'China with a Flaw in It' does something very different from 'The Great Exhibition and the Little One'. Morley sets out the historical framework for the readership, often mocking China's lack of progress, but if a country is of so little import, *why* would one bother to criticise it or to reference in such a meticulous fashion the points of change brought about by the Opium Wars? Morley recognises China's thriving manufacturing industry and its ability to add value by transforming its natural materials into commodities that Britain, as a consuming nation, buys. Equally, Morley engages with the 'internal distractions of the Chinese empire', which he suggests may benefit Britain in terms of trade and progress.[8] Clearly, however, the article's focus remains on securing access to the ports, which the British determinedly went about gaining in earlier years through the introduction of opium, a substance explicitly banned by China's rulers. The ports subsequently opened to British trade after the Opium War gave Britain access to the goods it wanted. Yet,

---

[7] Catherine Waters, *Commodity Culture in Dickens's Household Words: The Social Life of Goods* (Aldershot: Ashgate, 2008), p. 3.
[8] Henry Morley, 'China with a Flaw in It', *Household Words*, Vol. V, No. 119 (3 July 1852), 368-74 (p. 369). All subsequent references will appear in the text.

despite the partial military control brought about by the war, Britain still had something to fear. Morley states that:

> Taking the matter, however, on its own ground, we are disposed to doubt whether the evil of the Chinese war will lead to so much good as our conceit in the character of Europeans caused us to imagine. No wonders have happened in the way of commerce with the external world, and the internal state of China, since the war ('China with a Flaw in It', p. 369).

That the war achieved 'no wonders' suggests a feeling of futility on the part of the British. Despite empire-building successes elsewhere, the Chinese resolve to maintain agency is still a powerful force. China's attachment to its own culture and its resistance to British influence is a source of unease. Morley also notes that:

> If it should hereafter appear, as possibly it may, that the chief result of the Opium War is the overthrow of the Tartar influence, and the restoration of the dynasty of Ming, or any other set of Chinese emperors, then it will be pretty certain that the prospects of a friendly commerce with China have not been cleared, but rather clouded, by our thunder ('China with a Flaw in It', p. 370).

It is interesting to note that Morley recognises the fragile moment of power the British are enjoying. The notion that 'friendly commerce' is achievable shows a surprising level of optimism, which fails to recognise the effects of excessive taxations on the Chinese. Morley then moves on to consider the Chinese lack of a thorough knowledge of European ways, stating that:

> Before the war with England the Chinese were very ignorant of European ways, and knew little or nothing of European geography. They had no clearer idea of the distance between Manchester and Liverpool, than many of us have of the distance between Ladak and Penjinsk ('China with a Flaw in It', p. 369).

The concluding sentence bears further attention as Morley appears to recognise that the Chinese lack of knowledge of British geographical distances is mirrored by a British ignorance of transnational distances. It is also noteworthy that Morley uses Ladak, a place already colonised by the British, to represent a foreign geographical space.

The challenges created by the war are also explored, although significantly the financial implications are refocused on China, with Morley stating that:

> The cost of the defence against the English taxed to the utmost the imperial resources; and when they were still further taxed during the peace to pay for the expense of the attack by which they had been subdued, the Emperor was fairly smothered with pecuniary difficulties, and forced into shifts and schemes of the most perilous description ('China with a Flaw in It', p. 370).

While the war was essentially initiated by the British, of fundamental importance is the fact that China is ultimately made to pay. China's pecuniary difficulties are caused by Western intrusion rather than Eastern financial difficulties. Regenia Gagnier states that:

> India and China did not enter modernity as the helpless 'lands of famine' enshrined in Western imagination. They were made so by British policy on trade deficits and export drives, over taxation and merchant capital, foreign control of key revenues and developmental resources, imperial and civil warfare, and a gold standard favouring Britain.[9]

China's seeming lack of progress is not due to a lack of ingenuity but instead a determined effort by Britain to challenge the smooth trading passage of China by taxation.

Morley's agenda in relation to this is clear as he emphasises the significance of past Chinese trade restrictions on Britain, the importance of the reduction of Chinese strength and the ways in which Britain can exert continued control over this space. He states that:

> Our trade with China, since the war, has not increased with any great rapidity. The Chinese authorities do what they can to force the teas down to the port of Canton, where the people are riotous, the geographical situation is inconvenient and the harbour is bad; ships cannot approach the town itself, but anchor at Whampoa, eight or nine miles lower down. Canton being, moreover, the old trading port to which old-fashioned traders, whose ideas run in a groove, have always been accustomed, ships are still sent out to Canton, that

---

[9] Regenia Gagnier, *Individualism, Decadence and Globalization: On the Relationship of Part to Whole, 1859-1920* (Houndmills: Palgrave Macmillan, 2010), p. 22.

might be dispatched much more wisely to Shanghae ('China with a Flaw in It', p. 371).

Morley here situates the older ports as places of stasis, not convenient to British trade, and the Shanghai ports as ones that are infinitely preferable and clearly profitable.

Morley states in a series of tightly-made points the trading rules brought about by the new treaty. Firstly, the initial British trading disadvantage is '[t]he confinement of trade to the single port of Canton, at the southern extremity of China, far from the tea districts', which is then solved by the provision in the treaty that 'four ports should be open to our trade in addition to Canton: Amoy and Foo-chow-foo in Fokien province, Ning-po in Che-keang and Shanghae in Keang-nan' ('China with a Flaw in It', p. 371). This opening up of the borders enabled the British to make progress in trade and open up an area to which it had previously been denied admission. As point number three on this list states:

> It was provided by the treaty that there should be a fair and permanent tariff on export and import duties. On this head it ought to be noted, that no article at present entering China is taxed by the Chinese at more than five per cent, of its value, while we repress with a duty of two hundred per cent, the admission of tea into England ('China with a Flaw in It', p. 371).

This excessive taxation is further evinced by a document published by Hansard as part of a House of Commons debate on 26 April 1855:

> While we taxed the commodities imported from them at the rate of 180 per cent, we insisted on their taking ours at a Customs duty of only 6 per cent. [It was] feared that the increase of the duty on tea would materially check our trade with China.[10]

While seemingly the trade was not 'checked', this policy raises very serious questions about trading legislation and indeed the prudence of such fiscal policy. The fact that China was able to maintain its trade through the interest of the British in its commodities suggests a commercial resilience that goes against expectations and bestows, as Morley states, 'new lights on China'

---

[10] Mr. Gregson, 'The Customs Duties Bill, House of Commons, 26 April 1855, Vol. 137, cc. 791-805' in *Hansard 1803-2005* <http://hansard.millbank systems.com/commons/1855/apr/26/custom-dutiesbill#S3V0137PO_1855 _0426_HOC_38> [accessed 3 June 2011], p. 1793.

('China with a Flaw in It', p. 373). In this sense, China in the nineteenth century represents a growing commodity super power.

The articles I have considered represent a growing interest in China in a social, political and geographical sense. Despite Dickens's, Horne's and Morley's protestations about the lack of progress in China, the inward-looking nature of this locale could be both desirable and threatening. Far from revealing disinterestedness, the sustained criticism of this locale points instead to an interest heightened by the threat China posed, albeit from afar, through its refusal to conform to British will. By critiquing, cataloguing and privileging statistical information, 'The Great Exhibition and the Little One' and 'China with a Flaw in It' attempt to minimise the sense of China's strong cultural identity and the perceived threat from China and her diverse and highly desirable objects.

SECTION 3

A Defence of the Pen: The Figure of the Author Drawn by *Household Words*

Helen Mckenzie

We aspire to live in the Household affections, and to be numbered among the Household thoughts, of our readers.[1]

THE self-consciousness of *Household Words* is not unusual amongst mid-Victorian publications, but its intimate relationship with Dickens, and his popularity as a public figure, makes its construction of the author a particularly interesting one. This essay will examine the justification of the value of writing and of the profession of the writer contained within *Household Words*, focusing on the profound impact of the industrialisation of print upon the values ascribed to writing, to print, to creativity and to the writer. The commodification of printed material within Victorian society altered the status of writing, but it also radically altered the place occupied by authors in the public imagination. As a consequence, there was a significant re-evaluation of the values ascribed to writing, to print and, thus, to the writer. Scrutiny of writing led to scrutiny of the writer.

Mid-Victorian writers, including Dickens, actively participated in this redefinition of authorship in the wake of these transformations of the literary marketplace. The self-obsessed inwardness of nineteenth-century print culture was increasingly reified in the many column inches devoted to debates about what to read and how to read, arguments about the relative merits of different genres and styles, and fiercely opinionated reviews and

---

[1] [Charles Dickens], 'A Preliminary Word', *Household Words*, Vol. I, No. 1 (30 March 1850), 1-2 (p. 1).

commentaries.[2] As a consequence of this array of voices and viewpoints, conceptions of writing and of the role of the author were complex and often conflicting. The diversity of writers working in the mid-nineteenth century, when combined with the diversity of the reading public, produced a multitude of expectations and ideals that interacted to form the Victorian literary marketplace.

Household Words existed at the heart of these tensions and a consideration of its language and ideals illuminates many of the assumptions made about an author's role and responsibilities in Victorian society. My analysis will initially focus upon Dickens's aims for the periodical—as set out in 'A Preliminary Word' (30 March 1850)—reading this manifesto alongside an article by Wilkie Collins which conjectures about the reading public. The second focal point of my exploration of *Household Words* is the treatment of literary institutions in two articles, one by Dickens and one by Henry Morley. Through a scrutiny of the ideals and values that underpin the language of the periodical, this essay aims to illustrate the figure of the author that *Household Words* constructs for its readers.

I

Dickens explicitly voices his aims for *Household Words* in 'A Preliminary Word', which defines the nature of the relationship he intends to foster between the periodical and its readers. Through the vehicle of the publication he hopes 'to be admitted into many homes with affection and confidence' and for the magazine to become a familiar, everyday object.[3] Dickens illustrates a domestic scene and places his publication at its centre; in his vision, print is located at the heart of the private sphere and he imagines an informal and familiar relationship between the author and the reader.[4] But there is a simultaneous, yet contradictory, impression of the interaction between *Household Words* and the public that draws attention to its

---

[2] See, for example; 'Prospectus of a new journal', *Punch*, 9 May 1863, p. 193; 'Doubleday', 'Books and Their Uses', *Macmillan Magazine*, Vol. 2 (December 1859), 110-13; 'Periodical Literature', *Dublin Review*, June 1853, 541-66.

[3] [Dickens], 'A Preliminary Word', p. 1.

[4] In *The Sensation Novel and the Victorian Family Magazine* (Houndmills: Palgrave, 2001), Deborah Wynne examines the dynamic between the periodical press and the domestic group of the family, focusing on the 1860s and sensation fiction—a relationship that, in part, grew out of the influence of *Household Words* and *All the Year Round* in the 1850s and 1860s.

contractual nature: 'We know the great responsibility of such a great privilege'.[5] The implicitly business-like image employed here and the public nature of writing implied, stand in stark contrast to the intimate image of literature in the home. Despite the emotive language used, the clear sense of duty implied by the text also contrasts with the cosy domesticity of the image of fireside reading. This article, while recognising the philanthropic mission of *Household Words*, also emphasises writing as work: it is a 'solitary labour'.[6] In this depiction, authorship is not an unconstrained expression of an individual's aesthetic or artistic ambition; rather it is subject to the demands of the public and the desires of readers.

Dickens formulates a specific set of functions for *Household Words* and for its authors in relation to the imagined readership. He intends his writers to form an emotional bond with his readers and fulfil the roles of 'comrade and friend'.[7] But they must also fulfil a more authoritative position that carries enormous social and moral power and responsibility:

> We seek to bring into innumerable homes, from the stirring world around us, the knowledge of many social wonders, good and evil, that are not calculated to render any of us less ardently persevering in ourselves, less tolerant of one another, less faithful in the progress of mankind, less thankful for the privilege of living in this summer-dawn of time.[8]

The author is cast in a didactic role by Dickens and intended to direct readers' social understanding—and even their behaviour. He imagines for the Victorian author an intricate relationship with the public, proposing ideal roles that they must perform: they must be both friend and teacher, fireside companion and social commentator. These roles are based on relationships that recognise the necessity of the reader to constructions of the author. The publishing industry also importantly constructs this relationship as the fundamental bond at the heart of the literary marketplace—a depiction that recognises and further emphasises a marketplace based on economic transactions.

This complex ideal of the author and of print culture is implicit throughout *Household Words* and is present in every article and every page of the periodical as the assumed role that the writer fulfils. But some articles

---

[5] [Dickens], 'A Preliminary Word', p. 1.
[6] [Dickens], 'A Preliminary Word', p. 1.
[7] [Dickens], 'A Preliminary Word', p. 1.
[8] [Dickens], 'A Preliminary Word', p. 1.

tackle the position of print in Victorian society more directly, participating in the self-examination pervading the pages of *Household Words* as well as almost every periodical publication. One of the most interesting examples of such articles is an 1858 *Household Words* piece by Wilkie Collins entitled 'The Unknown Public' that seeks to identify the Victorian reading public including, or perhaps especially, those that read *Household Words*. This article is indicative of attempts to quantify the place of print in society and the landscape of nineteenth-century print culture. [9] In 1863, for example, Charles Allston Collins wrote an article in *Macmillan's Magazine* entitled 'Our Audience' which attempts, like 'The Unknown Public', to define the readers of periodical publications. Both pieces try to identify the nature of the readers and the ways in which they interact with print, such as where and how they buy reading material. There were also articles which explicitly sought to determine the place of the author within Victorian society, such as George Henry Lewes's 'The Condition of Authors in England, Germany, and France', published in *Fraser's Magazine* in 1847. Its opening line categorically states that '[l]iterature has become a profession. It has become a means of subsistence, almost as certain as the church or the bar'.[10] Interestingly, the emphasis here is on the financial rewards that writing can bring and, for Lewes, it is precisely this economic value that qualifies writing as a profession. The contentious yet intimate relationship between literature and commerce increasingly occupied a prominent position in periodical debates.

Collins's description of his changing perspective in 'The Unknown Public' is perhaps stylised and staged, but it is nevertheless valuable as it reveals many of the ideals shaping both the literary style and the business model behind *Household Words*. Collins opens by listing who he initially understood to be the reading public: 'the subscribers to this journal, the customers of book-clubs and circulating libraries, and the purchasers and borrowers of newspapers and reviews'.[11] The focus in this list of groups of figures and exchanges is on the commercial transactions that fuelled the mid-nineteenth-century press, thus revealing the monetary nature of the dissemination of print and the exchanges that formed the print industry. But,

---

[9] Such articles are exemplified by [Charles Allston Collins], 'Our Audience', *Macmillan's Magazine*, Vol. 8 (June 1863), 161-66.

[10] [G. H. Lewes], 'The Condition of Authors in England, Germany, and France', *Fraser's Magazine*, Vol. 35 (March 1847), 285-95 (p. 285).

[11] [Wilkie Collins], 'The Unknown Public', *Household Words*, Vol. XVIII, No. 439 (21 August 1858), 217-22 (p. 217).

he admits: 'I know better now. I know that the public just now mentioned, viewed as an audience for literature, is nothing more than a minority'.[12] Collins makes no attempt to deny the financial nature of the connection between the public and writing, but instead suggests that the place of reading in mid-Victorian society has been underestimated.

The interactions first mentioned by Collins are very formalised and deliberate ones, but the article goes on to explore the more accidental encounters between print and the public. He describes, very tangibly, the process of walking through London and the surrounding towns and villages and finding or stumbling across penny-novel journals in shop windows:

> Day after day, and week after week, the mysterious publications haunted my walks, go where I might [...]. I left London and travelled about England. The neglected publications followed me. There they were in every town, large or small. I saw them in fruit-shops, in oyster-shops, in lollypop-shops, Villages even—picturesque, strong-smelling villages—were not free from them.[13]

The intimate relationship between trade and print is represented in very visual terms here, emphasising the powerful physical presence of literature in Victorian streets. The text forcibly emphasises the pervasiveness of print through the personification of the 'mysterious publications', implying that print is neither passive nor neutral but is, instead, both dynamic and influential.

Collins imagines penny-novel journals as items of necessity in the shops, explicitly tying reading with consumption, or 'the human appetites'.[14] He describes an encounter with a publisher or bookseller, certainly exaggerated for humorous effect, but cogently dramatising the commodification of periodical writing. He asks for a recommendation about which penny-novel journal to choose:

> 'What about the stories in this one? Are they as good, now, as the stories in that one?'

---

[12] [Collins], 'The Unknown Public', p. 217.

[13] [Collins], 'The Unknown Public', p. 217.

[14] [Collins], 'The Unknown Public', p. 217. This image of consumptive reading is most strongly associated with sensation fiction and the dangers of reading, particularly for young women. See, for example, Pamela K. Gilbert, *Disease, Desire and the Body in Sensation Fiction* (Cambridge: Cambridge University Press, 1997) and Wynne, *Sensation Novel and the Victorian Family Magazine*.

The book seller replied: 'Well you see, some likes one, and some likes another. Sometimes I sells more of one, and sometimes I sells more of another. Take 'em all the year round, and there ain't a pin as I knows of, to choose between 'em [...]. Look what a lot of print in every one of 'em! My eye! What a lot of print for the money!'[15]

The value of print is expressed solely in monetary terms rather than aesthetic or literary ones; there is no mention of the style of the language or even the nature of the plots. The emphasis is entirely upon the amount of print in relation to its cost; the success or failure of the writing is measured in financial—not literary—terms. Collins criticises this form of mass-produced writing for its lack of artistic or literary talent: 'There seems to be an intense in-dwelling respectability in their dullness [... and] they lead to no intellectual result [...] and this sort of writing appeals to a monster audience of at least three million!'.[16] He focuses upon the sameness and repetition within periodical publications and criticises the value placed on the quantity, rather than the quality, of the writing in penny-novel journals. But, significantly, he cannot ignore either their existence or the existence of their readers.

The extent to which print has entered the public view and everyday experience is caricatured by Collins as he personifies the penny-novel journal, imagining it speaking to passers-by: '"Buy me, borrow me, stare at me, steal me—do anything, O inattentive stranger, except contemptuously pass me by!"'.[17] The identity of the penny journal is reliant upon its relationship with its readers; the desperation of the voice, while comic, implies that, rather than possessing any intrinsic artistic worth, the value of the text is entirely dependent upon its interaction with a reader. Interestingly, the author is not mentioned here at all, remaining a silent and invisible figure in this transaction. Although exaggerated for comic effect, this scene reveals the pervasiveness and also the visual power of printed materials in the nineteenth-century urban landscape. Collins also draws attention to the enormity, mystery and unknown quality of the readership of penny-novel journals, describing it as 'a public to be counted by millions; the mysterious, the unfathomable, the universal public'.[18] The impact of the proliferation of print is yet to be fully comprehended even by those most intimately involved in the process.

---

[15] [Collins], 'The Unknown Public', pp. 218-19.
[16] [Collins], 'The Unknown Public', p. 221.
[17] [Collins], 'The Unknown Public', p. 217.
[18] [Collins], 'The Unknown Public', p. 217.

The article does not seek to dismiss this multitude of readers. Instead, Collins identifies a need to educate and improve them and their reading: 'An immense public has been discovered: the next thing to do is, in a literary sense, to teach that public how to read'.[19] Collins's proposed mission of education is symptomatic of the didactic role that Dickens intended for *Household Words*: its authors were expected to teach the public how to read properly. As a further consequence of this multitudinous new public, Collins identifies a shift in the formulation of literary merit: it is no longer solely based on creativity, artistic integrity and good reviews, but also on commercial success and educational value. Recognising the huge numbers of readers, Collins draws attention to the increasing significance of the popularity of an author or a publication:

> To the penny journals of the present time belongs the credit of having discovered a new public. When that public shall discover its need of a great writer, the great writer will have such an audience as has never yet been known.[20]

Collins opens up the possibility of popularity as a measure of literary success and prowess, echoing the self-consciousness of the period and perhaps speaking of either himself or Dickens as that 'great writer'.

II

The dynamic between popularity and individual artistic integrity was further complicated by the specific conditions of the nineteenth-century periodical press. This period saw a shift towards a more intense and immediate writing experience with an increasingly public recognition that writers do not work independently or in isolation.[21] In consequence, the relationship between the individual writer and the publications that they wrote for is an interesting and complex one. Not only were authors constrained by their responsibility to the public but also to the political stance, style and character of that publication. *Household Words* is a particularly interesting example of this

---

[19] [Collins], 'The Unknown Public', p. 222.

[20] [Collins], 'The Unknown Public', p. 222.

[21] Any form of publication, both Jerome McGann and D. F. Mckenzie argue, is a social phenomenon, but the mid-nineteenth century saw an increasing recognition of the interconnected nature of the literary marketplace. See, Jerome McGann, *The Textual Condition* (Princeton: Princeton University Press, 1991) and D. F. Mckenzie, *Bibliography and the Sociology of Texts* (Cambridge: Cambridge University Press, 1999).

dynamic between the individual and the collective, as it was run under Dickens's name, both metaphorically and literally as his name appears at the top of every page. This tension is exemplified by articles that deal with literary establishments or institutions and the treatment of these organisations in *Household Words* is revealing about the structures of the mid-Victorian literary world and the role of the author within that world.

Dickens himself wrote a leading article for *Household Words* in 1851 entitled 'The Guild of Literature and Art' extolling its virtues. Together with Edward Bulwer-Lytton, Dickens was instrumental in the formation of this organisation, which aimed to provide a pension fund or financial assistance to authors and artists. Dickens explicitly sets out to establish authorship as a professional occupation aligned with commerce and in this article he poses the question:

> whether Literature shall continue to be an exception from all other professions and pursuits, in having no resource for its distressed and divided followers but in eleemosynary aid; or, whether, it is good that they should be provident, united, helpful of one another, and independent.[22]

His phrasing of this question is, of course, neither objective nor unbiased, and Dickens is unashamedly leading his readers to the answer that he would like to hear, namely that literature should not set itself apart from the economic realities of the marketplace. Dickens here proposes a unified profession, which acknowledges the financial pressure placed on writers to survive in a competitive industry. However, this formulation also reveals the paradox at the heart of his ideal conception of authorship: authors should be at once 'united' yet 'independent'.

In order to prevent The Guild of Literature and Art from simply being a charitable organisation, Dickens and Bulwer-Lytton aimed to foster 'prudence and foresight' by rewarding hard work and 'provident habits'.[23] The Guild explicitly states the contractual nature of the assistance given and the demands made of those helped by the Guild. The principal conditions of receipt of assistance are:

> Each member will be required to give, either personally or by a proxy selected from the Associates, with the approval of the

---

[22] [Charles Dickens], 'The Guild of Literature and Art', *Household Words*, Vol. III, No. 59 (10 May 1851), 145-47 (p. 146).
[23] [Dickens], 'The Guild of Literature and Art', p. 145.

Warden, three lectures in each year—one in London, the others at the Mechanics' Institutes, or some public building suited for the purpose, in the principle provincial towns.[24]

Significantly, these duties are very public ones implying an explicitly social role for the author that reflects the social responsibility Dickens intended for *Household Words*. These lectures are also, by being located in municipal or institutional buildings, associated with industrialism and institutionalisation. There is an interesting interaction here between science and commerce on the one hand and art and creativity on the other. Indeed, the very concept of a literary institution perhaps embodies the juxtaposition found in the mid-Victorian press and encapsulated in the dual aims Dickens sets forth for the literary profession to be both 'united' and 'independent'. These tensions participate not only in class issues but also in debates about individual autonomy and participation in an industrialised and urbanised world.

Dickens himself, through the very act of publishing this article in *Household Words*, engages with this paradox. As founder of the Guild and as 'Conductor' of the periodical, he is able to publish this article on the front page of the issue, clearly and very deliberately playing on the knowledge that his readers will know that he wrote the article and that he is instrumental within the institution. He plays on his popularity and on the knowledge that he is in control of the publication and that he can ultimately publish what *he* wants as he is not restricted by any conditions or requirements: he is 'independent' in the editorial control of *Household Words*. Dickens is, however, constrained by his readers, by his need to maintain his popularity and thus make a living as a writer. Conversely, the writers working for *Household Words* are 'united' but they are united under Dickens, his name, his fame and his artistic ambition: their independence is much more problematic. However, each of these writers is engaged in the 'solitary labour' Dickens imagines in 'A Preliminary Word' and they have a degree of control over whom they work for and the course of their own careers writing for other publications or writing fiction.[25] This ideal of the author is thus a paradoxical one that every author is forced to negotiate: every author is caught between artistic and creative autonomy, financial necessity and editorial control.

The complexity of the mid-Victorian press was intensified by an intricate and shifting network of loyalties between the writers themselves, typified by

---

[24] [Dickens], 'The Guild of Literature and Art', p. 146.
[25] [Dickens], 'A Preliminary Word', p. 1.

the very public, and now infamous, rivalry between Dickens and W. M. Thackeray. Thackeray heavily criticised the Guild for degrading the reputation of literary men in a very public and outspoken criticism at a Royal Literary Fund dinner on the same night as the first performance of Bulwer-Lytton's play *Not So Bad As We Seem*, which was performed to raise funds for the Guild on 16 April 1851 at Devonshire House before the Queen and Prince Albert.[26] Also, in a letter to Forster, Thackeray wrote, 'I don't believe in The Guild of Literature and Art, I don't believe in the Theatrical scheme; I think *that* is against the dignity of our profession'.[27] The vehemence of his criticism must at least in part be attributed to his personal rivalry with Dickens. Nevertheless, Thackeray's language emphasises the multiplicity of ambitions for, and conceptions of, the literary profession in the mid-century.

The opposition between the two men and the two institutions is complicated by Dickens's later involvement with the Royal Literary Fund and by the similarly paradoxical conception of the author at the heart of that institution.[28] In 1856, Henry Morley wrote an article for *Household Words* on the Royal Literary Fund's impersonality as an institution, thus contributing to Dickens's attempt to reform the Literary Fund when he became frustrated with the progress of the Guild. The article explores the impact of the conflict between the artistic nature of literature and institutionalism. Morley accuses the Royal Literary Fund of being a 'very stagnant institution', which has suffered 'under that insidious malady, Routine'.[29] The dynamic between

---

[26] 'Thackeray, in particular, took exception to this form of charity. On the very night of the first performance of *Not So Bad As We Seem,* he spoke at a dinner of the Royal Literary Fund to this effect "Literary men are not by any means, at this present time, that most unfortunate and most degraded set of people whom they are sometimes represented to be [...]"'. Peter Ackroyd, *Dickens* (London: Sinclair-Stevenson, 1990), p. 629.

[27] Thackeray wrote to Jane Welsh Carlyle, 'And don't you understand that there are a set of men who will be martyrs, who are painting their faces and asking for your money, who want to make literature a chronic beggary under the name of the Guild', quoted in Ackroyd, pp. 629-30. As Ackroyd notes on p. 1122, Thackeray's 'dismal response to the theatricals' is also discussed in Gordon Ray, *Thackeray: The Age of Wisdom* (London: McGraw-Hill, 1972).

[28] Michael J. Flynn addresses the class implications of the competition between Thackeray and Dickens and their involvement with the Royal Literary Fund in his essay 'Pendennis, Copperfield, and the Debate on the "Dignity of Literature"', *Dickens Studies Annual*, Vol. 14 (2010), 151-89.

[29] [Henry Morley], 'The Royal Literary Fund', *Household Words*, Vol. XIII, No. 311 (8 March 1856), 169-72 (pp. 169, 170).

creativity and work further problematises the relationship between the individual and the collective and exacerbates the conflict between the public and private roles of the author. Morley attributes this 'malady' to the Royal Literary Fund being run by committees after the death of its founder David Williams; the human and the individual elements of the institution have been eroded and corrupted by the mechanics and systems of the organisation. Morley argues that the balance has been lost between maintaining a focus on writing as a creative and artistic process on the one hand and participating in the literary marketplace as an economic system on the other.

Whilst Dickens clearly advocates the necessity of acknowledging the business element of the press, in his articles as well as in the way that he ran *Household Words* and marketed his fiction, he maintains a focus on the creativity of the profession. This attitude and Dickens's personal investment in *Household Words* is clearly felt in every article. Indeed as Morley observes,

> We do not write anonymously in reference to it, but place the responsibility of our remonstrance upon the name that appears at the head of every alternate page of this journal. We entreat the Public to consider what this institution is; what it spends; and what it does.[30]

Morley invokes Dickens's influence upon the attitudes expressed in the article and also writes the article, as 'we', as if from a collective united under Dickens. Dickens's persona engages the public, acting as the familiar and personal connection between the readers of *Household Words* and the matters it addresses, and once again we are reminded of the extent of his influence.

The mid-Victorian press was an industry attempting to define itself according to the ideals held by the diverse individuals working as writers, whilst also being intensely aware of the pressure of a public that was equally diverse and often contradictory. To fulfil the ideal that pervaded the mid-Victorian press, including *Household Words*, the author was required to occupy several conflicting, even paradoxical, roles or identities. An intrinsic contradiction exists between Dickens's identity as an author yet also a businessman. In every aspect of the author's role, and in every element of the literary marketplace, existed a fundamental tension between the author and his/her profession, the individual and the institution, and the artistic and the financial.

---

[30] [Morley], p. 172.

'Literary Adventurers': Editorship, Non-Fiction Authorship and Anonymity

Jasper Schelstraete

My dearest Katie,

It is nearly eight, and I have not yet even begun the Sketch; neither have I thought of a subject. Excuse the brevity of this note on that account and believe that it is only occasioned by my wish to see you as early as possible tomorrow.

I send you by George (who in Fred's absence on business, is kind enough to be the bearer of this) the volume which contains the Life of Savage. I have turned down the leaf. Now do read it attentively; if you do, I know from your excellent understanding you will be delighted. If you slur it, you will think it dry.[1]

IN October 1835, Catherine Hogarth received a copy of Samuel Johnson's *Lives of the English Poets* (1779-81) from Dickens. This gift from the young author to his blushing bride-to-be would not have lent itself well to making a good case for his ability to support a family. Dickens had marked out the 'Life of Richard Savage', specifically calling Catherine's attention to it in the enclosed letter by urging her, '*do* read it attentively'.[2] Savage offered a disturbing alternative to literary success, as a writer who—as Robert Douglas-Fairhurst puts it in his impressive study of Dickens's early career *Becoming Dickens* (2011)—'"drank away his talent", spent nights fretfully pacing the streets of London, and ended up as little more than a resentful

---

[1] To Catherine Dickens, October 1835, *The Letters of Charles Dickens*, ed. by Kathleen Tillotson, Graham Storey and others, Pilgrim Edition, 12 vols (Oxford: Clarendon, 1965-2002), Vol. I, p. 85 (original emphasis).
[2] *Letters of Charles Dickens*, Vol. I, p. 85 (original emphasis).

magnet for charity'.[3] Not, perhaps, the kind of future that would appeal to a sheltered twenty-year-old girl from a well-to-do family. Dickens was demonstrating the necessity of his work ethic, using Savage's life as a haunting vision of a potential future, a reminder of how precarious his position in the literary field was in that early stage of his career.

Years later, Savage appears in a different kind of publication by Dickens. He is mentioned in the unattributed article 'Literary Adventurers' published on 10 October 1863 in *All the Year Round*—no longer as a potential future, but as an example of a fate narrowly avoided. Savage appears alongside Thomas Chatterton, Oliver Goldsmith and, of course, Johnson, in a list of conspicuous eighteenth-century literary men, whose considerable talents did not guarantee comfortable subsistence. Like Johnson's *Lives*, 'Literary Adventurers' is mild in its account of Savage's life, attributing his debauched poverty to a problematic eighteenth-century literary marketplace:

> In those days, a large portion of working literary men were little better than outcasts [...] partly by their own vices, partly by the fact of their following a profession which had hardly acquired a recognised standing in the world, or found for itself a definite and indisputable sphere of usefulness. The reading public was not sufficiently large to maintain an excessive fraternity of writers; and the writers consequently often starved and broke their hearts in wretched garrets, or earned a despicable living by flattering the great.[4]

The article identifies two problems facing an eighteenth-century author like Savage. First, the marketplace was too limited to support many authors, which meant that an author either had to live in abject poverty as a bookseller's hack or 'debase his soul to the level of a parasite' by flattering a patron (p. 153), by whom he was 'half pitied, half despised' (p. 152). Second, authors lacked purpose, a well-defined role in society.

'Literary Adventurers' triumphantly declares that these obstacles have been overcome, claiming, '[t]he newspaper press has put an end to "the Poor Devil Author"' (p. 153). An increase in literacy rates over the first half of the nineteenth century meant a broader base of literary consumers, making

---

[3] Robert Douglas-Fairhurst, *Becoming Dickens: The Invention of a Novelist* (Cambridge, MA: Belknap Press of Harvard University Press, 2011), pp. 214-15.

[4] [Anon.], 'Literary Adventurers', *All the Year Round*, Vol. X, No. 233 (10 October 1863), 153-56 (p. 153). Further references to this article are given in parenthesis in the body of the text.

mass-production techniques practicable. Industrial improvements in printing, the decline of paper prices and the abolition of stamp and paper duty drastically reduced the production costs of publishing.[5] This made for a more open literary marketplace, which implies a 'decentering of literary authority'.[6] The second issue, however, concerned with the social standing and usefulness of authorship, remained unsolved. 'Literary Adventurers' hints at the 'duties' of an author as 'a member of the industrial world' (p. 155), but nowhere does it explicitly state what these duties might entail. The article derides the notion that periodical press authors should be primarily concerned with 'the abstract interests of the commonwealth of letters' (p. 154), but does not expressly offer up an alternative. In this paper, I aim to explore the article's remarkable, yet unspoken, positioning of authors within an explicitly market-driven literary field. Instead of being 'willing sacrifice[s] to literature,' who would be 'content to starve that the intellectual state might prosper' (154), some—particularly non-fiction—authors are recast as workmen in 'Literary Adventurers', dutifully catering to the demands of the marketplace. The article postures as a triumphant celebration of the nineteenth-century periodical press and its ability to support huge numbers of authors through a glossed-over notion of the equal division of wealth in an open marketplace. However, the preoccupation with pragmatic supply and the article's silence on issues of anonymity imply a much less inclusive project, introducing oppressive industrial factory models to literary non-fiction production, reducing authors to commodities at the disposal of the 'chief'.

In his neo-Marxist book *Towards a Sociology of the Novel* (1963), Lucien Goldmann distinguishes between the 'use value' and the 'exchange value' of objects. The former he describes as the 'natural and healthy relation between men and commodities [...] in which production is consciously governed by future consumption, by the concrete quality of objects', while the latter is 'the elimination of this relation with men's consciousness, its reduction to the implicit through the mediation of the new economic reality created by this form of [market] production'.[7] 'Literary Adventurers' attributes the

---

[5] Richard Altick, *The English Common Reader: A Social History of the Mass Reading Public 1800-1900* (Chicago: University of Chicago Press, 1957) pp. 277, 354.

[6] Paul Delaney, *Literature, Money and the Market: From Trollope to Amis* (Houndmills: Palgrave, 2002), p. 103.

[7] Lucien Goldmann, *Towards a Sociology of the Novel* [1963], trans. by Alan Sheridan (New York and London: Tavistock, 1975), pp. 7-8.

'failure' of authors from preceding eras to a fanciful disregard of the 'use-value' of their labour in society:

> It was long also before he himself [the author] acquired a just idea of his duties as a member of the industrial world. Too often he laid the foundation of his own failure by the sentimentalism of his views. Because it pleased him to write verses to Delia and Odes on Immortality, he took it into his head that that was his sole business in life, and that this rough toiling hard-handed world of ours was bound to stop, and hear him pipe, and reward him for his piping. Society, on the other hand, made the mistake of regarding the literary man as a sort of pleasant superfluity—an intellectual gipsy, to be played with on holiday occasions.[8]

The duties of an author, then, are not with 'pleasant superfluities', nor 'holiday occasions'. 'Literary Adventurers' posits the incompatibility of lofty, romantic authorship with an increasingly industrialised society. Periodical press authors should instead focus on the pragmatic 'use value' of their writing, providing their readers with information that would help them get ahead in society, chiming with the 'March of Mind' and the Victorian idea of self-help. The authors 'Literary Adventurers' is concerned with, then, are non-fiction authors, a distinction the article glosses over in its discussion of eighteenth-century writers.

Ella Ann Oppenlander describes *All the Year Round* as unique in its dealings with difficult non-fiction topics 'such as scientific advances, the postal system and the London water supply', presenting them 'in an attractive way that, while not patronising, was comprehensible to readers unaccustomed to making any intellectual effort'.[9] This project was also an integral part of *Household Words*, as becomes clear from 'A Preliminary Word', featured on the very first page of that journal:

> We seek to bring into innumerable homes, from the stirring world around us, the knowledge of many social wonders, good and evil, that are not calculated to render any of us less ardently persevering in ourselves, less tolerant of one another, less faithful in the progress of mankind, less thankful for the privilege of living in this summer-dawn of time. No mere utilitarian spirit, no iron binding of the mind

---

[8] Goldmann, pp. 155-56.
[9] Ella Ann Oppenlander, *Dickens' All the Year Round: Descriptive Index and Contributors List* (Troy, NY: Whitston, 1984), p. 28.

to grim realities, will give a harsh tone to our Household Words. In the bosoms of the young and old, of the well-to-do and of the poor, we would tenderly cherish that light of Fancy which is inherent in the human breast.[10]

Dickens's desire to educate his readers by presenting them with information in creative and fanciful ways remained strong throughout the run of *Household Words*. On 31 October 1852, Dickens wrote to Henry Morley, staff writer and a tireless contributor of useful non-fictional material, stressing the importance of what John Drew has called 'the spoonful of sugar principle':[11]

[T]he main trouble necessary to [Morley's contributions], is, the devising of some pleasant means of telling what is to be told. The indispensable necessity of varying the manner of narration as much as possible, and investing it with some little grace or other, would be very evident to you if you knew as well as I do how severe the struggle is, to get the publication down into the masses of readers.[12]

The same strategy was employed in *All the Year Round*, where titbits of useful knowledge were dolled up through illustrative anecdotes, allegories, dialogue and similar devices.[13] This is consistent with the famous argument Dickens made in a letter written to would-be *Household Words* contributor Emily Jolly (17 July 1855) that the author should cater to the marketplace—'You write to be read, of course'.[14] Writing for the periodical press is imagined here, as in 'Literary Adventurers', as producing a useful commodity, parcels of knowledge, 'mental food' ready for mass-consumption (p. 155), and with a guaranteed 'use value'. In return, the marketplace supports its authors, 'maintaining them in decency and comfort' (p. 155). 'Literary Adventurers' brushes aside hostile views of the marketplace, instead embracing it as the source of culture, explicitly associating literature with professionalism:

---

[10] [Charles Dickens], 'A Preliminary Word', *Household Words*, Vol. I, No. 1 (30 March 1850), 1-2 (p. 1).

[11] John M. L. Drew, *Dickens the Journalist* (Houndmills: Palgrave Macmillan, 2003), p. 110.

[12] To Henry Morley, 31 October 1852, *Letters of Charles Dickens*, Vol. VI, pp. 790-91 (p. 790).

[13] Oppenlander, p. 28.

[14] To Emily Jolly, 17 July 1855, *Letters of Charles Dickens*, Vol. VII, pp. 676-77 (p. 677).

The literary man is now a workman [...]. And, as if to show how well imagination harmonises with prosaic toil, this resort to steady working habits on the part of our pen-men has been accompanied by a development of the poetical faculty of which the Boyses and the Chattertons had but the feeblest glimpse. (156)

The duty of nineteenth-century periodical press authors was not just to convey prosaic, pragmatic information, but also to present it in an attractive way, using their 'poetical faculty' to facilitate it 'getting down into the masses'. Profitability, then, became a marker of literary quality, making 'literature a business—no small recommendation in a business land' (p. 156).

This is consistent with Dickens's overall project of tapping into a new middle-class readership for his periodicals. Lorna Huett has argued that Dickens shaped both *Household Words* and *All the Year Round* 'in opposition to the older, more established, highbrow monthly and quarterly reviews, which represented the literary tastes, reading practices and social rhythms of an earlier generation, and of a more leisured and secure upper class'.[15] The resulting format was in close proximity to that of the cheap press. This was not all that *All the Year Round* shared with the penny press: its implied reader, too, seemed to be 'not a discerning and educated man of taste, but rather [...] a willing consumer of the "useful and agreeable mental instruction"'.[16] The 'business' of the nineteenth-century periodical press author according to 'Literary Adventurers'—providing consumers with instruction, particularly instruction that would serve them in 'this rough toiling hard-handed world'—seems epitomised by cheap publications such as *Chambers's Journal of Popular Literature, Science and the Arts* (1854), which was, purportedly, equally committed to providing readers with quality fiction and journalism in a weekly format, just like *Household Words*. John Drew has pointed out that apart from *Chambers's* and *Howitt's Journal*—'probably the closest rival to *Household Words* in literary quality'—a range of similarly didactic weeklies were available at the time, most of which were characterised by 'bland paternalism and anodyne imagery'. Dickens remained well aware of the crucial brand difference separating his publications from the competition, something which becomes clear from the note he wrote to W. H. Wills in

---

[15] Lorna Huett, 'Among the Unknown Public: *Household Words*, *All the Year Round* and the Mass Market Weekly Periodical in the Mid-Nineteenth Century', *Victorian Periodicals Review*, 38:1 (2005), 61-82 (p. 72).
[16] Huett, p. 68.

1853, reminding him that, 'KEEP "HOUSEHOLD WORDS" IMAGINATIVE! is the solemn and continual Conductorial Injunction'.[17]

Dickens's unique selling point, however, was more than just the creative and imaginative ways in which his periodicals presented their didactic content. Dickens's publications were respectable, finding their way into aspiring working-class homes and middle-class drawing rooms alike, while periodicals such as *Chambers's* stayed in the sphere of 'the poor man'. The difference between the two was clearly more than the halfpenny in price. Richard Altick points out that it was the 'prestige of Dickens's name [which] helped break down further the still powerful upper- and middle-class prejudice against cheap papers'.[18] The 'exchange value' attached to Dickens's name was the guarantee for the respectability of his publications and, therefore, their success with middle-class audiences. Interestingly, while 'Literary Adventurers' stresses the importance of the 'use value' of non-fiction writing and its remuneration, it does not discuss the distinction any kind of writing could bring an author, glossing over the author function. Given the context in which 'Literary Adventurers' was published, as an anonymous non-fiction contribution 'conducted' by Dickens, the implications for authorial positioning within the marketplace are intriguing. This is especially remarkable, since Dickens was sensitive to the issue of anonymity as far as original fiction published in *All the Year Round* was concerned.

'Literary Adventurers', like most non-fictional items incorporated in *All the Year Round*, was published anonymously. While, at this time, neither Oppenlander's *Descriptive Index* nor *Dickens Journals Online* have a known author for 'Literary Adventurers', Dickens's micromanaging approach to editorship means the article can be read as at least maintaining Dickens's central editorial voice. In a letter to Elizabeth Gaskell written in 1850, Dickens explained that this use of anonymity in *Household Words* allowed all the contents to 'seem to express the general mind and purpose of the Journal'.[19] Dickens was by no means alone in this plea for a common identity. As Laurel Brake has pointed out, many Victorian periodicals,

---

[17] Drew, pp. 110-11; To W. H. Wills, 17 November 1853, *Letters of Charles Dickens*, Vol. VII, p. 200.

[18] Altick, p. 347.

[19] To Elizabeth Gaskell, 31 January 1850, *Letters of Charles Dickens*, Vol. VI, pp. 21-22 (p. 22).

adopted a policy of anonymity which [...] supports the corporate identity of the journal as a journal, and mitigates the differences of its individual contributors [...] such periodicals [...] present themselves to the reader as a whole, as a book does.[20]

Despite Dickens's stress on unity and collaboration, the—as Douglas Jerrold put it—'mononymous' nature of his publications meant that Dickens alone was credited with their contents. This situation eventually changed in *Household Words* and *All the Year Round* for the authors of original fiction, but non-fiction authors were not given the same privilege. For *Household Words*, Dickens's policy of anonymity had initially covered fiction and non-fiction alike, with Dickens claiming that any 'confusion of authorship [...] would be a far greater service than dis-service' to contributors.[21] Dickens's publications were contemporary with extended debates in the press concerning anonymity and the locus of literary authority and responsibility, which continued on well into the 1890s, even though the use of signature was, by that time, widespread, especially in monthly and quarterly publications.[22] In this climate, Dickens eventually changed his approach, feeling that long serial works benefited from having identifiable authors, and would help keep circulation up.[23] This conviction carried over into *All the Year Round*, where Dickens gave advance notice of the authorship of original serial fiction, often identifying the author in each instalment through by-lines. In the 10 October 1863 issue of *All the Year Round*, also containing 'Literary Adventurers', Charles Reade is identified as the author of *Very Hard Cash*—the serial that was running at the time—through the by-line 'By the Author of "It is Never Too Late to Mend"'. This privileging of serial fiction over non-fiction with regards to issues of authorship, anonymity and signature indicates that Dickens considered the authorship of novels to be culturally prestigious: not 'a workman's anonymous "prosaic toil"'—however well-presented—but' branded art.

In effect, Dickens had industrialised the patronage model: the swathes of non-fiction authors publishing in Dickens's publications were rewarded for their labour, and enjoyed the prestige and respectability Dickens's name

---

[20] Laurel Brake, *Print in Transition, 1850-1910: Studies in Media and Book History* (New York: Palgrave, 2001), p. 4.

[21] Drew, p. 118.

[22] Rachel Sagner Buurma, 'Anonymity, Corporate Authority, and the Archive: The Production of Authorship in Late-Victorian England', *Victorian Studies*, Vol. 50, No. 1 (2007), 15-42 (p. 21).

[23] Drew, p. 118.

brought, much as with traditional patronage. However, Dickens's remuneration came at the additional cost of anonymity, thereby divorcing the non-fiction author from his or her text, as far as the marketplace was concerned. Thus Dickens's name accrued additional 'exchange value', transforming his authorial persona into a brand, overshadowing his contributors and absorbing much of the prestige their writing might otherwise have brought them. This prevented these non-fiction authors from establishing an identifiable, and therefore potentially more valuable, signature.[24] 'Literary Adventurers' celebrates the periodical press author as a 'workman, in the best sense of the word', but remains silent on the importance of a signature on the author's 'prosaic toil' (156). By denying his non-fiction contributors a *hic fecit*, Dickens reduced them to commodified labour-power, incorporating them in the kind of industrial capitalist wage labour scheme 'Literary Adventurers' is celebrating: 'Journalism has made literature a business—no small recommendation in a business land' (p. 156).

'Literary Adventurers' is a veiled defence of the industrialised model of periodical publication. It claims that non-fiction authors writing for the periodical press have become respectable members of society, both because of their steady income as well as their independence from a 'debasing' patron. This 'escape' from patronage seems to be, in large part, artificial, as the author is recast as a workman, whose labour needs to have nothing but 'use-value', explicitly catering to a demographic of upwardly mobile lower- and middle-class readers. In effect, in 'Literary Adventurers', the periodical press non-fiction author seems reduced to commodified labour power. Professional respectability for these authors comes at the price of anonymity. As a result, cultural value shifts away from authorship in general onto authorship of original literary fiction and editorship. By becoming the overseer, whose presence guarantees quality and respectability, in what is essentially an industrial model of literary production, Dickens ensures that his publications can transcend the middle-class anxiety regarding the lower-class influx into periodical press readership, without him having to 'write it all'. Within the context of *All the Year Round*, Dickens's name absorbs all of the 'exchange value' that might otherwise have gone to the individual non-fiction contributors. Dickens, then, is the real literary adventurer, trail-blazing a new kind of presence, blending his authorial and editorial personas. The distinction Dickens made in his policy on anonymity between fiction and non-fiction is crucial. Authors of fiction are granted a brand of their

---

[24] Buurma, p. 22.

own, though still subordinate to that of the ubiquitous conductor. Non-fiction authors, on the other hand, are denied a signature and are apparently relegated to a dutiful respectability, elevated above penny-a-lining solely through the prestige and 'exchange value' connected to Dickens's name.

'Hunted and Harried by Pseudo-Philanthropists': Dickens, Martineau and *Household Words*

Iain Crawford

SOMETIME in the late nineties, Philip Collins came to speak at the university where I was then working. That semester I was teaching a seminar on the Victorian novel, and he asked me what we were reading. Knowing him as I did, I was a little reluctant to confess that we were currently in the midst of *Lady Audley's Secret* (1862). '*Lady Audley's Secret*? When you could be doing *Middlemarch*?' 'Oh, Philip,' I said, 'it's all about historicity and challenging students to think about canon formation'. An awkward pause ensued; clearly, he thought I had been in America far too long and was showing alarming signs of having gone native. So we left it at that, and off I went to hear him give one of those wonderful lectures that many of us still remember fondly.

When I began my current project on Dickens's editorial relationships I discovered, of course, that Philip had been there long before me, doing foundational work with the Research Society for Victorian Periodicals (RSVP) and examining the nooks and crannies of Dickens's journalistic life. Hearing his voice as I read these parts of his scholarship has been comforting, moving and, as always, illuminating. And so this paper is a

---

[1] Given the debt which scholars of Dickens and Victorian journalism owe to the late Philip Collins (1923-2007), who also founded the Centre for Victorian Studies at the University of Leicester which co-hosted the conference that gave rise to this collection, it was agreed that one of the plenary papers would be dedicated to his memory. Iain Crawford is one of many students whom Philip guided through their PhDs and on into successful academic careers.

belated response to Philip's question about what and how we should be reading. It draws, then, on the kinds of inquiry into primary and archival materials that he modelled so well and through which he produced the body of scholarship that continues to inform the ways in which we understand the Victorians.

Remembering his comment on Braddon, I am not entirely sure how he would feel about the fact that my project has evolved into a study of Dickens's relationship with another recovered woman writer, but I like to think he would appreciate the way I have gone about it. Like the larger project, this essay draws extensively upon archival research with both Dickens's own letters and the unpublished letters of those with whom he worked. At the same time, it also builds on the many recent studies of the emergence of the professional woman writer during the early Victorian years. And finally, of course, it owes a debt to that invaluable new resource *Dickens Journals Online*, so it is a special pleasure to thank its editorial team who allowed me to snag for proof-reading issue number 304 of *Household Words*, which is key to the discussion which follows.[2]

This number, which appeared on 19 January 1856, contains an article unlike any other in the journal's history. 'Our Wicked Mis-Statements' is a long and sustained assault upon the credibility of Harriet Martineau. Drafted by Henry Morley and revised by Dickens, the article responds to *The Factory Controversy* (1855), a pamphlet Martineau had published the previous month. She in turn was reacting against a series of essays by Morley on industrial safety and the need for parliamentary legislation. In her pamphlet, to be sure, Martineau had indeed offered a searing and very personal indictment of her opponents and, in particular, of Dickens himself—'He should not meddle with affairs in which rationality of judgment is required' was one of her milder comments, for instance.[3] Even so, his reply was still more hostile and more personally vindictive. Despite beginning by expressing reluctance to expose 'weakness in a sick lady whom we esteem', he goes on to build an unrelenting critique of both the substance and nature of her arguments.[4] He

---

[2] Over 1,000 volunteers proof-read, corrected and moderated the computer-read text of about 30,000 journal pages, enabling the *DJO* website to offer accurate text facsimiles alongside scans of the original pages.

[3] Harriet Martineau, *The Factory Controversy* (Manchester: The National Association of Factory Occupiers, 1855), p. 44.

[4] [Charles Dickens and Henry Morley], 'Our Wicked Mis-Statements', *Household Words*, Vol. XIII, No. 304 (19 January 1856), 13-19 (p. 13).

then closes the essay by claiming his and Morley's own propriety and suggesting something very different about Martineau's virtue:

> We have done. We hope we have not been induced to exceed the bounds of temperate and moderate remonstrance, or to prostitute our part in Literature to Old Bailey pleading and passionate scolding. We thoroughly forgive Miss Martineau for having strayed into such unworthy paths under the guidance of her anonymous friend, and we blot her pamphlet out of our remembrance.[5]

As Rush Limbaugh has recently confirmed, likening a female political opponent to a prostitute is a time-honoured strategy. Martineau, though, was no Georgetown law student and had no President Obama to call and defend her; we can only imagine how appalling she must have found Dickens's language. And what made his attack particularly awful was that, first, it came from someone with whom she had had a long personal and professional relationship, and, second, it was couched in such a way as to condemn all her hard-won authorial standing. Not content with brutally labelling her as a fallen woman in need of guidance—a mere streetwalker of journalism—Dickens asserts his intent to exert an ultimate editorial authority, to 'blot' her into oblivion, and to write her out of existence. There is no other such attack upon a writer or contributor in the entire run of *Household Words*, but in responding to Martineau's pamphlet the personal has for Dickens become inseparable from the public, his self-defence fused with defending his journalistic presence, his readiness to ignore conventional standards of decorum bound up with the authority he had claimed for himself and *Household Words* to shape the Victorian public sphere.

The received narrative of the Dickens/Martineau dispute has long been that it arose from two issues: first, their immediate disagreement over industrial safety; second, her belief that the editorial policy of *Household Words* was profoundly anti-Catholic, and that this bias had led Dickens and Wills to reject a story she had offered them in late 1854 for the special Christmas number. Scholars of both writers have accepted this narrative, prompted largely by the ways in which Martineau framed the dispute in her posthumously published *Autobiography* (1877), and this prevailing interpretation has remained broadly unchallenged. Clearly, the industrial safety issue was a substantive question and one on which Dickens and Martineau strongly disagreed. On the one side, she scornfully dismissed

---

[5] [Dickens and Morley], 'Our Wicked Mis-Statements', p. 19.

Dickens as a 'sentimental philanthropist' and labelled Morley's essays as 'philo-operative cant'.[6] On the other, Morley had frequently denigrated the factory owners as the 'pseudo-philanthropists' I refer to in my title.[7] Nevertheless, what I want to argue here is that both the factory safety issue and Martineau's claims of anti-Catholicism can more helpfully be seen as occasion rather than cause. For the dispute's underlying reasons have much more to do with Dickens's goals for *Household Words* and his expectations of his contributors, especially his female contributors. At the same time, for Martineau, refusing to give in to Dickens was essential to defending her role in shaping public discourse, and her response to him can most fully be understood in terms of the 'dread [of] being silenced' that she described in her *Autobiography* as her greatest fear.[8]

Working Together at *Household Words*, 1850–54

Despite the bitter end to their relationship, Martineau and Dickens had come together to work productively at *Household Words* during its early years. When Dickens recruited contributors for his new journal, he extended invitations to a number of woman authors that collectively indicate an intentional strategy to broaden the appeal of his new mass-market weekly. Perhaps not unmindful of her glowing comments about him in the recently published *A History of the Thirty Years' Peace* (1849), he sent one of these invitations to Martineau. While we have no record of his thinking about this and whether or not he had in mind the complementary talents she brought to his own strengths, the match certainly made sense on both sides: they had long known one another; they were broadly aligned in their progressive political views; she had a strong track record in writing serious material for the large popular audiences Dickens hoped to reach; and, even with the veil of anonymous publication, she brought to the new magazine her prestige and authority as one of the leading social commentators of the day. For Martineau, meanwhile, the decision to write for Dickens gave her a lucrative opportunity to reach a large reading public on contemporary social issues and to work with an author for whom she had a great deal of admiration. All

---

[6] Martineau, *The Factory Controversy*, pp. 35, 44-45.

[7] See, for example, [Henry Morley], 'Two Shillings per Horse Power', *Household Words*, Vol. XII, No. 285 (8 September 1855), 130-31 (p. 131). Martineau echoes this language in *The Factory Controversy*, p. 35.

[8] Harriet Martineau, *Autobiography* [1877], ed. by Linda H. Peterson (Peterborough, Ontario: Broadview Press, 2007), p. 569.

in all, each of them had ample reasons for extending their longstanding relationship into one of professional collaboration.

And, for almost four years, both the working and personal relationship appeared to fulfil this early promise: beginning with three lengthy pieces in 1850, Martineau went on to contribute a dozen items the following year and twenty-three in 1852, when her writings made up some 9% of the magazine's total columns. In both 1851 and 1852 she was also given high-profile placement by being included among the groups of authors who contributed to the thematically-defined special Christmas issue. Where Dickens comments on her work in his letters to W. H. Wills he is almost invariably positive and, when her contributions fell off in 1853 as she focused her energies on her translation of Comte's *Philosophie Positive*, he wrote to entreat to her to return to his pages:

My Dear Miss Martineau.

I *must* write a few words in reply to your note; first, for the pleasure of corresponding with you, however briefly; and secondly to say how very starry and stripy our little Bleaburn experience appears to me to be.

I am anxious to see the result of your Comte labors. I require a good deal to counterbalance your total abstinence from Household Words for so long a time, and have a selfish disposition to be mightily critical.[9]

Dickens goes on to pique her interest in returning to his columns by drawing her attention to a forthcoming article on his collaboration with Angela Burdett Coutts at Urania Cottage. Two years later, another round of correspondence involving Miss Coutts provides even more tangible evidence for the quality of the relationship. In March 1855, Martineau twice wrote to Dickens, and he shared her letters with Miss Coutts. Although they were reprinted in 1982, these letters have not subsequently been collected and have largely fallen out of the narrative about Dickens and Martineau's relationship despite the extent to which they provide compelling evidence for its quality just months before the great public quarrel. While their subject matter deals with proposals to improve working-class living conditions and diets, they also offer vivid testimony for the warmth of the relationship as

---

[9] To Harriet Martineau, 19 April 1853, *The Letters of Charles Dickens*, ed. by Kathleen Tillotson, Graham Storey and others, Pilgrim Edition, 12 vols (Oxford: Clarendon Press, 1965-2002), Vol. VII, pp. 67-68 (p. 67, original emphasis).

Martineau responds to Dickens's expression of concern over the news of the diagnosis she had just weeks earlier received of terminal congestive heart disease. Writing on her own illustrated stationery, she thus opens (see **Fig. 1**):

> Dear Mr. Dickens
>
> I write on this paper that you may see where I sit in the sun, in these bright afternoons;—viz, in an easy chair before the porch;—which porch is all grown over now with mixed evergreens & roses & honeysuckle, & really quite green already. You may understand the ladies on the terrace to be my nieces,—one head nurse, & the other house-keeper and second nurse. Two are necessary, as I am never left alone for a minute—I am so sorry that the Willses could not come to my little paradise while I could receive them.[10]

Ostensibly then, and to judge by both the working collaboration at *Household Words* and the epistolary evidence for their personal relationship, there seems little that would have predicted the bitter quarrel that would break out only months later. How, then, are we to explain this subsequent turn of events?

The answer, I suggest, lies in the divergent expectations and ambitions Dickens and Martineau had for their work together and, in particular, in the discrepancy between the kind of editorial relationship Martineau most valued and that which Dickens put in place for his contributors. Combined with Martineau's mingled awareness of the stature she had built for herself as a public commentator and her continuing vulnerability as a woman author in a profession where power was vested almost exclusively with male editors and publishers, these differences gradually coalesced between 1852 and 1855 and culminated in her extraordinary outburst of hostility in *The Factory Controversy* and Dickens's punitive counter-strike in the columns of *Household Words*.

Slipping towards Discord

Throughout her career, Martineau placed great value upon the relationships she developed with a series of editors. Beginning with her first publications in the *Monthly Repository* during the 1820s and the mentoring support she received from W. J. Fox, she went on to develop important partnerships with influential male editors, each of whom opened up opportunities for her and guided her to make the most of them. The best documented of these

---

[10] New York, Pierpont Morgan Library, MA1352:124775.

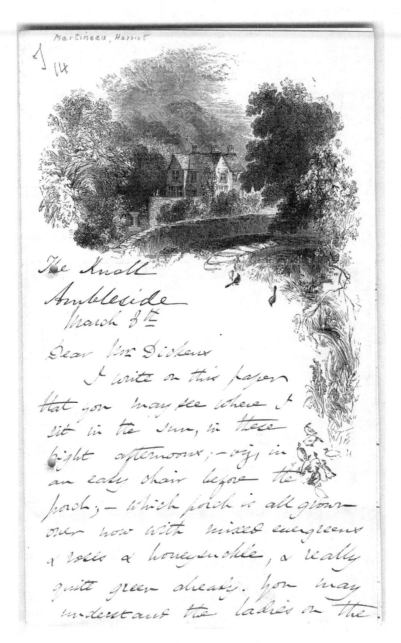

Fig. 1. Image © The Morgan Library and Museum, New York

ties and the one that had the most shaping influence on her career was that with Frederick Knight Hunt, who was also of course close to Dickens and who brought her on board as a leader writer for the *Daily News*, initiating a connection with the paper that would last a decade and a half and result in more than 1,600 pieces in its columns. A year into their work together, Martineau wrote to Hunt to pay tribute to all he had done for her:

> It is just a year now since you made me a 'gentleman of the press',— or Maid-of-all-work to D. News. I have enjoyed it very much,—the finding utterance for so much that was on my mind: &, through your kindness and courtesy, it has been very easy. I have only one anxiety,—the being so entirely alone, so far off,—that I can never be sure of being right, & doing what is best.—If at Whitsuntide, or any 'tide, you want a draught of fresh air, & relief from the din, you had better come here & refresh. It wd be a great gain to me & my work.[11]

In addition to the gratitude she expresses, however, we can also sense her anxiety and the continuing vulnerability she faced as she sought to become the first woman author to establish herself in such a major role in forming public opinion through the daily press.

However, while Martineau's connections with Dickens were certainly positive, they were also generally far less substantial than those she had with Fox or Hunt. Their surviving correspondence is limited and provides no indication of the kind of profound mentoring and personal support she drew from her other editors. And this difference can be largely accounted for by the very different conception of his editorial role that Dickens developed as he shaped *Household Words*. Indeed, to judge by comments he made to Emile de la Rue after giving up his position at the *Daily News*, Dickens appears to have developed his sense of this role several years before he founded the weekly magazine:

> I am again a gentleman. I have handed over the Editing of the Paper (very laborious work indeed) to Forster [...]. The Daily News is a great success—expenses at first, however, most enormous of course. It is very much respected by the good men of both parties who are exceedingly anxious that it should succeed, by reason of its forbearance and sense of responsibility. But I am not quite trustful in, or quite satisfied with, some of the people concerned in its

---

[11] *The Collected Letters of Harriet Martineau*, ed. by Deborah Logan, 5 vols (London: Pickering and Chatto, 2007), Vol. III, p. 276.

mechanical and business management, which is a very important part of such an undertaking. Therefore, I confine myself to writing, which is much more agreeable.[12]

Having learned from this previous experience, the business model he developed for his own journal thus vitally depended upon handing off the 'laborious work' to Wills, while both taking great pains to maintain his control over the final product and, like his own mentor, Francis Jeffrey at the *Edinburgh*, ensuring that his own writing was sufficiently present to set an overarching tone for the journal as a whole. In this model, most authors were treated simply as paid contributors and Martineau was no exception. Thus, after Dickens had initially recruited her in early 1850, he delegated the primary responsibilities for author relations to Wills and evidently limited his own involvement with her work to occasional copyediting, which he shared with his subeditor but which did not involve Martineau—indeed, as he proudly commented on one of her early contributions, 'I have cut Woodruffe as scientifically as I can, and I don't think Miss Martineau would exactly know where'.[13] Martineau liked Wills and she clearly enjoyed working with him, but, partly in consequence of this practical arrangement, she never developed the collaborative connection with Dickens that she had had with Fox and that she was, even as she wrote for *Household Words*, fostering with Hunt. Only when the larger relationship seemed in need of attention did she actually hear from Dickens himself—as in that letter of April 1853.

In the early 1850s, then, as Martineau was being shaped as a major journalist she was experiencing very different kinds of relationship with her respective editors and, also, very different kinds of relationship with the principal venues in which her work was appearing. Inevitably, given the profound differences in mission, format and audience among *Household Words*, the *Daily News* and the *Westminster Review*, she was called upon to write very different pieces, often on similar subjects. In particular, the kinds of writing she undertook for Dickens provided her with opportunities that were somewhat limited in scope and may well have become less of a match with her growing ambitions and abilities as a journalist. The majority of her contributions to *Household Words* fall into four major categories— descriptions of industrial processes; essays on domestic husbandry and diets;

---

[12] To Emile de la Rue, 16 February 1846, *Letters of Charles Dickens*, Vol. IV, pp. 497-99 (p. 498).

[13] To W. H. Wills, 21 August 1850, *Letters of Charles Dickens*, Vol. VI, pp. 153-54 (p. 153).

accounts of the disabled; and didactic fiction—and were types of writing that she had regularly produced previously. While these were all areas in which she certainly had an interest, the nature of a mass-market weekly magazine inevitably meant that the treatment called for was limited in depth and detail. Thus, for example, although she did write four pieces on Ireland for *Household Words* in 1852 and did touch upon the terrible consequences of the famine, these contributions have nothing like the range and weight of the twenty-seven 'Letters from Ireland' she wrote for Hunt and the *Daily News* that same year and quickly republished in volume form. By contrast, she waited a decade before collecting twenty-one of her *Household Words* essays and publishing them as *Health, Husbandry, and Handicraft* in 1861, which suggests an agenda driven far more by the opportunity to make good business use of her labour than by any sense of the pressing urgency of the work and the value of recirculating it.

Looking at the entire range of her journalism during the period between 1850 and 1854, then, it is clear that she was developing rapidly, growing in her confidence and ability to treat a wide range of major national issues. With Hunt's guidance, she was evolving into one of the most important leader writers for the *Daily News,* and, through another close editorial collaboration—that with John Chapman—she was becoming a semi-regular contributor to the *Westminster Review,* where she had an additional authority through her position as holder of the magazine's mortgage note. In embracing these new opportunities, however, she also found herself juggling their various demands and, as the record of her journalistic publishing in these years shows, she evidently made choices about where to concentrate her strength:

Year	*Household Words*	*Daily News*	*Westminster Review*
1850	3	0	0
1851	12	0	0
1852	23	67	1
1853	1	129	1
1854	7	183	3
1855	0	85	0

These figures suggest that, after a period of contributing successfully to *Household Words*, she quickly found that her work for the *Daily News*, leavened by the occasional piece for the *Westminster*, better suited her and gave her a more significant platform for shaping public discourse. It is perhaps no surprise, then, that intentionally or otherwise, she found herself moving away from writing for *Household Words*—and also that Dickens, presumably aware that he was in danger of losing one of his most important contributors, wrote as he did in April 1853 to try and win her back. It is also apparent that Hunt, rather than Dickens, was the winner here, since, until illness again affected her in 1855, the arc of her commitment continued to move towards increasing her presence in the *Daily News*.

Breaking Apart

The absence of a close editorial relationship, the fact that *Household Words* was, even with Dickens as its editor, only a mass-market weekly, increasing opportunities to write more substantive pieces for more prestigious venues and a deeply rewarding collaboration with Hunt—all these factors evidently combined to reduce Martineau's interest in contributing to Dickens's journal. In the ordinary course of events, she and Dickens might have quietly gone their separate ways, she expanding her work with other publications and he finding new contributors to replace her. But things, of course, did not end quietly and the way in which they fell apart shows what could happen when a woman author, increasingly confident of her powers and authority, yet also isolated by location, illness and social position, came into conflict with an editor whose temperament was as irascible as her own and with whom she did not have the kind of collaborative relationship that might have averted the cycle of mutually-assured destructiveness into which they became entrapped towards the end of 1855.

Two specific events were evidently responsible for precipitating the outbreak of hostilities and, in both instances, Dickens's absentee management style and organisational reliance upon his sub-editor played an important role in the sequence of events. First, in the autumn of 1854 and following a season in which she had not appeared in the special Christmas issue, Dickens and Wills invited Martineau to contribute once again. Unfortunately, Wills then communicated their rejection of the story she offered, 'Father D'Estelan's Christmas Morning', a narrative about the heroic self-sacrifice of a Jesuit priest sent on a papal mission to China. For Martineau, this unprecedented rebuff could hardly have come at a worse time: Frederick Knight Hunt's unexpected death on 18 November had left her grief-stricken and she herself was experiencing the symptoms that would lead to the diagnosis of terminal illness that she received early in 1855. Second, despite the rejection of her story, Martineau remained on good terms with Wills and, in September 1855, he and his wife paid a long-anticipated visit to Ambleside. During their stay, the issue of factory safety evidently came up and Wills drew Martineau's attention to Morley's *Household Words* essays. Martineau, who appears not to have been following the series, subsequently wrote to Chapman, asking him to send them to her, and he duly forwarded one of the volumes in which the essays had appeared.[14] When she read them, she was so angered that she began to plan the response that would eventually appear as *The Factory Controversy*. Poor Wills, then, had, without realising the consequences, had a hand in both the issues upon which Martineau's wrath would focus.

As we have already seen, Dickens was, as a matter of course, less engaged with author relations than Martineau preferred in her editors. During the period leading up to their quarrel, this tendency was reinforced by his own emerging emotional crisis and his habitual response to it—to move. Thus, in both 1854 and 1855, he shifted his entire family out of England for extended periods: much of the time between June and October 1854 was spent in Boulogne, while 1855 saw him go with the family, first, to Folkestone from July through October and then on to Paris, where they would stay until the end of April 1856. During these extended absences he became increasingly dependent upon Wills and then Morley to sustain the operations of *Household Words*. Thus, in the summer of 1855, he left London in early July, first on holiday and then to set up home in Paris in October. As his attention shifted to planning and then writing the early stages of *Little Dorrit* (1855-57), he delegated the day-to-day running of *Household Words* to Wills and only exercised overall control of the magazine through letters back to England. As a result, he almost certainly had no idea of what was in the offing with Martineau—in all the abundant surviving correspondence with Wills from these months there is no indication that he was at all aware of the emerging crisis.

For both Wills and Chapman, however, there was no such relief through ignorance, as their correspondence with Martineau between September and

---

[14] John Chapman to Harriet Martineau, 9 October 1855. Cadbury Research Library: Special Collections, University of Birmingham, H191. This, and subsequent quotations from the Harriet Martineau papers, are by kind permission of the Director of Special Collections.

November 1855 clearly shows. On returning to London from his visit to the Lake District, Wills may well have been surprised to receive Martineau's letter of 26 September responding to the invitation he evidently made while in Ambleside for her to contribute again to *Household Words*. Her reply, from which she extracts in the *Autobiography*, focuses upon the magazine's publication of Wilkie Collins's 'The Yellow Mask' (*Household Words*, 7-28 July 1855), a story that, on the basis of a description in a Philadelphia newspaper, she lambastes as anti-Catholic.[15] Not unreasonably, Wills, having chattily described returning alone to a London still largely quiet for the long vacation and having conveyed his thanks to Maria Martineau for some seeds she had sent him, asks in response whether Martineau has read the story herself and points out that she in fact does it considerable injustice. Unfortunately, he also rubs salt in the wound of what was clearly a related issue for Martineau as he goes on to refer to the rejection of 'Father D'Estelan' and reiterates that he felt 'perfectly justified in rejecting your Jesuit paper upon every principle, not only of duty, but of justice and common sense'.[16]

There is no evidence of any further correspondence between Martineau and Wills until 30 November, but, in the meantime, she was vigorously writing to John Chapman. Having composed her response to Morley's essays, she attempted to place it with the *Westminster Review*, only to find Chapman implacably resistant. During an extended exchange that includes half-a-dozen letters from him between 9 October and 16 November, Chapman refuses to budge from his fundamental point of objection, as expressed in his letter of 6 November:

> I shrink from printing your article as it stands. I should not like to publish the personal attacks on Dickens and Horner. An exposition of the law, of the difficulty of its application, and of its evil effects is valuable and telling and it seems to me that such an exposition would gain in force by being freed from all personal animadversion.[17]

---

[15] [Wilkie Collins], 'The Yellow Mask [i]', *Household Words*, Vol. XI, No. 276 (7 July 1855), 529-39; 'The Yellow Mask [ii]', *Household Words*, Vol. XI, No. 277 (14 July 1855), 565-73; 'The Yellow Mask [iii]', *Household Words*, Vol. XI, No. 278 (21 July 1855), 587-98; 'The Yellow Mask [iv]', *Household Words*, Vol. XI, No. 279 (28 July 1855), 609-19.

[16] W. H. Wills to Harriet Martineau, 28 September 1855, Birmingham, HM1026.

[17] Birmingham, HM193.

Refusing to contribute again for Dickens and refused here by Chapman, with the added gall of such resistance coming from a man who was her mortgagee, Martineau found the masculine world of mid-Victorian London editing set against her and had to turn to a much less significant venue for her essay. For only the second time in her career, she published exclusively outside London, finding an outlet in Manchester under the imprint of The National Association of Factory Occupiers, an organisation whose umbrella can only have been seen as partisan and one that aligned poorly with her hard-won status as an authoritative journalistic voice whose writing was ordinarily in such high demand in the best national venues.

Even now, despite the intensity of the feeling expressed in the pamphlet and her accumulated frustration with both *Household Words* and the *Westminster Review*, Martineau had neither broken with Wills nor yet given up entirely on Dickens. For she wrote to Wills on 30 November, opening her letter with 'My dear friend', to let him know in advance of the pamphlet's publication and indicating that she continued to hold Dickens the novelist in high regard. It was, as it had been since the very early years of their relationship, with Dickens the social commentator and editor that she differed, as she reiterated the point, and indeed the language, of the pamphlet in expressing her hope that,

> the loss of influence wh [Dickens] has incurred on all occasions of meddling with social subjects wh he does not understand will in time induce him to apply his fine genius to works in wh he can do nothing but good, and where he has a whole share of Art to himself.[18]

Still in Paris, finishing up the fourth number of *Little Dorrit* (March 1856), Dickens appears to have known nothing of the conflicts brewing back in England and he makes no mention of Martineau's essay until 3 January 1856, when his often-cited comment on her 'vomit of conceit' occurs.[19] But, revealingly, even at this point he also notes that he has not read the essay itself or even seen Morley's draft response, and he expresses a preference to do neither and indeed would 'rather (if only for the mortification it would cause her) not notice it at all'.[20] Matters subsequently evolved very rapidly, however, and just three days later he had read Morley's article, 'gone very

---

[18] *Collected Letters of Harriet Martineau*, Vol. III, pp. 376-77.
[19] To W. H. Wills, 3 and 4 January 1856, *Letters of Charles Dickens*, Vol. VIII, pp. 6-7 (p. 6).
[20] *Letters of Charles Dickens*, Vol. VIII, p. 6.

closely over that part of it which refers to Miss Martineau', and thought that 'it should be printed, and go into the opening of the next No. as I have arranged it in the enclosed proof'. He then moves to his last, often-quoted, comment on the matter:

> Miss Martineau, in this, is precisely what I always knew her to be, and have always impressed her upon you as being. I was so convinced that it was impossible that she *could* be anything else, having seen and heard her, that I am not in the least triumphant at her justifying my opinion. I do not suppose that there never was such a wrong-headed woman born—such a vain one—or such a Humbug.[21]

But, while this passage has often been quoted, it is hardly consistent with any of his earlier comments on Martineau and hardly consistent with all the positive evidence we have about their relationship. As such, it, and indeed the entire letter, seems less the considered judgement they have often been taken to be than the vituperative private venting of an irascible editor and author notoriously thin-skinned about any criticism and who, as Lillian Nayder has shown, was viscerally resistant to any show of female opposition.[22] Its very irascibility, however, also suggests that Martineau had good reason for being so concerned about the vulnerability of her standing as a professional author.

Unfortunately, and for their relationship fatally, the intemperance on both sides was amply evident in their public utterances. For Martineau's pamphlet was, as Chapman had feared, remarkable for the personal hostility of its attack on Dickens. Arguing that Dickens had assumed a new kind of responsibility 'when he set up "Household Words" as an avowed agency of popular instruction and social reform', she rebukes him for sentimental intrusion into serious topics and suggests that 'he should not meddle with affairs in which rationality of judgment is required'.[23] Although in this assessment Martineau was consistent with her long-held private views of

---

[21] To W. H. Wills, 6 January 1856, *Letters of Charles Dickens*, Vol. VIII, pp. 9-10 (p. 9, original emphasis).

[22] Lillian Nayder, *The Other Dickens: A Life of Catherine Hogarth* (Ithaca, NY and London: Cornell University Press, 2011).

[23] *The Factory Controversy*, pp. 36, 44.

Dickens, such a public statement was bound to sting and Dickens went to great lengths with his response. He clearly meant what he wrote to Wills about carefully arranging the proof of the 19 January issue of the magazine, for, even though he does not lead off the number with his response as he had initially suggested, he does preface 'Our Wicked Mis-Statements' by preceding it with Adelaide Anne Procter's poem, 'Murmurs':

Why wilt thou make bright music
Give forth a sound of pain?
Why wilt thou weave fair flowers
Into a weary chain?[24]

Positioning Procter as a woman writer who complied with his expectations of the lady author, he thus uses the questions with which her poem opens to interrogate, and by implication undermine, Martineau's more wayward authorial voice. Then, despite beginning his own article by expressing reluctance to expose 'weakness in a sick lady whom we esteem' he goes on to build the long and sustained assault upon her over the course of seven pages that ends with his desire to 'blot' her 'out of remembrance'.[25]

Number 304 of *Household Words* thus culminates a long and complicated engagement between Dickens and Martineau that has itself largely fallen out of remembrance. Re-examining their dispute, however, allows us to recognise that the longstanding focus upon their disagreement over the height of safety fences around industrial machinery and Martineau's allegations about the editorial biases of *Household Words* has obscured other, more significant questions. Underlying these questions of substance, that is, we can see the dispute as indicating a much larger and deeper struggle for control of Victorian public discourse. In particular, it illustrates one way in which the closed masculine world of Victorian publishing responded to the challenge posed by the emergence of professional women writers, confident in their abilities and determined to be heard. Driven by an utterly characteristic combination of inner emotional demons, unassailable conviction in the rightness of his own beliefs, and sharp business acumen, Dickens went after his opponent unsparingly, savaging her in ways that put

---

[24] [Adelaide Anne Procter], 'Murmurs', *Household Words*, Vol. XIII, No. 304 (19 January 1856), p. 13.
[25] [Dickens and Morley], 'Our Wicked Mis-Statements', pp. 13, 19.

aside years of friendship and collaboration in an effort to restore his own authority. If he thought Martineau had been silenced, however, he was destined to be disappointed, for she would exact a long and complicated revenge upon him—but that must be a story for another day.

The *Household Words* Journalist as Ethnographer: G. A. Sala's 'Phases of "Public" Life'

Catherine Waters

WITH his scenes of 'every-day life and every-day people', begun as a series of sketches in magazines appearing from 1833, Boz established Dickens's fascination with London street life. Openly avowing his partiality for 'amateur vagrancy', Boz travels through the city observing and describing its inhabitants, grouping and cataloguing them so as to produce a veritable ethnography of urban types and relishing the striking contrasts he discovers in the urban scene. In 'Gin Shops', for example, he moves from the slum dwellings near Drury Lane—with their '[w]retched houses with broken windows patched with rags and paper: every room let out to a different family, and in many instances to two or even three'—to the adjacent gin palace where

> All is light and brilliancy. The hum of many voices issues from that splendid gin shop which forms the commencement of the two streets opposite; and the gay building with the fantastically ornamented parapet, the illuminated clock, the plate-glass windows surrounded by stucco rosettes, and its profusion of gaslights in richly gilt burners, is perfectly dazzling when contrasted with the darkness and dirt we have just left.[1]

The 'amateur vagrancy' practised by Boz continued to influence later urban sketch writers and can be seen in the metropolitan travel writing published by Dickens in *Household Words*. While the journal published city sketches by a range of contributors—John Hannay, William Blanchard Jerrold, John

---

[1] Charles Dickens, 'Gin Shops', in *The Dent Uniform Edition of Dickens' Journalism*, ed. by Michael Slater and others, 4 vols (London: J. M. Dent, 1994-2000), Vol. I, 180-85 (p. 183).

Hollingshead, as well as Dickens himself—it is arguably George Augustus Sala who is *Household Words'* pre-eminent urban spectator. His series on 'Phases of "Public" Life' attests to his skills in cataloguing metropolitan types.

Boz's visit to a London 'Gin Shop' was undertaken with an explicitly social reformist aim, alerting his middle-class readers to social miseries lying beyond their ken. The 'inordinate love of plate glass, and a passion for gaslights and gilding' are described as a new mania, and the dazzling splendour of the gin shop evokes Benjamin's methodological concept of the 'dream house', projecting an alluring collective fantasy.[2] From the description of this glittering interior, Boz proceeds to sketch the wretched customers— the two old washerwomen seated to the left of the bar, the 'two old men who came in "just to have a drain"' and who are now 'crying drunk' and the 'knot of Irish labourers at the lower end of the place'—in order to argue that

> until you improve the homes of the poor, or persuade a half-famished wretch not to seek relief in the temporary oblivion of his own misery, with the pittance which, divided among his family, would furnish a morsel of bread for each, gin-shops will increase in number and splendour.[3]

Gareth Cordery has shown how this sketch is bound up with Victorian anxieties about the relationship between public and private life in the construction of modern subjectivity, manifesting 'the crude beginning of a structure central to making money, maintaining control and at the heart of a panoptical public house in an age of capitalism'.[4] But when Sala came to revisit the subject of the public house in a series of essays for *Household Words* on the 'Phases of "Public" Life' some seventeen years later, he was concerned not with the spatial instabilities unsettling the ideology of separate spheres, but rather with surveying the pub as an urban 'type'. Attempting 'a mild classification of the peculiar social characteristics of the different

---

[2] See Walter Benjamin, *The Arcades Project*, trans. by Howard Eiland and Kevin McLaughlin (Cambridge, MA and London: Harvard University Press, 1999), pp. 388-415.

[3] *Dickens' Journalism*, Vol. I, pp. 183-84.

[4] Gareth Cordery, 'Public Houses: Spatial Instabilities in *Sketches by Boz* and *Oliver Twist* (Part 1)', *Dickens Quarterly*, 20:1 (2003), 3-13 (p. 10).

metropolitan "publics"',[5] Sala provides an ethnography of 'London on Tap' that inverts subject-object relations—a narrative strategy that is in keeping with *Household Words'* imaginative engagement with a developing commodity culture.[6] The series appeared in three instalments, the first two published in May and the third in October 1852, and was followed by a number of separate articles on further drinking establishments in 1853.

Our first stop with Sala on his exploration of the 'Phases of "Public" Life' is a gin palace, notable for its promiscuously diverse architectural styles—'We have Doric shafts with Corinthian capitals—an Ionic frieze— Renaissance panels—a Gothic screen to the bar-parlour' ('Chapter the First', p. 226)—and its

> sundry little placards, framed and glazed, and printed in colours telling in seductive language of 'Choice Compounds,' 'Old Tom,' 'Cream of the Valley,' 'Superior Cream Gin,' 'The Right Sort,' 'Kinahan's L.L.,' 'The Dew Off Ben Nevis' [and] the 'Celebrated Balmoral Mixture, patronised by his Royal Highness Prince Albert' ('Chapter the First', p. 227).

Ironically, however, and in contrast to the variety of compounds dispensed, what most distinguishes the gin palace is the stereotyping and homogeneity evident in its customers:

> Like plates multiplied by the electro-process—like the printer's 'stereo'—like the reporter's 'manifold'—you will find duplicates, triplicates of these forlorn beings everywhere. The same woman giving her baby gin; the same haggard, dishevelled woman, trying to coax her drunken husband home; the same mild girl, too timid even to importune her ruffian partner to leave off drinking the week's earnings, who sits meekly in a corner, with two discoloured eyes, one freshly blacked—one of a week's standing. The same weary little man, who comes in early, crouches in a corner, and takes standing naps during the day, waking up periodically for 'fresh drops' ('Chapter the First', p. 227).

---

[5] [George A. Sala], 'Phases of "Public" Life: Chapter the First', *Household Words*, Vol. V, No. 13 (22 May 1852), 224-30 (p. 225). Subsequent page references are to this edition and appear in the text.

[6] I have discussed this aspect of the journal in Catherine Waters, *Commodity Culture in Dickens's 'Household Words': The Social Life of Goods* (Aldershot: Ashgate, 2008).

Rendered indistinguishable by their forlorn subjection to gin, these customers resemble the 'drainings, overflowings, and outspillings of the gin-glasses' that are allowed to drop through the perforated pewter counter to be 'collected with sundry washings, and a dash, perhaps of fresh material, [which] is, by the thrifty landlord, dispensed to his customers under the title of "all sorts"' ('Chapter the First', p. 227).

Sala's next stop, the Green Hog, belongs to 'a class of publics, becoming rapidly extinct in London': 'one of the old, orthodox, top-booted, sanded-floored taverns' ('Chapter the First', p. 228). Taverns enjoyed their heyday in the seventeenth century, facing competition after the Restoration in 1660 from the increasingly fashionable coffee houses. Symptomatic of the old-fashioned tavern they frequent, the customers of the Green Hog are of the '"old school,"—men who yet adhere to the traditional crown bowl of punch, and the historical "rump and dozen", who take their bottle of wine after dinner, and insist upon triangular spittoons' ('Chapter the First', p. 228). Men like Mr Tuckard:

> [A] round old gentleman, supposed to be employed in some capacity at the Tower of London, but whether as a warder, an artillery-man, or a gentleman jailer—deponent sayeth not. He appears regularly at nine o'clock every morning, eats a huge meat-and-beer breakfast, orders his dinner, re-appears at six o'clock precisely, eats a hearty dinner, drinks a bottle of port, and smokes nine pipes of tobacco, washed down by nine tumblers of gin-and-water [...]. He rarely speaks but to intimate friends (with whom he has had a nodding acquaintance for twenty years perhaps) [...]. He occasionally condescends to impart, in a fat whisper, his opinions about the funds and the weather ('Chapter the First', p. 228).

As a representative specimen of the 'comfortable and old-fashioned customers' who patronise the Green Hog, Mr Tuckard is a metropolitan type who is at the same time given the features of an individual. His sketch is both generalised and particularised as part of the ethnographic account of a participant observer, whose claim to expertise is that he has 'graduated in Beer' ('Chapter the First', p. 225).

A similar combination of abstraction and individuation is found in the account of the theatrical public house located 'over the way' from the Theatre Royal, Barbican. This 'house of call for Thespians' is patronised by the actors of the Theatre Royal, 'their friends and acquaintances, being actors at other theatres', as well as 'comedians, dancers and pantomimists' ('Chapter the First', p. 229). Having defined the class of customers, Sala proceeds to identify some of the individuals who compose it:

> At the door, you have Mr Snartell, the low comedian from Devonport, and Mr Rollocks, the heavy father from the Bath Circuit, who affects, in private life, a low-crowned hat with a prodigious brim (has a rich though somewhat husky bass voice), and calls everybody 'My son.' These, and many more dark-haired, close-shaven, and slightly mouldily-habited inheritors of the mantles of Kean, Dowton, or Blanchard, wait the live-long day for the long-wished-for engagements. [...] Then there is a little prematurely aged man, Doctor Snaffles, indeed, as he is called, who did the 'old man' line of business, but who does very little to speak of now, except drink ('Chapter the First', pp. 229-230).

The tension between group classification and analysis of individual types in the theatrical pub is compounded by the mixing of roles in public and private life and the sorting of performers into the sub-genres of their profession: low comedy, heavy father, old man and so on. Sala's sketch is an engaged reading of its customers that offers sociological insight into the struggles of those on the fringes of mid-century metropolitan life. Whatever the individual differences observable in the 'various classes of theatrical publics', writes Sala, 'there is common to them all a floating population of old play-goers, superannuated pantomimists, decayed prompters, actors out of engagement, and order-hunters and actor-haunters' ('Chapter the First', p. 230).

Amongst the many varieties of painters who frequent the 'artistic public house'—'grey-headed professors of the old school', 'spruce young fellows who have studied in Paris', 'moody disciples of that numerous class of artists known as the "great unappreciated"'—Sala picks out one who 'very rarely condescends to visit' such a venue:

> [T]hat transcendent genius Mr Cimabue Giotto Smalt, one of the P.P.P.B. or 'Pre-painting and Perspective Brotherhood.' Mr Smalt, in early life, made designs for the Ladies' Gazette of Fashion, and was suspected also of contributing the vigorous and highly-coloured illustrations to the Hatchet of Horrors—that excellent work published in penny numbers by Skull, of Horrorwell Street. Subsequently awakening, however, to a sense of the hollowness of the world, and the superiority of the early Italian school over all others, he laid in a large stock of cobalt, blue, gold leaf, small

wooden German dolls, and glass eyes, and commenced that course of study which has brought him to the proud position he now holds as a devotional painter of the most aesthetic acerbity and the most orthodox angularity.[7]

This looks at first glance like overdrawn satire at the expense of the Pre-Raphaelite Brotherhood. But the figure of Mr Cimabue Giotto Smalt is actually an ironic self-portrait of sorts—at least to the extent that Sala himself had served the same apprenticeship that is comically described here in his early life. He had accepted a commission to design some of the 'patterns' and fashion-plates that featured in the *Lady's Newspaper*, a journal launched in 1849 by the engraver Ebenezer Landells, and he subsequently worked for the best part of a year as a draughtsman illustrating Edward Lloyd's gory penny dreadfuls. According to his biographer, Ralph Straus, 'although it is impossible to identify his work it is known that he was responsible for the cuts in *The Heads of the Headless* [...] and for those in another "horror" with the appropriate title of *Murder Castle*'.[8] Thus despite the satiric Pre-Raphaelite cliché with which Mr Cimabue Smalt is lampooned—'He paints shavings beautifully, sore toes faultlessly' and 'dresses in a sort of clerico-German style'—Sala ironically infuses him with individual particulars drawn from his own life.

Equally ironic is his description of the artists' models, whose identity is paradoxically established through the versatility of their posing:

> Another pattern is refreshing himself with mild porter at the bar, being no other, indeed, than the well-known Caravaggio Potts, Artiste-modèle, as he styles himself. He began life as Jupiter Tonans, subsequently passed through the Twelve Apostles, and is now considered to be the best Belisarius in the model world. His wife was the original Venus Callipyge, of Tonks, R.A., but fluctuates at present between Volumnia and Mrs Primrose ('Chapter the Second', p. 251).

The description recalls Dickens's ironic tale (in the first volume of *Household Words*) of the bachelor whose perception of the same artist's model being

[7] [George A. Sala], 'Phases of "Public" Life: Chapter the Second', *Household Words*, Vol. V, No. 14 (29 May 1852), 250-55 (p. 250). Subsequent page references are to this edition and appear in the text.

[8] Ralph Straus, *Sala: The Portrait of an Eminent Victorian* (London: Constable, 1942), p. 57.

used for the various portraits hung in the Royal Academy is experienced as a haunting by 'The Ghost of Art'.[9] The versatile function of the artist's model as a 'pattern' or 'text-book' for comically incongruous portrait subjects captures the tension between abstraction and particularity that distinguishes the metropolitan sketch tradition. Like the mixture of public and private identities performed by the patrons of the theatrical public house, the artists' public house blends group classification with the detailed delineation of individual types.

Richard Sennett attributes the rise of urban sketches to the problem of coping with an environment of strangers in the wake of the great migrations to the cities that marked the nineteenth century.[10] Brought on not only by the agricultural crises throughout the century associated with new commercial and technological conditions, but also the revolutionary outbreaks that troubled Europe after Napoleon, these migrations gave London a cosmopolitanism reflected in its designation as a 'world' rather than a city.[11] Sala captures this cosmopolitan aspect as he moves on to sketch 'one of the foreign hostelries of London—the refugees' house of call':

> Herr Brutus Eselskopf, the landlord, is a refugee himself, a patriot without a blot on his political scutcheon. He has been a general of brigade in his time; but he has donned the Boniface apron, and affiliated himself to the Boniface guild, and dispenses his liquors with as much unconcern as if he had never worn epaulettes and a cocked hat, and had never seen real troops with real bands and banners defile before him ('Chapter the Second', p. 253).

His pub is located 'in the centre of that maze of crooked, refugee-haunted little streets between Saint Martin's Lane and Saint Anne's Church, Soho'. 'No marked difference can at first be discerned, as regards fittings and appurtenances, between the refugees' and any other public house', says Sala. But 'five minutes' observation of the customers' will reveal that the 'little

---

[9] [Charles Dickens], 'The Ghost of Art', *Household Words*, Vol. I, No. 17 (20 July 1850), 385-88 (pp. 385-87).

[10] Richard Sennett, 'Foreword', in *A Human Comedy: Physiognomy and Caricature in Nineteenth-Century Paris*, ed. by Judith Wechsler (London: Thames and Hudson, 1982), pp. 7-8.

[11] Tanya Agathocleous examines the literary techniques used to transform the city into an image of the world in Tanya Agathocleous, *Urban Realism and the Cosmopolitan Imagination in the Nineteenth Century: Visible City, Invisible World* (Cambridge: Cambridge University Press, 2011).

back parlour is filled, morning, noon and night, with foreigners under
political clouds of various degrees of density, and in a cloud of uniform
thickness and of strong tobacco, emitted in many-shaped fumes from pipes
of eccentric design'. Sala's sketch of the customers at Herr Eselkopf's reveals
his own cosmopolitan sympathies, as he considers how many of them

> have lost everything in the maintenance of what they conscientiously
> believed to be the right against might, live quietly, honestly,
> inoffensively, doing no harm, existing on infinitesimal means,
> working hard for miserable remuneration, willing to do anything for
> a crust, teaching languages for sixpence a lesson, painting portraits
> for a shilling apiece, taking out lessons on the flute or pianoforte in
> bread and meat! ('Chapter the Second', p. 254).

The limits of his cosmopolitan sympathies are, however, evident in the
stereotyping shown in the third and final chapter of 'Phases of "Public"
Life', where the 'chief object' of the customers who frequent the 'Judaical
public-house' of a Sunday morning 'is the buying or selling of [...]
merchandise'.[12] These patrons are described alongside sketches of a 'fighting'
public house (the 'Bottleholder and Sponge')—distinguished by the signs of
damage inflicted during former bouts of fisticuffs—and a servants' public
house (the 'Cocked Hat and Smalls') characterised by the petty squabbles of
flunkeyism.

This third chapter ended the series, but Sala returned to the task of
surveying the phases of public life five months later in 'My Swan', a sketch
that Dickens considered to be 'so excellent' that he advised W. H. Wills, his
subeditor, to publish it as the leader for the issue of 26 March 1853. It
describes a fishing public-house 'on the little fishing river Spree', whose
landlord, Groundbait, we're told, is 'the *arbiter piscatorium*, the oracle, the
expert juré of angling': Sala's ostentatious flourish of cod Latin and French
sets the mock heroic tone for the description.[13] The parlour of the Swan is
replete with 'badges and trophies of the piscatorial craft':

> Rods of all shapes and sizes, eel spears, winches, landing nets,
> Penelopean webs of fishing tackle, glistering armouries of hooks,
> harpoons, panniers, bait-cans; and in a glass case a most wonderful

[12] [George A. Sala], 'Phases of "Public" Life: Chapter the Third', *Household Words*,
Vol. VI, No. 134 (16 October 1852), 101-05 (pp. 102-03).
[13] [George A. Sala], 'My Swan', *Household Words*, Vol. VII, No. 157 (26 March 1853),
73-76 (p. 73). Subsequent page references are to this edition and appear in the text.

piscatorio-entomological collection of flies—flies of gorgeously tinted floss silk, pheasants' feathers, and gold and silver thread—flies warranted to deceive the acutest of fish. ('My Swan', p. 74)

Such lavish inventorying of the contents of the parlour is typical of *Household Words*' handling of advertising and commodity culture. Sala clearly enjoys expatiating upon the peculiar displays of the fishing pub: seemingly esoteric exhibits that serve simultaneously to portray the type and yet at the same time to mark its particularised individuality. Thus 'My Swan' can boast the possession of some unique honours:

Over the fire-place is the identical rod and line with which J. Barbell, Esq. hooked the monstrous and European-famed jack in the river Dodder, near Dublin, and in the year of grace eighteen hundred and thirty-nine; in one corner are the shovel and bucket with and in which at the same place and time the said jack [...] was ultimately landed. Conspicuous between the windows is the portrait of J. Barbell, Esq., a hairy-faced man, severely scourging a river with a rod like a May-pole; beneath that, the famous jack himself *in propria persona*, in a glass case, stuffed, very brown and horny with varnish, with great staring glass eyes (one cracked), and a mouth wide open grinning hideously ('My Swan', p. 74).

The mock-heroic effect of Sala's account of these 'trophies' comes from his emphasis upon their authenticity, their identity as originals, and his assumption of their universal renown while at the same time suggesting their localism. They are described in a comic crescendo that culminates in no mere representation, but the prize catch itself: '*in propria persona*'. The stuffed fish, preserving a life-like form but 'swimming vigorously through nothing at all', and having an unnaturally 'neat fore-ground of moss and Brighton-beach shells and a backing of pea-green sky', shares its unrealistic aspect with the portrait of its captor, J. Barbell, and his improbably large fishing-rod. Such exhibits establish the distinctiveness of this public house, alongside the 'varied and eccentric' members of the angling company who frequent it, the whole scene laying itself open to the ethnographic gaze of a spectator like Sala, who is not so much detached, as comfortably at home in this setting:

If you come to the Swan merely as an observer of the world, how it is a wagging, as I do, you may take your half-pint of neat port with Groundbait, or shrouding yourself behind the cloudy mantle of a pipe, study character among the frequenters of the Swan ('My Swan', p. 75).

What do these accounts of mid-Victorian public houses tell us then about metropolitan sketch writing in *Household Words*? 'Comparison in urban history is best conducted at the level of particular institutions within the town, rather than between towns as a whole', argues Brian Harrison, and the 'pub and the temperance society, which can be found in most Victorian towns, demand such an approach'.[14] Sala's survey of the 'Phases of "Public" Life' adopts such a comparative approach to give a lively ethnographic survey of contemporary London life. The public house is an evolving institution whose various manifestations, as sketched by Sala, provide an interesting mixture of urban types. Unlike Benjamin's painter of modern life who remains unconscious of his similarity to the commodities upon which he casts his *flâneurial* gaze, Sala's ethnographic portraits are distinguished by a self-conscious awareness of the tension between the classification of a type and the delineation of individual features. Their mode is comic or ironic, and they manifest a narrative blend of journalistic and literary technique that, as I have argued elsewhere, is distinctive of *Household Words* in its imaginative handling of non-fictional prose.[15]

---

[14] Brian Harrison, 'Pubs', in *The Victorian City: Images and Realities*, ed. by H. J. Dyos and Michael Wolff (London: Routledge and Kegan Paul, 1973), p. 161.
[15] See Waters, *Commodity Culture in Dickens's 'Household Words'*.

Morley was alive: to begin with. The Curious Case of Dickens and his Principal Household Wordsmith

Daragh Downes

Dickens' journal does not seem my element.[1]

IN 1833, at the age of ten-and-three-quarters, London boy Henry Morley was sent by his father to a progressive Moravian brothers' school in the German town of Neuwied on the Rhine. His two years there would be happy ones. One episode in particular stayed with him:

> I remember once having written a tale in my copy-book instead of the Latin exercise for which it was intended—I was rattle-brained enough for anything. It was before I had acquired the language of the place, and so the tale was writ in English. Being detected in the contumacious act, I was prepared to suffer accordingly—but quite the contrary. The master understood English, and read my tale instead of the exercise. So soon as the school hours were over, he called the boys to silence, and sat him down and translated it to them—with improvements, I have no doubt, of his own, or I should not have got quite so much credit by the matter. The by no means critical boys thought it something tremendously first-rate.[2]

Exercise versus tale, task work versus creative writing, left-brain duty versus right-brain play: already in this rather touching incident we see dramatised a tension that will remain live well into Morley's thirties. The schoolmaster's generous-spirited response to Henry's 'contumacious act' of furtive

---

[1] Henry Morley, Letter to fiancée Mary Anne Sayer, 1851 in Shaen Solly, *The Life of Henry Morley, LL.D* (London: Edward Arnold, 1898), p. 150.
[2] Solly, p. 27.

fabulation gave the sensitive young lad his first taste of official encouragement on that head. It was not however his first taste of peer applause. During an earlier stint at a school in Chichester he had attained a Copperfield-like status in the eyes of his fellow boarders, whose coaxing at bedtime gave him license to tap an already fertile fairy-tale imagination. 'There was no squeamish taste to please in myself or my hearers', he would recall years afterwards, 'and I was glad to weave, as they to hear, my stock of knights, dragons, castles, forests, fairies, and so forth, into combinations perpetually new'.[3]

The happy reception of Morley's stories at Chichester and Neuwied helped salve a wound that had been inflicted at his first boarding school at Stony Stratford. He had been sent to this ghastly institution at the tender age of six or seven:

> I had […] longed to be allowed to contribute [to the storytelling at bedtime]. Only once they suffered me, and I distinctly remember how, elated with the honour, I began—scorning even then to draw upon the story-books—with, 'Once upon a time there was a parrot', and I was going on to say, 'in a great wood', when a shout of derision stopped my mouth for aye.[4]

The derision was all the more hurtful as Morley had come to Stony Stratford full of insecurity about the strangeness of his own psyche. He was, as he would later put it, 'a perfect visionary', prone to uncanny experiences that his adult self would try to write off in sound Victorian-rationalist fashion as mere visual and auditory hallucinations.[5] In fact the worry never left him that such experiences—which persisted well into adulthood—were related to a hereditary 'trace of insanity'. His biographer and son-in-law Henry Shaen Solly spots the crucial connection here: 'The vividness of his childish illusions, and the vigorous creativeness of his imagination in afterdays, indicate at once a real danger and a source of literary power'.[6] Allied to this visionary quality was what Morley himself would recall as:

> [A] remarkable power of half-abstraction. On one occasion I remember that I walked to school in this unconscious state, without

---

[3] Solly, p. 21.

[4] Solly, p. 21.

[5] Solly, pp. 12-13. See also Morley's 'New Discoveries in Ghosts', *Household Words*, Vol. IV, No. 95 (17 January 1852), 395-97.

[6] Solly, p. 37.

missing my way, and went through a great part of the morning's routine, until in the middle of a class—perhaps spurred by some question—I woke up as out of sleep, and was completely unable to remember anything either of having left home, or of what I had done since I arrived at school, although I must have read books, have answered questions, and possibly said lessons through. In such a case, if no one observed my look of momentary amazement on recovering myself, I never told how I had been wool-gathering. I never got any consolation for such intelligence on the few occasions when I did volunteer it, and so I kept my dreamland to myself.[7]

Not surprisingly, Morley became an avid reader of fairy tales at a very early age. They, and they alone, seemed to offer refuge from his 'dreamland' isolation and reassurance that his experiences in that private virtual reality were not wholly without precedent or value.

From popular derision at Stony Stratford to popular demand at Chichester to official approbation at Neuwied: we do well to ponder the early schoolboy progress of Henry Morley, *conteur*, as we prepare to ponder the later career of Henry Morley, *conteur*, at Charles Dickens's *Household Words*. For—put simply—there was no such career to speak of. Dickens's response to Morley's fantastical offerings grimly inverted that of the Moravian schoolmaster: he closed Morley down with unceremonious speed.

When Morley first came onto Dickens's radar in 1850 it was not as someone with long-cherished literary ambitions but as a qualified medical doctor whose witty pieces on public health had been noticed by John Forster at *The Examiner*. This seems to have led Dickens to construe Morley too narrowly as a dependable facts-and-issues man. In thus pigeonholing Morley, Dickens was merely picking up where Morley's surgeon father had left off a couple of years earlier. Morley's adolescence and the first phase of his adult life had been dominated by a paternally-imposed medical vocation that was ultimately to prove uncongenial. After a disastrous partnership in a practice at Madeley, Shropshire, Morley had courageously reinvented himself as an independent schoolmaster, first in Manchester and then (thanks to a timely intervention by Elizabeth Gaskell's husband) at Liscard near Liverpool. It was at Liscard, as he described to his fiancée Mary Anne Sayer, that his fairy-tale talent had had its most profuse flowering to date:

---

[7] Solly, pp. 14-15.

[A]s I've no time for reading fairy tales to tell the children, and it is part of my plan to tell them, I've been driven to rely upon my own invention. The last thing before we part, during the twenty minutes before five o'clock, you will be generally right in picturing me seated in the chimney corner, telling outrageous marvels to my childish circle. I start a new tale on Monday, and make it last the week; and as I know their tastes, I find that my own inventions amuse the children more than if I get them out of memory of print.[8]

It was to these end-of-school-day sessions that most of Morley's remarkable *Kunstmärchen* owe their origin. Just how remarkable these tales are is perhaps only now beginning to be appreciated.[9] Indeed there is a case to be made that it is as the originator of such dementedly anarchic tales as 'My Wonderful Adventures in Skitzland', 'Baron Bletch, of the Hammer' and 'The Lettered Mackerel' that Henry Morley reaches out to us at his most compelling. Reading these and other stories gathered in the collections *Fables and Fairy Tales* (1859) and *Oberon's Horn* (1860), it is hard to dismiss as flattery the words of his illustrator Charles H. Bennett: 'Your fairy tales are fuller of notions, conceits, and good honest daring absurdity than anything modern that I know'.[10] At their best, these stories look back to Swift, Hoffmann and Gogol and forward to Carroll, Barrie and even Kafka. My purpose in the present paper, however, is not to praise Morley the storyteller but to ask why Dickens all but buried him.

The numbers are shocking. Morley was the single most prolific contributor to the pages of *Household Words*, and by some distance. Between 1850 and 1859 he was responsible, as sole or chief writer, for no fewer than 320 items—an output of some 1,081,000 words. The number of original tales contained within this prodigious feat of textual production: 13, or some 4% of total output (4.6% if calculated by word-count rather than number of articles). But even this meagre figure masks the true scale of Dickens's under-exploitation of Morley's imaginative gifts. Fully 7 out of those 13 original tales were submitted in the first few months of Morley's association with the journal. If we exclude his freelance contributions for 1850 and begin our reckoning from 1851, the year in which he became a salaried staff-member, his total output falls to 303 items. Of these 303 items a mere 6—

---

some 2% (or, in word-count terms, 2.5%)—are original tales. (In considering these figures, it is worth bearing in mind that—according to John Drew's estimate—roughly one third of *Household Words* consists of original poetry and fiction).[11]

But even this does not tell the full story. If one restricts one's list of original Morley tales to those that might meaningfully be designated 'fantasy tales'—narratives, that is, in which the fantasy element is ample and dominant in the signature Morley manner, in which (to borrow from Morley's own appreciation of the Countess D'Aulnoy) 'the writer shakes off all common regard for possibilities, and gives up [his] entire mind without reserve to the extravagance of fairyland'—then the total number of such tales between 1850 and 1859 falls from 13 to 7.[12] This represents a decrease from 4% of total output to 2.2% (or, in word-count terms, from 4.6% to 2.4%). Now of these 7 original fantasy tales, a grand total of 1 ('Much Too Good Boys') dates to the post-1850 period—and even that one tale is presented essayistically as a parody rather than a *bona fide* work of fantasy.[13]

This means that between January 1851 and late February 1859 *not a single original Morley fairy tale or fantasy story was published in the pages of Household Words*.[14] What happened? The basic sequence of events is not too hard to reconstruct. We must go back to Morley's published contributions for that all-important first year of 1850. The pivotal text is 'The Water-Drops'.[15] Before its publication, Morley's substantial prose pieces had fallen into two categories: free-radical fantasies (for example, 'My Wonderful Adventures in Skitzland' and 'The Golden Fagots') and issue-driven pieces presented in the kind of 'upside-down' satirical mode that was already going down well at Forster's *Examiner* (such as 'Letter from a Highly Respectable Old Lady' and

---

[11] John M. L. Drew, *Dickens the Journalist* (Houndmills: Palgrave Macmillan, 2003), p. 115.

[12] 'The School of the Fairies', *Household Words*, Vol. XI, No. 275 (30 June 1855), 509-13 (p. 511).

[13] 'Much Too Good Boys', *Household Words*, Vol. XIX, No. 466 (26 February 1859), 309-12.

[14] 'The Night Porter' does boast supernatural elements but is too firmly grounded in narrative realism to be convincingly categorised as a Morleyan fairy tale or fantasy. 'The Night Porter', *Household Words*, Vol. XVI, No. 401 (28 November 1857), 513-18.

[15] 'The Water-Drops', *Household Words*, Vol. I, No. 21 (17 August 1850), 482-89. Subsequent references are to this edition and will appear in the body of the text.

'Improving a Bull').[16] 'The Water-Drops' marks Morley's first foray into what we might call the alienated fairy-tale—the fairy-tale that has been enlisted wholly to the cause of 'Serviceable Information'.[17]

'The Water-Drops' opens on an authentic fairy-tale premise:

> Far in the west there is a land mountainous, and bright of hue, wherein the rivers run with liquid light […] it is well known in many nurseries, that the bright land we speak of, is a world inhabited by fairies. Few among fairies take more interest in man's affairs than the good Cloud Country People; this truth is established by the story I am now about to tell.

> Not long ago there were great revels held one evening in the palace of King Cumulus, the monarch of the western country. Cirrha, the daughter of the king, was to elect her future husband from a multitude of suitors ('The Water-Drops', pp. 482-83).

The tale soon falls to earth, however, and in a double sense, when Nebulus and Nubis from the neighbouring principality of Nimbus are sent down as part of a contest to win Princess Cirrha's hand in marriage. The two suitors are put through a series of adventures illustrative of the principles of water hygiene:

> Nubis, in the meantime, had commenced his day with hope of a more fortunate career. On falling first into the Thames he had been much annoyed by various pollutions, and been surprised to find, on kissing a few neighbour drops, that their lips tasted inky. This was caused, they said, by chalk pervading the whole river in the proportion of sixteen grains to the gallon. That was what made the water inky to the taste of those were accustomed to much purer draughts. 'It makes,' they explained, 'our river-water hard, according to man's phrase; so hard as to entail on multitudes who use it, some disease, with much expense and trouble.'

> 'But all the mud and filth,' said Nubis, 'surely no man drinks that?'

---

[16] 'My Wonderful Adventures in Skitzland', *Household Words*, Vol. I, No. 10 (1 June 1850), 225-29; 'The Golden Fagots', *Household Words*, Vol. I, No. 12 (15 June 1850), 288; 'Letter from a Highly Respectable Old Lady', *Household Words*, Vol. I, No. 8 (18 May 1850), 186-87; 'Improving a Bull', *Household Words*, Vol. I, No. 19 (3 August 1850), 450-51. See also Solly, p. 151.

[17] To borrow a regular rubric from Morley's future *Household Words Almanac*.

'No,' laughed the River-Drops, 'not all of it. Much of the water used in London passes through filters, and a filter suffers no mud or any impurity to pass, except what is dissolved. The chalk is dissolved, and there is filth and putrid gas dissolved.' ('The Water-Drops', p. 484)

Morley even offers footnotes at several points referencing recent medical reports. One would like to suppose such a bizarre shotgun wedding of escapist fancy and edifying fact to be beyond parody were it not for the inclusion in later numbers of *Household Words* of two pitch-perfect parodies of just this brand of crude fairy-tale didacticism. The writers of these parodies? Charles Dickens and Henry Morley.[18] The aesthetic violence that Morley has done to himself in 'The Water-Drops' will be revealed when he publishes a very different version of the tale in 1859 under the title 'Dropped From the Clouds'. That version protects its fairy-tale character from any polluting infusion of public health information.[19]

After the publication of 'The Water Drops', Morley never looked back—he had already been turned to salt. His two October 1850 pieces show the scale of his artistic demoralisation. 'The Irish Use of the Globe' takes a promising fantasy idea—a hermit bringing a world-weary traveller into his cave and showing him a magic globe that offers a window on events in the world—and turns it into a banal vehicle for discussing the political economy of Irish farming. Morley's original draft of the next article, 'The Penny Saved', evidently contained a strong fantasy element too. It was returned to him with a blunt directive: 'cut out the fairies'.[20] An exasperated Morley was forced to throw away weeks of work and recast the article as a catechistic dialogue. The result is every bit the hotch-potch the original version must have been:

Rising Young Operative. 'Please, father, what is a blue-book?'

Paternal Operative. 'A blue-book is a thick heavy catechism done up in blue covers.'

---

[18] [Charles Dickens], 'Fraud on the Fairies', *Household Words*, Vol. VIII, No. 184 (1 October 1853), 97-100; [Morley], 'Much Too Good Boys'.

[19] Henry Morley, *Fables and Fairy Tales* (London: Chapman & Hall, 1859; repr. 1860), pp. 93-106. Internal evidence leads me to the tentative conclusion (with due deference to James Fowler, p. 247, n. 9) that the unadulterated fairy-tale version was composed before the version published in *Household Words*.

[20] Solly, p. 163.

'What is it for?'—'Why, when Parliament sets some of its Members to inquire about a subject, and hear evidence quietly in a room for to get at facts, they print the evidence and so on, and send it to all the other Members, so that they may read and know the facts.'

'What is the blue-book you have borrowed to read?'—'It is all about Savings Banks.'[21]

The few short months since 'My Wonderful Adventures in Skitzland' saw a steady devolution. That tale, which had (according to Wills) made 'a sort of sensation' in the office,[22] represents not just Morley's second paper for *Household Words* but the first and last truly autonomous fantasy of his that Dickens would entertain.[23] 'The King of the Hearth' (published in the 30 November 1850 number) did, it is true, elicit something approaching warm interest from Dickens himself.[24] But the exemption of this particular tale from Dickens's customary allergic reaction probably stemmed less from aesthetic pluralism than from a mild bout of narcissism: 'The King of the Hearth' is a blatant composite imitation of the Gabriel Grub story in *The Pickwick Papers* (1836-37) and the Christmas books *A Christmas Carol* (1843), *The Cricket on the Hearth* (1845) and *The Haunted Man* (1847). Not that Morley will ever be invited to contribute to one of the Christmas extra Numbers. There is a poignant error on this score in Solly's biography:

> Special efforts were made to plan and publish an extra good Christmas number of *Household Words* [for 1851], and the matter was discussed at a couple of dinners to which Dickens invited the staff. This consisted, in addition to himself, of W. H. Wills, R. H. Horne, Charles Knight, and Henry Morley. All were anxious to do their best of this occasion, and Mr. Morley, besides having 'a bothering Christmas paper from Naples to dress up,' wrote one which assuredly may be identified with the first paper in the number, entitled 'What Christmas Is As We Grow Older.[25]

---

[21] 'The Penny Saved; A Blue-Book Catechism', *Household Words*, Vol. II, No. 30 (19 October 1850), 81-84 (p. 81).

[22] Solly, p. 161.

[23] The tale had actually been written several years earlier (Solly, p. 154).

[24] Solly, p. 168.

[25] Solly, pp. 199-200.

The actual author of 'What Christmas Is, As We Grow Older' was, of course, Dickens. [26]

'The King of the Hearth' does not, then, pass muster as a quite genuine Morley article. It is, however, a Morleyan fantasy that is allowed to present itself without apology as a fantasy. *Household Words* never played host to another such.[27]

Morley's two pieces in the 28 December 1850 number represent his decisive re-entry into generic no-man's-land. The bulk of the satirical 'Mr. Bendigo Buster on Our National Defences against Education' was written by Morley, but Dickens tried to salvage the piece through comprehensive editing, amending and interpolation. The finished version is a veritable Frankenstein's monster of a text. Despite Dickens's best efforts at damage limitation, it keeps forgetting that it is supposed to be delivered in a vocal tone of sustained irony. Much of it—far too much of it—is a dry digest of Joseph Kay's just-published *The Social Condition and Education of the People in England and Europe*.[28] At times the joins between Dickensian irony and straight Morleyan exposition are almost comically obvious:

> [*Irony on*:] Well, but I haven't yet fully exposed the enormity of the offence committed by these Germans against wholesome Ignorance. Just see what pains they give themselves to fit a man for office as a teacher. [*Irony off*:] In the first place, he is generally of the peasant class, and, though educated like a gentleman, he is at no time raised

---

[26] See Dickens's rather tart reference to Morley in a letter to Wills of 16 December 1854: 'I would fence off this paper of Morley's (which is quite out of the question), by writing him that we have done with Xmas for this year'. To W. H. Wills, 16 December 1864, in *The Letters of Charles Dickens*, ed. by Kathleen Tillotson, Graham Storey and others, Pilgrim Edition, 12 vols (Oxford: Clarendon Press, 1965-2002), Vol. VII, p. 485.

[27] A fact which makes Morley's lengthy—though drastically abridged—retelling of Goethe's verse fable 'Reineke Fuchs' across two numbers in August 1851 such a dispiriting read: see 'The Story of Reineke the Fox', *Household Words*, Vol. III, Nos. 73-74 (16-23 August 1851), 484-91, 524-27. For later examples of second-hand storytelling by Morley see 'Frozen and Thawed', *Household Words*, Vol. VIII, No. 202 (4 February 1854), 533-39; 'Shot Through the Heart', *Household Words*, Vol. X, No. 240 (28 October 1854), 245-48; and 'Wild Legends', *Household Words*, Vol. X, No. 243 (18 November 1854), 315-19.

[28] Joseph Kay, *The Social Condition and Education of the People in England and Europe: Shewing the Results of the Primary Schools, and of the Division of Landed Property, in Foreign Countries*, 2 vols (London: Longman, Brown, Green, and Longmans, 1850).

above that sympathy with his own class which is necessary to his full influence in after life.[29]

Whether Dickens or Morley is responsible for the two sentences I have marked as ironic is not established. Harry Stone tentatively ascribes them to Morley.[30] I suspect that they may actually be a continuation of a Dickensian interpolation that Stone has identified as beginning three sentences earlier. What seems beyond question, however, is that the passage I have marked as non-ironic is from Morley.

If Morley's earlier brace of Highly Respectable Old Lady pieces had come perilously close to rhetorical meltdown with their maladroit medley of comic female patter and solemn didactic purpose, then Bendigo Buster goes all the way. A different but related complaint can be made of 'The Death of a Goblin'. It starts out promisingly enough as the story of a haunting but ends on a ponderous note of rationalist explanation:

> A dark cellar had a very little daylight let into it,—we could just see the floor covered with filth, in which some of the planks had sunk and disappeared. 'There,' said the old lady, 'there's the stuff your ghost had in his cup. There's your Sir Godfrey who poisons sleepers, and cuts off your children and your girls. Bah! We'll set to work, Peggy; it's clear your ancestors knew or cared nothing about drainage. We'll have the house drained properly, and that will be the death of the Goblin.'[31]

This moment marks the death not just of a goblin but of the goblin principle itself in Morley's *Household Words* fictions. He has not simply cut out the fairies; he has banished his entire dream-world population. From this time forth his Dickens-licensed forays into fancy will see him forcing dry, expository discourse aboard one rickety pseudo-fictive vehicle after another. Disconnected from the well-springs of his native storytelling talent, he will again and again replace fable with conceit, character with (part-time) satirical persona and magic with 'fanciful' machinery. That his account for 1851 will

---

[29] [Henry Morley and Charles Dickens], 'Mr. Bendigo Buster on Our National Defences against Education', *Household Words*, Vol. II, No. 40 (28 December 1850), 313-19 (p. 317).

[30] 'Introduction' to Charles Dickens' *Uncollected Writings from Household Words 1850-1859*, ed. by Harry Stone, 2 vols (Bloomington and London: Indiana University Press, 1968), Vol. I, p. 191.

[31] 'The Death of a Goblin', *Household Words*, Vol. II, No. 40 (28 December 1850), 335-36 (p. 336).

open with the first instalment in the six-part 'Phantom Ship' series is dismally fitting: that series will offer one interminable geographical, historical or scientific lecture after another, presented under cover of a painfully-thin fanciful premise.[32] The keynote for Morley's career as an emasculated storyteller at *Household Words* has been struck.[33]

But might not the suite of texts we have been looking at be viewed as intriguing or even charming instances of *Household Words* hybridity? Might they not be taken as faithful representatives of the Dickensian programme of writing fictively and fancifully about facts? And might they not at least be of socio-historical interest as instances of a mid-Victorian attempt to counteract an increasingly hegemonic utilitarian worldview? These are tempting lines of analysis, but only the third seems to me to have traction. To affirm these pieces on aesthetic grounds would surely be to miss just how embarrassingly out of his element Morley is in them. Having come to *Household Words* as a self-directing and heterodox storyteller, he is now reduced to anticipating the demand of his Conductor (or *auteur*) for a continuous blend of fancy and fact.[34] In the strong majority of cases, the result will be a sub-Dickensian *and sub-Morleyan* hotch-potch.

This is not to say that Morley's work at *Household Words* is a complete write-off. Far from it. There is some fine crusading journalism. One thinks for instance of the imperishable demolitions of Harriet Martineau and her friends at the National Association of Factory Occupiers,[35] or the whip-smart exposés of charlatans like the headmaster of a nominally Free

---

[32] 'Our Phantom Ship: Negro Land', *Household Words*, Vol. II, No. 43 (18 January 1851), 400-07.

[33] Later that year (1851), Morley will have a paper on the political economy of 'combination' sent back: 'Dickens, bother him! wants the combination paper altered from a cheerful dialogue to a grave essay. I thought the subject better treated in the other way, and think so still, but I must put my taste in my pocket' (Solly, p. 196).

[34] See John Drew, Hazel Mackenzie and Ben Winyard, '*Household Words*, Volume I March 30–September 21, 1850', *Dickens Quarterly*, 29:1 (March 2012), 50-67 (p. 51).

[35] 'Ground in the Mill', *Household Words*, Vol. IX, No. 213 (22 April 1854), 224-27; 'Fencing with Humanity', *Household Words*, Vol. XI, No. 264 (14 April 1855), 241-44; 'Death's Cyphering-Book', *Household Words*, Vol. XI, No. 268 (12 May 1855), 337-41; 'Deadly Shafts', *Household Words*, Vol. XI, No. 274 (23 June 1855), 494-95; 'More Grist to the Mill', *Household Words*, Vol. XI, No. 279 (28 July 1855), 605-06; 'Two Shillings per Horse-Power', *Household Words*, Vol. XII, No. 285 (8 September 1855), 130-31; and with Dickens, 'Our Wicked Mis-Statements', *Household Words*, Vol. XIII, No. 304 (19 January 1856), 13-19.

Grammar School[36] or the ballyhooed American medium who offers private sittings in London for an honorarium of one guinea per person.[37] But it is telling that such triumphs tend to come precisely when Morley suspends his hapless quest for a contrived fanciful angle and simply goes for the jugular. Morley's command of topics from the spheres of science and political economy can be masterly and, on those occasions when he avoids the polar extremes of contrived fancy and dull penny-cyclopædia discourse, he is capable of writing potently.

But these palpable hits should not distract us from the formidable number of papers that fell into what Dickens elsewhere called 'a dreary, arithmetical, Cocker-cum-Walkingame dustyness that is powerfully depressing'.[38] Hence the pertinence of a letter from Dickens to Morley of 31 October 1852:

> I am afraid you do not give sufficient consideration to some of your papers in Household Words. They are not to be done without trouble; and the main trouble necessary to them, is, the devising of some pleasant means of telling what is to be told. The indispensable necessity of varying the manner of narration as much as possible, and investing it with some little grace or other, would be very evident to you if you knew as well as I do how severe the struggle is, to get the publication down into the masses of readers, and to displace the prodigious heaps of nonsense and worse than nonsense, which suffocate their better sense [...] what I particularly want to impress upon you is, that it is not enough to see a thing and go home and describe it, but that the necessity is, for ever upon us of patiently considering *how* to describe it, so as to give it some fanciful attraction or some new air.[39]

---

[36] 'A Free (and Easy) School', *Household Words*, Vol. IV, No. 86 (15 November 1851), 169-73.

[37] 'The Ghost of the Cock Lane Ghost', *Household Words*, Vol. VI, No. 139 (20 November 1852), 217-23.

[38] To W. H. Wills, 16 October 1851, *The Letters of Charles Dickens*, Vol. VI, p. 522. Harry Stone explains Dickens's disparaging reference: Edward Cocker and Francis Walkingame were 'authors of well-known arithmetics' ('Introduction' to *Uncollected Writings*, Vol. I, p. 33).

[39] To Henry Morley, 31 October 1852, *The Letters of Charles Dickens*, Vol. VI, pp. 790-91. Compare Dickens's complaint to Wills over a decade later about Morley's continued tendency to enumerate facts and figures without sufficient 'grace of

These words constitute a valuable programmatic statement from Dickens on the style he is striving for in his still young weekly journal. But the eye of the Morley admirer will be caught by what comes next:

> I was particularly pleased with the Pic Nics in the Prairies [*sic*], which I thought very spiritedly and admirably done. But frequently it appears to me that you do not render justice to your many higher powers, by thinking too slightingly of what you have in hand, instead of doing it, for the time being, as if there were nothing else to be done in the world—the only likely way I know of, of doing anything.[40]

What exactly has Morley done in 'Pic-nics in the Prairie' to earn such high commendation from his Conductor? He has robotically put together an almost word-for-word digest of highlights from Edward R. Sullivan's recently published book *Rambles and Scrambles in North and South America*.[41] This is no isolated instance. On a conservative estimate, a good quarter of Morley's total output at *Household Words* falls under the rubric of 'book or report digest'. But the reality is that a great many more of his papers (such as the 'Phantom Ship' series mentioned above) are comparably regurgitative, being research projects involving little or no original input by Morley himself. Morley's polymath intellectual range and commensurate research skills made him matchlessly serviceable to Dickens. In Morley, Dickens was blessed with a one-man diffusion machine;[42] in Dickens, Morley was cursed with an editor who saw him as just that and no more.[43]

---

handling' (To W. H. Wills, 29 January 1865, *The Letters of Charles Dickens*, Vol. XI, pp. 12-13).

[40] *The Letters of Charles Dickens*, Vol. VI, p. 791.

[41] See To W. H. Wills, 7 October 1852, *The Letters of Charles Dickens*, Vol. VI, p. 774: 'Morley's (I suppose) resumé of the Prairie book, is as well done as a paper of that kind can be. Quite a model'.

[42] I take this felicitous characterisation from John Sutherland's essay, 'Journalism, Scholarship, and the University College London English Department', in *Grub Street and the Ivory Tower: Literary Journalism and Literary Scholarship from Fielding to the Internet*, ed. by Jeremy Treglown and Bridget Bennett (Oxford: Oxford University Press, 1998), pp. 58-71 (p. 64).

[43] On the more general problem of the surprising number of unimaginative articles in *Household Words*, and the question this raises as to the intensity of Dickens's supervision, see Shu-Fang Lai, 'Fact or Fancy: What Can We Learn about Dickens from His Periodicals, *Household Words* and *All the Year Round*?', *Victorian Periodicals Review*, 34:1 (Spring 2001), 41-53.

To euphemise Dickens's effective silencing of the creative Morley would, I submit, be a critical and indeed ethical error. The story of Morley's years as a Household Wordsmith is the story, at least in part, of a certain sorry misrecognition by one delightfully idiosyncratic fabulist of another. Dickens may have helped pluck the younger man from a pedagogical career of provincial marginality, but much of the work he put him to in London was of a piece with the work he had been doing as a schoolmaster (a fact confirmed by the range of topics enumerated in Morley's January 1849 Manchester school prospectus and the schedule of 'Wednesday Evening Lectures' advertised therein).[44] When Morley turned to Forster for advice in June 1851 over whether to accept Dickens's startling invitation to move to London and join the staff of *Household Words*, he was advised to choose once and for all between the occupations of teaching and writing.[45] In truth, though, he never did make the choice—or was blocked from doing so. The line of continuum from his time as a schoolmaster through his years at *Household Words* and on to his final self-reinvention as a Professor of English Literature is all too straight.

Dickens consistently prized his protégé's analytical and explanatory talents over his potential as a literary original. Instead of allowing Morley to keep the magisteria of fact and fancy non-overlapping, and instead of taking extra pains to mentor him in the latter domain, he bellowed 'Now, what I want is, Facts!' in one ear and 'Keep *Household Words* imaginative!' in the other.[46] Morley, not being Dickens, could not meet such an impossible double injunction. Lacking the capacity for self-assertion that Dickens himself had displayed a decade-and-a-half earlier when Chapman and Hall had sought to tie him to a restrictive format for *The Pickwick Papers*, he quickly became Dickens's low-maintenance anti-Bartleby, ever ready to oblige with the next research project. (This was not just a matter of Morley's genuine uncertainty as to his own proper vocation: his experience of dealing with contributors as editor of *King's College Magazine* back in 1841-42, coupled with an early signal from Wills that fractious behaviour from contributors did not go down well at *Household Words*, decided him against chafing openly under Dickens's regime).[47] His efforts to imitate the Inimitable and effect a

---

[44] See Solly, p. 102.
[45] Solly, p. 190.
[46] See To W. H. Wills, 17 November 1853, *The Letters of Charles Dickens*, Vol. VII, p. 200.
[47] Solly, p. 161.

magical fusion of fact and fancy led him again and again into journalistic banality.[48]

The magnitude of the calamity of the *Household Words* years for Morley's own artistic development is ultimately incalculable. The counterfactual story of what he might have achieved as a storyteller had Dickens never heard of him—or, having heard of him, taken him under his wing and moderated his research-project workload—will forever lie buried in what Nassim Nicholas Taleb would call 'the unseen cemetery of invisible consequences'.[49] Critics Elaine Ostry and James Fowler have done important work in taking Morley seriously as a fairy-tale writer, but their account of the relationship between Morley's move to *Household Words* and his progress as a fairy-tale writer is governed by a teleology that is a little too gladsome to ring true.[50] The opportunity cost of that move was dreadfully heavy.

Morley would finally escape his journeyman existence in the mid-sixties, but only at the cost of 700 pounds per annum—and the far higher cost of spending the rest of his life discoursing copiously about literature rather than generating new literature of his own. There is no little pathos in the picture we have of Morley travelling the provinces to deliver English Literature extension lectures to packed halls at just the time that Dickens is off on his own reading tours. As John Sutherland and John L. Kijinski have shown, a relentlessly taxonomic, unimaginative and sub-critical approach to the study of literature came to be the stock-in-trade of the man dubbed 'Professor More-and-Morley' by *Punch*.[51]

It would of course be naïve to deprive Morley of all agency in this affair by suggesting that he himself bore no responsibility for his own creative decline. The point rather is that Dickens failed in his duty of care to his young employee by over-exploiting what was already becoming a

---

[48] As Harry Stone notes (*Uncollected Writings*, Vol. I, pp. 34-35), Morley was not the only staff member to suffer the ill effects of Dickens's demand that contributors emulate his distinctive brand of fancy.

[49] Nassim Nicholas Taleb, *The Black Swan: The Impact of the Highly Improbable* (London: Allen Lane, 2007), p. 111.

[50] See Elaine Ostry, *Social Dreaming: Dickens and the Fairy Tale* (New York and London: Routledge, 2002), pp. 112-25 and Fowler, '"Telling Outrageous Marvels"', p. 244.

[51] Sutherland, 'Journalism, Scholarship', p. 64; John L. Kijinski, 'Securing Literary Values in an Age of Crisis: The Early Argument for English Studies', *English Literature in Transition, 1880-1920*, 31:1 (1988), 38-52 (pp. 40-41).

dangerously hypertrophied left side of the brain. Dickens released a genius only to put him right back in the lamp.

Champagne, *All the Year Round* and Henry Vizetelly

David Parker

ON 10 October 1868, a paper called 'The Glorious Vintage of Champagne' appeared in *All the Year Round*.[1] Until now no author has been identified, but now it is possible to do so, after comparison of the paper with two classic books on the subject. Even though the identification is beyond reasonable doubt, in itself this is no great achievement. More is gained, though, by the glimpse it affords into the way the mid-Victorian periodical press was evolving.

In *Household Words*, Dickens published papers on wine by a number of authors, known or easily identifiable. Among them, Edmund Saul Dixon (1809-93) stands out. A Cambridge graduate, and rector of Intwood with Keswick in Norfolk, Dixon enjoyed a comfortable income of £350 a year from his living, hired a curate to undertake parish duties, and lived for some years in France. He busied himself with writing, doubtless to augment his income, but also, evidently, to document personal interests. Poultry, gardening and cooking were among his favourite topics, and he contributed to a wide range of journals.[2] For *Household Words* he wrote many papers, including ones on cognac, claret, French vineyards and French drinking establishments. Published on 17 February 1855, 'A Bottle of Champagne' has been identified as his work by Anne Lohrli and prompts the thought that Dixon was also author of 'The Glorious Vintage of Champagne'.[3] It is as

---

[1] [Henry Vizetelly], 'Leaves from the Mahogany Tree: The Glorious Vintage of Champagne!', *All the Year Round*, Vol. XX, No. 494 (10 October 1868), 424-26.

[2] 'Author Index', *Dickens Journals Online*
 http://www.djo.org.uk/indexes/authors.html> [accessed 25 April 2012].

[3] [Edmund Saul Dixon], 'A Bottle of Champagne', *Household Words*, Vol. XI, No. 256 (17 February 1855), 51-56; Anne Lohrli, *Household Words: A Weekly Journal 1850-*

well to remember, though, that thirteen years elapsed between the two papers and to note the different attitudes they exhibit towards their subject.

'The Glorious Vintage of Champagne', I believe, can in fact be attributed to Henry Vizetelly (1820-94), a very different kind of contributor. Lohrli proposes Vizetelly as the author of 'A Lynch Trial in California', published in *Household Words* in September 1851.[4] The office contributor book records the piece as having been written by a Mr Brooks, but Brooks was a pseudonym Vizetelly had used in 1849, on the title page of a book about California (see below) and Dickens had form for using it as well, in *David Copperfield* (1849-50). If Vizetelly's autobiography, *Glances Back through Seventy Years* (1893), is to be believed, he was also a contributor to *All the Year Round*, though of course no contributor book for *All the Year Round* survives to confirm authorship, nor has any paper in it been ascribed to Vizetelly on other grounds.[5]

Vizetelly was baptised in the parish church of St Botolph without Bishopsgate, London in 1820. His forebears, who originally spelled their name 'Vizzetelli', had migrated, probably from Venice, at the end of the seventeenth century and set up as printers in London, a trade the family still followed. Young Henry trained as a wood-engraver and, after coming of age, became a partner in the business, with his elder brother James. In 1842 he assisted Herbert Ingram in founding the *Illustrated London News* and the family firm produced wood engravings for it. Characteristically, though, Vizetelly spotted an opportunity. The following year, with his elder brother and Andrew Spottiswoode, the twenty-three-year-old launched the *Pictorial Times*, organised like its rival around wood engravings and the rotary press. Among the contributors were Mark Lemon, Douglas Jerrold, Gilbert à Beckett and W. M. Thackeray. The periodical survived until 1848, when it was bought up by Ingram.

It was in 1844 that Vizetelly first encountered Dickens, in the waiting room at the offices of the publisher Longman. Dickens went in to see Thomas Longman before Vizetelly, and the fact of their interview triggered typical speculation in the mind of the young entrepreneur. He thought of

---

1859, Conducted by Charles Dickens. Table of Contents, List of Contributors, and their Contributions (Toronto: University of Toronto Press, 1973), pp. 256-61.
[4] [Henry Vizetelly], 'Chip: A Lynch Trial in California', *Household Words*, Vol. III, No. 78 (20 September 1851), 611-12.
[5] Henry Vizetelly, *Glances Back through Seventy Years* (London: Paul, Trench, Trübner, 1893), p. 139. Subsequent references to the book identify it as *Glances Back* and are given in parenthesis.

Dickens's quarrel with Chapman and Hall in 1844 and of his switching to Bradbury and Evans:

> I could not help connecting this visit of his to Longman and Co. with the change which was then in contemplation; and I marvelled how it could possibly have happened that the great Paternoster-row house had failed to come to terms with the popular novelist who was then at the zenith of his fame (*Glances Back*, p. 204).

Vizetelly first tried his hand at authorship—pseudonymously—in *Four Months among the Gold-Finders in Alta California: Being the Diary of an Expedition from San Francisco to the Gold Districts*, published in London by David Bogue in 1849, the year of the Californian gold rush. The author was declared to be one J. Tyrwhitt Brooks, M. D., who was said to have recorded the account of a Captain Sutter. The success of the book, which was also published in New York and translated into several foreign languages, brought it to the attention of Captain Sutter himself, who denounced it as fictitious. Vizetelly acknowledges his authorship in *Glances Back* (p. 346). It was *Four Months among the Gold-Finders* that persuaded Lohrli to propose Vizetelly as the author of 'A Lynch Trial in California'.

In 1852 Vizetelly ventured into book publishing, issuing a cheap reprint of *Uncle Tom's Cabin* (1852). Nor was the contracting work of the family firm discontinued: its most notable successes, indeed, were achieved in the early 1850s, with engravings for David Bogue's editions of Longfellow and fifty or so volumes of the National Illustrated Library. In 1855, with Bogue, Vizetelly sought to seize a chance offered by the imminent abolition of newspaper stamp duty. He corresponded with Dickens over the abolition, but failed to persuade him to be active in the campaign for this. Nothing daunted, he was instrumental in launching a second rival to the *Illustrated London News*, the twopenny *Illustrated Times*, which enjoyed an initial circulation of over 200,000—double that of the *News*. If Vizetelly's boast is to be believed, he made a profit of £1,200 from engravings for a single issue, devoted to the marriage of the Princess Royal in January 1858. Edmund Yates and George Augustus Sala were among the contributors and Hablôt Knight Browne was among the illustrators. Ingram reacted to this renewed competition by purchasing a one-third share in the *Illustrated Times* in 1857 and buying Vizetelly out completely two years later for more than £4,000, but retaining him as editor on the handsome annual salary of £800 (DNB).

From 1865, when the *Illustrated Times* ceased publication, until the end of 1877, Vizetelly lived in Paris, working as a correspondent for the *Illustrated*

London News. He also contributed articles on French subjects, he declares, to 'various London periodicals, notably "All the Year Round"' (*Glances Back*, p. 139). He made himself an authority on wine during his stay in France, producing four monographs on the subject and serving as a wine juror at the Vienna Exhibition of 1873 and the Paris Exhibition of 1878. From his Paris base he continued to supervise publishing ventures at home, including a translation of Dumas's *The Man in the Iron Mask* (1847-50) in 1870 (DNB).

On his return to England in 1878, with renewed vigour, Vizetelly threw himself once more into publishing, specialising in translations of French and Russian novelists such as Flaubert, Daudet, Dostoyevsky and Tolstoy—not all of which pleased Mrs Grundy, who was positively affronted by the translations, between 1884 and 1888, of seventeen novels by Émile Zola. This venture led to fines and a short imprisonment for Vizetelly who, at the age of 69, prudently withdrew from the literary fray, to enjoy a few years of retirement before his death on 1 January 1894 (DNB).

Changes in the London-based periodical press during the third quarter of the nineteenth century alone prompt the supposition that Vizetelly was the author of 'The Glorious Vintage of Champagne'. Two distinct kinds of contributor were emerging: on the one hand there were old-fashioned gentlemanly men of letters; on the other, hard-boiled professionals, metropolitan and entrepreneurial. In a letter to Wilkie Collins of 25 January 1864, about the death of Thackeray, Dickens resisted this distinction, but though he might have matched neither, many writers fitted one category or the other.[6] Dixon strikingly exemplifies the one type, Vizetelly the other type.

And there was a reason why a professional like Vizetelly was needed for 'The Glorious Vintage', rather than a gentlemanly scribbler like Dixon. The market for champagne had changed and expanded. There was a new kind of buyer, in need of advice. In 1855, champagne and other French table wines were scarcely affordable except by the rich—as had been the case since the end of the seventeenth century. The middle-class readers targeted by *Household Words* would doubtless have enjoyed Dixon's article, as people do stylish descriptions of unaffordable luxury, but they would for the most part have drunk fortified Iberian wines. In 1860, however, the treaty of commerce with France, and budget measures that followed upon it, changed matters. Tariffs were adjusted to match strength, so that French table wine

---

[6] To Wilkie Collins, 25 January 1864, *The Letters of Charles Dickens*, ed. by Kathleen Tillotson, Graham Storey and others, Pilgrim Edition, 12 vols (Oxford: Clarendon Press, 1965-2002), Vol. X, pp. 346-47. See also Gordon N. Ray, *Thackeray: The Age of Wisdom, 1847-1863* (New York: McGraw Hill, 1958), pp. 154-55.

became more affordable, Iberian fortified wine less so. As a result, by 1880 imports of French wine had increased more than tenfold, compared to what they had been in 1850.[7] Readers of *All the Year Round*—puzzled and no doubt delighted—had to be instructed about a product suddenly within their means, in an 1862 article entitled 'Light Wines'.[8] The 1868 article on champagne was further instruction.

Dixon was a man of letters on the eighteenth-century model—a country rector with gentlemanly hobbies, which he documented with readers equally gentlemanly in mind. He was a sound journalist, to be sure. Not always entirely pleased with his contributions, Dickens nevertheless appreciated Dixon's readiness to supply readers with abundant information. Take his account of the procedure for ridding champagne bottles of sediment:

> The bottles have to be placed sur pointe, as it is called, in their bottle-racks; that is, leaning with their necks downward, at an angle of not quite forty degrees. The sediment has thus a tendency to sink towards the cork. Each individual bottle has then to be moved or slightly twisted, with the least perceptible shock, or coup de main (increasing the inclination from time to time), every day for a month or six weeks, according to the season and the quality of the wine. It seems an endless and impossible job to treat in this way the multitudinous contents of such a cellar as M. Moët's; but one clever active man can turn and shake, upon a stretch, as many as fifteen thousand bottles a day. At last, when the dark deposit is all got down to the cork, the wine is ready to submit to the operation called 'dégorger,' or disgorging. The workman, or dégorgeur, who performs it is remarkably light-fingered. Each bottle is handed to him, and taken from him, by an attendant slave on either side. He holds it horizontally, removes the wire or the iron clasp, takes out the cork, lets a spoonful of froth spurt out with a fizz (carrying with it the ugly dregs), raises the bottle perpendicularly, replaces the cork, and the feat is done.[9]

But abundance of information notwithstanding, Dixon's readiness to wonder at the skill of the working man and his moments of whimsy—the attendant

[7] James Nicholls, 'Wine, Supermarkets and British Alcohol Policy', *History and Policy* <http://www.historyandpolicy.org/papers/policy-paper-110.html> [accessed 25 April 2012].

[8] [Anon.], 'Light Wines', *All the Year Round*, Vol. VII, No. 170 (26 July 1862), 476-80.

[9] [Dixon], p. 56.

slaves, for instance—gives his piece something of the character of remarks made by the wine secretary of a gentlemen's club.

His seigneurial tone was not right for the subject of champagne in 1868. The right tone, however, came naturally to Vizetelly—man on the make, artisan and entrepreneur, and, variously, printer, illustrator, author, editor, publisher, correspondent and jobbing journalist. He was in the forefront of those seeking a wider readership, not just of gentlemen and their ladies; in the forefront of those seeking to reach that readership by procuring the abolition of stamp duty and lowering prices; in the forefront of those taking advantage of new technology, such as wood-engraving and the rotary press.

It would not be true to say that Dickens was seeking a different kind of contributor in the 1860s. He used both gentlemanly scribblers and inky professionals, published both *belles-lettrist* rumination and gritty accounts of fact. Both Dixon and Vizetelly were among the early contributors to *Household Words*. It is likely that Dixon, who survived Dickens, was among the contributors to *All the Year Round*, so many of them unidentified. Even so, the voice of Vizetelly on champagne, in *All the Year Round* in 1868, is a sign of the way the periodical press was evolving.

The emphasis was changing. Dickens's own contributions to *All the Year Round*, to be sure, continue to exemplify the traditional conception of the periodical essay primarily as a record of adjustment to the writer's sensibility. But there was a call, ever louder, for investigation as an end in itself. There was a demand, ever more insistent, from an expanded readership that wanted to be told things and guided in its judgement.

Vizetelly could do whimsy, could do the stylistic flourish, but, more than Dixon, he kept in mind his readers' need for elementary instruction. 'The Glorious Vintage of Champagne' teaches them about the history of champagne, the ecology of the champagne country, techniques for growing, harvesting and producing champagne, varieties of champagne, sales of champagne and the great names of the champagne industry. But whatever else it is, it is also a shopper's guide:

> In the first-class of champagne stands Sillery, pale amber, with dry taste, rich body, and fine bouquet. The best is the Vin du Roi, grown in the vineyards of Verzenay and Mailly, which stud the north-eastern slopes of a chain of hills that separate the Marne from the Vesle. These vineyards formerly belonged to the Marquis de Sillery, who has thus delightfully immortalised his name. The wine was long known as the wine de la Marechale, from the Marechale d'Estrées, who watched over its careful manufacture; but the marquis has long

since ungallantly expelled the memory of la Marechale. Sillery is allowed to be the most spirituous and choice, besides being the strongest, most durable, and most wholesome, of the Champagne wines. It is unquestionably the highest manifestation of the divinity of Bacchus in all France.[10]

The very title of 'The Glorious Vintage of Champagne' shows it to be a celebration of the beverage. 'A Bottle of Champagne', in contrast, is sceptical about it. Champagne, Dixon says, is 'a factitious thing' made out of who knows what, who knows where:

Champagne's real place is not at a dinner, but at a ball. A cavalier may appropriately offer, at propitious intervals, a glass now and then to his danceress. There, it takes its fitting rank and position amongst feathers, gauzes, lace, embroidery, ribbons, white satin shoes, and eau de Cologne. It is simply one of the elegant extras of life [...]. It ought not to push into the background of neglect and disesteem, the more solid and generally useful elixirs of life.[11]

Elixirs constituted by other and better wines, he means.

'A Bottle of Champagne' we must again recall, was written thirteen years before 'The Glorious Vintage of Champagne'. A man may change his mind in thirteen years. What he writes about, indeed, may change and call forth a different response. But in this instance it would be a radical reversal. The case for Vizetelly, moreover, is ratified by another circumstance. Close examination reveals that 'The Glorious Vintage of Champagne' is a preliminary sketch upon which Vizetelly's subsequent books on the subject are based. Echoes of the wording of 'The Glorious Vintage' are to be found again and again in his *Facts about Champagne* (1879) and in the luxurious redaction, *A History of Champagne* (1882).[12]

Consider two of these echoes:

In the year 1397, Wenceslaus, King of Bohemia, came to France under pretence of negotiating a treaty with Charles the Sixth. He reached the fatal city of Rheims, famous for its cathedral—and its Champagne. The great Bohemian drank, and got drunk. He drank again, and got drunk again. [...] He never got sober any more; he

---

[10] [Vizetelly], 'The Glorious Vintage of Champagne', p. 425.
[11] [Dixon], pp. 52, 57.
[12] Henry Vizetelly, *Facts about Champagne* (London: Ward, Locke, 1879); *A History of Champagne* (London: Scribner & Welford, 1882).

remained soaked in Champagne, forgot all about Bohemia, all about the treaty, all about Charles the Sixth and the disputed claims, all about everything, but drank until he saw a bill that sobered him and terrified him into departure.[13]

King Wenceslaus of Bohemia, a mighty toper, got so royally drunk day after day upon the vintages of the Champagne, that he forgot all about the treaty with Charles VI, that had formed the pretext of his visit to France, and would probably have lingered, goblet in hand, in the old cathedral city till the day of his death, but for the presentation of a little account for wine consumed, which sobered him to repentance and led to his abrupt departure.[14]

We all know a glass of good dry Champagne. It is indeed what Dr. Druitt sensibly calls 'a true stimulant to mind and body, rapid, volatile, transitory, and harmless'.[15]

Dr. Druitt, equally distinguished by his studies upon wine and his standing as a physician, pronounces good champagne to be 'a true stimulant to body and mind alike, rapid, volatile, transitory, and harmless'.[16]

The possibility of plagiarism, admittedly, has to be considered, but that would call upon us to elaborately suppose that Vizetelly plagiarised an article written by some anonymous other, upon one of his own specialisations, published thirteen years previously in a periodical to which he himself contributed. We note, moreover, that the same echoes, plus others, appear in *A History of Champagne* three years later: 'Nay, the Americans have actually made Champagne from petroleum' becomes, 'A sweet champagne can be produced from the most ordinary raw wine—the Yankees even claim to have evolved it from petroleum'.[17] Vizetelly evidently deemed these anecdotes and observations his own. The repetition is persuasive.

'The Glorious Vintage of Champagne' was Vizetelly's work, we can conclude, and, as such, it marks a development in periodical publishing

---

[13] [Vizetelly], 'The Glorious Vintage of Champagne', pp. 424-25.

[14] Vizetelly, *Facts about Champagne*, p. 14.

[15] [Vizetelly], 'The Glorious Vintage of Champagne', p. 425.

[16] Vizetelly, *Facts about Champagne*, p. 166.

[17] [Vizetelly], 'The Glorious Vintage of Champagne', p. 426; Vizetelly, *Facts about Champagne*, p. 258.

during the third quarter of the nineteenth century, acknowledged, at least in practice, by Dickens.

Unfamiliar in their Mouths: The Possible Contributions of Fitz-James O'Brien to Household Words

Pete Orford

FITZ-JAMES O'Brien was born in Ireland in 1828 to a land-owning family of proud descent. As a young man he had his poetry published in the Irish journals. Then, at the age of 21, he received an inheritance of £8,000 and moved to London for two and a half years, from mid-1849 to early 1852, where he continued to write poetry in addition to observational pieces and some early fiction. He then lived in New York up until his early death in 1862 and it is here he made his reputation, partly for some plays he wrote early in his American career, though his main literary output was once again in the journals, to which he contributed poetry, short stories, theatre reviews and observational accounts from his travels around the city. But if this last description sounds like a bearded fellow from Portsmouth who might be familiar to the reader, I should stress that in terms of work ethic and attitude, Dickens and O'Brien were poles apart. A lover of wine, women and song (and a bit of a bar-room brawler), O'Brien lived a life of extravagance. His £8,000 inheritance with which he arrived in London (around £600,000 in modern currency) was spent by the time he left London, after which a constant motivation for his writing was the urgent need to pay off debt. There are several stories in New York of his turning up at a friend's house destitute, locking himself away and writing through the night before emerging the next morning with a new work for the publishers, only then, as soon as it had been accepted, to go straight out with the earnings and buy a lavish dinner for all and sundry.[1] He made little, if any, revisions to such

---

[1] For the modern equivalent of O'Brien's inheritance I have taken my cue from Michael Slater's 'Note on Monetary Values', which offers a rough conversion from nineteenth-century to modern currency by multiplying the former by 75—see Michael Slater, *Charles Dickens* (London: Yale University Press, 2009; repr. 2011), p.

writings, so many that appeared in print were essentially first drafts, which is both a testament to his skill and an indictment of his attitude. When the American Civil War (1861-65) broke out he volunteered for the Union army and Lieutenant O'Brien died of an infected gunshot wound at the grand old age of thirty-three.

It was 1880, 18 years after his death, before a collection of his work appeared in print, which shows that his friends were as organised as he was. William Winter's *Plays and Poems of O'Brien* included in its prefatory material a number of recollections from Winter and O'Brien's other American friends. Consequently we have a fair insight into his life in the States, but our details of his life in Ireland and England consist purely of what his American friends had been told in turn by O'Brien himself; this isn't much to begin with as they all noted a general reticence in him when speaking of his earlier life— and even when he did, sometimes O'Brien lied. Winter recalls one piece of

> serious waggery on the part of O'Brien, who liked to amuse himself by ascertaining how much certain solemn persons would believe. Thus, on one occasion, at table in the Manhattan Club, when the overwhelming Count Gurowksi was shooting forth his knowledge of court etiquette, O'Brien dissented from that nobleman's views, and was promptly challenged for his authority by the growling and spluttering diplomatist. To this he replied, with entire gravity, 'I was for several months a resident at the Court of St. James, as maid of honour to the Queen'.[2]

This leaves us treating any information of O'Brien's pre-New York life with caution. Unverified stories include his serving in the British Army and studying at Trinity College Dublin, while his reason for leaving London was an affair with the wife of a soldier and that said soldier was returning with haste from the wars to have a serious word with O'Brien.[3]

The claim of particular interest to these proceedings first appeared in print in the *New York Times* just after O'Brien's death, which recounted how, in London, O'Brien 'rose speedily to the dignity of a contributor to Dickens' *Household Words*', while the unidentified L. H. B. later specified in *The Round*

---

xvii. For details of O'Brien's last-minute, late-night writing sessions, see William Winter, *Old Friends* (New York: Moffat, Yard and Company, 1909), pp. 70-71.

[2] William Winter (ed.), *The Poems and Stories of Fitz-James O'Brien*, Vol. I (Boston: James R. Osgood and Company, 1881), p. xxxviii.

[3] Francis Wolle, Fitz-James O'Brien: *A Literary Bohemian of the Eighteen-Fifties* (Colorado: University of Colorado, 1944), pp. 27-28.

Table that 'O'Brien had contributed several articles to the first two volumes'.[4] No further developments were made on this until the 1940s when Francis Wolle published his biography *Fitz-James O'Brien: A Literary Bohemian of the Eighteen-Fifties* (1944). Wolle was able to uncover O'Brien's genealogy and compile a bibliography of his works in the Irish and English press. It is an impressive work and commendable for the many discoveries Wolle made, yet his treatment of the *Household Words* claim is rather fleeting. Wolle states 'It has been my privilege to go through the original manuscript office book of Household Words wherein are listed the names of the contributors and the sums paid to each, and O'Brien's name is not there'.[5] He then goes on to say his study of the accounts did yield three anonymous works written during O'Brien's time in London: the short-story 'An Arabian Nightmare' and the poems 'An Abiding Dream' and 'A Child's Prayer'.[6] Of the latter, said Wolle:

> I should like to assign definitely to O'Brien. It is the same in its subject matter and its sweetly religious mood as the earlier 'My Childhood's Prayer' (an earlier poem by O'Brien). The typically O'Brien note, however, is the stanza about the robin's song. Being convinced, therefore, that 'A Child's Prayer' is O'Brien's, I see no reason for hesitating to claim as his the other two pieces which come so close to it in time and in method of recording.[7]

To claim one work on the basis of only one parallel is questionable at best; to claim a further two separate works on top beggars belief. But as the sole biography of O'Brien it remains the authoritative voice, while the obscurity of O'Brien has left Dickens scholars unaware of the whole argument, so the attribution of these works to O'Brien remains either unknown or unchallenged—until now.

My aim has been to try and make as objective and scholarly an analysis as possible to determine whether O'Brien truly had any hand in *Household Words*. One advantage that the modern scholar has over Wolle is Anne

---

[4] *New York Times*, 10 April 1862; Wolle, p. 26.

[5] Wolle, p. 26.

[6] 'An Arabian Nightmare', *Household Words*, Vol. IV, No. 85 (8 November 1851), 166-68; 'An Abiding Dream', *Household Words*, Vol. IV, No. 86 (15 November 1851), 182-83; 'A Child's Prayer', *Household Words*, Vol. IV, No. 90 (13 December 1851), 277.

[7] Wolle, pp. 26-27.

Lohrli's sterling work on W. H. Wills's account book for *Household Words*.[8] A look at this work identifies an error in Wolle's study; there are a lot more than three anonymous works written during O'Brien's time in England. Discounting those for which subsequent authors have been suggested, or for which the content matter automatically excludes O'Brien (such as 'Degree Day at Cambridge' in which the author self-identifies as a Cambridge man),[9] still leaves a total of eight poems and six prose works written between 1849 and 1852 for which we do not know the author:

Poetry

Earth's Harvests (22 June 1850)
Battle with Life! (21 Sept. 1850)
A Lesson for Future Life (12 Oct. 1850)
A Memory (26 Oct. 1850)
Aspire! (25 June 1851)
An Abiding Dream (15 Nov. 1851)
A Child's Prayer (13 Dec. 1851)
A Cry from the Dust (28 Feb. 1852)

Prose

Curious Epitaph (11 May 1850)
The Old Churchyard Tree (13 July 1850)
Innocence and Crime (27 July 1850)
The Bush-Fire Extinguisher (13 Sept. 1851)
An Arabian Night-Mare (8 Nov. 1851)
My Uncle and My Aunt (3 Jan. 1852)

(Titles in italics indicate those which Wolle attributed to O'Brien.)

My study of the prose is ongoing and subject to more tests; this article is therefore going to present my findings on the authorship of the poetry. I offer these findings with the caveat that, with the lack of external evidence, any claims made solely upon internal evidence is never going to provide absolute fact, but always opinion: the best we can achieve is to make that opinion as educated and informed as possible, to find such a degree of parallels between the anonymous work and O'Brien's that goes beyond coincidence and suggests common authorship. To this end I studied thirty-three poems by O'Brien, all written in the years around the *Household Words* poems (see **appendix one**). I also analysed two test poems which appeared in *Household Words* during this time and for which the authorship *is* known. Comparing O'Brien's poems with two that I knew not to be by him allowed

---

[8] Anne Lohrli, *Household Words: A Weekly Journal 1850-1859, Conducted by Charles Dickens. Table of Contents, List of Contributors and their Contributions* (Toronto: University of Toronto Press, 1973).

[9] 'Chips: Degree Day at Cambridge', *Household Words*, Vol. II, No. 47 (15 February 1851), 491-92.

me to assess what constitutes a normal level of parallel and what breaks the coincidence barrier to identify the poem as O'Brien's.

Having selected these texts as test cases, the next step was stylometry. For this I am indebted to the advice and guidance of my colleague Will Sharpe, whose research on Shakespeare's apocrypha follows in the footsteps of MacDonald Jackson, a leading light in early-modern authorship studies.[10] Jackson champions a nuts-and-bolts approach to the language to avoid tenuous conclusions—such as Wolle made—and instead to make judgments as objective as possible. This can go too far the other way and, while Jackson's faith in recent years in computer analysis certainly minimises the prejudices of human interpretation, nonetheless I feel that, for all the pitfalls of subjectivity, human intuition can allow us to identify connections that a computer would miss. Nonetheless, in the absence of external evidence these tests offer our best chance for any indication of authorship, so, using Sharpe and Jackson's methodologies as a starting point, I made some alterations to allow for differences in sixteenth- and nineteenth-century texts (for example, the identification of unique spellings in Renaissance works is irrelevant in a post-dictionary age where spelling is widely homogenised), arriving at these characteristics with which to analyse each poem:

1. Contractions (it's, o'er, ev'ry, etc.)
2. Exclamations (any use of the exclamation mark, but specifically Oh! Ah! Lo!, etc.)
3. Stylised language (thou, hast, dost, etc.)
4. Rhyme scheme—for example, cross rhyme (abab) or envelope rhyme (abba)
5. Rhyme endings—are they masculine or feminine?
6. Rhyming pairs—what words did O'Brien use to rhyme with one another?
7. Metre—what is the beat of the poem?
8. Form—what's the length and structure of the stanzas and does it follow a recognised form?

---

[10] Will Sharpe, 'Authorship and Attribution', in *William Shakespeare and Others: Collaborative Plays*, ed. by Jonathan Bate, Eric Rasmussen and others (Basingstoke: Palgrave Macmillan and The RSC Shakespeare, 2013). For more on Jackson's approach to stylometry, see MacDonald P. Jackson, *Defining Shakespeare: Pericles as Test Case* (Oxford: Oxford University Press, 2003) and MacDonald P. Jackson, *Studies in Attribution: Middleton and Shakespeare* (Salzburg: Institut Für Anglistik und Amerikanistik, 1979).

9. Parallel passages—are there any images or ideas in the anonymous poems that coincide with those within O'Brien's?

Each of these can offer conscious or subconscious traits of the author; the writer's preference for contracting certain words or using particular exclamations and so on can be the written equivalent of dialect, betraying the author's voice even through the anonymity of print. With this in hand I was able to build some sort of profile of O'Brien's writings. It is hampered by the common recognition not only that O'Brien frequently adapted to suit the needs and tastes of whichever journal he was writing for, but, moreover, the criticism that much of O'Brien's poetry lacked a rigid structure or style. Nonetheless:

- With contractions it is clear he favoured 'o'er', ''tis' and ''twas' above others. 'O'er' appears a total of 33 times in 16 of the poems, ''tis' appears 15 times in 9 of the 33 and ''twas' appears 10 times, also in 9 poems. Other contractions used by O'Brien generally appear only once or twice in total.
- Exclamations are certainly used by O'Brien—all but 6 poems had them—and 16 of those used 'Oh!' in particular, which appeared 38 times in all.
- Of the stylised language the most common appearances were 'thy', 'thou' and 'thee'. This corresponds to O'Brien's tendency to use stylised language predominately when speaking to someone, either in dialogue or when addressing the reader directly.
- O'Brien's use of rhyme scheme is erratic; often poems will have a combination of cross-rhymes and envelope rhymes in a variety of order. Of the rhyme endings, O'Brien used both masculine and feminine, though he favoured the former: 25 used a majority of masculine endings, compared to 3 predominately feminine poems, while 5 contained an equal number of each.
- He favoured iambic above other beats, and tetrameter was his most common measure, though you can also see a surprising range—from dimeter up to heptameter—and frequently poems use a combination of 2. By far the most common stanza length in his poetry is the octain.

With this established I could then assess the anonymous poems. Again, this is not without its flaws. In particular, there are three fundamental problems that arise from looking at these poems, each stemming from the fact that they are being assessed in their final print form rather than as a manuscript. Firstly, as a final, printable copy, each has been potentially honed and worked over by the author and such revisions can minimise any subliminal traits. Secondly, by appearing in *Household Words* the eight anonymous poems are conforming to a house style and tone that would limit the range of individual characteristics (much as O'Brien's work for other journals can also reflect the political slant of the editor and readership). Finally, and perhaps most significantly, given our knowledge of Dickens's tendency to revise his contributors' works, quite aggressively on occasion, we must also bear in mind that many of these poems may well be the product of at least two authors: the original author and either Dickens or one of his colleagues.

Nonetheless, with all such warnings in mind, I began comparisons of the anonymous poems with O'Brien's to look for any tell-tale signs. Let us take 'A Child's Prayer' as an opening example, given that it was this poem which was the lynchpin in Wolle's argument:

> The day is gone, the night is come,
> The night for quiet rest:
> And every little bird has flown
> Home to its downy nest.
>
> The robin was the last to go
> Upon the leafless bough
> He sang his evening hymn to God,
> And he is silent now.
>
> The bee is hushed within the hive
> Shut is the daisy's eye;
> The stars alone are peeping forth
> From out the darkened sky.
>
> No, not the stars alone; for God
> Has heard what I have said:
> His eye looks on His little child,
> Kneeling beside its bed.
>
> He kindly hears me thank him now
> For all that he has given,

For friends, and books, and clothes, and food:
But most of all for Heaven,

Where I shall go when I am dead,
If truly I do right;
Where I shall meet all those I love,
As Angels pure and bright.[11]

It is written in iambic tetrameter, which O'Brien favoured, and it has four-line stanzas and cross-rhyming, all of which are common enough and have examples in O'Brien's work. There is no use of stylised language, contractions or exclamations to make comparisons with. There are two rhyming pairs that match others found in O'Brien's poems: the pairing of 'eye' and 'sky' appears in 'To a Captive Seagull' and 'The Famine', while 'given' and 'heaven' are matched in 'The Epicurean'. But the robin parallel that Wolle found is really the only one in the text, and the comparison to O'Brien's 'My Childhood Prayer' draws up more differences than similarities. Most damning of all though is a piece of external evidence discussed by B. W. Matz. Wills's account book shows payment was made to George Meredith for this poem, although the entry was subsequently crossed out and the name replaced by Richard Horne. But this, argues Matz, is typical of Meredith, as money for his poems was frequently paid to Horne who then passed it on to him. Anne Lohrli cautiously suggests this 'may point to Meredith's authorship, but of itself is not an indication of his authorship'.[12] However, I would certainly argue that the evidence in the account book for Meredith is more compelling than the scant parallels seen within the text for O'Brien. Overall there is not sufficient evidence to counter Matz's observations to the contrary: I would recommend O'Brien is not considered the author of this poem.

To further justify this it is prudent to consider one of the other anonymous poems—'A Memory'—which offers a great deal more indication of shared authorship.

Sometimes in halls of beauty and of love
Where many fair and many proud ones be,
And where the reckless and the thoughtless move,

---

[11] For this, and all poems reproduced from *Household Words*, I am indebted to the *Dickens Journals Online* project for making such material freely available.
[12] See Lohrli, p. 480.

I picture thee.

Thy memory comes to my lone heart enfolden
In strains of sweetest music; murmuring low,
Strange tales of dames and knights in pageants olden,
And courtly show.

The lonely wind that sighs in murmurs deep
Round some old ruin dear to love and fame,
Luring the passer-by to pause and weep,
Might breathe thy name!

I picture thee the spirit of some spot
Beautifully haunted by an olden spell;
Some waving wood, or silver-streaming grot,
Or perfumed dell.

Ever retiring in thy simple grace,
A gentler, dearer presence, never shone
From mortal figure or from lady's face,
Than thy dear one.

A very rose-bud to the gazer's eye,
Yet to the sense thou art a blooming flow'r,
Pouring thy fragrance on the summer sky
At evening hour.

Ever in dreams thou com'st. I may not trace
In waking hours the presence of that spell
Which holds me bound with such a winning grace.
—Farewell![13]

Once again the form is not unique; it has iambic pentameter, while the use of quatrains and cross rhymes is nothing too distinctive. This time the poem does have stylised language, and 'thee', 'thy' and 'thou' (O'Brien's favourites) all appear in number. There is also an eye rhyme in 'love' and 'move' (so it looks the same but does not sound the same), which is a technique O'Brien

---

[13] [Anon.], 'A Memory', *Household Words*, Vol. II, No. 31 (26 October 1850), 112.

was not averse to using in his other poems. In addition there is a specific contraction in 'flow'r' that O'Brien previously used in 'An Ode to the Divinest of Liquors', but these indications alone are still incidental rather than compelling. However, the number of rhyming pairs that match O'Brien's is much greater than in 'A Child's Prayer': 'be' and 'thee' appears in 'The Loves and the Fates of the Dragon-Fly and the Water-Lily'; there are three rhyming pairs that appear in 'Forest Thoughts' ('spell/dell', 'grace/face', 'trace/grace'); while again, 'eye' and 'sky' (present also in 'A Child's Prayer') can be seen in two of O'Brien's poems, as can 'flower' and 'hour' (in 'An Ode to the Divinest of Liquors' and 'To an Infant'). Finally, and most intriguingly, there are the parallel passages (see **appendix two**). Though not exclusive to O'Brien's poetry, this poem's imagery—of having visions of a loved one (stanzas one and seven), these visions travelling directly to the author's heart (stanza two), and the spell-binding power of love—all have a precedent in O'Brien. In particular, however, the idea of low murmuring as associated with love (stanza two) is very common in O'Brien, as is the lonely, hushed or whispering wind (stanza three), and O'Brien had twice drawn on the ruins of a castle near his family home as a piece of imagery (stanza three), while silver is his colour of choice for idyllic settings (stanza four), and the imagery in 'A Memory', both of flowers in the evening and fragrant air as connected to beauty and love (stanza five), is again a familiar idea in O'Brien's poetry. In summary, when we look at this poem we see a far more comprehensive overlay of parallels with fifteen of the O'Brien poems considered; a higher level of crossovers than might be expected and grounds for considering this poem as O'Brien's.

Taking a look at all the anonymous poems then, of these eight my analysis has identified two as almost certainly O'Brien's—'A Memory' and 'Battle with Life!' (for which justification follows below)—with three—'A Lesson For Future Life', 'A Child's Prayer' and 'A Cry From The Dust'— that I would rule out at this stage (due to a low level of parallels), and a remaining three for which it is worth pursuing further investigation. Of these three, 'Earth's Harvests' and 'Aspire' both have a moderate comparison of rhyming pairs and parallel passages, but neither too much nor too little to argue convincingly either way. 'An Abiding Dream', which Wolle attributed to O'Brien not on any evidence within it, but because he was attaching it with 'A Child's Prayer', actually has a strong number of matching rhyming pairs, while the motif used within of an inanimate object, in this case the deceased mother's chair, as a focal point for an emotional theme is used conspicuously by O'Brien in three poems—'Our Old Garden Chair', 'The

Lonely Oak' and 'The Shadow by the Tree'—though again, there is not quite the same number of crossovers, such as can be seen in 'A Memory', as to be fully conclusive.

Having done all this, the dreaded question, which all academics fear, is, 'so what?' What does this information offer us? Certainly the benefit to O'Brien studies is greater than that to Dickens studies; it has been noted that O'Brien's early writings follow a Dickens model and this gives substance to that idea.[14] Also the kudos of a connection to Dickens was felt enough by O'Brien for him to overcome his usual reticence and tell his American friends about his work for *Household Words*, which demonstrates the cultural currency of Dickens even in his own lifetime. In contrast, there is no mention of O'Brien in Dickens's letters or any of his writings and the absence of his name from the account book suggests a lack of personal connection with either Wills or Dickens. That said, the benefit of identifying the authors of these anonymous works is certainly of benefit to Dickens studies from a 'completionist' perspective and it provides a fuller picture of the contemporaries and characters Dickens and his works were interacting with.

However, the primary benefit of all of this can be best explained when we look at the other poem that I would definitely attribute to O'Brien, 'Battle with Life!'

> Bear thee up bravely,
> Strong heart and true!
> Meet thy woes gravely,
> Strive with them too!
> Let them not win from thee
> Tear of regret,
> Such were a sin from thee,
> Hope for good yet!
>
> Rouse thee from drooping,

---

[14] O'Brien's first confirmed work of fiction, *The Phantom Light* (published in *The Home Companion* from January to February 1852) is especially conspicuous for the way in which the style varies between O'Brien's own and an elaborate imitation of Dickens (with grateful acknowledgments to Ellie Collins of OUP for her help and assistance in providing me with a copy of this story).

Care-laden soul;
Mournfully stooping
'Neath grief's control!
Far o'er the gloom that lies,
Shrouding the earth,
Light from eternal skies
Shows us thy worth.

Nerve thee yet stronger,
Resolute mind!
Let care no longer
Heavily bind.
Rise on thy eagle wings
Gloriously free!
Till from material things
Pure thou shalt be!

Bear ye up bravely,
Soul and mind too!
Droop not so gravely,
Bold heart and true!
Clear rays of streaming light
Shine through the gloom,
God's love is beaming bright
E'en round the tomb![15]

To briefly summarise the general analysis: it has iambic dimeter and trimeter, which has O'Brien precedents, as does the predominately masculine endings, while the eight-line stanza was the most common type among the O'Brien poems I analysed. It has some contractions, all of which have been used by O'Brien elsewhere, and exclamations are in full force, as is stylised language (note the many appearances of 'thee', 'thou' and 'thy'). However, there was only one rhyming pair that matched O'Brien ('light/bright' is used in 'The Fisher's Lay'), so the links were mainly reliant on parallel passages (see **appendix three**). Again, there were a number of these, although overall they only matched with eight of the O'Brien poems I'd analysed.

---

[15] [Anon.], 'Battle with Life!', *Household Words*, Vol. I, No. 26 (21 September 1850), 611.

However, the clinching argument for this as O'Brien's work is one poem in particular, 'A Lyric for Life', which appeared in the London journal the *Family Friend* in August 1850, just one month before 'Battle with Life!' was published in *Household Words*:

> The winter had swollen a deep-rolling river,
> And it rush'd with a thousand wild shouts to the main;
> And its waves in their chainless disdain sought to shiver
> An oak-tree of ages that guarded the plain.
> But in vain round its broad trunk the billows came leaping,
> In vain did they toss their white plumes in despair;
> Each leaf lay as still as if Winter was sleeping,
> And Summer's faint music was haunting the air.
>
> And I thought 'twas a lesson which weak soul might borrow,
> That man should bear up with a spirit as brave,
> Nor bend like a reed when the waters of sorrow
> Come threatening to sweep him along to the grave.
> For life is a combat, and hearts that are strongest
> Will conquer all trials, and win every prize;
> And the day ever breaks when the night is the longest—
> And the tree in its peril still turn'd to the skies!

The poem describes an image of an oak tree withstanding the current of an overflowing river (either based on an actual event witnessed by O'Brien, or simply an idea he was struck with). It is in the second stanza, where O'Brien expands upon the meaning of this image, that we can see the origins of 'Battle with Life!' The phrase 'life is a combat' is perhaps the first clear indicator, but then further comparison of the two poems side-by-side identifies a startling focus of correlations: 'Man should bear up with a spirit as brave' becomes 'bear thee up bravely'; 'hearts that are strongest' becomes 'strong heart and true'; 'brave' and 'grave' prompt 'bravely' and 'gravely', while 'strongest' and 'longest' can be seen in 'stronger' and 'longer'; and the conclusion, with the break of dawn and the tree in its peril still steadfastly looking to the skies, informs the line, 'light from eternal skies show us thy worth'. The close proximity of each poem's publication, in connection with the aforementioned parallels with other O'Brien poetry, suggests shared authorship rather than plagiarism. Seeing these two poems together clearly identifies O'Brien as the author of the second poem, but this identification is not the end of the discussion but the beginning, for the flow of ideas from the first poem to the second now informs our reading of it; we can see how the original image of the oak tree in the river is continued in the first two stanzas of 'Battle with Life!', developing the first poem's suggestion that this image is a lesson to mankind, and expanding upon it in the last two stanzas with the imagery of eagle's wings and the soul's ascent.

It is important to consider that, with the exception of the Christmas numbers, each issue of *Household Words* was a diverse and disjointed collection of writings by different authors that can create a jarring effect, especially to the modern reader, as we can struggle without a context for each article and poem. Anonymous works in particular are at a disadvantage because we have no concept of the author's ideals or other works that might inform our reading. But here, 'A Lyric for Life' enriches our understanding of 'Battle with Life'. By identifying the authorship of the poem we have access to a wider context of works, allowing us to better understand and appreciate it; and that, for me, is the fundamental benefit of naming an author to these poems at last.

Appendix One

Poems known to be by O'Brien to which the anonymous poems were compared, arranged according to the journal in which they appeared and including date of first publication.

The Nation

- Oh! Give a Desert Life to Me! (15 March 1845)
- Epigram on Hearing a Young Lady Regret Her Eyes Being Bloodshot (28 March 1845)
- Loch Ina (26 July 1845)
- The Famine (7 March 1846)
- The Boatmen of Kerry (14 March 1846)
- Excelsior! (13 March 1847)

Cork Magazine

- An Ode to the Divinest of Liquors (July 1848)
- My Childhood's Prayer (August 1848)
- Una of Lough-Ine (August 1848)
- Serenade (September 1848)
- Impromptu to a Lady (September 1848)
- The Loves and the Fate of the Dragon-Fly and the Water-Lily (September 1848)
- The Fisher's Lay (October 1848)
- Where Shall We Dwell? (October 1848)
- The Epicurean (November 1848)
- Forest Thoughts (December 1848)

Family Friend

- Lines Addressed to a Young Lady about to Depart for India (15 July 1850)
- A Lyric for Life (15 August 1850)

Parlour Magazine

- To a Captive Seagull (3 May 1851)
- Impromptu on Hearing a Young Lady Complain That Her Eyes Were Bloodshot (21 June 1851)
- Our Old Garden Chair (21 June 1851)
- The Lonely Oak (12 July 1851)
- Dawn—A Sonnet (2 August 1851)
- To an Infant (23 August 1851)
- Hateful Spring (30 August 1851)
- Fortune in the Fire (20 September 1851)

Dublin University Magazine

- The Wish; or, the Fall of the Star (August 1851)

American Whig Review

- Madness (August 1852)
- Pallida (September 1852)
- The Song of the Immortal Gods (September 1852)
- The Old Knight's Wassail (September 1852)
- The Shadow by the Tree (October 1852)
- Oinea (December 1852)

Appendix Two

Parallel passages between 'A Memory' and O'Brien's poetry

'A Memory'	Poems by O'Brien
'I picture thee'	'visions come o'er me Of love and thee' ('The Fisher's Lay')
'Thy memory comes to my lone heart enfolden'	'my young heart unfearing [...] Thy dear voice comes singing In love-dreams to me' ('The Fisher's Lay')
'In strains of sweetest music; murmuring low, Strange tales'	'whisperings of love' ('The Loves and the Fate of the Dragon-Fly and the Water-Lily')
	'Whispers are straying Around me and saying She is now praying Thy path may be bright' ('The Fisher's Lay')
	'Have I low whispered' ('Pallida')
	There is a music [...] That wreathes the soul with strange impassioned spells' ('Forest Thoughts')
	'the caves of the deep Murmur their solemn melodies' ('Where Shall We Dwell?')
	'deep low murmurs' ('Madness')
'The lonely wind that sighs in murmurs deep	'the rustling sigh [...] When the wind swept by'

Round some old ruin'

('The Loves and the Fate of the Dragon-Fly and the Water-Lily')

'hushed winds'
('The Fisher's lay')

'no chants, save when the wind
Sweeps the tall arches of the trees'
('Forest Thoughts')

'The summer breeze
Through the distant trees
Murmurs in fragrant breathings o'er'
('Loch Ina')

'Round some old ruin dear to love and fame'

'On its grassy side
In ruined pride
A castle of old is darkling seen'
('Loch Ina')

'Never does my memory dwell
Upon the ruins sleeping there
With such calm joys as when the spell
Recalls my childhood prayer'
('My Childhood's Prayer')

'silver-streaming grot'

'silver sand'
('Loch Ina')

'silvery shore'
('Una of Lough-Ine')

'A very rose-bud to the gazer's eye,
Yet to the sense thou art a blooming flow'r,
Pouring thy fragrance on the summer sky
At evening hour.'

'the sun [...] is sinking [...]
Our brows may catch the fragrant air'
('Our Old Garden Chair')

'life is a garden whose roses are fading
The blue sky above it soon clouds

will hide
Let us cull then its buds'
('The Epicurean')

'all round thee should breathe of
flowers'
('To an Infant')

'The summer breeze
Through the distant trees
Murmurs in fragrant breathings o'er'
('Loch Ina')

'flowers are sending
Their oderous sighs on the breezes
of night'
('Serenade')

'Ever in dreams thou com'st'   Thy dear voice comes singing
                                      In love-dreams to me'
                                      ('The Fisher's lay')

                                      'I flew
                                      Weaving sweet dreams of love and
                                      you'
                                      ('The Loves and the Fate of the
                                      Dragon-Fly and the Water-Lily')

'that spell   'And if I hear thy tender tones
Which holds me bound'   That move me like a spell'
                                      ('Where Shall We Dwell?')

Appendix Three

Parallels between 'Battle with Life!' and O'Brien's poetry

<u>'Battle with Life!'</u>   <u>Poems by O'Brien</u>

'Tear of regret
Such were a sin for thee'

'we weep o'er our degraded land'
('Oh! A Desert Life for Me!')

'hope for good yet'

'no hope for thee'
('Forest Thoughts')

'Care-laden soul […]
Clear rays of streaming light
Shine through the gloom'

'The thought dispelling sunlight that
beguiles the soul from deep
reflection'
('Forest Thoughts')

'o'er the gloom that lies
Shrouding the earth
Light from eternal skies'

'as when on sorrowing brows first
gleams the birth
Of joys for years estranged […]
so steals the silent dawn upon the
sleeping earth'
('Dawn—A Sonnet')

'shadows cold and dun
Flit between thee and the sun'
('To an Infant')

'gazing through that sunny cloud
[…]
Up to this time my life has been a
shroud'
('Pallida')

'A shadow stealing on a summer sea'
('Madness')

'light from eternal skies'

'summer skies, whose face
May smile eternal'
('Forest Thoughts')

'Let care no longer

'my soul is longing to be free

Heavily bind
Rise on thy eagle wings
Gloriously free'

Without the weight of chains it bore'
('Oh! A Desert Life for Me!')

'Bird of the wild far-sweeping wing
[…]
Thy home is where the free winds
sing'
('To a Captive Seagull')

'one free singing bird'
('Forest Thoughts')

SECTION 4

'A Glimpse of Passing Faces': Dickens, the Streets and the Press[1]

Judith Flanders

THE narrator who opens *The Old Curiosity Shop* (1840-41) might be read as an authorial stand-in:

> Night is generally my time for walking [...] it affords me greater opportunity of speculating on the characters and occupations of those who fill the streets [...] a glimpse of passing faces caught by the light of a street-lamp or a shop window is often better for my purpose than their full revelation in the daylight.[2]

Previous essays about London, by Charles Lamb, Leigh Hunt and others, had been filled with history, with learned asides, with a great panoply of education. Dickens, in his first essays into essays, with *Sketches by Boz* (1833-36), truly did sketch what he saw: the people of the streets, and the world that these people lived in. It was with Sam Weller, whose knowledge of London was much like that of his creator—'extensive and peculiar'—that Dickens found his subject and his audience.[3] For the rest of his career, Dickens continued to find his subjects in the streets, or in journalistic descriptions of the streets.

Sometimes the connections seem likely, but whether or not Dickens would have seen them cannot be known. In *Dombey and Son* (1846-48), Rob the Grinder is a working-class boy sent to a charity school and obliged to wear a specific, old-fashioned uniform. The *Illustrated London News* had

---

[1] Some of this essay appears, in different form, in *The Victorian City: Everyday Life in Victorian London*, published by Atlantic Books, 2012.
[2] Charles Dickens, *The Old Curiosity Shop* [1840-41], ed. by Angus Easson (Harmondsworth: Penguin, 1985), p. 43.
[3] Charles Dickens, *The Pickwick Papers* [1836-37], ed. by Mark Wormald (Harmondsworth: Penguin, 1999), p. 266.

printed a series of engravings of these outfits four years before the novel was begun.[4] Sometimes the likelihood that Dickens read something is fairly clear. In *Our Mutual Friend* (1864-65), Gaffer Hexam, who dredges bodies out of the river, the dustmen who collect waste and Betty Higden, the itinerant pedlar, all have their street-equivalents in Henry Mayhew's interviews in the *Morning Chronicle* (1849-50).[5] The inclusion of all three makes the probability high. And sometimes it's a certainty. As Dickens was writing *Our Mutual Friend*, James Greenwood, the 'Amateur Casual', visited a casual-ward in the guise of a labourer out of work. His report caused a sensation, even toned down as it had been by the *Pall Mall Gazette*'s editor, 'to avoid suspicion of exaggeration'.[6] Although, oddly, the clearly homoerotic elements were left in, causing much shocked comment, and it has been suggested that this influenced Dickens's depiction of the friendship between Mortimer Lightwood and Eugene Wrayburn. He certainly he knew of the report and *All the Year Round* published several articles critiquing the workhouse system around the same time.[7]

Then there were the times when Dickens reported directly on something he had seen in his journalism and therefore allows us to see how it fed back into his fiction: in *Household Words* he described a woman who had roamed Berners Street in his childhood, who was said to have lost her mind when abandoned by her fiancé, wearing her wedding dress ever after.[8] Sometimes, he reversed the trick: when Oliver Twist first arrives in London, the route he follows is 'across the classic ground which once bore the name of Hockley-in-the-hole', which many would recognise as a district in *The Beggar's Opera*

---

[4] *Illustrated London News*, 28 May 1842, pp. 44-45.

[5] Harland S. Nelson, 'Dickens's *Our Mutual Friend* and Henry Mayhew's *London Labour and the London Poor*', *Nineteenth-Century Fiction*, Vol. 20, No. 3 (December 1965), 207-22; Harvey Peter Sucksmith, 'Dickens and Mayhew: A Further Note', *Nineteenth-Century Fiction*, Vol. 24, No. 3 (December 1969), 345-49; and Richard J. Dunn, 'Dickens and Mayhew Once More', *Nineteenth-Century Fiction*, Vol. 25, No. 3 (December 1970), 348-53.

[6] Seth Koven, *Slumming: Sexual and Social Politics in Victorian London* (Princeton: Princeton University Press, 2004), p. 35.

[7] See, for example, [Joseph Charles Parkinson], 'A Workhouse Probe', *All the Year Round*, Vol. XVIII, No. 449 (30 November 1867), 541-45; [Joseph Charles Parkinson], 'Another Workhouse Probe', *All the Year Round*, Vol. XVIII, No. 450 (7 December 1867), 558-64; and [Joseph Charles Parkinson], 'A Country Workhouse', *All the Year Round*, Vol. XIX, No. 451 (14 December 1867), 16-20.

[8] [Charles Dickens], 'Where We Stopped Growing', *Household Words*, Vol. VI, No. 145 (1 January 1853), 361-63 (pp. 362-63).

(1728), that eighteenth-century celebration of rogues and thieves. Here, Dickens is signalling his chosen genre through a real route in literature.[9]

Even more common, though, are when Dickens took events not from one source, but simply from things that routinely happened. A handful of cases of middle-class children abducted, stripped of their clothing and turned back onto the streets, appear in the *Illustrated London News* every year or so. Sometimes, though, a more interesting case appears. Three years before *Dombey* began to be published, a woman applied to a workhouse for relief and the workhouse surgeon thought the three-year-old boy with her was in some way 'superior'. So puzzling did he appear that he was, ultimately, interviewed by the Lord Mayor in his home, where the toddler recognised a piano and a watch-guard—notably middle-class objects. He said he had a mother in the country who was kind to him and called him Henry, while this woman, whom he called his straw-yard mother, had taken away his clothes, which he itemised and which were the clothes worn by middle-class children. A search was instituted for the child's family, but without success. Henry was raised by the workhouse surgeon, and ultimately they emigrated to Melbourne.[10]

Sometimes, of course, Dickens uses the sheer repetition of items as part of his fiction. When, at Mr Podsnap's, 'a stray personage of a meek demeanour' makes a 'reference to the circumstance that some half-dozen people had lately died in the streets', many readers would have read a reference to this in the press.[11] An example, culled again from the mainstream, middle-class, middle-brow *Illustrated London News*, is from an inquest held in Walthamstow during the Hungry Forties, but similar incidents continued to appear, albeit less frequently, throughout the period. The jury heard that this man, 'name unknown, aged 52' had been out of work for weeks, but had managed to scrape a living selling congreves (matches), until the police had threatened to arrest him as a beggar. He was too frightened to go out selling in the streets again and bartered his remaining stock for stale crusts and dregs of tea, as well as a place to sleep on the floor in a room. Then he vanished for four days, until he was found crouched outside: he said he had left because he had nothing left to barter. His 'landlord' helped him in and gave him some gruel and ale, but he died

---

[9] Charles Dickens, *Oliver Twist* [1837-39], ed. by Philip Horne (London: Penguin, 2002), p. 63.

[10] *Illustrated London News*, 21 August 1852, p. 135.

[11] Charles Dickens, *Our Mutual Friend* [1864-65], ed. by Adrian Poole (Harmondsworth: Penguin, 1997), p. 143.

the next day. Verdict: 'That the deceased died from want of the common necessaries of life and exposure to the cold.'[12] These are the stories that would have been in readers' minds as Mr Podsnap gestured the 'stray personage's' comments away as 'not in good taste'.

It is therefore essential that we understand the conditions of the time, both in reality, as seen through the newspapers, and as people remembered them—all three, of course, not always overlapping. A useful example of this tripartite view is perhaps the idea that the slums were so dangerous they were all but impassable to the 'respectable'.

These areas were presented by journalists to middle-class readers as a voyage into the unknown and references to the confusion created by the mazes of courts and alleys were commonplace. Early in his career, even Dickens did it: in *Sketches by Boz* a stranger in Seven Dials is faced with alleys that 'dart in all directions' before they vanish into an 'unwholesome vapour', like a ship at sea moving into the foggy distance.[13] Anyone even attempting to navigate the courts would find themselves 'irretrievably lost', warned Dickens's protégé G. A. Sala, who, despite living in Great St Andrew Street (roughly where Charing Cross Road is today), declared, 'I never yet knew the exact way, in or out of that seven-fold mystery'.[14] Memoirs too harped on this theme of unspeakable danger. Donald Shaw, a sporting upper-class gent with a military background, described going to the 'dens of infamy' in the 1860s, and enjoyed himself enormously by imagining that the 'motley groups' of drunken sailors he passed all had 'deadly knives at every girdle', watched by 'constables in pairs'—that is, he is specific that these were places where constables did not patrol singly, because of the danger. He and his friends were taken to an East End pub said to be 'the most dangerous of all the dens', and he was thrilled to be told,

> We've got a mangy lot here tonight; they won't cotton to the gents. If they ask any of their women to dance it will be taken as an affront, and if they don't ask them it will be taken as an affront.

---

[12] *Illustrated London News*, 14 December 1844, p. 371.

[13] Charles Dickens, 'Seven Dials', in *Sketches by Boz* [1836], ed. by Dennis Walder (Harmondsworth: Penguin, 1995) pp. 90-96 (p. 92).

[14] [G. A. Sala], 'Bright Chanticleer', *Household Words*, Vol. XI, No. 262 (31 March 1855), 204-09 (p. 204).

But the leader of his group had only to shout out, 'What cheer [...] my hearties' and all settled down to drink together.[15] (Shaw appears not to notice that this rather invalidates his shivery thrill at the danger.)

Field Lane, in Clerkenwell, was renowned as 'occupied entirely by receivers of stolen goods'.[16] Thomas Trollope claimed that in 1818, aged eight, he had visited the notorious street.[17] If his story is true, an eight-year-old child could make his way through such a place without hindrance, much less violence. After his early sketches, Dickens was frequently sharp on the notion of no-go areas. Even in failing health, in the year before he died, he routinely visited these districts with no trouble at all:

> How often [...] have I been forced to swallow, in police-reports, the intolerable stereotyped pill of nonsense, how that the police-constable informed the worthy magistrate how that the associates of the prisoner did [...] dwell in a street or court which no man dared go down.[18]

Much of the middle-class's belief in these no-go areas came from incomprehension, owing to increasing separation of the classes, and I need to make a diversion here to describe what was happening to London as Dickens was writing.

At the beginning of the century, there were a dozen or so large slum districts: in the centre of town, St Giles ran south from Tottenham Court Road and Bloomsbury, with Soho on its western edge, down to Seven Dials

---

[15] [Donald Shaw], *London in the Sixties (With a Few Digressions) 'by One of the Old Brigade'* (London: Everett and Co., 1908), pp. 92-94. These memoirs I have approached with more than usual caution. There is little that can be verifiably checked in them, but when there is, it does tend to be misremembered. Shaw writes of Valentine Baker, who was discharged from the army after a scandal; he joined the Ottoman army, before becoming head of the Egyptian police. Shaw claimed to have seen him in Egypt in 1894 and, seemingly unaware of his post-British career, described his friend as 'a broken man', as well he might have been, for when Shaw ostensibly saw him Baker had been dead for seven years. Given this, I have relied on Shaw not for facts, but simply for how people remembered, or wanted to remember, things.

[16] William Hepworth Dixon, *The London Prisons* (London: Jackson and Walford, 1850), p. 227.

[17] Thomas Adolphus Trollope, *What I Remember* (London: Richard Bentley, 1887), p. 11.

[18] [Charles Dickens], 'New Uncommercial Samples [Uncommercial Traveller xxxiv]: On an Amateur Beat', *All the Year Round*, N.S. Vol. 1, No. 13 (27 February 1869), 300-03 (p. 300).

on the east; St Martin-in-the-Fields ran westwards from the church to Swallow Street, off Piccadilly; and the Devil's Acre, around Tothill Fields, and Old and New Pye Streets, clustered near Parliament. Heading east, there was Clare market, from High Holborn to the Strand, more or less where the London School of Economics is now; Saffron Hill and Field Lane were in Clerkenwell, running along the side of the Fleet ditch; Smithfield held more tenements and back-courts; as did the area around Golden Lane and Whitecross Street. Further east still, around Shoreditch, Old Nichol was a slum district, as were increasing areas of Bethnal Green, Whitechapel and Spitalfields. South of the river, Old Mint was in Bermondsey, as was Jacob's Island, a swampy area where the River Neckinger met the Thames. Several of these districts were used in *Oliver Twist* (1837-39): Fagin's 'ken' is 'in the filthiest part of Little Saffron-Hill' and his second hideout is 'in the neighbourhood of Whitechapel', while Sikes lives in Bethnal Green, possibly in Old Nichol Street, and his last hideout is Jacob's Island.[19]

But the situation altered—and worsened—throughout the first half of the century. Two words were used regularly to describe the destruction of neighbourhoods where the poor predominated: 'improvements' and 'ventilation'. Both involved the building of wide new streets through a poor neighbourhood, to allow the prosperous access to better districts on either side, and, more specifically, to drive the poor out. In the 1840s *The Times'* leader-writer thought that, 'As we cut [...] roads through our forests, so it should be our policy to divide these thick jungles of crime and misery.' He could not, he said, understand why the poor chose to live in such squalid conditions and locations: it must be the 'attraction of misery to misery'.[20]

From the 1840s, the railways drove these clearances at an ever-faster pace. Property-owners and long-leaseholders were compensated if their buildings were destroyed, but those who rented day-to-day, or even week-to-week, received nothing. They simply had to shift for themselves, finding new lodgings which were likely to be more expensive, as nearby cheap rooms became scarcer. In 1846 a Parliamentary Select Committee heard that rents increased by 25 per cent in many of the districts surrounding improvement schemes.[21] Behind the new Farringdon Street station a resident said 'a thousand houses have been pulled down for the railway within half a mile'

---

[19] Dickens, *Oliver Twist*, pp. 116, 153.
[20] *The Times*, 2 March 1861, p. 8.
[21] 'House of Commons Select Committee, Royal Commission on Metropolis Railway Termini' (1846), cited in John R. Kellett, *The Impact of Railways on Victorian Cities* (London: Routledge and Kegan Paul, 1969), p. 36.

and those residents had all moved into his street 'because there's nowhere else'.[22] In 1841, in one street near the Pye Street slum, 655 people lived in 27 houses; six years later, after Victoria Street had been built, 1,095 people occupied the same 27 houses.[23] And the pattern was repeated. By 1851, Hampstead had 5.3 people per acre, Kensington had 16.2, Westminster had 71.5 and the Strand had 255.5.[24] 'What', worried *Household Words*, 'must be the results of these London improvements, when the roofs of a hundred wretched people are pulled down to make room for perhaps ten who are more prosperous'?[25] '[W]e make our New Oxford Streets, and our other new streets', Dickens had earlier written, 'never heeding, never asking, where the wretches whom we clear out crowd'.[26] And of course the fictional representation of all of this is the crossing-sweeper Jo, in *Bleak House* (1852-53), who won't move on, because, as he says, there is nowhere for him to move on to.[27]

The words 'rents' or 'courts' were enough to identify a slum in nineteenth-century London, meaning as it did housing built behind other buildings, using the passageway that had originally been designed to give access to stabling, 'a covered alley, not wider than an ordinary doorway', or even half that, compelling visitors 'to walk in sideways'.[28] Frying-Pan Alley, one of Field Lane's nearly three dozen courts, had an entrance that measured two feet, six inches across—not wide enough to get a coffin through, said the scandalised reporter.[29] Twenty feet long, the court contained twenty houses. Around these dead-end courtyards houses were built against three walls, with windows on just one side. Sometimes these courts had more buildings thrown up behind them, with, therefore, no windows at all. Houses

---

[22] James Greenwood, *The Wilds of London* (London: Chatto and Windus, 1874), p. 72.
[23] Cited in Roy Porter, *London: A Social History* (Harmondsworth: Hamish Hamilton, 1994), p. 268.
[24] Henry Mayhew and John Binny, *The Criminal Prisons of London and Scenes of Prison Life* (London: Charles Griffin, [1862]), p. 15.
[25] [Henry Morley], 'Life and Death in Saint Giles's', *Household Words*, Vol. XVIII, No. 451 (13 November 1858), 524-28 (p. 526).
[26] [Charles Dickens], 'On Duty with Inspector Field', *Household Words*, Vol. III, No. 64 (14 June 1851) 265-70 (p. 263).
[27] Charles Dickens, *Bleak House* [1852-53], ed. by Norman Page (Harmondsworth: Penguin, 1985), p. 275.
[28] Thomas Archer, *The Pauper, The Thief, and the Convict; Sketches of Some of their Homes, Haunts, and Habits* (London: Groombridge and Sons, 1865), p. 11.
[29] George Godwin, *London Shadows: A Glance at the 'Homes' of the Thousands* (London: George Routledge, 1854), p. 13.

with windows that received some ambient light after dark were a luxury. In *Bleak House*, when Charley locks her siblings in their room while she is at work, she notes with pride, 'When it comes on dark, the lamps are lighted down in the court, and they show up here quite bright—almost quite bright'.[30] 'Almost quite bright' made their room not a slum at all, but ordinary working-people's lodgings.

Charley was simply living in a fictionalised version of Dickens's 1830s St Giles sketch, where a shopkeeper's family lived in the shop and the back parlour, with an Irish labourer and his family in the back kitchen and a 'jobbing man—carpet-beater and so forth' and his family in the front kitchen. 'In the front one-pair' lived another family, and, in the back one-pair 'a young 'oman as takes in tambour-work, and dresses quite genteel'; another family occupied the front attic, and 'a shabby-genteel man' in the back attic.[31] They were not, by any means, the type of people that most writers, and most readers, thought of when they heard the word 'slums': the un-nuanced idea of a seething population consisting entirely of layabouts, drunkards and thieves. A look at a small slum in Kensington at mid-century affirms what Dickens found. In Jennings' Buildings, made up of eighty-three two-storey late-eighteenth-century houses built around five small courts off Kensington High Street, 1,000 residents lived with no running water, no drains and forty-nine privies between them. Yet many were in long-term employment and the courts supported social clubs, pubs and a savings club, while the residents resorted to the magistrates to bring cases against neighbours—that is, they saw themselves not as the middle class saw them, as an unruly and potentially dangerous underclass, but as part of the law-abiding majority.[32]

Lodging-houses, by contrast, had beds that were rented by the night, each room having several beds occupied by strangers. In *The Pickwick Papers* (1836-37), Sam Weller told of a 'twopenny rope' in some lodging-houses: the beds were made of coarse sacking, stretched across ropes, and 'At six o'clock every mornin'' they let's go the ropes at one end, and down falls the lodgers'.[33] While I have found no mention of this outside fiction (except in Orwell in the twentieth century), many lodging-houses were brutally basic in

---

[30] Dickens, *Bleak House*, p. 263.

[31] Dickens, 'Seven Dials', pp. 94-95.

[32] Jennifer Davis, 'Jennings' Buildings and the Royal Borough: The Construction of the Underclass in Mid-Victorian England', in *Metropolis London: Histories and Representations since 1800*, ed. by David Feldman and Gareth Stedman-Jones (London: Routledge, 1989), pp. 11-39 (pp. 20-21).

[33] Dickens, *Pickwick Papers*, pp. 212-13.

their amenities and desperately overcrowded. In *Household Words* in 1851 Dickens described a St Giles lodging-house, where, as the door opens, the visitor is 'stricken back by the pestilent breath that issues from within': 'Ten, twenty, thirty—who can count them! Men, women, children, for the most part naked, heaped upon the floor like maggots in a cheese!'[34]

In many cases lodging-houses were small terraced houses, letting out beds in a few rooms. In the 1840s, one lodging-house had a shop in its front room, a parlour behind, which the lodgers used as a communal kitchen, and two rooms with two beds at sixpence each, for married couples, and two rooms for single people, housing altogether twenty-four lodgers (plus children, uncounted, on the floors). Another small house had six rooms, for men only: two rooms with six double beds, sleeping three each, at two-pence per person, and four rooms sleeping ten each, at three-pence.[35] As late as the 1870s, after legislation had been passed regulating the number of people per room, Flower and Dean Street in the East End had thirty-one lodging-houses occupied by 902 lodgers, or thirty people per house.[36]

Given this type of density of occupation, one of the biggest problems was sanitation, which Dickens mentions only sideways. Oliver Twist washes himself 'and made everything tidy by emptying the basin out of the window', as directed by Fagin.[37] This no doubt raised a smile in middle-class readers, but really what else was Fagin to do in his Clerkenwell slum? Few houses had any drainage, water supplies ranged from scarce to non-existent and there were few privies. Sometimes landlords let an elderly or infirm person have a bed rent-free in return for washing down the privy daily. In one court, when the landlord did not, the residents arranged for the most impoverished to take on the task and as payment supplied her with broken bits of leftover coal.[38]

In 1849 a letter was published in *The Times*, from fifty-four residents of a court in St Giles, begging:

> We are Sur, as it may be, livin in a Willderniss, so far as the rest of London knows anything of us, or as the rich and great people care about. We live in muck and filthe. We aint got no priviz, no dust

---

[34] [Dickens], 'On Duty with Inspector Field', pp. 266-67.

[35] Thomas Beames, *The Rookeries of London: Past, Present, and Prospective* (London: Thomas Bosworth, 1850), p. 79.

[36] Jerry White, *London in the Nineteenth Century: 'A Human Awful Wonder of God'* (London: Jonathan Cape, 2007), pp. 324, 236.

[37] Dickens, *Oliver Twist*, p. 69.

[38] Greenwood, p. 75.

bins, no drains, no water-splies, and no drain or suer in the hole place [...]. We all of us suffur [...] and if the Colera comes Lord help us.

Up to sixty people lived in a single cellar, they said, ending, heartrendingly, 'make these landlords of our houses [...] make our houses decent for Christions to live in [...]. Preaye Sir com and see us, for we are living like piggs, and it aint faire we shoulde be so ill treted'.[39]

The Times did as the writers suggested, and visited, seeing in one room a child dressed only in a sack, eaten up with fever, and lying next to a woman with cholera. 'A strange boy' was also sleeping in the room; no one knew where he had come from, or what his name was. 'He had had nothing to eat for two days except a crust of bread given him by a woman who pitied him, though she could ill-spare the morsel.'[40] It is hard to imagine that Dickens, with his confirmed interest in slums and living conditions, did not see this *Times* article, and *Bleak House*, with its picture of the slum of Tom-all-Alone's, and the fever-wracked Jo helped by the brick-makers' wives who can ill spare him food, springs obviously to mind.

Three years later, another Jo appeared, as if one even needed to look for them. In 1852 at a Ragged School dormitory Dickens recorded seeing an elderly printer, alcoholic and starving, and, next to him, 'an orphan boy with burning cheeks and great gaunt eager eyes, who was in pressing peril of death too'.[41] Both were taken to the workhouse to die. For Dickens, there was no difference between fiction and non-fiction. As he wrote the following year: 'Dead, your Majesty. Dead, my lords and gentlemen [...]. Dead, men and women, born with heavenly compassion in your hearts. And dying thus around us every day.'[42]

---

[39] *The Times*, 5 July 1849, p. 5 (all spelling as in the original). One contemporary historian has suggested that the publication of this letter was arranged—and possibly part-written, or at least elaborated—by Charles Cochrane, a sanitary-health agitator. See also James Winter, *London's Teeming Streets, 1830-1914* (London: Routledge, 1993), pp. 130-31.

[40] *The Times*, 9 July 1849, p. 3.

[41] [Charles Dickens], 'A Sleep to Startle Us', *Household Words*, Vol. IV, No. 103 (13 March 1852), 577-80 (pp. 579-80).

[42] Dickens, *Bleak House*, p. 705.

Household Words and the Crimean War: Journalism, Fiction and Forms of Recuperation in Wartime

Holly Furneaux

THIS paper comes out of a broader project on Victorian military masculinity. In that project I ask why a particularly gentle soldier is the hero of so many Crimean War narratives and why the cultural response to this famously mismanaged war should feature an unexpected figure, the military man of feeling.

In this context I have been particularly fascinated by Dickens's improbably named Richard Doubledick, the hero of Dickens's contribution to the 1854 Christmas number of *Household Words*, 'Seven Poor Travellers'. Doubledick, a disgraced recruit to the ranks, features in a tale of soldierly rehabilitation, told through the story of his friendship with an exemplary officer, Taunton. Conceived and written in the months from October 1854, in which dire reports of the condition of the British troops in the Crimea emerged, the tale responds directly to this crisis with a Napoleonic Wars narrative. Dickens rewrites class and national antagonism through a powerful celebration of the transformative nature of male friendship. Here I will look at this neglected tale within the context of a broader journalistic response to the Crimean War, particularly within *Household Words*. I will consider the way in which this journal uses a politicised presentation of gender, specifically a range of representations of appropriate soldierly masculinities, to mobilise its critique of the army system, and the administration more widely.

'Seven Poor Travellers' was multi-authored in a style that had become familiar to readers in the three previous years since the inauguration of *Household Words*. This collaboration brought together short tales by Dickens, George Augustus Sala, Adelaide Anne Procter, Wilkie Collins and Eliza Lynn Linton, under a loose framing device of the narratives told by those seeking refuge in an Almshouse on Christmas Eve. Dickens's traveller, having supplied the others with a festive meal, begins the storytelling with an account of his relative Private Richard Doubledick. Doubledick has enlisted, in a familiar narrative of army recruitment, in desperation after a mysterious disgrace, which has prevented him from marrying his beloved fiancé, and lives as a soldier 'with a determination to be shot':

> There was not a more dissipated and reckless soldier in Chatham barracks, in the year 1799, than Private Richard Doubledick. He associated with the dregs of every regiment, he was as seldom sober as he could be, and was constantly under punishment.[1]

Doubledick, with an alacrity suitable to this condensed form of narrative, is swiftly redeemed by his encounter with his commanding officer, Captain Taunton. Taunton has a firm belief that a military career can offer a democratic form of moral redemption, by offering each soldier, even of the lowest rank, ready opportunities to regain their own self respect, and earn that of their regiment. Through the powerfully charismatic figure of Taunton, Dickens deftly configures war as an opportunity for personal and social reformation. Doubledick's moral restoration is effected through his reaction to his Captain, and their swiftly developing friendship:

> Now the captain of Richard Doubledick's company was a young gentleman not above five years his senior, whose eyes had an expression in them which affected Private Richard Doubledick in a very remarkable way. They were bright, handsome, dark eyes [...] the only eyes now left in his narrowed world that Private Richard Doubledick could not stand (p. 577).

F. A. Fraser chose to illustrate the reforming power of Taunton's gaze in the figure he produced for the 1871 collected edition of the Christmas numbers, as the single illustration for 'Seven Poor Travellers'. Fraser's illustration depicts both Captain and Private as men of fine feeling, taking the moment at which Doubledick begins to weep and physically documenting, in Taunton's upraised hand, the reaching out that redeems him. Fraser captures Dickens's emphasis on the two as men of feeling, both in tactile and emotional terms; their capacity for deep emotion and for forms of restorative touch is registered through a narrative of intense friendship. With a 'bursting heart' Richard asks Taunton to be the witness of his reformation, and Taunton agrees, in appropriately visual terms, to be a

---

[1] [Charles Dickens], 'The Seven Poor Travellers: The First', *Household Words*, Vol. X, Extra Christmas Number (25 December 1854), 573-82 (p. 577). All subsequent references appear within the text.

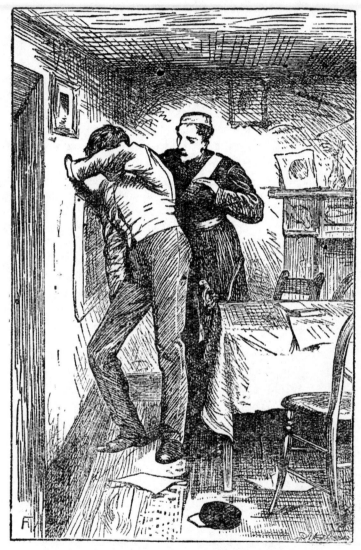

THE SEVEN POOR TRAVELLERS.

F. A. Fraser (1871)

'watchful and a faithful one': 'I have heard from Private Doubledick's own lips, that he dropped down upon his knee, kissed that officer's hand, arose and went out of the light of the dark, bright, eyes, an altered man' (p. 578). Doubledick ruminates variously on the transformative effect of the man who 'saved me from ruin, made me a human creature, won me from infamy and shame. O God forever bless him!' (p. 579).

The traveller's tale closest in content to Dickens's in this Christmas number is supplied by Adelaide Anne Procter, who also wrote a number of Crimean War poems in her regular contributions to the journal. Procter closes the number with a poem about a young woman who learns that her home town is going to be attacked and rides through the night and the Rhine to save it.[2] Like Dickens's story Procter's poem considers the thorny question of allegiance in wartime. Procter's 'Tyrol maid' instinctively aligns herself with her Austrian birth-land when she discovers the plan of attack in the Swiss valley where she has lived and worked 'More peaceful year by year' (p. 606). Her enjoyment of this life, however, presents no dilemma: 'What were the friends beside her? / Only her country's foes!' (p. 607). Dickens's tale, as we will see, has to strain somewhat harder to endorse a fledgling Anglo-French alliance as a natural, instinctive loyalty. Both contributions, too, are concerned with the appropriate gendering of military heroism and the personal characteristics of a hero. The Bregenz maid adopts a simpler model of sacrificial duty to that worked out through Doubledick and Taunton:

> Before her eyes one vision,
> And in her heart one cry,
> That said, 'Go forth, save Bregenz,
> And then, if need be, die!' (p. 607).

The number, then, is bounded by some surprising war heroes, from eminently feeling men to a patriotic cowgirl.

Dickens's tale follows the friendship of Doubledick and Taunton through the military campaigns of thirteen years, and Dickens is precise in both his recording of the longevity of this bond and in his dating of their encounters with the French throughout the sporadically fought Napoleonic Wars. In India in 1801, Doubledick, who has been promoted to Sergeant, is

---

[2] [Adelaide Anne Procter], 'The Seven Poor Travellers: The Seventh', *Household Words*, Vol. X, Extra Christmas Number (25 December 1854), 606-07. All subsequent references appear within the text.

invariably 'close to' Taunton, 'ever at his side, firm as a rock, true as the sun' (p. 578). In an 1805 campaign against the French in India, Doubledick's heroism in saving the regimental colours and 'rescu[ing] his wounded Captain who was down' is rewarded by another promotion. Dickens is insistent on cataloguing Doubledick's promotions, at one point interrupting the narrative to list the ranks through which he has progressed: 'Private, Corporal, Sergeant, Sergeant Major, Ensign, [...] Lieutenant' (p. 579). By the end of the story Doubledick has become a Major.

Dickens's emphasis on army promotion would have made immediate sense to regular readers of *Household Words* who would have read Eustace Grenville Murray's article 'Army Interpreters' two weeks earlier in the 16 December issue. Murray provided several other articles for the journal, specifically on the Crimea, under his *nom de plume* 'The Roving Englishman'. His work provided part of *Household Words'* substantial coverage of aspects of the conflict; the *Dickens Journals Online* index lists 88 articles for the journal in total under the heading 'Crimean War'. These articles tend to focus, as Sabine Clemm has summarised in her work on Dickens's journalism and ideas of nationhood, on the cultures and people of the Crimea and criticism of the British government for its handling of military matters.[3] Though overt comment on international politics was not the journal's usual mode, Grace Moore has shown how *Household Words* demonstrated clear support for the war in its early stages through a number of articles that explored Turkish civilisation, refuting myths of Eastern barbarism, and some material inciting 'animosity against the Czar'.[4] Eliza Lynn's (later Lynn Linton) 'The True Story of the Nuns at Minsk', which was published on 13 May 1854, less than two months after Britain and France had formally joined with the Ottoman Empire in the war against Russia, explicitly seeks to 'convert' those in Britain still partisan to the Czar.[5] Once, though, the appalling conditions endured by the British Army in the Crimea became apparent, the journal's coverage focused on the British government's mismanagement of the campaign, critiquing hierarchies and attitudes in the Cabinet and the army.

Murray's 'Army Interpreters' opens with a scorching satirical account of a British blunder that results in the taking prisoner of Turkish allies in the

---

[3] Sabine Clemm, *Dickens, Journalism and Nationhood: Mapping the World in Household Words* (London and New York: Routledge, 2009), p. 103.

[4] Grace Moore, *Dickens and Empire: Discourses of Class, Race and Colonialism in the Works of Charles Dickens* (Aldershot: Ashgate, 2004), p. 77.

[5] [Eliza Lynn], 'The True Story of the Nuns at Minsk', *Household Words*, Vol. IX, No. 216 (13 May 1854), 290-95 (p. 290).

mistake that they are Russian enemies. The interpreter is unable to understand them, as 'these stupid people', the report sarcastically comments, 'could not speak English'.[6] More darkly presented is the treatment of these prisoners:

> The affair occasioned a good deal of sparkling conversation, and gave birth to a joke of Cornet Lord Martingale's, which has quite made his reputation as a wit in the aristocratic regiment to which he belongs. 'We always shut up turkeys towards Christmas,' said his lordship; 'it makes them fatter for killing.' The point of the young peer's jest, however, was blunted by the haggard appearance of the prisoners, who having had nothing but salt pork served to them, had supported themselves merely on the bread which was given with it, according to a regulation which the interpreter had a dim idea was somehow or other connected with their religious tenets.

This example of witless aristocratic inhumanity is developed in a critique of the promotion system in public offices: 'Our public servants [...] are born, not made'. The piece closes with a warning to new entrants to Her Majesty's service hoping to advance through study and hard work:

> Let him rather seek to enter the great British cousinocracy by marriage if he really wish to get on. Let him resolutely and perseveringly address himself to gaining the affections of some good old Whig family, and all these things will be given to him.[7]

In this context the political impetus behind Doubledick's striking, and historically highly unlikely, progress from Private to Major is clear. Characteristically, the connections between tales in the Christmas number itself were less transparent. As well as Procter's closing poem, which does examine some similar concerns, contents include Sala's disturbingly anti-Semitic portrayal of a magical diamond fair, Collins's detective story, and a grisly tale of domestic abuse and murder by Lynn. Dickens's part of the number, however, speaks in a clear dialogue with material in concurrent numbers of *Household Words*. Readers were encouraged to make a connection between Grenville Murray's 'Army Interpreters' and 'Seven Poor Travellers', by the immediate continuation from Murray's article—the final in its issue—

---

[6] [Eustace Clare Grenville Murray], 'Army Interpreters', *Household Words*, Vol. X, No. 247 (16 December 1854), 431-32 (p. 431).
[7] [Murray], 'Army Interpreters', p. 432.

into an advertisement for the special Christmas number.[8]

More explicitly, both Dickens's tale and Murray's article participate in the wider campaign for administrative reform. Galvanised by Crimean mismanagement, the Administrative Reform Association was established four months after the publication of this Christmas number. Its resolutions were reported in Dickens's sister publication to *Household Words*, *The Household Narrative of Current Events*, a monthly news digest:

1. 'That the disasters to which the country has been subjected in the conduct of the present war are attributable to the Inefficient and practically irresponsible management of the various departments of the state, and urgently demand a thorough change in the administrative system.'

2. 'That the true remedy for the system of maladministration which has caused so lamentable a sacrifice of labour, money, and human life, is to be sought in the introduction of enlarged experience and practical ability into the service of the state; that the exclusion from office of those who possess in a high degree the practical qualities necessary for the direction of affairs in a great commercial country is a reflection upon its intelligence and a betrayal of its interests; that while we disclaim every desire of excluding the aristocratic classes from participation in the councils of the crown, we feel it our duty to protest against the pretensions of any section of the community to monopolise the functions of administration.'[9]

While the war was the immediate catalyst for the foundation of the Association, its aims were wider—the reduction of jobbism in the military and all areas of government, so that roles were allocated according to ability rather than social rank. The largely middle-class membership of the Association promoted the efficiency of industry as more successful than

---

[8] The advert which follows that for 'Seven Poor Travellers' is for the continuing serialisation of Elizabeth Gaskell's *North and South* (1854-55). Stefanie Markovits has made a convincing case that Gaskell's novel, published from 2 September 1854 to 27 January 1855, can best be understood within the context of the journal's Crimean War coverage. Markovits gives particular attention to the relationship between Gaskell's novel and Adelaide Anne Procter's numerous Crimean War poems, which explore the attractions of pacifism and ideas of just war [*The Crimean War in the British Imagination* (Cambridge: Cambridge University Press, 2009), pp. 92-93].

[9] [Anon.], 'Narrative of Parliament and Politics', *The Household Narrative of Current Events*, Vol. VI, No. 5 (May 1855), 97-110 (p. 110).

leadership based on aristocratic hierarchy and ability to pay. While the association was short-lived, some of its aspirations were later realised in the 1870s Cardwell reforms, which abolished the purchase of commissions.

In his speech at the opening meeting of the Association, Dickens explicitly linked William Howard Russell's Crimean dispatches for *The Times* to the widespread awareness of the campaign as a national disaster:

> When the TIMES newspaper proved its then almost incredible case, in reference to the ghastly absurdity of that vast labyrinth of misplaced men and misdirected things, which had made England unable to find on the face of the earth, an enemy one twentieth part so potent to effect the misery and ruin of her noble defenders as she has been herself, I believe that the gloomy silence into which the country fell was by far the darkest aspect in which a great people had been exhibited for many years.[10]

Dickens, as Stephanie Markovits notes, admired Russell, whose reports clearly influenced Dickens's most famous response to Crimean mismanagement in his depictions of circumlocution in *Little Dorrit* (1855-57). Dickens encouraged Russell to undertake a lecture tour on his return from the Crimea and later wrote to him: 'I have always followed you closely, and have always found new occasions to express my sense of what England owes you for your manly out-speaking and your brilliant description'.[11] Though it doesn't have the profile of *Little Dorrit*, Dickens's 1854 Christmas tale is clearly concerned with reform on a national institutional level, as well as a personal one. Despite the historical unlikelihood of a cross-class friendship between Captain and Private, Dickens endorses a command model of moral influence and cross-rank sympathy through the exemplary figure of Taunton. Through Doubledick's promotion from common soldier to officer, Dickens is also determined to figure the army as a site of social aspiration, with opportunities for betterment through individual hard work and heroism, insisting that Ensign Richard Doubledick had 'risen through the ranks' (p. 578).

The genre of the Christmas number is a significant one, given Dickens's established reputation for these seasonal redemptive narratives. The 1854 number cites Dickens's best-known Christmas book of a decade earlier, *A Christmas Carol* (1843). The traveller who narrates the tale of Taunton and

---

[10] 'Administrative Reform Association, 27 June, 1855', *The Speeches of Charles Dickens*, ed. by K. J. Fielding (Oxford: Clarendon Press, 1960), 197-208 (p. 201).
[11] Markovits, p. 36.

Doubledick reminds us that 'Christmas comes but once a year—which is unhappily too true, for when it begins to stay with us the whole year round, we shall make this earth a very different place', echoing the lesson that Scrooge has learnt: 'I will honour Christmas in my heart and try to keep it all the year'.[12] In 1854 the opportunity for moral redemption is presented not by supernatural experiences, but by a reformed, meritocratic army system. The number, then, constitutes a sentimental, fictional deployment of the arguments made in broader journalism in Dickens's periodicals, and beyond, at this time which called for administrative reform. By placing 'Seven Poor Travellers' in this context, the politics of seasonal sentiment are laid bare. The political mobilisation of 'gentle' Christmas feeling is more readily associated with Dickens's Christmas books of a decade earlier, such as the attack on utilitarian thought in *The Chimes* (1844). Sally Ledger has written about the particular resonance in the 'Hungry Forties' of Dickens's emphasis on the 'regenerating power of human fellowship'.[13] In this Crimean Christmas number we see a similar focus on forms of regeneration—capable of crossing class and national boundaries—via intimate fellowship.

'Seven Poor Travellers' is engaged in a wider remaking of national attitudes, worked out through Doubledick's reaction to the suitably heroic French Officer, a 'courageous, handsome, gallant officer of five and thirty' (p. 578), who gives the command for the fire in which Taunton is killed. Doubledick becomes 'a lone, bereaved man' (p. 579), living only to deliver a packet of Taunton's hair to his mother and to avenge his friend's death through an encounter with this Frenchman. While Doubledick receives some comfort in forming a posthumous brotherhood to Taunton, whose mother feels that 'in her bereavement' in Doubledick 'she had found a son' (p. 579), vengeance threatens to become Doubledick's predominant response to his loss: 'A new legend now began to circulate among our troops; and it was, that when he and the French officer came face to face once more, there would be weeping in France' (p. 579).

This promised revenge plot is a conventional accompanying narrative to the typical plot of wartime camaraderie. Dickens disrupts these conventions in his unusually detailed vocalising of the emotional connection between these men, and then completely breaks with them in re-routing the revenge plot into a second plot of to-death-and-beyond friendship. Having returned

---

[12] Melisa Klimaszewski draws out this parallel in her edition of *The Seven Poor Travellers* (London: Hesperus, 2010), p. viii.

[13] Sally Ledger, 'Christmas', in *Charles Dickens in Context*, ed. by Sally Ledger and Holly Furneaux (Cambridge: Cambridge University Press, 2011), pp. 178-93 (p. 179).

to his regiment and suffered a serious head injury, Doubledick is conveyed to a hospital in Brussels, where, after some time, he regains consciousness: 'It was so tranquil and so lovely, that he thought he had passed into another world. And he said in a faint voice, "Taunton are you near me?"' (p. 580).

This death-longing reverie of physical proximity to the lost beloved is interrupted by a more conventional nursing romance plot of a type Florence Nightingale abhorred, as Doubledick's former fiancé, Mary, finds and heals him.[14] This redirection of Doubledick's emotional emphasis is variously unconvincing—he fails to remember that in his fever, 'at the point of death', he married Mary that he might call her 'Wife before he died' (p. 581).[15]

Mary's arrival only temporarily interrupts the main plotline by which Doubledick will continue to develop his relationship with Taunton through an encounter with the French officer who gave the fatal command. Through a lucky coincidence Mrs Taunton has become the guest of the French officer's family, and Doubledick, joining her, finds that his host is his cherished enemy. Doubledick's perplexity about how to react allows Dickens space to remake Anglo-French relations in a manner befitting the new alliance of these nations in the Crimean War. The allegiance between the British and the French was so novel that British officers and men made repeated slips of the tongue in which the French were conflated with the enemy. Famously Lord Raglan, who commanded the campaign and had served on the Duke of Wellington's Staff during the Peninsular War of 1808-14 and lost an arm at Waterloo, would absent-mindedly refer to the French,

---

[14] In her 1859 *Notes on Nursing*, Nightingale attacks the proliferation of nurse romance plots in Crimean narratives: 'Popular novelists of recent days have invented ladies disappointed in love or fresh out of the drawing-room turning into the war hospitals to find their wounded lovers, and when found, forthwith abandoning their sick-ward for their lover, as might be expected. Yet in the estimation of the authors, these ladies were none the worse for that, but on the contrary were heroines of nursing' [*Notes on Nursing: What It is and What It is Not* (London: Duckworth, 1970), p. 75].

[15] The scene where Mary reminds Doubledick that she shares his name anticipates Eugene Wrayburn's similarly muted enthusiasm for what he believes will be a final act, again a reparative one which will correct past wrongs, of deathbed marriage to Lizzie in *Our Mutual Friend* (1864-65). The structures of a reluctant (or in Doubledick's case, apparently unconscious) marriage in contrast to an emotional enthusiasm for a beloved male friend are also paralleled. I've discussed Eugene's subdued capitulation to marriage and his explicit love for his boyhood friend Mortimer Lightwood in *Queer Dickens: Erotics, Families, Masculinities* (Oxford: Oxford University Press, 2009), pp. 101-02.

rather than the Russians, as the current enemy.[16] This kind of widespread confusion is cited in another *Household Words* piece a couple of weeks after 'Seven Poor Travellers': 'The Rampshire Militia'. This piece presents a fictional account of the mustering of a volunteer force, including farm workers, such as Ned Barry: 'Ned Barry, for one, did not know who the enemy were, though he felt sure there was one coming—Rooshan or French, or somebody—to take Westerleigh, and burn down our house'.[17]

In 'Seven Poor Travellers' Dickens reflects on the historical enmity between the countries as the narrator laments that in the aftermath of the Napoleonic conflicts, 'unhappily many deplorable duels had been fought between English and French officers, arising out of the recent wars' (p. 582). On encountering the French officer though, Doubledick's desire for vengeance immediately evaporates and he thanks the spirit of his departed friend for 'these better thoughts [...] rising in [his] mind' and for showing him 'the blessings of the altered time': 'It is from thee the whisper comes that this man did his duty as thou didst—and as I did, through thy guidance, which has wholly saved me, here on earth—and that he did no more' (p. 582).

In this final moment of epiphany, Doubledick recognises that rather than the further bloodshed of a vengeful duel, sincere friendship between the former enemies, and unqualified forgiveness, is the most fitting reaction to Taunton's death. In a highly idealised ending Dickens offers the vision of a friendship between these former adversaries that continues beyond death through future generations, who, like Doubledick and Taunton, recognise their bond through unbreakable battlefield allegiance:

> The time has since come when the son of Major Richard Doubledick, and the son of that French officer, friends as their fathers were before them, fought side by side in one cause: with their respective nations, like long-divided brothers whom the better times have brought together, fast united (p. 582).

This fraternal image of unity clearly had a political dimension in celebrating the Anglo-French military alliance and it is also informed by Dickens's own enthusiasm for French culture. As John Drew has shown, Dickens was particularly sensitive about the representation of the French during the Crimean War period. In October 1854 he held over G. A. Sala's comic article

---

[16] Alastair Massie, *The National Army Museum Book of the Crimean War: The Untold Stories* (London: Sidgwick and Jackson, 2005), p. 11.

[17] [Harriet Martineau and ?James Payn], 'The Rampshire Militia', *Household Words*, Vol. X, No. 251 (13 January 1855), 505-11 (p. 505).

on French military dandyism, explaining to Wills that it came 'painfully upon the Battle Field accounts in *The Times* [...]. I would rather say nothing about France unless I had plenty to say about its gallantry and spirit'.[18] In this explanation we can see how W. H. Russell's dispatches for *The Times* helped to shape *Household Words*, informing the journal's critiques of mismanagement *and* Dickens's editorial decisions about appropriate content. He preferred firmly Francophile material, publishing 'Our French Watering Place', a glowing account of Boulogne and the chivalry of her citizens, proud to billet troops free of charge, as the lead article of the 4 November issue, the day before the Battle of Inkerman. The conclusion of 'Our French Watering Place' anticipates that of 'Seven Poor Travellers', with a celebration of Anglo-French unity, praising the 'long and constant fusion of the two great nations there', which 'has taught each to like the other, and to learn from the other, and to rise superior to the absurd prejudices that have lingered among the weak and ignorant in both countries equally'.[19]

In its fairly heavy-handed endorsement of the Anglo-French alliance and calls for a meritocratic army, 'Seven Poor Travellers' uses the figure of the gentle military man in the service of reformist social journalism. Taunton and Doubledick are part of a wider literary cast of gentle military men who come to particular prominence in the Crimean War. Dickens's pre-Crimea novel, *Bleak House* (1852-53) features a gentle soldier, Trooper George, who anticipates the more detailed account of Doubledick's army reformation: '[I] went away and 'listed, harum-scarum, making believe to think that I cared for nobody, no not I, and that nobody cared for me', describing himself as an 'idle dragooning chap who was an encumbrance and a discredit to himself, excepting under discipline'.[20] George, after his army career, is most notable for the physical and emotional care he offers to those suffering, across a social spectrum.[21] During 1854 *Bleak House* was published in translation in two Russia periodicals, *Sovremenik* (*The Contemporary*) and *Otechestvennye Zapinksi* (*Annals of the Fatherland*), giving those on the opposite side of the war an insight into Dickens's determinedly curative presentations

---

18 Quoted in John M. L. Drew, *Dickens the Journalist* (Houndmills: Palgrave Macmillan, 2003), p. 117.

19 [Charles Dickens], 'Our French Watering Place', *Household Words*, Vol. X, No. 241 (4 November 1854), 265-70 (p. 582).

20 Charles Dickens, *Bleak House* [1852-53] (London: Penguin, 1996), p. 845, 846.

21 I discuss Trooper George's nursing care and the transformation of his shooting gallery into a military hospital in Chapter Six of *Queer Dickens*.

of the military man.[22] Dickens later returns to the figure of a gentle soldier, and to the happy memories of living near Boulogne and watching the French troops prepare for the Crimean War, which he had recorded in 'Our French Watering Place', in the 1862 Christmas number of *All the Year Round*. Dickens's contribution to this number, 'His Boots', is set in a French fort town and features a French soldier who adopts a neglected child and provides her with exemplary care.[23]

While many of Dickens's first British readers might have seen a continuity between *Bleak House*'s Sergeant George and the gentle soldiers of 'Seven Poor Travellers', others might have recognised a connection with the hero of William Makepeace Thackeray's novel published serially throughout the Crimean War, *The Newcomes* (1853-55). Thackeray's Colonel Newcome is another exemplary military man of feeling, invariably described in terms of his almost excessive kindness to others and sacrifice of self. Thackeray's and Dickens's simultaneous emphasis on the military man of feeling would have been particularly apparent for American readers, who read *The Newcomes* in *Harper's New Monthly Magazine* (in Britain the serial appeared in twenty-four monthly stand-alone instalments). Dickens's part of 'Seven Poor Travellers' was reprinted in the February 1855 issue under a title which emphasised the redemptive Christmas message, 'The Redeemed Profligate'; this was placed immediately before the monthly instalment of Thackeray's novel.[24]

In conclusion I want to speculate a bit further on the effects—both enabling and problematic—of the popular figure of the gentle military man at a time of war. *Household Words* was welcome reading for some of those serving in the Crimea. Nathaniel Steevens, for example, of the Connaught Rangers, says in his Crimean campaign reminiscences for January 1855, 'during this month I fortunately picked up several numbers of *Household Words*'.[25] This is a particular relief to Steevens, who has commented repeatedly in earlier parts of the journal on the difficulty of getting any decent reading material. In May 1854, for example, he writes 'we greatly felt

---

[22] Veronica Shapovalov, 'They Came From *Bleak House*', *Dostoevsky Studies*, 9 (1988), 202-07 (p. 206). These translations were by V. Butszor and I. Biriler. Biriler's translation, Shapovalov records, was published as a separate book in 1855.

[23] [Charles Dickens], 'His Boots', *All the Year Round*, Vol. VIII, Extra Christmas Number (25 December 1862), 578-85.

[24] Charles Dickens, 'The Redeemed Profligate', *Harper's New Monthly Magazine*, Vol. X, No. 57 (February 1855), 371-77.

[25] Nathaniel Steevens, *The Crimean Campaign with 'The Connaught Rangers', 1854-1856* (London and Edinburgh: Griffith and Farran, 1878), p. 177.

the want of books to read; the few that could be purchased were trashy novels, and very dear'. He reiterates this in July 1854: 'We much felt the want of books to while away the many spare hours; and newspapers were most eagerly read and reread'.[26] This reference to the re-reading of newspapers suggests a considerable multiplier effect at work, so that the issues of *Household Words* he mentions were likely to have had considerable circulation. Improving supply routes to the Crimea, which Steevens also mentions in January 1855, make it just possible that one of the issues he was reading that month was the recent Christmas number. Though (sadly!) he doesn't pass comment on Doubledick and Taunton, he does at least give his impression of *Household Words*: 'I found this periodical to be very acceptable reading in leisure moments'.[27]

A cycle in which serving soldiers read such narratives of military men is represented by John Everett Millais's *Peace Concluded* (1856). Millais's painting depicts, in part, the competing forms of wartime reading as a returned Crimean officer reads the announcement of peace in *The Times*, having discarded a number of Thackeray's *The Newcomes* in its distinctive, yellow wrapper. Colonel Newcome and Dickens's emotionally and physically sensitive soldiers make for some surprising models of soldierly behaviour in a time of war, which demand a complication of our vision of military masculinity. On one level the celebration of the figure of the feeling soldier endorses an unexpected model of masculinity, in which sensitivity and restorative kindness is celebrated. I was initially drawn to Dickens's persistent portraits of gentle soldiers as examples of the complexity and emotional richness of Victorian representations of masculinity, even in the most militaristic of contexts. However, we can see how these military men of feeling are also deployed in the service of militarism. Like Dickens, Thackeray was a member of the Administrative Reform Association. The Colonel's caring behaviour, like that of the emotionally literate Taunton and

---

[26] Steevens, pp. 23, 62-63.

[27] Steevens, p. 177. Dickens's fiction was particularly popular reading for soldiers in this period. Dickens, alongside others including Jane Austen, Edward Bulwer-Lytton and Henry Fielding, was named on a list of authors receiving the 'highest degree of popularity' in J. H. Lefroy's 1859 *Report on the Regimental and Garrison Schools of the Army, and on Military Libraries and Reading Rooms* (London: Stationary Office), cited in Sharon Murphy, '"Quite Incapable of Appreciating Books Written for Educated Readers": The Mid-Nineteenth Century British Soldier', in *A Return to the Common Reader: Print Culture and the Novel, 1850-1900*, ed. by Beth Palmer and Adelene Buckland (Aldershot: Ashgate, 2011), pp. 121-32 (p. 126).

the reformed Doubledick, is suitable for a democratised army. Reading 'Seven Poor Travellers' within its journalistic context exposes the political mobilisation of these characters as appropriate figure-heads for a reformed army. Taunton, and the reformed Doubledick and Trooper George, can also work to promote the army as a more respectable career. More broadly, by bridging the gap between civilian and military values, these figures endorse a militarised society.

This is a conundrum that I am encountering throughout this research: representations of the gentle soldier very often work to make militarism more palatable. Dickens's expansive definition of a military masculinity, which can encompass deep feeling and tenderness, works not to critique a militarised society per se, but to critique the inefficiencies of the current system. Counter to the effect we might expect of a narrative in which soldiers weep, express the intensity of their friendship and mourn for one another, this narrative also campaigns for the greater efficiency of the war machine.

By way of a less disturbing conclusion I want to come back to the range of possible effects of Dickens's 'Seven Poor Travellers'. As we have seen through this example, the figure of the military man of feeling was put to various uses, public and private; these ranged from calls for army and administrative reform, to making camp and battlefield life more manageable for individual soldiers. While such narratives participated in a wider debate that culminated in the significant reforms to army hierarchy in the decade after Dickens's death, they might also, for some readers, have called into question the value of conflict. While in many ways 'Seven Poor Travellers' straightforwardly supports the Administrative Reform Association case for the more effective waging of war, Dickens's moving emphasis on the power of male bonds, capable of overcoming a long history of national antagonism and reworking a private desire for vengeance, allows for more complex responses. The abrupt reversal, which the tale dramatises, of the historic enmity with France into an unbreakable alliance, exposes the arbitrary nature of military allegiance, and might call into question the new hostilities of the Crimean war, while Doubledick's poignant mourning of his beloved friend killed in action shows, unequivocally, its costs.

Our Hour: Dickens's Shifting Authorial Personae

Paul Schlicke

DICKENS first shot to fame in the character of 'Boz', who presented himself to his readers in the editorial first person, as 'we'. Although his first eight sketches, dating from December 1833 when he was twenty-one years old, were published anonymously, and the twelve which appeared in *Bell's Life* in 1835-36 were attributed to 'Tibbs', all the selections published in the two series of *Sketches by Boz* by Macrone in 1836 were attributed to 'Boz', as were those in the collected edition published in 1839 by Chapman and Hall, which established the content and order in which the sketches have appeared ever since. In every case, 'Boz' was 'we'.[1]

Pickwick Papers (1836-37) was also narrated by an editorial 'we'. The 'Boz' of *Oliver Twist* (1837-39), however, was 'I'. The title page of the first volume edition of *Pickwick Papers* (November 1837) and that of the second issue of the first edition of *Oliver Twist*, 12 months later, both announced Charles Dickens as author, but it was as 'Boz' that Dickens edited *Bentley's Miscellany*; it was as 'Boz' that he was hailed during his first visit to America in 1842, and it was as 'Boz' that serialised parts of his novels were issued as late as the final double number of *Martin Chuzzlewit* (1843-44) in July 1844.[2]

---

[1] The 1839 Chapman and Hall edition of *Sketches by Boz* initially appeared in monthly serial parts between November 1837 and June 1839. Neither the part issues nor the title page printed in No. 20 identified 'Boz' as Dickens. For a full listing of original publication details for Dickens's early sketches see 'The First Publication of Dickens's Sketches in Serial and Volume Form', in *The Dent Uniform Edition of Dickens' Journalism*, ed. by Michael Slater and others, 4 vols (London: J. M. Dent, 1994-2000), Vol. I, pp. xxiii-xxvi.

[2] Robert Douglas-Fairhurst mistakenly claims that it was with the second issue of the first edition of *Oliver Twist* in November 1838 that Dickens 'start[ed] signing his work "Charles Dickens"' [*Becoming Dickens: The Invention of a Novelist* (Cambridge, MA: Belknap Press of Harvard University Press, 2011), p. 14]; in fact Dickens was

Sunday Under Three Heads (1836) was attributed to 'Timothy Sparks', and in *Master Humphrey's Clock* (1840-41) Dickens experimented unsuccessfully with the editorial persona of an old man. Sometime between 1845 and 1848 Dickens began, then abandoned, an autobiography, parts of which he incorporated in his first novel written in the first person, *David Copperfield* (1849-50). One further novel, *Great Expectations* (1860-61), has a first-person narrator, as do half of *Bleak House* (1852-53) and many shorter stories, sketches and articles. His journalism was published anonymously, with an editorial voice which varies between the singular 'I' and the editorial 'we'. Contributions to his journals, *Household Words* and *All the Year Round*, including his own pieces, were also unattributed, although both journals announced on every page opening that they were 'conducted by Charles Dickens'. 'The Uncommercial Traveller' presented himself in the first-person singular, as 'I'.[3]

In short, there is chameleon-like variety in the personae which Dickens adopted in his journalism and fiction throughout his career—to say nothing of the aliases under which he disguised himself as landlord to Ellen Ternan. In the present paper we—that is, I as its author and you as readers—will look at some of Dickens's narrative personae, and in particular at his choice between using 'we' and 'I' as narrators. At the end of the discussion I will speculate on possible cross-fertilisation between three works with which he was engaged around the same time, at the height of his powers: the serialisation of *David Copperfield*, the launch of *Household Words*, and the final, extensive revision of *Sketches by Boz*.[4]

Building on Walter Benjamin's discussion of Charles Baudelaire, Michael Hollington has described Dickens's characteristic perspective as that of a

---

identified by name in advertisements as early as July 1836 (in the *Athenaeum*), and on the title page of the first volume edition of *Pickwick* in November 1837.

[3] Dickens wrote thirty-six papers for *All the Year Round* as 'The Uncommercial Traveller', including sixteen papers that appeared from January to October 1860, a second series of twelve articles, which ran from May to October 1863, a stand-alone article entitled 'The Ruffian by The Uncommercial Traveller' (10 October 1868) and a third series of seven pieces under the heading of 'New Uncommercial Samples' which ran from December 1868 to June 1869. For full details of the original publication of the series see *Dickens' Journalism*, Vol. IV, pp. vii-xxxiii.

[4] *Sketches by Boz: Illustrative of Every-Day Life and Every-Day People*, Cheap Edition (London: Chapman and Hall, 1850).

flâneur, or stroller, a detached observer of city streets.[5] Martina Lauster has challenged this, insisting that the narrator of the *Sketches* is not the bohemian outsider of Baudelaire, but rather 'one of a countless number of ordinary city-dwellers who read the metropolitan surfaces'.[6] Certainly, 'Boz' is no cynical dandy, but an earnest apologist, who cares passionately about what he describes in his subtitle as 'every-day life and every-day people'. The Parish sketches, which originally appeared under the title 'The Parish', were re-designated 'Our Parish' when they were gathered at the head of the collected edition.[7] '*We* may smile at such people', 'Boz' comments, 'but they can never excite *our* anger'; their behaviour, he insists, is 'surely more tolerable than the precocious puppyism in the Quadrant, whiskered dandyism in Regent Street and Pall Mall, or gallantry in its dotage anywhere' [my italics].[8] He satirises affectations, but his attitude to squalor and drunkenness is pity and understanding rather than condemnation; he finds 'strange chords in the human heart', which despite 'depravity and wickedness' will 'vibrate at last'.[9] Tolerance, sympathy and understanding (and ridicule of pretensions) characterise the 'Boz' of the *Sketches*.

But, as Angus Easson has shown, 'Boz', the narrator, is far from a fully-rounded character. He is 'more than a pen name', but unlike Mr Spectator or Charles Lamb's Elia, he is 'not a consistently realised persona'. Rather, he is a perceiving eye, a responsive mind, and a creative imagination.[10] Moreover, his personality evolves as Dickens revised his texts for later editions. In their first appearance, in newspapers and periodicals, the sketches were laced with

---

[5] Michael Hollington, 'Dickens the Flâneur', *Dickensian*, 77 (1981), 71-87; 'Nickleby, Flanerie, Reverie: The View from Cheerybles', *Dickens Studies Annual*, 35 (2005), 21-43.

[6] Martina Lauster, *Sketches of the Nineteenth Century: European Journalism and its Physiologists, 1830-50* (Houndmills: Palgrave Macmillan, 2007), p. 9.

[7] The Parish sketches include 'The Beadle—The Parish Engine—The Schoolmaster', *Evening Chronicle*, 28 February 1835; 'The Curate—The Old Lady—The Half Pay Captain', *Evening Chronicle*, 19 May 1835; 'The Four Sisters', *Evening Chronicle*, 18 June 1835; 'The Election for Beadle', *Evening Chronicle*, 14 July 1835; 'The Broker's Man', *Evening Chronicle*, 28 July 1835; 'The Ladies' Societies', *Evening Chronicle*, 20 August 1835; 'Our Next-Door Neighbour', *Evening Chronicle*, 18 March 1836.

[8] 'Thoughts about People', *Evening Chronicle*, 23 April 1835, repr. in *Dickens' Journalism*, Vol. I, pp. 211-15 (p. 215).

[9] 'The Pawnbroker's Shop', *Evening Chronicle*, 30 June 1835, repr. in *Dickens' Journalism*, Vol. I, pp. 186-93 (p. 192).

[10] Angus Easson, 'Who is Boz? Dickens and His Sketches', *Dickensian*, 81 (March 1985), 13-22.

profanity and indelicacy. As his target audience broadened, however, Dickens took steps to avoid bringing a blush to the cheek of the young person, systematically eliminating curses and invocations of God and the devil. Retained in the 1836 selections, about half of the 'damns' were edited out for the 1839 edition, and by 1850 all but a couple were eliminated, as was any mention of a brothel.

Not only did he systematically clean up his texts, he also took care to depict 'Boz' as a more decorous persona, fit company for a family audience. Where he had described himself 'quaffing our grog' in the opening paragraph of the *Bell's Life* version of 'The New Year', for the volume publication he more studiously presented himself 'penning this article'. And in the same sketch he eliminated entirely the original final paragraph, which saw him drinking in the New Year:

> But twelve has struck, and the bells ring merrily out which welcome the new year. Away with all gloomy reflections. We were happy and merry in the last one, and will be, please God, in this. So as we are alone, and can neither dance it in, nor sing it in, here goes our glass to our lips, and a hearty welcome to the year one thousand eight hundred and thirty-six say we.[11]

Even more telling are changes introduced to his own self-portrait as guide and commentator in 'A Parliamentary Sketch'. He was content to leave his narrator unchanged for the Second Series (December 1836), but by the time of the 1839 edition he clearly felt the need to upgrade his image. In 'The "House"', Boz buttonholes his reader, 'You must often have seen him in the box-lobbies during the vacation'. This cajoling bit of camaraderie is deleted in revision, as is the sly confidence, 'you may peep into the House for one instant, but not longer, for it's against orders our being there at all'. Similarly, in the description of Nicholas, the butler at Bellamy's, Dickens markedly reduces the emphasis on his own intimacy with the functionary. Instead of insouciantly explaining that 'many a time, long after day-break on a summer's morning have we amused ourselves in drawing the cautious old man out', he removes all reference to himself, stating merely, 'and then for the edification and behoof of more juvenile questioners, he would stand for an hour together, answering deferential questions'. [12]

---

[11] 'The New Year', *Bell's Life in London*, 3 January 1836, repr. in *Dickens' Journalism*, Vol. I, pp. 221-25 [excludes quoted paragraph].
[12] 'The "House"', *Evening Chronicle*, 7 March 1835 [not repr. in *Dickens' Journalism*].

In the first versions of two of the last *Sketches by Boz* to be written, 'The Hospital Patient' and 'Hackney Cabs and their Drivers' (both originally published in the *Carlton Chronicle*), Boz presented himself in the first-person singular, as 'I'. Otherwise his narrator consistently referred to himself in the less individuating editorial form, as 'we'.[13] At the first opportunity, some three months after the *Carlton Chronicle* pieces had appeared, when the Second Series was in preparation, the 'I' of these sketches was brought into line with the others and changed to 'we'.

The linguist Emile Beveniste has observed that first- and second-person pronouns constitute a unique element in language in that they have no definable class of reference, but can be defined only in terms of their location within an act of discourse: '"I" can only be identified by the instance of discourse that contains it, and by that alone'. Each 'I' has its own specific reference, 'valid only in its uniqueness'. This is immediately clear in reported conversation, in which the 'I' and 'you' shift back and forth between speakers, each referring to him- or herself as 'I' and to the person addressed as 'you'. 'I' is the person who utters the present instance of discourse containing that pronoun; 'you' is the individual spoken to in the discourse containing that instance of 'you'. Greg Urban further distinguishes between the 'I' pointing to an everyday self and the 'I' pointing to an imaginary or assumed self: 'In the latter case, the individual speakers to whom the "I" points are in fact anaphoric substitutes for characters in a narrative text'. Further, '[t]he anaphoric "I" is a metaphoric "he"'.[14]

Such distinctions become slipperier, however, when the first-person speaking voice adopts the plural form, 'we'. At its simplest, the editorial or authorial 'we' refers to the singular speaker or author, while avoiding the specifying personal reference. This usage, which arose in early nineteenth-century periodicals, left the individual writer unidentified, but lifted him into a 'corporate discourse'. As Jon Klancher notes, '[t]he monthly and quarterly journals had begun to absorb their writers into the discursive mode of each journal, often merging writer, editor, and publisher into a corporate,

---

[13] 'The Hospital Patient', *Carlton Chronicle*, 6 August 1836, repr. in *Dickens' Journalism*, Vol. I, pp. 236-40; 'Hackney Cabs and their Drivers', *Carlton Chronicle*, 17 September 1836 [not repr. in *Dickens' Journalism*].

[14] Emile Beveniste, 'The Nature of Pronouns', in *Problems in General Linguistics*, trans. by Mary Elizabeth Meek (Coral Gables: University of Miami Press, 1966; repr.1971), pp. 217-22 (p. 218); Greg Urban, 'The "I" of Discourse', in *Semiotics, Self, and Society*, ed. by Benjamin Lee and Greg Urban (The Hague: Mouton de Gruyter, 1989), pp. 27-52 (pp. 49, 35).

collective "author" institutionally set apart from its readers'.[15] In the partisan political environment of early nineteenth-century journalism, this procedure not only brought the weight of the journal to bear on what was written, but also invited license for scurrilous attacks and misinformation—a practice which infuriated Dickens. Responding to an attack on his friend John Elliotson in 1841, he wrote to Macready,

> [W]hen I think that every dirty speck upon the fair face of God's creation, who writes in a filthy, bawdy newspaper—every rotten-hearted pander who has been beaten, kicked, and rolled in the kennel, yet struts it in the Editorial We once a week—every vagabond that an honest man's gorge must rise at—every live emetic in that nauseous drug-shop, the Press—can have his fling at such men and call them knaves and fools and thieves, I grow so vicious that with bearing hard upon my pen I break the nib down, and with keeping my teeth set, make my jaws ache.[16]

Two decades later Dickens was still—albeit more decorously—reiterating this complaint. Responding to an attack on *Little Dorrit* (1855-57) by James Fitzjames Stephen in the *Edinburgh Review*, he wrote, 'even party occupation, the reviewer's license, or the editorial plural, does not absolve a gentleman from a gentleman's duty, a gentleman's restraint, and a gentleman's generosity'.[17]

Dickens nevertheless found great flexibility for himself in the possibilities available in the first-person plural pronoun. Randolph Quirk identifies a variety of special uses for it: an editorial 'we' avoids the personal; an inclusive 'we' brings together author and reader; a generic 'we' includes the speaker, addressee and third parties; a rhetorical 'we' collectively extends to the party or nation; a condescending 'we' speaks from a posture of superiority; and a royal 'we' is used by a monarch—the last alone finding no

---

[15] Jon Klancher, *The Making of English Reading Audiences, 1790-1832* (Madison: University of Wisconsin Press, 1987), p. 48.

[16] To William Charles Macready, 24 Aug 1841, *The Letters of Charles Dickens*, ed. by Kathleen Tillotson, Graham Storey and others, Pilgrim Edition, 12 vols (Oxford: Clarendon Press, 1965-2002), Vol. II, p. 368.

[17] [Charles Dickens], 'Curious Misprint in the Edinburgh Review', *Household Words*, Vol. XVI, No. 384 (1 August 1857), 97-100 (p. 100).

place in Dickens.[18] In *Sketches by Boz* alone Robert Patten distinguishes among the comradely 'we', the ethical 'we', the authorial 'we', the sympathetic 'we', the guide 'we', the repetitious 'we' and the pluralised identity.[19]

The most obvious reason for any author to favour 'we' over 'I' is that it deflects attention away from the individual person who has written an article, and allows the writer both to extend authority for what he says to the publishing house that has produced his work and, either implicitly or explicitly, to invite solidarity with his readers. At the height of his career, as the most famous writer in the English language, he could (and did) assume that readers would be as interested in himself as observer as they were in what he observed. In both the autobiographical fragment and *David Copperfield*, Dickens identifies his speaking voice as 'I'. There is one exception, when Miss Mowcher uses a condescending 'we' in teasing David: 'Oh, my goodness, how polite we are!' she exclaims in response to David's declaration that he feels honoured to meet her.[20] Otherwise in these works Dickens reserves 'we' as a plural pronoun to include others in addition to the speaker. The later 'Uncommercial Traveller' sketches, developing a narrator largely undifferentiated from the author, are all presented by the Traveller as 'I'. But at the outset of his career, unknown to the public, and hoping to gain recognition for his sketches, it would have been inappropriate for Dickens to draw attention to himself as writer and narrator, even under a pseudonym. His focus there was upon observed scenes, characters and tales and not on himself as observer.

Support for this interpretation is to be found in the history of the prefaces that Dickens wrote for his works. All of the prefaces that he wrote between 1836 and 1841—for *Sketches by Boz, Pickwick, Oliver Twist, Nicholas Nickleby* (1838-39), and *The Old Curiosity Shop* (1840-141)—were presented in the third person, referring to himself as 'the Author'. The preface for Macrone's second series of the *Sketches*, published in December 1836, includes a humorous dialogue between author and publisher, but that too is introduced not by 'I' or 'we' but by 'the Author'. Only with the 1841 edition

---

[18] Randolph Quirk, Sidney Greenbaum, Geoffrey Leech and Jan Svartvik, *A Comprehensive Grammar of the English Language* (London and New York: Longman, 1985), pp. 335-57.

[19] Robert L. Patten, *Charles Dickens and 'Boz': The Birth of the Industrial Age Author* (Cambridge: Cambridge University Press, 2012) pp. 63-64.

[20] Charles Dickens, *David Copperfield*, edited by Nina Burgis [1849-50] (Oxford and New York: Oxford University Press, 1997), p. 320.

of *Oliver Twist*, in what Kathleen Tillotson describes as 'Dickens's longest and most ambitious preface, an important critical manifesto', does Dickens step forward authoritatively as 'I'—a stance which he invariably follows in every subsequent preface that he wrote.[21] Initial diffidence gives way to confident pronouncement, in acknowledgement of his position of eminence. But self-effacing humility is the stance of the early sketches and prefaces.

The 'we' of *Pickwick*, Bradley Deane proposes, evolves, as the novel progresses, from representing the voice of an anonymous editor to that of a personalised author, reflecting Dickens's growing convictions about authorship. As Deane notes, Dickens dedicated the novel to Thomas Talfourd, who was struggling, even as Dickens was writing, to secure copyright legislation that would transfer rights from publisher to author.[22] But even before *Pickwick*, Dickens was forging intimacy with his characters and his readers. Repeatedly in the *Sketches* he remarks on the interest afforded by the sights he witnesses and expresses his desire to share his own fascination with his readers: 'we wish', he writes at the end of one, 'that we could impart to others any portion of the amusement we have gained for ourselves'.[23]

The news articles that Dickens contributed to the *Morning Chronicle* were sometimes presented from 'I', more often as 'we', and the voice of his contributions to the *Examiner* in the 1840s was routinely 'we'. His experiment with a characterised speaker in *Master Humphrey's Clock* was a failure on two counts: the crippled old man, uninteresting in himself, lacked the versatility necessary for the narrator of the two novels that took over the planned miscellany, and he was too specifically a Dickensian character to be handed over to other contributors. Jonathan Grossman proposes an ingenious but unconvincing case for Master HHumphrey's narrative role in *The Old Curiosity Shop*, based on Humphrey's declaration that he is himself Nell's great-uncle, brother to her grandfather. Despite Dickens's heroic

---

[21] 'Introduction', in Charles Dickens, *Oliver Twist* [1837-39], ed. by Kathleen Tillotson (Oxford: Clarendon, 1966), p. xxviii.

[22] Bradley Deane, *The Making of the Victorian Novelist: Anxieties of Authorship in the Mass Market* (New York and London: Routledge, 2003), pp. 27-57. See also Rob Allen, '"Boz Versus Dickens": Paratext, Pseudonyms and Serialization in the Victorian Literary Marketplace', in *From Compositors to Collectors: Essays on Book-Trade History*, ed. by John Hinks and Matthew Day (New Castle, DE: Oak Knoll Press for The British Library, 2012), pp. 155-80.

[23] 'Omnibuses', *Morning Chronicle*, 26 September 1834, repr. in *Dickens' Journalism*, Vol. I, pp.138-41 (p. 141).

attempt to tie up loose threads after the initial false start to the novel, the robust Single Gentleman is so patently not the same character as the crippled old man by his clock-case that the claim of identity is ludicrous.[24] Conceived of as a means to release himself from the burdens of writing monthly instalments of an extended prose tale, the *Clock* soon involved even greater labour as Dickens found himself singlehandedly committed to producing weekly instalments of first one and then a second novel.

Quickly abandoning his next editorial project with the *Daily News*, Dickens meditated on a narrative strategy for a new miscellaneous periodical. Writing to Forster, he proposed the concept of

> [A] certain SHADOW, which may go into any place, by sunlight, moonlight, starlight, firelight, candlelight, and be in all homes, and all nooks and corners, and be supposed to be cognisant of everything, and go everywhere, without the least difficulty [...] a character [...] which any of the writers may maintain without difficulty [...] cheerful, useful, and always welcome.[25]

By the time he launched *Household Words* six months later, the Shadow had vanished, but he instituted a house style that allowed the anonymous contributors harmoniously to share the editorial 'we', picking up issues, motifs and styles that coherently reflect a journal 'conducted by Charles Dickens'.

A number of Dickens's own contributions to *Household Words* are presented in the first-person singular. Many of these voices are sharply differentiated from that of the author, much as the characters in Robert Browning's dramatic monologues patently speak for themselves and not for Browning. Cobbs, the 'I' figure in 'The Toady Tree', 'Tapenham', the speaker in 'Cheap Patriotism', and the Raven in 'Perfect Felicity' are examples in which Dickens ventriloquises voices, much as he does so inimitably in his fiction.[26]

---

[24] Jonathan Grossman, *Charles Dickens's Networks: Pubic Transport and the Novel* (Oxford: Oxford University Press, 2012), pp. 91-154.

[25] To John Forster, 7 October 1849, *The Letters of Charles Dickens*, Vol. V, p. 622. See Jonathan V. Farina, '"A Certain Shadow": Personified Abstractions and the Form of *Household Words*', *Victorian Periodicals Review*, 42:4 (Winter 2009), 392-415.

[26] 'The Toady Tree', *Household Words*, Vol. XI, No. 270 (26 May 1855), 385-87; 'Cheap Patriotism', *Household Words*, Vol. XI, No. 272 (9 June 1855), 433-35; 'Perfect Felicity. In a Bird's Eye View', *Household Words*, Vol. I, No. 2 (6 April 1850), 36-38.

Other speaking voices in the journalism, however, purport to represent the outlook of Dickens himself. Whereas there seems to be no clear rationale for his choice between 'I' and 'we' in much of his journalism, he does tend to employ the first-person singular pronoun when he wishes either to emphasise his personal engagement with a subject or to speak with particularly emphatic authority. In 'Gaslight Fairies', for example, an article about the hard off-stage lives of the extras in pantomimes, he writes sympathetically as 'I, the writer' and in 'A Nightly Scene in London', recounting an incident when he came upon a group of miserably poor wretches shut out of the Workhouse, his outrage boils over as 'I, the Conductor of this journal'.[27] It is as 'I' that he declares 'my position' in 'The Noble Savage' and reports his conversation with 'Mr. Snapper' in 'On Strike'.[28] Some of the quasi-autobiographical pieces, such as 'Gone Astray', 'A Flight', 'Lying Awake', and 'A Walk in a Workhouse' use the first-person singular, as (of course) does his ill-advised 'Personal' statement about the break-up of his marriage.[29]

On the other hand, other articles, in which one might expect emphasis on Dickens's personal engagement, drop into the editorial 'we'. 'A Preliminary Word', with which he opens his new journal, is presented by 'we', as are his attack on the coddling of 'Pet Prisoners', his account of meeting with 'A Detective Police Party', his satire on Bloomerism ('Sucking Pigs'), his defence of traditional fairy stories ('Frauds on the Fairies'), his celebration of childhood pleasure ('Where We Stopped Growing'), and many others.[30]

---

[27] 'Gaslight Fairies', *Household Words*, Vol. XI, No. 255 (10 February 1855), 25-28 (p. 25); 'A Nightly Scene in London', *Household Words*, Vol. XIII, No. 305 (26 January 1856), 25-27 (p. 25).

[28] 'The Noble Savage', *Household Words*, Vol. VII, No. 168 (11 June 1853), 337-39 (p. 339); 'On Strike', *Household Words*, Vol. VIII, No. 203 (11 February 1854), 553-59.

[29] 'Gone Astray', *Household Words*, Vol. VII, No. 177 (13 August 1853), 553-57; 'A Flight', *Household Words*, Vol. III, No. 75 (30 August 1851), 529-33; 'Lying Awake', *Household Words*, Vol. VI, No. 136 (30 October 1852), 145-48; 'A Walk in a Workhouse', *Household Words*, Vol. I, No. 9 (25 May 1850), 204-07; 'Personal', *Household Words*, Vol. XVII, No. 429 (12 June 1858), 601.

[30] 'A Preliminary Word', *Household Words*, Vol. I, No. 1 (30 March 1850), 1-2; 'Pet Prisoners', *Household Words*, Vol. I, No. 5 (27 April 1850), 97-103; 'A Detective Police Party [i]', *Household Words*, Vol. I, No. 18 (27 July 1850), 409-14; 'A Detective Police Party [ii]', *Household Words*, Vol. I, No. 20 (10 August 1850), 457-60; 'Sucking Pigs', *Household Words*, Vol. IV, No. 85 (8 November 1851), 145-47; 'Frauds on the

Occasionally he shifts between the editorial 'we' and the personal 'I' within the same sketch. 'Whole Hogs' opens with 'I' attacking various societies, but concludes with recommendations from 'we'. The narrative voice of 'Gone to the Dogs' moves in the opposite direction; it changes from 'we' to 'I'. And sometimes he abandons both forms, leaving out all mention of himself as writer, or referring to himself in the third person by name. In 'Curious Misprint in the Edinburgh Review', he declares that 'the hand of Mr. Dickens writes this paper'. But this sort of procedure is less congenial, as he explains in 'Cheap Patriotism', an article which begins in the third person, from 'the writer of this paper' but already in the second paragraph reverts to the first person, a dramatised 'I', 'in consequence', he declares, 'of the great difficulty of sustaining the third'.[31]

When all is said, the choice between 'we' and 'I' as narrator often appears arbitrary, both when Dickens writes as editor and when he writes of what are purportedly his own experiences, but he clearly found the editorial 'we' a usage of great versatility. At its simplest, it is little more than a modest substitute for 'I', as indicated when he describes himself as 'we, the writer'.[32] The voice of 'we' is authoritative, but not always omniscient. Describing an annual sale of china, for example, the narrating voice declares:

> Where the china comes from, where it goes to, why it is annually put up to auction when nobody ever thinks of bidding for it, how it comes to pass that it is always the same china, whether it would not have been cheaper with the sea at hand, to have thrown it away, say in eighteen hundred and thirty, are standing enigmas.[33]

Often this singular usage glides smoothly into a plural to include the reader as well as the speaker. 'Let none of us be ashamed', he urges his reader, 'If we can only preserve ourselves from growing up, we shall never grow old, and the young may love us to the last'. Such inclusiveness easily expands to include the whole nation, as when he refers to 'We English people', but it

---

Fairies', *Household Words*, Vol. VIII, No. 184 (1 October 1853), 97-100; 'Where We Stopped Growing', *Household Words*, Vol. VI, No. 145 (1 January 1853), 361-63.

[31] 'Whole Hogs', *Household Words*, Vol. III, No. 74 (23 August 1851), 505-07; 'Gone to the Dogs', *Household Words*, Vol. XI, No. 259 (10 March 1855), 121-24; 'Curious Misprint', p. 97; 'Cheap Patriotism', *Household Words*, Vol. XI, No. 272 (9 June 1855), 433-35 (p. 433).

[32] 'Where We Stopped Growing', p. 361.

[33] 'Our Watering Place', *Household Words*, Vol. III, No. 71 (2 August 1851), 433-36 (pp. 433-34).

can also exclude those who disagree with a stated stance. '*We* are the sensible, reflecting, prompt Public, always up to the mark', he writes (italicising 'we' for emphasis), 'whereas that other Public persists in supinely lagging behind, and behaving in an inconsiderate manner'. And sometimes he has fun playing with the ambiguities, as in 'Our School', in which he refers to himself and his schoolfellows in the plural, as 'we', and then goes on to remark in what can only be singular usage, that 'we had the honour to attain and hold the eminent position of first boy'.[34]

Dickens also plays with the versatile possibilities of the second-person pronoun, generally using it to refer directly to his readers, but sometimes it slips into generic usage, referring to everyone in general, or even as a further indirection for self-reference. This is clearest in his *Sketches by Boz* piece 'Early Coaches', in which he writes

> Who has not experienced the miseries inevitably consequent upon a summons to undertake a hasty journey? You received an intimation from your place of business—wherever that may be, or wherever you may be—that it will be necessary to leave town without delay. You and your family are forthwith thrown into a state of tremendous excitement; an express is immediately dispatched to the washerwoman's; everybody is in a bustle; and you, yourself, with a feeling of dignity which you cannot altogether conceal, sally forth to the booking office to secure your place.[35]

And so on. Knowing as we do now about Dickens's youthful experiences as a newspaper reporter, we can be certain that the event recounted here has strong autobiographical resonance, but even for his first readers, wholly unacquainted with the author's personal life, it is clear that the 'you' of this passage is no more than a deliberately transparent stratagem for veiled self-reference.

I have been surveying some of the strategies adopted by Dickens in deploying speaking voices in his writing. In my final remarks, I want to turn briefly to a tantalising instance of intertextuality: the possibility that Dickens's final major revisions of his earliest published imaginative work

---

[34] 'Where We Stopped Growing', p. 363; 'Insularities', *Household Words*, Vol. XIII, No. 304 (19 January 1856), 1-4 (p. 1); 'That Other Public', *Household Words*, Vol. XI, No. 254 (3 February 1855), 1-4 (p. 1); 'Our School', *Household Words*, Vol. IV, No. 81 (11 October 1851), 49-52 (p. 49).

[35] 'Early Coaches', *Evening Chronicle*, 19 February 1835, repr. in *Dickens' Journalism*, Vol. I, pp. 133-37 (pp. 133-34).

may have impacted directly on some of the most distinguished of his journalistic writing at the height of his career. Specifically, I want to suggest that his return to the 'Our Parish' sketches for the Cheap Edition, published in November 1850, may have influenced the speaking voice in some of his *Household Words* contributions, in particular four in the series of 'Our' sketches, beginning with 'Our Watering Place' in August 1851, and continuing with 'Our School', 'Our Vestry', and 'Our French Watering Place' in November 1854. Other sketches by Dickens on 'Our' subjects—'Our Bore', 'Our Honorable Friend' and 'Our Commission'—being trenchantly satiric, deploy a quite different editorial voice.[36]

Sketches by Boz was the most extensively reworked of all Dickens's writings. Between the appearance of the first sketch in December 1833 and the publication of the Cheap Edition seventeen years later, Dickens undertook major revision on five separate occasions. The most substantial of these occurred sometime between 1847, when the project of a collected edition was inaugurated, and 1850, when the latest revision of the sketches was published.[37] Unquestionably, Dickens's developing artistry up to mid-century, in particular the writing of *David Copperfield* and the launch of *Household Words*, fed into the revision of *Sketches by Boz*. More intriguingly, his return to the sketches at that time is likely to have influenced some of the sketch writing he undertook for *Household Words*.

'Our Parish' contains seven sketches, set in an unnamed community in which the speaker is resident. As the pronoun 'our' indicates, the 'Boz' of these sketches expresses a sense of belonging, although, as Easson notes, he acts entirely as an observer, never as a participant.[38] Four of the parish sketches describe local characters and societies, with a brief account of the parish fire engine in action. A satirical sketch relates the election for beadle. Another, after an introduction by 'Boz', is largely given over to a tale about an execution on a property, as reported by the broker's man. The final sketch

---

[36] 'Our Vestry', *Household Words*, Vol. V, No. 127 (28 August 1852), 549-52; 'Our French Watering Place', *Household Words*, Vol. X, No. 241 (4 November 1854), 265-70; 'Our Bore', *Household Words*, Vol. VI, No. 133 (9 October 1852), 73-76; 'Our Honorable Friend', *Household Words*, Vol. V, No. 123 (31 July 1852), 453-55 and 'Our Commission', *Household Words*, Vol. XII, No. 281 (11 August 1855), 25-27. Dickens also published twenty-one further sketches in *Household Words* by other hands with 'Our' subjects named in the titles.

[37] The number of variants in later editions published with Dickens's authority drops so dramatically that the texts of *Sketches by Boz* are virtually stable from 1850.

[38] Easson, p. 15.

develops a facetious theory of door knockers and moves into a comic description of the lodgers in the house next door, concluding with an emotional account of a mother's anguish over the lingering death of her young son. The tone of the series, which varies from amusement and ridicule to pathos, depends on the complex modulation of response by 'Boz', who is both part of and apart from what he describes. Long ago J. B. Priestley described humour as 'tender mockery, as found in a loving family', and it is just such a fusion of simultaneous attachment and detachment that defines the distinctively Dickensian quality of the observing persona in these sketches.[39]

This persona, which, as I have been explaining, is only one of many that Dickens deploys throughout his career, is recreated in the *Household Words* sketches which I have named, and it is conducive to some of his most attractive writing. 'Our Watering Place' opens with a warm appreciation of the setting as 'a blessed spot', which inspires the observer to 'a lazy inclination to sketch'. He expresses admiration for the clergyman and the naval officer and amused tolerance for the townspeople who claim that they face ruin even when all the lodgings in town are let. 'We' treats the scene as animate, even magical, and describes a trivial altercation as a storm in a teacup, just like the competing ladies' societies in 'Our Parish'. The sketch ends with an upbeat celebration of life, beauty and sparkling sunshine.[40]

'Our School', whose proprietor Dickens described elsewhere as 'by far the most ignorant man I have ever had the pleasure to know, who was one of the worst-tempered men perhaps that ever lived' is presented without bitterness, but rather with vaguely romantic and gently ridiculing recollections of schoolmates.[41] Although the narrating voice concludes that the world is a better place since the school closed, his memories are nostalgic, even charming:

> The boys trained the mice much better than the masters trained the boys. We recall one white mouse, who lived in the cover of a Latin dictionary, who ran up ladders, drew Roman chariots, shouldered muskets, turned wheels, and even made a very creditable appearance on the stage as the Dog of Montargis. He might have achieved greater things, but for having the misfortune to mistake his way in a

[39] J. B. Priestley, *English Humour* (London: Longmans, 1929), p. 16.
[40] 'Our Watering Place', p. 433.
[41] 'Warehousemen and Clerks' Schools, 5 November 1857', *The Speeches of Charles Dickens*, ed. by K. J. Fielding (Oxford: Clarendon Press, 1960), p. 240.

triumphal procession to the Capitol, when he fell into a deep inkstand, and was dyed black and drowned.[42]

In 'Our Vestry', Boz makes his relationship to the community explicit: 'We have a Vestry in our borough', he writes, 'and can vote for a vestryman— might even *be* a vestryman, if we were inspired by a lofty and noble ambition. Which we are not'. The sketch is a spoof on the self-importance of local politicians, reprising the Lilliputian party rivalry of 'The Election for Beadle' in 'Our Parish'. He underlines his sense of the unimportance of the heated debates by observing that it was 'no fun at all' when two of the disputants left the hall.[43]

Finally, the editorial 'we' of 'Our French Watering Place' looks back on his holidays there with warm affection, in particular for his landlord, M. Loyal, whom he describes as a faintly ridiculous but wholly admirable character. The place stimulates his imagination, so that he fancies that a child climbing up stairs on the cliff edge 'might conceive himself another Jack, alighting on enchanted ground from another beanstalk'. He declares:

> We have no doubt whatever, standing looking at their uphill streets, house raising above house, and terrace above terrace, and bright garments her and there lying sunning on rough stone parapets, that the pleasant mist on all such objects caused by their being seen through the brown nets hung across on poles to dry, is, in the eyes of every true young fisherman, a mist of love and beauty, setting off the goddess of his heart.[44]

In each of these sketches, the speaking persona stands as a member of the community, gently mocking its absurdities, affectionately appreciating is beauties and imaginatively stimulated by what he sees. The charm of the observations is crucially dependent on the complex attitude of the editorial 'we', sharply observant, alert to the silliness of much that he sees and hears and prompted to fanciful speculation about it all. Dickens creates a pronominal presence in his writing of rich variety, subtlety and fascination.

---

[42] 'Our School', pp. 50-51.
[43] 'Our Vestry', pp. 549, 551.
[44] 'Our French Watering Place', p. 267.

The One and the Many

Robert L. Patten

What translated a discourse into tables and a distinction into a fixed category was the emergence of the state as the dominant force in the provision of literacy.

—David Vincent[1]

IN style, in topic, in playfulness, in variety, in stunning success and rather serious failures, above all, in whatever Dickens thought he was doing in fiction and journalism, the 'Uncommercial Traveller' papers challenge received opinion about Dickens's writing. They have been most often read for autobiographical revelations. But given the number of pieces that claim to be based on experiences that Dickens could not have had, that mode of reading may be limited. John Drew and Michael Slater make a similar point in their 'Introduction' to volume four of *The Dent Uniform Edition of Dickens' Journalism* (2000). Noting that '[John] Forster does not apply the term "autobiographical"' to the 'Uncommercial', they stress that several of their headnotes indicate divergences from 'a strictly autobiographical or historiographical account'.[2]

These *All the Year Round* papers are written documents, with their own truth status and affect purposes. If the structure of an issue of Dickens's last periodical was to open with fiction, why should we not begin a consideration of his contributions to that periodical by asking, what is their status as fiction and/or journalism? It is odd how we celebrate Dickens's imagination by

---

[1] David Vincent, *The Rise of Mass Literacy: Reading and Writing in Modern Europe* (Cambridge: Polity Press, 2000), p. 5.
[2] Michael Slater and John Drew (eds), *The Dent Uniform Edition of Dickens' Journalism, Vol. 4: 'The Uncommercial Traveller' and Other Papers, 1859-70* (London: J. M. Dent, 2000), p. xvi.

wanting to pin everything he ever said down to a 'source', a person he knew, an event he witnessed, a sensation he himself felt. We don't want to allow his imagination any kind of free rein and so we take any reference to places, persons and situations similar to ones Dickens might have known as transcriptions of his own life.

That is a very Victorian assumption. And the way in which Dickens's fiction first intermingled with journalism illustrates the possibility of confusing our contemporary categories of truth/reality/reporting versus fiction/imagination/inventing with the blurrier status of writing in Dickens's time. The generic distinction between news and fiction in newspapers is difficult to detect through typography, location within the paper or information provided. The by-line 'Boz' at the close might mark that distinction, though often the pages with news also contain letters signed by the correspondent, which might be thought to be, if not 'true' in some general journalistic sense, 'true' insofar as the opinion and facts of the undersigned are concerned. So signed pieces might be as veridical as unsigned ones. And Dickens, of course, contributed both during his early career writing for the *Morning* and *Evening Chronicle*—writing many anonymously-authored stories about political dinners and reviewing plays at legitimate and popular theatres, as well as contributing realistic fictional 'sketches' undersigned 'Boz'.

In short, journalism in the Victorian period had as variable a relation to 'hard fact' as it seems to have today. Journalism mixes fact and fancy, or at least clothes naked facts in fancy dress. If we understand the art of journalism in these terms, we will perhaps be better attuned to the effects of Dickens's rhetoric in the 'Uncommercial'.

Another fundamental aspect of journalism is its attempt to represent its subject and its subscribers, the diverse worlds of its audience. When Dickens collected his six parish sketches, he changed the title from 'The Parish' of his first story to 'Our Parish', the title of the others. By the simple use of a possessive plural pronominal adjective, 'our', the title rhetorically insists that the world of the text and the world of the reader are the same, or at least are homologous—the same thing in a different setting. Which gets us to the key question if we don't read his journalism as covert autobiography: how does a journalist image 'our' world?

To image 'our' world is to find representations that work equally well in the reporter's universe and the reader's: the same thing in different worlds. And since no newspaper can contain the world's variety, reporters, like the rest of us, have to identify representative instances of that homology shared between writer and consumer. There is the rub. For any time an individual is picked out as representative, she is thereby rendered categorically unrepresentative: no one person can personify the unrepresented. Jo, the *Bleak House* (1852-53) crossing sweeper, comes pretty close to ground zero of human possibility, and so he has become visibly celebrated for being nearly invisible. Most recently, he has been discovered as the subject of a very early moving picture—where he doesn't himself move, having frozen to death.[3]

There's a passage early on in *Bleak House* that eloquently makes my point about representing the one and the many. The thirteen-year-old daughter of a deceased minor court functionary, Charlotte 'Charley' Neckett, is responsible for maintaining her two younger siblings and herself. She runs out to work as a washerwoman while Esther Summerson, John Jarndyce, Harold Skimpole, Mrs. Blinder and the reader watch 'her run, such a little, little creature,' Esther says, 'in her womanly bonnet and apron, through a covered way at the bottom of the court; and melt into the city's strife and sound, like a dewdrop in an ocean'.[4] What gives Charley distinction, singles her out, her energy and determination and womanly bonnet and apron, become lost when she merges with the general strife and noise, like a drop of water in the sea. On her own she is scarcely representative, being very particularised. The medium, Esther's narration, makes her a heroic individual. But then she melts into the general and becomes unrepresentable again.

In her important book *The Anthology and the Rise of the Novel* (2000), Leah Price points out that Victorian reviews alternated excerpts with plot summaries.[5] What was picked out as representative of a text might therefore become exceptional. Depending on the disposition of the reviewer, editor or publisher of the journal, the passage quoted could be a good example of an otherwise bad book, a bad example of an otherwise good book, a bad example of a bad book, a good example of a good book, a characteristic

---

[3] Cole Abaius, 'Movie News: British Film Institute Discovers World's Oldest Dickensian Movie', *Film School Rejects*, 9 March 2012, <http://www.filmschoolrejects.com/news/british-film-institute-discovers-worlds-oldest-dickensian-movie-the-death-of-poor-joe-1901.php> [accessed 9 March 2012]; G. A. Smith, director, *The Death of Poor Joe* [sic] (1901).

[4] Charles Dickens, *Bleak House* [1852-53], ed. by George Ford and Sylvère Monod, Norton Critical Edition (New York: W. W. Norton, 1977), p. 195.

[5] Leah Price, *The Anthology and the Rise of the Novel* (Cambridge: Cambridge University Press, 2000).

sample of the book's political slant, or an uncharacteristic sample—in either case, to be praised or damned depending on the article's politics. Indeed, the example could be unrepresentative of the book as a whole, quoted to make the article's point, not the book's. In sum, 'representative' always embeds a point of view, not a neutral sign. And Dickens is a great artist at investing nominally neutral signs with significance—a distinction and affect that communicate the book's point of view. Charley is, if anything, a little heroine, not an indistinguishable molecule in the flood of humanity.

Early on in his reporting, Dickens understood that people are different. His recognition is the antithesis of an alternative way of dealing with individuality: the grossing up of particulars into a general whole. As in 'the greatest good for the greatest number', the mantra shaping Utilitarian legislation for half a century. An attempt to parse that 'greatest number' produces incoherence—as we see in any revenue code that tries to accommodate all the exceptions taxpayers could imagine being rightfully theirs. If the first distinctions Dickens might have observed closely were between clerks and masters, subjects and MPs, he soon learned to distinguish Whigs from Tories—at a time in the early 1830s when these distinctions themselves were loosening and shifting. And as he walked the streets and studied the bustling company, he began to categorise folks. That was a typical urban activity. Indeed graphic prints of various 'types'—market woman, parish beadle—were staples of 1820s and 1830s stationers' shops. One figure stood for the occupation as a whole. And this slippage was the more readily accepted because different trades seemed to bear distinctive marks: the dustman's two-brimmed hat, the stage coachman's whip.[6]

The 1830s was a time for enumerating the types that made up urban society. Boz the reporter made this his specialty, picking out types from regions of society untravelled by the middle and governing classes. As he said at the conclusion of 'Thoughts about People', first published in the *Evening Chronicle* on 23 April 1835:

> There are so many classes of people in London, each one so different from the other, and each so peculiar in itself, that we find it time to bring our paper to a close before we have well brought our subject to a beginning. We are, therefore, induced to hope that we may calculate upon the permission of our readers to think about people again at some future time.[7]

---

[6] George Cruikshank, *London Characters* (London: Joseph Robins, 1828).

[7] Charles Dickens, 'Thoughts about People,' *Evening Chronicle*, 23 April 1835.

He gives us further instances of these classes, 'each so peculiar in itself': the parish beadle, the old lady, the retired captain on half-pay, the draper's assistant attempting to pass for fashionable buck, the spinster, the hen-pecked husband, the *nouveau-riche* family, the victim of fatal domestic abuse.

This variety is chock full of disappointed lives. The reviewers of *Sketches by Boz* (1836) identified the journalist Boz as a teller of truths about the lower echelons of society.[8] However, perhaps insulated by their economic and social capital, affluent readers found the trials and tribulations of lesser mortals comic. There was a politics at work in introducing such subjects for the perusal of the literate. *Sketches by Boz* initiated Dickens's life-long commitment to making ordinary lives noticeable and worthy. But these portraits are, on the whole, if not condescending, still distanced. How could reviewers think that these scenes constituted Boz's humour: pawning one's last treasured possessions for bread, or witnessing a condemned man's last night, or hearing the final gasps of a beloved son dying of disease and malnutrition, or watching the even more horrifying spectacle of a mother seeking medical assistance in reviving her son, hanged a few hours previously? There was something in that reportage that kept a transparent shield between the scenes of suffering offered as typical and the consumers of those stories: something called style. 'Bozzes' came to be the denomination of a certain mixture of text and picture (by George Cruikshank), dirt and discovery, pathos and bathos, by which one class became acquainted with another.

We know that Dickens inherited Pickwickian types that he transformed into individuals. We know that he took the Hogarthian contrasted apprentices, industrious and idle, and recast those comparisons in brilliantly imaginative ways in *Oliver Twist* (1837-39) and *Nicholas Nickleby* (1838-39). Oliver is both the idle apprentice at Fagin's and eager to prove himself industrious, though his industry threatens to get him hanged. Nicholas, Kate, Miss Knag, the Mantalinis, the Crummles troupe, Newman Noggs, all play industrious and idle roles in that complicated account of what it means to be in business. But these figures are so individualised—Squeers being an outstanding instance—that one of the most insightful of Dickens's critics, J. Hillis Miller, discerned in *Nicholas Nickleby* something like the refutation of any notion that society might be expressed by representative examples. Miller perceived in the novel a multitude of unique grotesques, a kind of philosophical nominalism in which 'the character really exists as a kind of

---

[8] Philip Collins (ed.), *Dickens: The Critical Heritage* (London: Routledge and Kegan Paul, 1971), pp. 27-30.

generalised form or abstract idea of himself'. The collision of these figures within an urban space yields 'sheer chaos, an inextricable jumble of objects and people in ceaseless motion, multiplied inexhaustibly, without order or direction'. In sum, the more one refines the distinctions within general classes, the more one asks any particularised individual to stand as a representative, the closer one draws to an uncountable pluralism of monads 'multiplied inexhaustibly, without order or direction'.[9]

By the time he wrote the 'Uncommercial', Dickens had at his command an extraordinary range of rhetorical strategies that could be deployed to represent 'our'—that is, his and his readers'—world. The setting of these travel accounts within the double-columns of *All the Year Round* already contextualised them as participating in a printed issue devoted to both fiction and fact—to use a crude binary for the moment. Within the print and conceptual context, the 'Uncommercial' tries multiple ways of representing Britain and Britons, in their own right or as contrasted to foreigners. And to draw those representations, he employs various syntactic and definitional tricks. They all have in common two aspects: what I call 'the array' and what I want to identify as a nineteenth-century version of the trope of *copia*. Let me give definitions first, examples thereafter.

'Array' became a way of attempting to schematise the multitudinousness of Victorian society. It was a mode of accounting for variety and for sorting it out. Consider the title page to volume one of the 1861–62 collected edition of Henry Mayhew's four-volume *London Labour and the London Poor*, most of which had been originally published as newspaper articles not dissimilar to 'The Parish', and which he collectivised and arrayed in categories and subcategories, each entry separate and yet a part of a larger whole (see **Fig. 1**).[10] There is no wholly transparent reason why these portraits are arranged in this order, but Mayhew has attempted a series that progresses in complexity or reductiveness.

---

[9] J. Hillis Miller, *Charles Dickens: The World of His Novels* (Cambridge, MA: Harvard University Press, 1958), pp. 88-89.

[10] Henry Mayhew, *London Labour and the London Poor* [1851], 4 vols (London: Griffin Bohn & Co., 1861–2), vol. I (1861).

LONDON LABOUR

AND THE

LONDON POOR;

A

CYCLOPÆDIA OF THE CONDITION AND EARNINGS

OF

THOSE THAT *WILL* WORK,
THOSE THAT *CANNOT* WORK, AND
THOSE THAT *WILL NOT* WORK.

BY

HENRY MAYHEW.

THE LONDON STREET-FOLK;

COMPRISING,

STREET SELLERS.	STREET PERFORMERS.
STREET BUYERS.	STREET ARTIZANS.
STREET FINDERS.	STREET LABOURERS.

WITH NUMEROUS ILLUSTRATIONS FROM PHOTOGRAPHS.

VOLUME I.

LONDON:

GRIFFIN, BOHN, AND COMPANY,

STATIONERS' HALL COURT.

1861.

Fig. 1. Title page of *London Labour and the London Poor*, Vol. I, [1851] 1861

CONTENTS.

THE AGENCIES AT PRESENT IN OPÉRATION WITHIN THE ME-
TROPOLIS, FOR THE SUPPRESSION OF VICE AND CRIME.

By the Rev. William Tuckniss, B.A.

Fig. 2. Contents page of *London Labour and the London Poor*, Vol. IV, 1862

Next, look at the title page for the fourth volume of this edition (1862), which was a joint project by Mayhew, the Reverend William Tuckniss and others, detailing among other things *The Agencies at Present in Operation within the Metropolis, for the Suppression of Vice and Crime*. Here heads and subheads are more clearly indicated (see **Fig. 2**).[11]

The study begins with a rationale and justification: the 'Universal Desire for Investigation'. Mayhew's section starts by foregrounding his taxonomies of types: 'Introduction and Classification'. Thus the 'array' is becoming more sophisticated and self-conscious, providing its justification as an investigation in the public interest and, following that, a report that has a system governing its operation and presentation. Collaborative sociological investigation becomes almost a signature of mid-Victorian blue books and journalism. In his periodicals Dickens contributes to the trend in several ways: by commissioning writers and specifying the subject matter, by very considerable editorial revising, by jointly composing articles and by gathering together a company of writers who contribute separate stories fitted within the overall outline and setting supplied by Dickens for his Christmas numbers. Collaboration requires some sharing of rules and protocols, so that an investigation undertaken by a collective—as Mayhew's original volume four was—has from the start a programme to follow and a canvas to be filled in. Order cannot come after the notes are taken, but before they are taken, which makes the project more complete and, at the same time, more determined in outcome by the directives provided at the start.

Now we are beginning to get at the heart of our subject. As David Vincent says at the outset of his canonical study *The Rise of Mass Literacy* (2000), 'what translated a discourse into tables and a distinction into a fixed category was the emergence of the state as the dominant force in the provision of literacy'.[12] I am not sure of all he means by this sentence, but among its meanings is the connection between literacy and tabulation, instigated by the state that creates those tables. Take an 1881 census form (see **Fig. 3**). When all these categories are filled in by the census taker, the Public Record Office knows the birthplace, age, family composition, marital status and occupation of every person in Britain, and from those data— adjusted to limit the variety of categories—can be written the laws

---

[11] Henry Mayhew, *London Labour and the London Poor*, 4 vols (London: Griffin Bohn & Co., 1861–2), vol. IV (1862), p. iii.

[12] Vincent, p. 5.

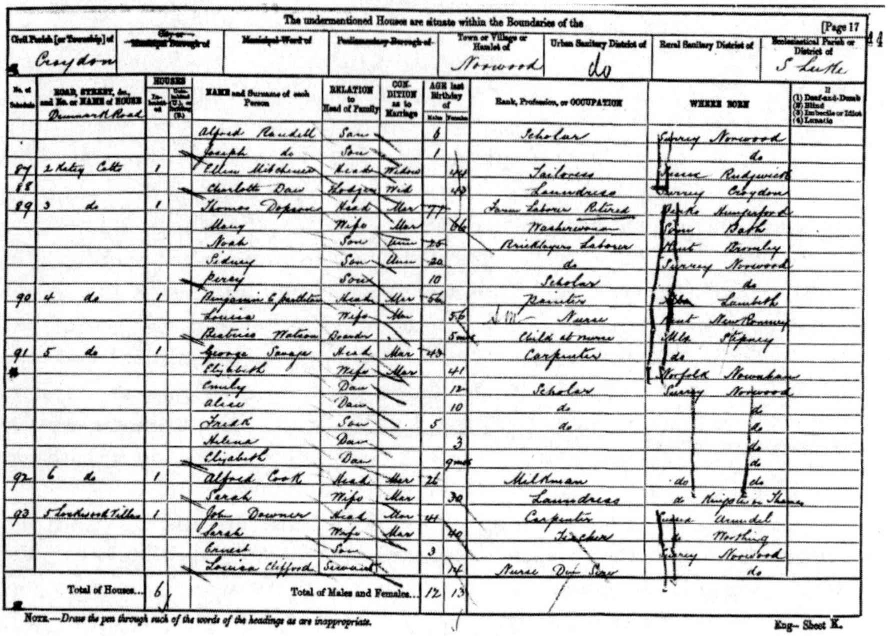

The undermentioned Houses are situate within the Boundaries of the [Page 17

Civil Parish [or Township] of Croydon | City or Municipal Borough of | Municipal Ward of | Parliamentary Borough of | Town or Village or Hamlet of Norwood | Urban Sanitary District of do | Rural Sanitary District of | Ecclesiastical Parish or District of S Luke

No. of Schedule	ROAD, STREET, &c., and No. or NAME of HOUSE (Denmark Road)	HOUSES Inhabited	HOUSES Uninhabited (U.), or Building (B.)	NAME and Surname of each Person	RELATION to Head of Family	CONDITION as to Marriage	AGE last Birthday of Males	AGE last Birthday of Females	Rank, Profession, or OCCUPATION	WHERE BORN	(1) Deaf-and-Dumb (2) Blind (3) Imbecile or Idiot (4) Lunatic
				Alfred Randell	Son		6		Scholar	Surrey Norwood	
				Joseph do	Son		1			do	
87	2 Katey Cotts	1		Ellen Mitchener	Head	Widow		44	Tailoress	Sussex Rudgwick	
88				Charlotte Daw	Lodger	Wid		48	Laundress	Surrey Croydon	
89	3 do	1		Thomas Dopson	Head	Mar	77		Farm Laborer Retired	Berks Hungerford	
				Mary	Wife	Mar		66	Washerwoman	Som Bath	
				Noah	Son	Unm	25		Bricklayers Laborer	Kent Bromley	
				Sidney	Son	Unm	20		do	Surrey Norwood	
				Percy	Son		10		Scholar	do	
90	4 do	1		Benjamin C Partleton	Head	Mar	56		Painter	Mdx Lambeth	
				Louisa	Wife	Mar		56	Nurse	Kent New Romney	
				Beatrice Watson	Boarder			5 mo	Child at nurse	Mdx Stepney	
91	5 do	1		George Savage	Head	Mar	43		Carpenter	do	
				Elizabeth	Wife	Mar		41		Norfolk Newnham	
				Emily	Dau			12	Scholar	Surrey Norwood	
				Alice	Dau			10	do	do	
				Fredk	Son		5		do	do	
				Helena	Dau			3		do	
				Elizabeth	Dau			9 mo		do	
92	6 do	1		Alfred Cook	Head	Mar	26		Milkman	do do	
				Sarah	Wife	Mar		30	Laundress	do Kingston on Thames	
93	5 Lockwood Villas	1		John Downer	Head	Mar	41		Carpenter	Sussex Arundel	
				Sarah	Wife	Mar		40	Teacher	do Worthing	
				Ernest	Son		3			Surrey Norwood	
				Louisa Clifford	Servant			14	Nurse Dom Serv	do	
	Total of Houses...	6		Total of Males and Females...			12	13			

NOTE.—Draw the pen through such of the words of the headings as are inappropriate. Eng– Sheet K.

Fig. 3. Sample page from the 1881 census; image courtesy of *In Their Shoes* http://partleton.co.uk/Benjamin1825.htm

promoting the greatest good and the books expounding the composition of the British public. Moreover, if one wants a further breakdown, say what percentage of residents in Lancashire were employed in 1851 as handloom weavers, those numbers can be abstracted and calculated.[13] The result is a complete count of those weavers, a record that shows great variation in the percentage of workers in each parish employed in weaving—from two to fifty percent—and, paradoxically, an enumeration and comparison of individuals that supplies no individuating characteristics whatsoever. Not even the gender of those labourers at the loom. These are ones grossed up into the many—or the few.

The other key term to be defined is *copia*. In *De duplici copia verborum ac rerum commentarii duo* (*On Copia of Words and Things*, 1512) Erasmus argued that

[13] Geoffrey Timmins, *The Last Shift: The Decline of Handloom Weaving in Nineteenth-Century Lancashire* (London: Manchester University Press, 1993). See pp. 217 and 226 for the images cited.

to reach all readers one needed to deploy varieties of style and subject matter. Variety, he tells the students for whom his book was originally written and published, 'is so powerful in every sphere that there is absolutely nothing, however brilliant, which is not dimmed if not commended by variety'.[14] At one point Erasmus supplies 146 varieties of sentences based on 'Your letter pleased me greatly'.[15] And in Book Two, he insists that varieties of subject matter and treatment involve 'the assembling, explaining, and amplifying of arguments by the use of examples, comparisons, similarities, dissimilarities, opposites, and other like procedures'.[16] While I doubt that Dickens was a close reader of Erasmus, teachings deriving from Erasmus about the need for variety to reach and persuade a variety of readers may well have been principles he learned in school. *De Copia* was originally composed for John Colet, Dean of St Paul's Cathedral and for the choirboys in the Cathedral school; by 1824 at least 180 editions plus a like number of digests had been printed.[17] Dickens does seem to know, instinctively perhaps or from his observations of parliamentary and legal oratory, how important it is to supply many voices (rhetorics addressed in Erasmus's first volume) and subjects (examples addressed in the second volume) to persuade. In addition, his journalism surely prompted him to think about how he might speak about and to the whole of society through multiple subjects, of the sort that cram the columns of his two mid-Victorian periodicals. So for my purposes we can consider *copia* as a synonym for abundance and variety of subjects and rhetorics aiming in some way or other to present both the individuals comprising Victorian society and their larger agglomerations into classes, populations (urban and rural, for instance) and the polity as a whole.

If mid-Victorian journalism aimed to draw a picture of contemporary society, the 'Uncommercial' supplies snapshots—many of them. And as Dickens draws sketches and drafts scenes we can spot him making attempts to solve the knotted challenge of portraying the individual, the representative, the type, the subclasses, the whole class and the whole

---

[14] Desiderius Erasmus, 'Copia: Foundations of the Abundant Style (De duplici copia verborum ac rerum commentarii duo)', in *Collected Works*, ed. by Craig R. Thompson (Toronto: University of Toronto Press, 1978), Vol. XXIV, p. 302.
[15] Virginia W. Callahan, 'The *De Copia*: The Bounteous Horn', in *Essays on the Works of Erasmus*, ed. by Richard L. DeMolen (New Haven and London: Yale University Press, 1978), pp. 99-109 (p. 101).
[16] Erasmus, p. 301.
[17] Callahan, p. 102.

population. His strategies can be compressed and clever, expanded and elaborate and everything in between. Let us look at some.

Distinction within Classification

'John Nightingale, William Thrush, Joseph Blackbird, Cecil Robin, and Thomas Linnet!' cried Friar Bacon.

'Here, sir!' and 'Here, sir!' And Linnet, Robin, Blackbird, Thrush, and Nightingale, stood confessed.[18]

Here we have individual farm labourers clubbing together to buy a pig to raise and butcher. They join in groups of five and borrow the purchase money, £1, from the owner of the estate, for complicated reasons denominated Friar Bacon, as if he embodies three centuries of scientific efforts. Each labourer is given a full Christian and paternal name. And yet they are barely individuated. Indeed, all surnames are the names of birds. And those birds are called in a different order from their subsequent line-up, indicating either their lack of differentiation or how they assemble in the reverse of their call-up order. Or, in my unsporting hypothesis, Dickens looked at his copy and just transcribed the names from the last he had written back to the first, without worrying at all about the implications of the sequences.

So we have two homologous classification systems: the *genera* agricultural labourers and birds of the field. And we have five species of each *genus*: John, William, Joseph, Cecil and Thomas—labourers; Linnet, Robin, Blackbird, Thrush and Nightingale—avians.

Sampling

Another way of intimating coverage of the whole by representing a part is sampling. In 'The Shipwreck' (28 January 1860), Dickens quotes from letters he had borrowed from a clergyman, the Rev. Stephen Roose Hughes, responsible for burying many of those drowned in a shipwreck on the Welsh coast the previous October.[19] Dickens prints samples of the tributes to the

---

[18] [Charles Dickens], 'The Poor Man and His Beer', *All the Year Round*, Vol. I, No. 1 (30 April 1859), 13-16 (p. 15).

[19] [Charles Dickens], 'The Uncommercial Traveller [i]', *All the Year Round*, Vol. II, No. 40 (21 January 1860), 321-26 (pp. 324-26). This article was re-titled 'The Shipwreck' in volume editions of *The Uncommercial Traveller*, 1861 [1860] *et seq*.

Rev. Hughes's services on behalf of the dead penned by the bereaved. He quotes 'a mother', 'a husband', two widows, a father, several guests who spent a night at the Rectory, the Old Hebrew congregation of Liverpool and a Jewish gentleman. Each excerpt instantiates the locution and personality of the writer, embodying a class of correspondent in an individual voice. The 'Uncommercial' also notes the kinds of identifying marks found on the bodies of passengers and sailors—another sampling. One man had a printed charm, others wore lockets encasing portraits of women or locks of hair, and sailors were identified by their tattoos. Again, the class is that of corpses marked with identifying traces; within that class, some marks were common, others particular to individuals. The text samples all varieties, providing specifics that stand for many.

Developmental Categories

There is very little indication in 'The Poor Man and His Beer' of how these avians and human beings got to this farm and beer-club, though considerable evidence that Friar Bacon has established a system of patronage that supports and maintains the work, health and pleasure of those labourers who have arrived. Some classifications, however, depend on one's growing into, staying in, or declining from that class: a labourer who can no longer work belongs to a different category than one who refuses to work, though able-bodied (yet another category more unfavourable to human sympathy or government assistance). So how does one get or hold a place in a classification, as opposed to being one of many corpses in a Welsh cemetery?

> The first strong external revelation of the Dry Rot in men, is a tendency to lurk and lounge; to be at street-corners without intelligible reason; to be going anywhere when met; to be about many places rather than at any; to do nothing tangible, but to have an intention of performing a variety of intangible duties tomorrow or the day after [...]. As it is in wood, so it is in men [homology]. Dry Rot advances at a compound usury quite incalculable.[20]

This second quotation is quite clearly an analysis of a type: those susceptible, as wood is, to Dry Rot. But the type is one of movement. The homology here is between animal and vegetable, with the former gradually declining

---

[20] [Charles Dickens], 'The Uncommercial Traveller [xii]', *All the Year Round*, Vol. III, No. 65 (21 July 1860), 348-52 (p. 350). This article was re-titled 'Night Walks' in subsequent editions of 'The Uncommercial Traveller'.

into the latter. 'Men' become less animate—'lurk' and 'lounge'. They lose their mental faculties—'without intelligible reason'. They circulate without purpose, almost like cells in a fluid moving as the fluid moves—'going anywhere'. That motion turns into a kind of stasis—'do nothing tangible, but have an intention of performing' on another day. And they grow petrified and rotten at a compound rate.

This is a passage from one of the finest 'Uncommercial' pieces: 'Night Walks' (21 July 1860). The Uncommercial's survey of the houseless of the city by night is both idiosyncratic and representative; that is, being subjected to an idiosyncratic personal 'inability to sleep', he 'finished [his] education in a fair amateur experience of [the category of] houselessness'. Note that the comprehensiveness of his survey is nuanced by 'fair' and 'amateur'; nonetheless, the invocation of a 'finished [. . .] education' suggests something substantially complete and adequately covered. Moreover, the rhetoric of the piece is overtly, at the start, affective: his night walk 'brought [me—and will bring his readers] into sympathetic relations with people who have no other object [than the experience of houselessness] every night in the year'—'Our' world.

Group Subjects with Individuation

'Night Walks' is strategised and narrated as a journey through London's streets. It is therefore a progressive narrative, extending from night until dawn. The 'Uncommercial' passes individuals, walking or lounging or sleeping, along the way, one-by-one. But the intention and, to some extent, the effect of the total narration is to account for the houseless population of the metropolis, in all its subdivisions, rather like the subdivisions Mayhew supplies of people who work. Dickens applies a different strategy of enumerating the one and the many in another 'Uncommercial' essay, 'Tramps' (16 June 1860). Here he speaks about a subcategory of tramps, hop-pickers:

> They come in families, men, women, and children, every family provided with a bundle of bedding, an iron pot, a number of babies, and too often with some poor sick creature quite unfit for the rough life, for whom they suppose the smell of the fresh hop to be a sovereign remedy. Many of these hoppers are Irish, but many come from London. They crowd all the roads, and camp under all the hedges and on all the scraps of common-land, and live among and upon the hops until they are all picked, and the hop-gardens, so

beautiful through the summer, look as if they had been laid waste by an invading army.[21]

In this piece, it is the subjects that are moving, not the observer. This is an interesting example of group representation coupled with individuation: families with bedding, babies and 'some poor sick creature', Irish but also coming from London, which sounds like two categories but needn't be, as many Irish moved to London and could be both. While individual characteristics are picked out within the paragraph, it begins and ends with collective nouns: 'They' and 'families' at the outset, 'an invading army' at the end. And that 'army' is homologous to the 'families': alike in different settings in their effect on the land and crops.

Conspectus of Society

I will move forward to my last and most complex example, which comes from the final run of 'Uncommercial' essays, 'New Uncommercial Samples' written for the New Series of *All the Year Round* in 1868 through 1870:

As we walked by the softly lapping sea, all the notabilities of Namelesston, who are for ever going up and down with the changelessness of the tides, passed to and fro in procession. Pretty girls on horseback, with detested riding-masters; pretty girls on foot; mature ladies in hats—spectacled, strongminded, and glaring at the opposite or weaker sex. The Stock Exchange was strongly represented, Jerusalem was strongly represented, the bores of the prosier London clubs were strongly represented. Fortune hunters of all denominations were there, from hirsute insolvency in a curricle, to closely buttoned-up swindlery in doubtful boots, on the sharp lookout for any likely young gentleman disposed to play a game at billiards round the corner. Masters of languages, their lessons finished for the day, were going to their homes out of sight of the sea; mistresses of accomplishments, carrying small portfolios, likewise tripped homeward; pairs of scholastic pupils, two and two, went languidly along the beach, surveying the face of the waters as if waiting for some Ark to come and take them off. Spectres of the George the Fourth days flitted unsteadily among the crowd, bearing

---

[21] [Charles Dickens], 'The Uncommercial Traveller [x]', *All the Year Round*, Vol. III, No. 60 (16 June 1860), 230-34 (p. 234). This article was re-titled 'Tramps' in subsequent editions of 'The Uncommercial Traveller'.

the outward semblance of ancient dandies [...]. Alone stationary in the midst of all the movement the Namelesston boatmen leaned against the railings and yawned, and looked out to sea, or looked at the moored fishing-boats and at nothing. Such is the unchanging manner of life with this nursery of our hardy seamen.[22]

This is a long paragraph from 'A Little Dinner in an Hour' (2 January 1869), in which the Uncommercial strolls around a seaside town waiting for dinner. The town, Namelesston, may stand in for Brighton, though it is doubtful if any hotel in that fine seaside resort could summon up such a combination of inadequate waiters, foul atmosphere, dirty linen, noxious food and dyspeptic sherry, as the Uncommercial and his friend Bullfinch experience in their 'ill-served, ill-appointed, ill-cooked, nasty little dinner' at the Hotel Temeraire.[23] Still, this report of the townspeople precedes the dinner; the Uncommercial and Bullfinch are still mildly hopeful of a satisfying 'little dinner in an hour'.[24] So our guide anatomises the citizens of the town, takes an inventory of the residents in this seaside resort, with good humour, expecting satisfying refreshment shortly.

He offers his readers a census of citizenry, noting the copious varieties of inhabitants. Each class is denominated (females, males, children). Some occupy more individuated categories (young, pretty, on horseback) than others (Stock Exchange strongly represented). The survey picks out particular accessories (spectacles, doubtful boots), particular movements (tripping homeward, walking languidly), particular vehicles (horse, foot, curricle) and particular examples of species (bores, ancient dandies). But the whole is framed by suggestions of a kind of timelessness: all the notabilities 'are for ever going up and down with the changelessness of the tides', while the stationary boatmen lean, yawn, look at boats or nothing. 'Such', the paragraph concludes, 'is the unchanging manner of life' here. These are not people who change category.[25]

This feels like a piece of writing that at first simply fills out a census form for the hour of waiting for that little dinner. I imagine my students skipping over it, even anathematising it as a perfect example of Dickens's unrelenting

[22] Charles Dickens, 'New Uncommercial Samples: A Little Dinner in an Hour [The Uncommercial Traveller xxxii]', *All the Year Round*, N.S. Vol. I, No. 5 (2 January 1869), 108-11 (p. 109).
[23] Dickens, 'New Uncommercial Samples: A Little Dinner in an Hour', p. 111.
[24] Dickens, 'New Uncommercial Samples: A Little Dinner in an Hour', p. 108.
[25] Dickens, 'New Uncommercial Samples: A Little Dinner in an Hour', p. 109.

wordiness. It says nothing, advances no plot, brings no interesting feature of the landscape or a person in the town to life. It passes time for the Uncommercial, uses up time for the reader.

But I would ask such readers to reconsider. For what we might all agree on is that, at the end of this paragraph, we have a very good idea, if we read it all, about what this seaside town looks like and who lives there. And somehow it seems like what we know so well, if not from experience, then from other travel journalism and fictions: how drab and restless and variegated and ill-assorted are those who congregate in holiday coastal towns. Mature ladies do wear hats to keep the sun off their foreheads and noses; sharpers are on the lookout for idle youths with jingling pockets. Think of the experience we gain from reading about the visit of the young gentlemen at Blimber's Academy when they go to the seaside in *Dombey and Son* (1846-48). I suspect even careful readers tend to elide the details, to use them as prompts to call up their own analogues, different in specific matters but homologous in general. And so we come away with something different from, and in some ways better than, a complete census of the inhabitants, a complete account of every occupation and what percentage of the population is engaged in each trade. We have a sense of classes and categories and even subcategories of persons, each with its own generalised but distinguishing characteristics (see **Fig. 4**). And we have a sense of the whole human aggregation of this town; what it feels like to be there as resident or visitor, student or teacher, married or single, honest or dishonest, modern or ancient, landlubber or sailor. Dickens in this piece of writing manages to meld the inclusive with the representative, without narrowing down to the individualised or the exclusive example.

Moreover, while nothing here seems exaggerated or unrealistic, it would be impossible from this account, however panoptic it seems to be, to frame any law for the greatest good of the greatest number of these people. And while we see no one closely enough, or long enough, to know a history and to care about a future, we are to some extent prompted to empathy, if not sympathy, for individuals. The Uncommercial has more empathy, I feel, for the males, some of whom come in for a fair amount of abuse, than for the females so conventionally drawn as young and pretty or mature and bespectacled. Still, they are more than statistics, more than entries on a census form, even though I have charted them to demonstrate the relation to those other forms of accounting, enumeration and tabular reporting increasingly demanded by a government that 'just wants to know'.

PRIMARY CATEGORY	PRIMARY CHARACTERISTIC	SECONDARY ATTRIBUTE
Females		
Young	Pretty	On horseback
	Pretty	On foot
Mature	In hats	Spectacled
Mistresses of accomplishments	Carrying small portfolios	Tripping homeward
Males		
Riding-masters	Detested	
Stock Exchange	Strongly represented	
Jerusalem	Strongly represented	
London Clubs, Bores of	Strongly represented (Prosier ones)	
Fortune Hunters	All denominations	
	Hirsute insolvency	Curricle
	Buttoned-up swindlery	Doubtful boots
Young gentleman	Disposed to play	Billiards
Masters of languages	Finished lessons	Going home
Spectres of the George the Fourth days	Flitting unsteadily	Resembling ancient dandies
Namelesston boatmen	Leaning against railings	Yawning, looking
Children		
Scholastic pupils	Two by two	Walking languidly

Fig. 4. All the notabilities of Namelesston

David Vincent has just completed a wonderful book about Paul Pry, the eponymous principal in John Poole's 1825 farce.[26] Pry, with his striped pants, hessian boots, top hat, tailcoat and umbrella, becomes the personification of curiosity, of a busybody; his image was stamped on china and handkerchiefs and he and his descendants—who might include Cruikshank's Mrs. Toddles and Dickens's Sairey Gamp and Rosa Dartle—continue to peer and peek and excuse themselves for intruding for another two centuries. Vincent identifies Pry as the figure on which nineteenth-century anxieties about the competing claims of domestic privacy and governmental inquiry coalesce. Ministers want to know exactly who you are and what you are doing, especially in bed, though they pretend that is not their subject. And private lives want to remain private, even if they do parade on boardwalks and sit a horse beautifully while riding along Rotten Row.

---

[26] David Vincent, *I Hope I Don't Intrude: Privacy and its Dilemmas since 1800* (forthcoming).

What Dickens tries to do, I am suggesting, especially in these 'Uncommercial' pieces, is devise a set of rhetorical strategies to bring the private—the very private as in the descriptions in 'Poor Mercantile Jack' (10 March 1860) of Liverpool slums and brothels—and individuated into conversations with larger aggregations and categories, in order to produce something like an account of the nation, but with feeling, not statistics, with persons, not categories, as the fundamental component of society.[27] To do so requires melding fact with fancy, finding analogies and homologies (Friar Bacon, Dry Rot in men), managing to make the particular representative of a greater whole without distorting either side of the equation. If we ask, 'What can journalism be in a Utilitarian age?', when summative categories, not personalised ones, constitute the basis of 'fact', the Uncommercial has an answer. If we ask, 'Of what use are essays to mid-Victorian imperial industrialisation?' the Uncommercial has an understated but powerful response. If we ask 'Why should we care for those who are not a significant part of commercial enterprise, like the sick and the poor, tramps and the houseless?' Dickens calls out to us to give the answer ourselves.

Those same questions drive governments today. I do not hear many journalists adopting the Uncommercial's copious rhetorics of appeal.

---

[27] [Charles Dickens], 'The Uncommercial Traveller [iv]', *All the Year Round*, Vol. II, No. 46 (10 March 1860), 462-66. This article was re-titled 'Poor Mercantile Jack' in subsequent editions of 'The Uncommercial Traveller'.

Our Island's Story: Dickens's Search for a National Identity

David Paroissien

'WE should be devilish sharp in what we do to children', Dickens reflected, in a reference to Mrs Pipchin's establishment in Chapter Eight of *Dombey and Son* (1846-48). His fictional account of her educational regime, he assured John Forster, was far from exaggerated. 'It is from the life', Dickens explained, writing from Lausanne in November 1846, 'and I was there—I don't suppose I was eight years old'. He then added: 'Shall I leave you my life in MS. when I die?'.[1]

Additional personal and professional interests seem to lurk behind the question put to Forster. Writing about Paul's early progress coincides with matters Dickens had raised with Miss Coutts about schools for Charley, his eldest son, and also about a project simultaneously under consideration with Dr James Kay-Shuttleworth to set up 'an experimental Normal Ragged School'.[2] What should pupils be taught, by whom and what role should the state play in funding educational opportunities? On these and matters related to 'the Education of the People, [and] the elevation of their character', Dickens wrote to another correspondent, 'I think I could do good service [...] and enter with my whole heart'.[3] Dickens spoke with conviction, I think, because he understood the importance of schooling and the implications of educational policy for society.

A further concern has an earlier origin and can be traced to an exchange between Dickens and Douglas Jerrold in May 1843. Writing to the latter on

---

[1] To John Foster, 4 November 1846, *The Letters of Charles Dickens*, ed. by Kathleen Tillotson, Graham Storey and others, Pilgrim Edition, 12 vols (Oxford: Clarendon Press, 1965-2002), Vol. IV, p. 653.

[2] To Dr James Kay-Shuttleworth, 28 March 1846, *The Letters of Charles Dickens*, Vol. IV, p. 527.

[3] To Lord Morpeth, 20 June 1846, *The Letters of Charles Dickens*, Vol. IV, p. 566.

the third, Dickens thanked the radical journalist for a present of books and for a copy of the first number of Jerrold's recently published *Illuminated Magazine*. The prospectus of this new monthly promised a far-reaching programme. It would comment on 'our social abuses and social follies', decline to shrink 'from any subject with a social wrong at its core' and speak directly to 'the MASSES of the people'.[4] In fulfilment of this pledge, Jerrold launched the new enterprise with his own essay in the first number, 'Elizabeth and Victoria', an ironical description of those who deplored change and progress and who correspondingly lamented the loss of 'the good old days'.[5] Unsurprisingly, Dickens praised Jerrold's sentiments, finding them wise, sharp and written with 'the finest end of that iron pen of yours'.[6]

Subsequent comments amplify Dickens's enthusiasm. Shortly before receiving a copy of the first issue of the *Illuminated Magazine*, Dickens had attended a charity dinner. It had been held in London and hosted by the capital's 'City aristocracy', whose sentiments, volubly expressed in after-dinner speeches, had driven him to madness with their 'conservative or High church notions'. 'I vow to God', Dickens continued, 'If ever I destroy myself, it will be in the bitterness of hearing those infernal and damnably good old times, extolled'. Deeply upset by such sentiments, Dickens reached a conclusion similar to Jerrold's: that the time had come to confront 'the Parrots of Society'.[7] In Dickens's lexicon this derisive phrase stood for members of the affluent middle class—'monied interest—flushed—highly respectable, Stock Exchange, perhaps—City, certainly'—people insular in outlook and ignorant of history.[8] As Dickens later portrayed them in *Bleak House* (1852-53), they wanted to stop 'the hands upon the Clock of Time' directing life back to England's *ancien régime* rather than forward into the 'Iron country' of Mr Rouncewell. Venting 'wrath' against those who stood firm against progress, Dickens went on to describe his plan to combat the advocates of stasis. 'I am writing a little history of England for my boy, which I will send you when it is printed for him'. 'I have tried to impress upon him [...] the exact spirit of your paper', he added.[9] Nothing is known

---

[4] To Douglas Jerrold, 3 May 1843, *The Letters of Charles Dickens*, Vol. III, p. 481, n.

[5] Douglas Jerrold, 'Elizabeth and Victoria', *The Illuminated Magazine*, Vol. I (1843), 3-8.

[6] *The Letters of Charles Dickens*, Vol. III, p. 481.

[7] *The Letters of Charles Dickens*, Vol. III, pp. 481-82.

[8] [Charles Dickens], 'A Flight', *Household Words*, Vol. III, No. 75 (30 August 1851), 529-33 (p. 529).

[9] *The Letters of Charles Dickens*, Vol. III, p. 482.

about the relationship of this early draft to the work Dickens later issued serially in *Household Words*. It is, however, the first clear reference to *A Child's History of England*, a project Dickens took to heart and turned over in his mind in the following years.

The absence of a surviving manuscript, coupled with a paucity of references to *A Child's History* in Dickens's letters, raises problems about the precise dating of the work. Circumstantial and contextual evidence, however, suggest that he continued to engage with the project he described to Jerrold in May 1843 up to the publication of the first instalment in *Household Words* on 25 January 1851. This eight-year interval, I think, is significant, suggesting a lengthy genesis of *A Child's History of England* and the possibility of its enrichment by reading and reflection, aided further by extended periods spent abroad, from which perspective distance on the nation and its history could be gained.

Questions about the interrelationship between *A Child's History of England* and *Bleak House* point to a third context worth exploring about which I have written elsewhere.[10] For the present, therefore, I will characterise the views that emerge from Dickens's 'little book'. I will also offer an explanation for the trenchant tone of his meditation on the politics of power and the behaviour of England's ruling elite. What he assembles is a doleful story, no match for the tales of 'the old Bards', whom Dickens describes as going about in Saxon times 'from feast to feast' recounting stories of virtue and bravery.[11] Rather the muse he summons inspires a blunt account of vain tyrants and bloody rulers whose brutality to labouring men he will not forgive.

Dickens made no secret of the revisionist agenda that controls his survey of royal rule from Alfred the Great to the deposition of James II and the Glorious Revolution of 1688. Referring to *A Child's History* in a letter to Emile de la Rue in December 1853, he spoke of his intention to present 'the Truth respecting certain English Kings, whom it has been thought a kind of

---

[10] David Paroissien, "'Dedlocked': The Case Against the Past in *Bleak House* and *A Child's History of England*', in *Charles Dickens: L'Inimitable The Inimitable*, ed. by Christine Huguet (Paris: Democratic Books, 2011), pp. 123-61.

[11] [Charles Dickens], 'A Child's History of England [ii]', *Household Words*, Vol. II, No. 48 (22 February 1851), 524-28 (p. 525). The 'History' was published irregularly in thirty-nine parts, from 25 January 1851 to 10 December 1853, covering Volumes II-VIII of *Household Words*.

religious gentility to lie about'.[12] He might well have added English queens. In the chapter on Elizabeth I, offered as an attempt to understand 'what kind of woman she really was', he dismisses her insistence on the Crown's discretionary powers of Prerogative, for example, and confesses himself tired of the way she thought it 'very pleasant and meritorious' to repeat her determination to live and die 'a maiden Queen'.[13] More generally, deference to the Tudors, who had brought unity to a country earlier ravaged by civil wars—a familiar theme since Shakespeare's history plays—has no place in the chapters that chronicle their unbroken reign from 1485 to 1603. With little to say about Henry VII, a dull king whose years Dickens fills out with a lively account of the conspiracies that troubled his vulnerable regime, he signs off by saying that if Henry had lived much longer (he died at 52) he would have made many more enemies among the people than he did, 'by the grinding exaction to which he constantly exposed them, and by the tyrannical acts of his two prime favorites in all money-raising matters, EDMUND DUDLEY and RICHARD EMPSON'.[14] 'We now come to King Henry the Eighth', Dickens announces with obvious relish, 'whom it has been too much fashion to call "Bluff King Hal," and "Burly King Henry," and other fine names'. Determined to redress the balance, he wastes no time in calling him plainly 'one of the most detestable villains that ever drew breath'.[15]

The chapters that follow remove all the bloom that had gathered over the sun-lit landscape of 'Merrie England', deposited by those who looked back nostalgically on the pageants and processions monarchs knew their arbitrary rule required. Rather, in Dickens's account the reign of the Tudors stands out as remarkable for the blood that was shed and bodies burned, for the greater part instigated by the crowned heads working collaboratively with archbishops, priests and other powerful representatives of the 'three great sects of religious people' who held sway in post-Reformation England.[16]

---

[12] To Emile de la Rue, 4 December 1853, *The Letters of Charles Dickens*, Vol. VII, p. 221.

[13] [Charles Dickens], 'A Child's History of England [xxvii]', *Household Words*, Vol. VII, No. 164 (14 May 1853), 261-64 (p. 261, 263).

[14] [Charles Dickens], 'A Child's History of England [xxii]', *Household Words*, Vol. VI, No. 141 (4 December 1852), 284-88 (p. 288).

[15] [Charles Dickens], 'A Child's History of England [xxiii]', *Household Words*, Vol. VI, No. 146 (8 January 1853), 404-08 (p. 404)

[16] [Charles Dickens], 'A Child's History of England [xxviii]', *Household Words*, Vol. VII, No. 167 (4 June 1853), 332-36 (p. 334).

Leaders from all three feel the lash of Dickens's scorn. His intolerance for the Papacy and its agents in England, for example, comes as no surprise to anyone familiar with his comments on the Papal States in *Pictures from Italy* (1846). But he is equally severe with those who set out to reform the Roman Church, attacking the Act of Six Articles (1539) as the duplicitous work of Henry VIII for embodying 'the very worst parts of the monkish religion' while the Puritans, with their more radical theological agenda, he pronounced 'for the most part an uncomfortable people, who thought it highly meritorious to dress in a hideous manner, talk through their noses, and oppose all harmless enjoyments'.[17] Admittedly, improvements to the Anglican Church occurred under Edward VI, who reversed some of the excesses of Henry VIII, as images were removed from churches, people informed that they were no longer required to confess themselves to priests unless they chose, and a common prayer-book drawn up in the English language, 'which all could understand'.[18] Further gains occurred under Elizabeth, whose reign Dickens describes as great 'for the Protestant religion and for the Reformation which made England free'. But what truly made her rule glorious and forever memorable was the contribution of 'the distinguished men who flourished in it': the great voyagers, statesmen and scholars and, of course, 'the names of BACON, SPENSER, and SHAKESPEARE'.[19]

England's crowned heads in Dickens's view merit little respect for their intellectual achievements. Hunting animals and other sports aside, waging wars against France or Spain and taxing the poor to finance them are more to the taste of our royalty than reading or writing books. It is not surprising therefore that he had to reach back 900 years to find a monarch he unequivocally admired. During the thirty years he reigned, Alfred the Great studied philosophy, translated important Latin works 'into the English-Saxon tongue', made just laws, founded schools, 'heard causes himself in his court of Justice', and did right to all his subjects, motivated by 'the great desires of his heart [...] to leave England better, wiser, [and] happier in all ways, than

---

[17] [Charles Dickens], 'A Child's History of England [xxiv]', *Household Words*, Vol. VI, No. 151 (12 February 1853), 524-28 (p. 527); 'A Child's History of England [xxviii]', p. 334.

[18] [Charles Dickens], 'A Child's History of England [xxv]', *Household Words*, Vol. VII, No. 155 (12 March 1853), 45-48 (p. 46).

[19] [Charles Dickens], 'A Child's History of England [xxix]', *Household Words*, Vol. VII, No. 169 (18 June 1853), 382-84 (p. 384).

he found it'.[20] One is tempted to wonder if this extended tribute flickered through Dickens's mind as a testimonial to his own life's work.

At this point questions will rise. What motivates the anger in Dickens's exposure of the politics of royal power and his account of the complicity of clerics in the perpetration of tyranny and misrule? Are the ghosts present in his narrative of England's story those of the country's past? Or do they belong to the author or perhaps to my own collusion in welcoming a strain of republican sentiment in *A Child's History of England*? 'I think the Stuarts were a public nuisance altogether', Dickens comments, looking back on the successors to the Tudors, whose legacy of 'hanging, beheading, burning, boiling, mutilating, exposing, robbing, transporting, and selling into slavery' he briefly chronicles.[21] His use of the phrase is nicely ironic given the way 'public nuisance' has been employed by the crown and its authorities over the centuries to describe conduct that if not strictly illegal proved nevertheless unreasonable and injurious to the general public. Who suffered at the hands of England's ruling elite? *A Child's History of England* leaves readers in no doubt: the poor people, of course, time and time again, compelled to wage wars not of their making and certainly not to their advantage, compelled to believe what they were told because they were denied access to the doctrines that constituted their beliefs, compelled to contribute taxes to the public purse, which rich and selfish monarchs and their confederates controlled. Can we wonder then that Alfred stands out as England's only truly decent ruler and Wat Tyler as the unsung hero of a confrontation with the establishment no common man could win? In a eulogy delivered after his account of Tyler's defiance of the poll-tax in 1380, Dickens writes:

> Wat was a hard-working man, who had suffered much, and had been foully outraged [when a tax collector sexually assaulted his daughter]; and it is probable that he was a man of a much higher nature and a much braver spirit than any of the parasites who exulted then, or have exulted since, over his defeat.[22]

---

[20] 'A Child's History of England [ii]', pp. 527-28.
[21] [Charles Dickens], 'A Child's History of England [xxxviii]', *Household Words*, Vol. VIII, No. 192 (26 November 1853), 307-12 (p. 310); [Charles Dickens], 'A Child's History of England [xxxix]', *Household Words*, Vol. VIII, No. 194 (10 December 1853), 360-61 (p. 360).
[22] [Charles Dickens], 'A Child's History of England [xvi]', *Household Words*, Vol. V, No. 116 (12 June 1852), 304-08 (p. 306).

Why, however, *this* version of England's story, a tale of hard times tailored for the times in which it was incubated? I would like to suggest two possible explanations. First, Dickens began work on *A Child's History* during an epoch when multiple voices came together to look to the past for guidance and inspiration. Benjamin Disraeli and his Young England supporters, discontented clerics in Oxford senior common rooms, architects, interior designers and painters—representatives of all three groups engaged in retrospection, looking back to the past as if to avert the present. Pugin's *Contrasts* (1836) provides a single defining visual image of attitudes deeply entrenched, which played out at political, cultural and social levels and which Dickens felt impelled to challenge.[23] A second motivation, to summarise my earlier point, originated in Dickens's determination to combat ideas he feared might contaminate his own son. This began as a personal project whose expansion over time broadened into a public mission to educate readers of *Household Words* with a 'true' history of England rather than one masked in genteel lies.

Taken together, these concerns find common ground in a principled resistance to 'slavish adulation' typical of Dickens's thinking. Writing in *Household Words* in 1856, he subsequently labelled this English trait 'one of our Insularities', especially if we have a royal or titled visitor 'among us'. England's history of course is stuffed with royals and also with sycophants, toadies and tuft-hunters, who delight in all the flummery and mummery essential to life in court and aristocratic circles. No one else paid out so many 'doubtful compliments' as the English, Dickens thought, and we would not pay them, he argued, 'if we had a little more self-respect'. 'Through our intercourse with other nations', he added, 'we cannot too soon import some'.[24]

The United States Dickens visited in 1842 fell short of the republic of his imagination and while Dickens's affection for post-Bourbon France deepened, Napoleon III repelled him. But the time Dickens spent in both republics clearly taught him something about the importance of self-respect. 'Half-a-dozen dukes and lords, at an English county ball, or public dinner, or any tolerably miscellaneous gathering', he observes in 'Insularities',

---

[23] Augustus Welby Northmore Pugin, *Contrasts; Or, A Parallel Between the Noble Edifices of the Fourteenth and Fifteenth Centuries, and Similar Buildings of the Present Day, Shewing the Present Decay of Taste: Accompanied by Appropriate Text* (London: Printed for the Author and Published by Him, 1836).

[24] [Charles Dickens], 'Insularities', *Household Words*, Vol. XIII, No. 304 (19 January 1856), 1-4 (p. 3).

are painful and disagreeable company; not because they have any disposition unduly to exalt themselves, or are generally otherwise than cultivated and polite gentlemen, but because too many of us are prone to twist ourselves out of shape before them, in contortions of servility and adulation.[25]

Take *A Child's History of England* to heart and you will please David Copperfield's Aunt Betsy by not twisting and turning like Uriah Heep. Teach that to school children today and they will learn something valuable, in spite of the version of our island's story recommended by Michael Gove. Agree with this clownish Minister of Education, whose idea of an appropriate gift to one of the world's richest women in times of immense public austerity is a new yacht, and you'll endorse attitudes Dickens vigorously opposed. Better therefore to adapt John Masefield's advice to a different context and suggest that if the Windsors yearn to go down to the lonely sea again to escape 'this boastful island', let them buy their own tall ship.

---

[25] [Dickens], 'Insularities', p. 3.

How the Dickens Scandal Went Viral

Patrick Leary

ATTENTIVE readers of Dickens's *Dombey and Son* (1846-48) in the summer of 1858 might well have been struck by the following passage:

> The barrier between Mr. Dombey and his wife was not weakened by time. Ill-assorted couple, unhappy in themselves and in each other, bound together by no tie but the manacle that joined their fettered hands, and straining that so harshly, in their shrinking asunder, that it wore and chafed to the bone. Time, consoler of affliction and softener of anger, could do nothing to help them. Their pride, however different in kind and object was equal in degree; and, in their flinty opposition, struck out fire between them which might smoulder or might blaze, as circumstances were, but burned up everything within their mutual reach, and made their marriage way a road of ashes.[1]

Those readers could have encountered this passage in any of a number of editions of the novel that had appeared since its debut ten years before. But some of them would have encountered it in newspapers like the *Congregationalist* of Boston, which prefaced it with a pointing finger and the comment, 'The following passage from *Dombey & Son* (the author, Charles Dickens, having just separated from his wife) is singularly striking at this moment.' Others might have come across it in the *Charleston Courier* of South Carolina, which found the description of Mr and Mrs Dombey similarly striking, 'apropos of the Dickens Scandal'. The *Daily State Journal* of Madison, Wisconsin, making the reasonable assumption that its readers were already well-informed about the state of the Dickens marriage, simply printed the

---

[1] Charles Dickens, *Dombey and Son* [1846-48], ed. by Andrew Sanders (London: Penguin, 2002), p. 699.

passage beneath the ominous boldfaced title: 'Coming Events Cast their Shadow Before'.[2]

For in the course of that summer, Charles Dickens's separation from his wife, along with all of the purported and imagined reasons for that separation, became matter for comment in the newspaper press all over the English-speaking world. In our own internet-inflected terms, the 'Dickens scandal', as it was often called, went viral. Spreading all over Britain within a few days of Dickens's extraordinary public announcement in June (the 'Personal' statement), the scandal had crossed the Atlantic a mere ten days later and begun to spread to the farthest reaches of the American hinterland. Thereafter, it would become a transatlantic phenomenon, shaped and filtered by the distinctly different cultures of the American and British newspaper press. The circulation and reception of the scandal was also importantly shaped by Dickens's own continued intervention, particularly the startling first appearance in America—and thereafter, of course, in Britain and elsewhere—of what would come to be known to his biographers as the 'Violated Letter', composed by him in May but not published until August.

Dickens biography has not paid much attention to these developments.[3] While only slight notice has been taken of the interestingly varied reactions to the 'Personal' statement in the British press, the circulation of reports about the Dickenses' marriage in the American press has been almost entirely ignored. One result of this neglect has been a curiously blinkered view of the scandal that has, over many years, perpetuated various misconceptions about how much contemporaries knew about the matter. For example, the standard view has always been that the story of the 'misdirected jewels' that precipitated the separation was privately known only to a few, who preserved it in records that were not published until decades

---

[2] *Congregationalist*, 9 July 1858; *Charleston Courier*, 17 July 1858; *Daily State Journal*, 8 July 1858. While some of the newspapers and periodicals mentioned in this article were consulted on microfilm, most were found in collections of digital facsimiles, including: Gale Cengage's '19th Century UK Newspapers', '19th Century U.S. Newspapers', '19th Century UK Periodicals', '*Illustrated London News* Historical Archive'; '*The Times* Digital Archive'; ProQuest's 'Historical Newspapers', 'Early British Periodicals' and 'C19: The 19th-Century Index'; the '*Scotsman* Archive'; Readex's 'Early American Newspapers'; and 'NewspaperArchive.com'.

[3] An important early treatment can be found in K. J. Fielding, 'Dickens and the Hogarth Scandal', *Nineteenth-Century Fiction*, Vol. 10, No. 1 (June 1955), 64-74. Michael Slater's *The Great Dickens Scandal* (London: Yale University Press, 2012) gives the fullest account yet of the course of the scandal from its inception to the present day.

later. More significant is the traditional understanding that Dickens's mistress, Ellen Ternan, was an 'invisible woman' (the title of Claire Tomalin's fine biography), whose role in Dickens's life had been so thoroughly suppressed that it remained completely unknown to the reading public before beginning to emerge, controversially, in the 1920s and thereafter. Neither of these assertions can survive a closer look at the news and commentary that actually appeared in American newspapers, much of it derived from London sources. That many of these details failed to re-cross the Atlantic to appear in Britain suggests how decisively the differing cultures of the two countries affected what kinds of information and opinion were made available to their respective readers. Quite apart from its import for students of Dickens's life, tracing the course of the Dickens scandal's journey through the nineteenth-century press helpfully illuminates important aspects of that press as a circulatory system.

The 'Personal' Statement

By the spring of 1858, the impact on Dickens's increasingly unhappy marriage of his infatuation with eighteen-year-old Ellen Ternan, whom he had met in Manchester in 1857, had proven decisive and he determined to live apart from his wife. Matters came to a head in May, amid a flurry of legal moves and Dickens's growing concern that his domestic arrangements, and indeed his own personal conduct, had become a widespread subject of gossip. He was right—they had. William Makepeace Thackeray, for instance, wrote to his mother of walking into the Garrick Club one day and hearing men talking about Dickens as having separated from his wife because of an intrigue with his sister-in-law, Georgina. 'O no!' chimed in Thackeray helpfully, 'it's with an actress'; Thackeray had heard all about it at the races at Epsom Downs.[4] Dickens's first response to news of such rumours about his behaviour was an energetic campaign to quash them at their source, beginning with his wife's mother and her youngest sister, Helen, who had made no secret of being furious at the way Catherine had been treated. Holding up the settlement of Catherine's income and house, he demanded and got their signatures on a statement repudiating any suggestion of misconduct on his part. On 25 May, he wrote a long, self-servingly disingenuous account of his marriage that began with the statement that he

---

[4] To Mrs. Carmichael-Smyth [May 1858], in *The Letters and Private Papers of William Makepeace Thackeray*, ed. by Gordon Ray (Cambridge, MA: Harvard University Press, 1945-46), Vol. IV, pp. 85-87.

and his wife, Catherine, had lived unhappily together for many years and that they were 'in all respects of character and temperament, wonderfully unsuited to each other'. The remainder of this extraordinary letter threw the entire blame for the failure of the marriage upon his wife, whom he described as suffering at times from a 'mental disorder' that had rendered her unfit both as wife and mother, and ended with a defence of the 'spotless' character of a 'young lady' who had been slandered by 'two wicked persons'. This letter he put into the keeping of Arthur Smith, the man in charge of the series of public readings that he would begin in June, with a cover letter urging Smith to show the letter 'to anyone who wishes to do me right, or to anyone who may have been misled into doing me wrong'.[5]

Now known to Dickensians as the 'Violated Letter', this document would appear in print in August under mysterious circumstances, with results to which we will return, but when it was composed in May it appears to have been one among several private or, at most, semi-public measures that Dickens had employed to beat back what he saw as a rising tide of private gossip about the separation. But he soon determined on an extraordinary course that Forster opposed but that John Delane of *The Times* supported: a fully public statement. Headed merely 'Personal', this open letter to his reading public was printed up as a 'card' and sent to the major London dailies for publication on 7 June, anticipating Dickens's publication of it on the first page of the number for *Household Words* that was dated 12 June but appeared on 9 June. It begins, 'Three-and-twenty years have passed since I entered on my present relations with the Public', and indeed the only relationship discussed in the statement is that between Dickens and his public. Of the actual occasion for this extraordinary declaration, he writes only that it concerns 'some domestic trouble of mine, of long-standing' that 'has lately been brought to an arrangement'. The main thrust of the statement is the urgency of contradicting the 'grossly false' gossip circulating concerning his 'domestic trouble', gossip that he imagines 'not one reader in a thousand' has been able to escape.[6] Dickens's main concern, as I have argued elsewhere, is to use the power of the press to stop people from talking about the separation; his target is not what appeared in the newspaper press itself, which had been entirely silent about the matter, but with the oral

---

[5] To Arthur Smith, 25 May 1858, *The Letters of Charles Dickens*, ed. by Kathleen Tillotson, Graham Storey and others, Pilgrim Edition, 12 vols (Oxford: Clarendon Press, 1965-2002), Vol. VIII, p. 568 and Appendix F (pp. 740-41).

[6] [Charles Dickens], 'Personal', *Household Words*, Vol. XVII, No. 429 (12 June 1858), 601.

transmission of gossip.[7] From the moment of the statement's appearance, however, the newspaper press, willingly or not, had become a party to the discussion of Dickens's private life.

It is no exaggeration to say that the publication of the 'Personal' statement stunned the British literary world. The range of press responses, from instinctive support to disapproval, is reflected even in the papers that first willingly printed it at his request. The *Morning Chronicle* prefaced the letter with the remark, 'We publish with regret, and at a special request, the following [...]'.[8] In the days to come, what struck most observers who commented editorially, in remarks that usually either prefaced or were appended to the statement itself, was Dickens's crucial vagueness about the precise nature of the 'domestic trouble' to which he had alluded. Most people, even among his most admiring readers, simply had no inkling of his private life, let alone the nature of the 'monstrous' rumours concerning it. The opening article in the *Critic*, reprinting the statement, doubtless spoke for many readers in asking, 'Now really we should be very much obliged to anybody who will inform us—what is all this about? What are the "misrepresentations"? What the "slanders"? What the precise nature of the "unwholesome air"?'[9] The *British Banner* coyly remarked, 'We are happy in being able to say that we are entirely in the dark as to what the nature of the scandal is.'[10] The *Era* noted, 'Mr. Dickens has written a letter to all the daily papers [...] in reference to some scandal [...] but to what member of Mr. Dickens's family the reported scandal attaches does not clearly appear'.[11] A number of papers combined disapproval of the impropriety of Dickens discussing such personal matters in print with utter perplexity about their nature. The *Aberdeen Journal* spoke for many in expressing regret that Dickens had 'felt compelled to come before the public, and defend himself from what he calls "abominably false rumours"', before going on to confess, 'What these are we have not yet heard'.[12]

Into this informational vacuum rushed the London correspondent of the *Scotsman*, which followed its printing of the statement with an editorial gloss that would be reprinted throughout the English-speaking world and would crucially shape responses to the scandal. The paper began by remarking on

---

[7] Patrick Leary, *The Punch Brotherhood* (London: The British Library, 2010), pp. 86-88.
[8] *Morning Chronicle*, 7 June 1858, p. 5.
[9] *Critic*, 12 June 1858, p. 287.
[10] *British Banner*, 10 June 1858, p. 13.
[11] *Era*, 13 June 1858, p. 9.
[12] *Aberdeen Journal*, 9 June 1858, p. 5.

how limited a circle might have been expected to have possession of information that Dickens had mistakenly assumed was well-nigh universal, before moving on to an insider's account of the matter at hand:

> As Mr Dickens' statement is apt to be somewhat unintelligible to those beyond the reach of the gossip of London and 'the literary world,' we may explain that the fact, as we are informed, is, that Mr Dickens has, by mutual agreement, separated from his wife, on the ground of 'incompatibility.' The name of a young lady on the stage has been mixed up with the matter—most cruelly and untruly, is the opinion, we hear, of those having the best means of judging [...]. We mention these facts to explain the allusions to which Mr Dickens has thought proper to give publicity.[13]

As a clue to how the correspondent came by this information, the most striking element of this summary is the phrase, 'as we are informed', followed by the grounds for the Dickenses' separation—'incompatibility'. The latter word, expanded by many newspapers into the phrase 'incompatibility of temper', would soon become a key part of the discussion of the Dickenses' marriage. Other newspaper accounts make clearer that Dickens himself, or someone close to him, had offered this explanation of his 'domestic trouble' privately as a kind of supplement to the 'Personal' statement. The most likely way for this explanation to have gained circulation would have been through private showings of the letter that he had drafted on 25 May and given to Arthur Smith with the admonition to show it to anyone who might benefit from seeing it; 'incompatibility of temper' is a fair paraphrase of the opening remarks of that letter. As *John Bull and Britannia* archly summed up the situation,

> [W]e are led to suppose that the 'trouble' which Mr. Dickens has succeeded in bringing to an arrangement was entirely an affair of incompatibility of temper. Plainly speaking [...] there have been Household 'Words,' at divers times between certain persons; but no Household Deeds of a discreditable kind.[14]

But of course the *Scotsman* had also mentioned, although it had quickly dismissed, vaguely discreditable deeds that provided an alternative explanation to mere 'incompatibility' for the dissolution of the Dickenses' marriage—an unnamed 'young lady on the stage'. The paper did not mention

---

[13] *Scotsman*, 9 June 1858, p. 4.
[14] *John Bull and Britannia*, 12 June 1858, p. 377.

the even more damaging rumours linking Dickens with Georgina Hogarth, his sister-in-law. *Reynolds's Newspaper* was not so delicate, remarking that 'The names of a female relative, and of a professional young lady, have both been, of late, so freely and intimately associated with that of Mr. Dickens as to excite suspicion and surprise'.[15] Most other papers kept their allusions to these other explanations for the separation less specific and gave credence to Dickens's strenuous denials of their truth.[16] In touching on the nature of those rumours, some of Dickens's defenders may, in their zeal, have made matters rather worse. The *Freeman's Journal* for example, boldly declared, 'It is due to the character of the great writer and public teacher to say that his friends (and they are legion) entirely acquit him of the charge of gross immorality so recklessly made and so industriously circulated.'[17] The *Hull Packet and East Riding Times* likewise prefaced its reprint of Dickens's statement (followed by the *Scotsman*'s editorial) in this way, 'Some slanders, imputing gross profligacy to Mr Charles Dickens, having been in circulation, he has published the following personal explanation in *Household Words* this week'.[18] Conjecturing that the rumours themselves might be responsible for the separation, the *Morning Chronicle* went so far as to openly urge a reconciliation between Mr and Mrs Dickens:

> Where all parties concerned are so really good and amiable, it will be indeed most lamentable if the exaggeration of scandalizing rumour amongst ignorant persons be allowed to widen a breach, which every experience of life shows not to be really so irreparable.[19]

Although most writers for the British press, with a few exceptions like Reynolds, were supportive of, or at least neutral about, the state of affairs of which Dickens wrote, almost all could agree that he had been ill-advised to issue a public statement on such a personal matter. The correspondent for the *Inverness Courier* remarked that 'though Dickens is a universal favourite, this egotistical manifesto of his is universally condemned'. (Unusually among

---

[15] *Reynolds's Newspaper*, 13 June 1858, p. 3.

[16] Typical of this supportive tone was the *Illustrated London News*, 12 June 1858, p. 583: 'A great author has this week thought it necessary to appeal in print to his fellow-authors against certain scandals—stupid, foul, and lying enough—which nobody of name believed for a single moment.'

[17] *Freeman's Journal*, 2 July 1858, p. 3. The *Freeman's* piece was reprinted in such papers as the *Birmingham Post* and *Trewman's Exeter Flying Post*.

[18] *Hull Packet and East Riding Times*, 11 June 1858, p. 8.

[19] *Morning Chronicle*, 11 June 1858, p. 5.

commentators at this time, the *Courier* also spared a few words of praise for Mrs Dickens as 'a kind, good-humoured Scotch lady'.)[20] Others remarked upon Dickens's curious delusion that 'not one reader in a thousand' would be ignorant of the rumours about his marriage, the *Era* estimating that 'out of the thirty millions of people in these islands, till he himself gave rumour her wings, there were not thirty individuals who knew anything of the matter'.[21] *John Bull and Britannia* fretted at the disillusioning effect upon Dickens's readers, who until now had imagined that he embodied in his own life the domestic virtues that he had extolled in his novels; by telling his readers 'how little, after all, he thinks of the marriage tie [...] he has quite spoilt our taste for the greatest of all fictions—Dickens himself'.[22] As press reactions to the statement trailed off toward the end of June, to be replaced by glowing reviews of Dickens's series of readings, the *Critic* took a last retrospective look at the subject that reflected the common opinion that Dickens had been misled by authorial vanity into stoking the fires of gossip:

> [Y]our literary man gets his head above the soil and imagines that the business of mankind mainly consists in looking at him. This is the error into which Mr. Dickens fell when he put forward that extraordinary document which, as we predicted [...] has set all the old women in the land inquiring what dreadful things the amiable author of 'Pickwick' has been doing.[23]

Glad to put the matter to rest, the *Era* had doubtless spoken for many in declaring that, 'In charity, we hope that Mr Dickens will write no more letters on family subjects'.[24] Yet it is a measure of how quickly and widely news and opinion could now circulate in the new mass press of the mid-nineteenth century that matters would not end there.

American Reaction

The news about Dickens's 'domestic trouble' reached the New York papers less than two weeks after its first appearance in Britain. The poles of the press reaction were represented by the two most successful papers in the city and, indeed, in the country: the *New York Tribune* and the *New York Herald*.

---

[20] Reprinted by the *Caledonian Mercury*, 21 June 1858, p. 3.
[21] 'Charles Dickens and His Letter', *Era*, 13 June 1858, p. 9.
[22] *John Bull and Britannia*, 12 June 1858, p. 377.
[23] *Critic*, 3 July 1858.
[24] 'Charles Dickens and His Letter', p. 9.

Both had been founded in the 1830s and both reflected the aims and personalities of their founders, each of whom continued to be deeply involved in the daily operation of their respective papers.[25] Horace Greeley's *Tribune* was above all a paper of views rather than news and those views were staunchly Republican, anti-slavery, patriotic and respectable. The paper's purpose was to improve the moral tone of American society. Newspaperman James Gordon Bennett had made the *New York Herald* essential daily reading for the New York business community by being the first to carry detailed commercial news of the doings on Wall Street, but he made his paper essential to a growing host of other readers with his reporting on sensational crime and scandal and his insistence on being the first with breaking stories. The *Herald*, like its owner, was cynical about politics, sceptical of authority, pro-Southern and Democratic in its sympathies. The two men despised one another. Greeley considered Bennett a scoundrel whose wallowing in unseemly scandal degraded the tone and purpose of the newspaper press as a whole. Bennett, in turn, thought his rival a moralising blockhead, memorably suggesting that if one could somehow galvanise a large New England squash, it would make just as capable a newspaper editor as Horace Greeley.[26]

Reprinting Dickens's statement elsewhere in the paper but offering no London reporting of its own, the *Tribune* added a brief and dignified editorial paragraph that echoed the *Morning Chronicle* in blaming the gossips and hoping that some sort of reconciliation could still be effected:

> Charles Dickens has met, by a full, emphatic denial, the scandals which certain London journalists and letter-writers have recently set afloat with reference to his family relations. Until further advised, we shall believe that he states the truth [...]. It seemed from the first improbable that he, the father of a family of grown-up children [...] could have deliberately exposed himself in the autumn of life, to such gossip. Most likely he had some momentary difference with his wife, which tale-bearers aggravated into a serious alienation, and then invented infidelity on his part to account for that alienation.[27]

---

[25] On differences between the British and American newspaper press during this period, see Joel H. Wiener, *The Americanization of the British Press, 1830-1914: Speed in the Age of Transatlantic Journalism* (New York: Palgrave Macmillan, 2011), especially his discussion of Bennett as one of the creators of the modern press (pp. 36-42).

[26] Harvey Saalberg, 'Bennett and Greeley, Professional Rivals, Had Much in Common', *Journalism Quarterly*, Vol. 49, No. 3 (September 1972), 538-50 (p. 541).

[27] *New York Tribune*, 21 June 1858, p. 4.

The *New York Herald*, by contrast, was all over the story and its account was widely reprinted by other papers. The report of the *Herald*'s anonymous 'London correspondent' was dated 4 June—before the appearance of the 'Personal' statement—but appeared in the paper on 18 June. The tenor of the lengthy article can be guessed from the italicised highlights at the top of the column: '*The Separation of Charles Dickens from His Wife—What the Gossips say about it—Miss Ternan implicated—Public Sympathy with Mrs. Dickens* [...] *What Some People Say about Mr. Dickens' Troubles'*. This was the sort of gossipy scandal that the *Herald* lived for and it seized upon the opportunity with evident relish, brushing aside Dickens's privately offered explanations:

> The great novelist, and delineator of the character of the inimitable Mr. Pecksniff, has separated from his wife. [...] It is given out that the cause of their separation is incompatibility of temper. That is all fudge. A married life of twenty-two years, nearly a dozen children, a spotless life on the part of the wife and mother, and now to have uncongenial temper cause a separation, is simply preposterous.

The correspondent went on to explain (with startling accuracy) that in the course of recruiting professional actors to assist in putting on private theatricals for charity in Manchester, Dickens had met

> a Miss Ternan, well known in Manchester, and latterly on the London boards [...]. A very pure and very platonic affection sprang up between this young lady and the author of Pickwick. [...] She is now charged with being the cause of the separation.[28]

The *Herald* correspondent was probably confusing two 'Miss Ternans' in his report; Ellen was scarcely 'well known' as an actress and her older sister Fanny would subsequently be mistaken by other gossips as the object of Dickens's affection. Nevertheless, the printing of these specifics—the actress's name, as well as the circumstances under which they met—instantly distinguishes the American paper's treatment of the scandal from that of even the boldest of its British counterparts.

The 'London correspondent' is a frequent and notable feature of the American coverage of the scandal, as it had been for some parts of the provincial press in Britain. While the major metropolitan dailies often paid

---

[28] *New York Herald*, 19 June 1858. Despite the date of 4 June at the head of the column, in a later paragraph the author may be referring to the 'Personal' statement in alluding to 'Mr. Dickens's statements', although it is possible that the reference is to the letter of 25 May given to Arthur Smith.

London writers to contribute regular reports, many much smaller newspapers could boast an occasional 'London letter' of some sort. Little is known about these correspondents, who almost always wrote anonymously. Some were London-based experts on politics or foreign affairs; Karl Marx, for example, was the *New York Tribune*'s London correspondent at this period, writing reports for the paper about European politics. Some portion of the trade, however, appears to have consisted of less formal arrangements between American papers and London journalists who picked up some extra income by retailing London club-land gossip to American readers, as Edmund Yates is known to have done for the *New York Times* in the 1860s. The course of the Dickens scandal in the American press makes clear that, while some papers were merely reprinting material and adding their own editorial commentary, others were featuring actual reporting from writers in London, as the *Herald* had done. Out of reach of the British law of libel and writing for a newspaper culture that was often considerably less restrained than the British press about reporting scandal, the 'London correspondent' frequently contributed material to American papers that would have been virtually unprintable at home. One startling result of this critical element of the scandal's circulation was that newspaper readers in tiny towns in rural America were often much more closely informed of the state of London gossip about Dickens's marital troubles than were readers in London itself.

The coverage of the role of the 'other woman' in the scandal offers a particularly striking instance of this contrast, as we have seen. Nor was the *Herald* the only American paper to mention the possibility of another woman's involvement in the case. The London correspondent of the *North American and United States Gazette* of Philadelphia, for example, informed American readers that the 'wicked rumours [...] refer to a pretty young actress, Miss T——, and as people are usually uncharitable, the worst actions and motives have been attributed to an acquaintance which, if it existed at all, may have been perfectly innocent'.[29] Under the heading, 'CHARLES DICKENS IN TROUBLE', the *Baltimore Sun* noted archly that 'Charles Dickens, the author, who did not like the moral habits of some of our countrymen, has just given the English world the opportunity to scan his own'. The *Sun* went on to report that 'Charles has had a taste for private theatricals, which threw him into frequent intercourse with a Miss Ternan, an actress of

---

[29] *North American and United States Gazette*, 21 June 1858.

celebrity. His attentions becoming something more than was required by a fictitious passion, Mrs. Dickens rebelled'.[30]

It was left to the London correspondent of the *Detroit Free Press*, however, to provide the most extensive reporting on this aspect of the scandal. Passing along rumours that Dickens has been sleeping in the office of *Household Words*, the paper's 'Letter from London' went on to give the proximate cause of the separation:

> I hear that Dickens has for some time been paying attention to an actress at the Haymarket. (Amy Sedgwick, it is thought.) So charmed was he with her that he went to Hunt & Roskell's and bought her a beautiful bracelet […] and had the lady's name engraved upon it. The trinket was unfortunately lost one night when he was taking her to a place of amusement and was found by some honest person, who took it to Hunt & Roskel's [sic], who at once sent it to Mr. Dickens, and as Mr. Dickens was out, Mrs. Dickens received the naughty tell-tale. She presented it to her lord when he came home, and simply said, 'Charles, I wish you would not be so open in these matters,' whereupon (as the lawyers say) the editor of *Household Words* went into a towering passion, and said he would not stay another minute in the same house with his wife.[31]

Devotees of Dickensian biography will instantly recognise this as a version of the 'misdirected jewels story' that most chroniclers agree was the immediate occasion for the separation between Charles and Catherine. Astonishingly, this published report in a Detroit newspaper is by far the earliest and the most detailed version that we have, one that appeared within weeks of the incident and was quickly reprinted in the *Charleston Courier* and other American papers.[32] True, it gets the name of the actress wrong—Amy Sedgwick, with whom Ellen Ternan had once worked as an understudy, was mentioned by more than one report about the scandal—but it admits that

---

[30] *Baltimore Sun*, 21 June 1858, p. 2.

[31] *Detroit Free Press*, 22 June 1858.

[32] There are several sources for the story, the most often cited being a book of reminiscences published in 1909 by John Bigelow, who recalled having heard the story at Thackeray's dinner-table in 1860. A few years ago, I came across another version in the unpublished diary of publisher Richard Bentley (Special Collections, University of Illinois at Urbana-Champaigne), who noted having heard it from Mr and Mrs Thomas Chandler Halliburton, who had in turn heard it from Mrs Gilbert Abbott à Becket. That diary entry is from 23 March 1859.

that information is uncertain, and unlike any of the other accounts that were published decades later, it gives the name of the jewellers.[33] No hint of this story in a British newspaper of the period has ever come to light.

Despite such reports as these, however, the American press's reaction to the scandal, taken as a whole, did not reflect a widespread conviction that Dickens had been unfaithful to his wife. To the contrary, his denials of such 'monstrous rumours' in the 'Personal' statement were generally believed, although the alternative reason advanced for the separation remained puzzling to many commentators. Dickens's popularity undoubtedly played a role in this reluctance to believe the worst. 'That the author of the immortal Pickwick, the hypocritical Pecksniff and the noble-hearted Cuttle; the creator of Little Nell, Little Dorrit, and Agnes', wrote the *Galveston Weekly News* 'should so far depart from his high duty as to violate the precepts he has been so many years teaching, is what we have no disposition to believe'.[34]

Some editorialists found the rumours simply hard to credit about a husband and father of Dickens's age. 'It seems scarcely probable', remarked the *Sandusky Register* of Sandusky, Ohio, 'that Mr. Dickens, who has lived with his wife some twenty-two years and […] who is father of nearly a dozen children, should at this advanced stage of life become enamored of a pert young actress'.[35] Nevertheless, while not joining the *New York Herald*'s correspondent in dismissing the 'incompatibility of temper' explanation as mere 'fudge', many other newspaper writers found that explanation hard to credit for the same reason. 'What strikes the public as remarkable in this case', wrote Cleveland's *Daily Herald*, 'is the fact that Dickens and his wife have lived for a quarter of a century together, and Mr. Dickens has just found out that there exists an "unconquerable incompatibility" of temper between them. No body will believe this story'.[36] In its 'Monthly Summary of Events' for July 1858, the *United States Democratic Review* listed the news item in this way: 'Charles Dickens has separated from his wife—cause, domestic

---

[33] This is indirectly confirmed by Richard Bentley, who in the recounting of the story in his diary refers to Hunt and Roskell by its former name, Hunt and Mortimer. In investigating possible candidates for the jewellers in the story, Katharine Longley, in her unpublished defence of Ellen Ternan, confirmed that the firm's records perished in the Blitz (Senate House Library, 'Pardoner's Tale', Chapter 6, note 12).

[34] *Galveston Weekly News*, 21 July 1858.

[35] 'Daily Commercial Register', 23 June 1858, p. 3.

[36] *Cleveland Daily Herald*, 22 June 1858.

difficulties and *incompatibility of temper*, discovered after living together 22 years, and bringing up a large family of children.'[37]

Remarkably, many papers took it upon themselves to bolster the otherwise implausible explanation of 'incompatibility' after so many years of marriage by holding up Dickens's domestic difficulties as typical of the man of genius. The young Walt Whitman, writing in the *Brooklyn Daily Times*, condoled with Dickens's many disillusioned readers who 'had imagined that their favorite author enjoyed some such domestic bliss as he has himself pictured in his "Copperfield"'. Citing the recently reported scandal attaching to Edward Bulwer-Lytton, whose own unhappy marriage had been much in the news, Whitman averred that, 'Of all the calamities of authors—of all the infelicities of genius—it strikes us that their domestic difficulties are the worst'.[38] The same comparison occurred to the editorialist of the *Louisville Journal* of Louisville, Kentucky:

> It is rather melancholy that the two greatest living novelists, Dickens and Bulwer, are separated from their wives. Each of the two seem to be idolized by almost every lady in the world except the one he interchanged vows with at the altar.[39]

The *Philadelphia Enquirer* offered up a column on the larger theme entitled, 'Ill-Assorted Marriages; Or, Genius Not Domestic', while the *Plain Dealer* of Cleveland, in a widely reprinted piece, expounded, 'From the days of the poet Job, whose wife was the original Mrs. Caudle, down to Socrates and Xantippe, and so on down to Byron, and finally to Dickens, matrimonial unhappiness has ever attached itself to literary men'.[40] *Frank Leslie's Illustrated Newspaper*, in a long, gossipy report of the scandal, advised its female readers 'not to marry men of genius!', a species of advice echoed by the *Richmond Whig*, which excoriated men of letters like Dickens as 'the most irritable of all human beings' and cautioned any woman against marrying one 'unless she is prepared to burn incense to his vanity for the rest of her life'.[41]

---

[37] *United States Democratic Review*, July 1858, p. 93.
[38] 'The Private Lives of Great Men', quoted in *The Uncollected Poetry and Prose of Walt Whitman*, ed. by Emory Holloway (New York: Doubleday Page, 1921), Vol. II, p. 18.
[39] As reprinted in the *Baraboo Republic* (Baraboo, Wisconsin) of 15 July 1858, giving the *Journal* as its source; also reprinted without attribution in the *American Citizen* of Jackson, Michigan, 5 August 1858, p. 4.
[40] *Philadelphia Inquirer*, 1 June 1858, p. 3; *Plain Dealer*, 26 June 1858, p. 2.
[41] *Frank Leslie's Illustrated Newspaper*, 3 July 1858; *Richmond Whig*, 13 July 1858.

Authorial vanity became a popular theme in American press reports of the separation, one that in some instances was coupled with highly-coloured imaginings of what had gone on inside the Dickenses' marriage. The *Springfield Republican* in Massachusetts was not the only paper to offer a capsule history of the Dickenses' marriage, but the account of its 'London correspondent' was the one most widely reprinted in other American papers:

> For some years they lived very happily together; but Mr. Dickens, having become a great man, flattered and courted, finds that his domestic felicity is not as great as could be desired.—She is not intellectual.—He reads his works to her, and she, absorbed in needlework, inquires abstractedly what he means by some of his most brilliant passages. In short, she is not a companion to him, so the brilliant novelist and actor separates on the ground of 'incompatibility' from her whom he vowed before God to love and cherish.[42]

The circulation of this account also illustrates the speed with which articles or simply paragraphs about the Dickens scandal were picked up and reprinted, often moving quickly from papers on the Eastern seaboard to towns large and small throughout America, following along major transportation routes. Within little more than a week, the Springfield paper's article had moved west to the Great Lakes and south to Richmond, Virginia, soon to reach the Gulf coast (Alabama's *Mobile Register*) and such small Midwestern towns as Kenosha, Wisconsin (*Kenosha Times*) and Fort Wayne, Indiana (*Weekly Republican*).[43] Striking, too, is how many smaller papers were capable of originating material that would be widely reprinted in major metropolitan dailies, such as a report from the London correspondent of Boston's *Atlas and Bee* that claimed that the separation could be explained by disagreement between the Dickenses over the religious education of their daughters.[44]

---

[42] *Springfield Republican* of Springfield, Massachusetts, reprinted first in the *Detroit Free Press*, 18 July 1858 and thereafter in many other papers.

[43] Similarly, a long article on the scandal, entitled 'Incompatibility' and meditating on the lessons to be learned from the Dickens matter, appeared in the *Cleveland Daily Herald* on 23 July and shortly thereafter was published on the front page of the *Superior Chronicle*, the paper of the tiny hamlet of Superior, Wisconsin at the far western edge of the Great Lakes.

[44] See, for example, the reprinting of this article in the *New York Times*, 29 June 1858.

As it had in Britain, American newspaper coverage of the Dickens scandal dwindled within a matter of weeks. By the end of July, few papers had anything more to say about it. Coverage of Dickens's readings rarely mentioned anything about his marital difficulties and anticipation ran high over reports that he might soon embark on a reading tour of America. The following month, however, a letter appeared that brought the whole matter up again.

The Violated Letter

The circumstances surrounding the appearance in August, in a New York City newspaper, of the letter that Dickens had written in May explicitly blaming Catherine for the separation, remain a mystery. What little scholars thought they knew about it, derived from John Forster's biography of Dickens (1872-74), turns out to be mistaken. In Forster's account, Dickens's readings manager, Arthur Smith, gave a copy of the letter to 'the London correspondent of the *New York Tribune*', where it appeared on 16 August 1858. However, we now know that the *Tribune* was not the first paper to publish it: the letter had already appeared the day before in the rival *New York Herald* under the heading, 'The Dickens Domestic Affair', prefaced only by the comment, 'The following letters are in circulation among the friends of Mr. and Mrs. Dickens. They speak for themselves'.[45] The *Tribune* reprinted the *Herald*'s version under the same title and in the same four-part form in which it would subsequently appear throughout the American and British press: the statement that the letters were circulating among 'friends' and speak for themselves; Dickens's cover letter to 'My Dear Arthur', urging him to show the letter to all and sundry; the long letter itself; and the appended statement exculpating Dickens and signed by the Hogarths. The whole ends with the initials 'D. J. A.', a signature that has never been plausibly explained.[46] Dickens would subsequently claim that the letter had appeared in print without his knowledge or consent—hence the term 'violated

---

[45] *New York Herald*, 15 August 1858, p. 8.

[46] The late Katharine Longley's suggestion of 'Delaware Journalists Association' has no evidence to support it; no such organisation has been traced and initials printed at the ends of columns in American newspapers almost always appear to have referred to individuals. Longley was, however, the first scholar to notice that the *Tribune* editorial's reference to the letter having 'got into print' suggested that it had already appeared elsewhere. See her letter to the editor of the *Dickensian* (August 1989), pp. 128-29.

letter'—but the expansive tone of his cover note to Smith suggested to many observers, from that day to this, that if he had not specifically connived at its publication he had certainly given Smith the kind of blanket permission that had made that publication likely, if not inevitable.

Although it had not been the first to print the letter, the *Tribune* did publish a separate editorial on the matter that contrasted sharply with its sympathetic support of the 'Personal' statement:

> Mr. Dickens has recently felt constrained to separate from his wife of some twenty-odd years. That wife has said nothing, and, so far as the public is aware, has instigated others to say nothing, about the matter [...]. Mr. Dickens was stung by the circulation of anonymous scandals to publish [...] his solemn, emphatic denial [...]. There he should have stopped. [...] Yet he has been tempted to write again, ostensibly for private circulation only, but his letter has got into print, as such letters always will. [...] In a case of matrimonial abrasion, the public sympathy instinctively takes the side of the weaker party—that is, the wife [...]. One more uncalled-for letter from Mr. D. will finish him.[47]

As before, the material was quickly reprinted, appearing in the *New York Times* on 17 August under the weary heading, 'The Dickens Scandal Again', before rapidly surfacing in Philadelphia (17 August), Charleston, South Carolina (20 August), Raleigh, North Carolina (25 August) and many other papers, large and small, throughout the United States. Although commentary was restrained, perhaps as a result of readers' satiation with a distasteful subject, much of what there was echoed the *Tribune* editorial's exasperated disapproval. As the *Gazette* of Alexandria, Virginia remarked, 'We should think that it was about time that this subject should be excluded from the newspapers.'[48]

Michael Slater, in *Dickens and Women* (1983), gives a brilliant and completely persuasive analysis of the psychology of the 'violated letter' and how writing it met Dickens's need to cast himself, by proxy through his own children, as a child neglected by an uncaring mother.[49] Likewise, Catherine Waters points to the letter's ideological dimension, in the urgency with which

---

[47] *New York Tribune*, 16 August 1858, p. 4.

[48] *Alexandria Gazette*, 18 August 1858.

[49] Michael Slater, *Dickens and Women* (Stanford: Stanford University Press, 1983), pp. 145-48.

it argues that Catherine Dickens had failed in her proper domestic sphere.[50] But looking at what might be called the media ecology surrounding the letter's appearance in print offers yet another vantage point. Dickens's 'Personal' statement had puzzled many readers and the subsequent explanations failed to satisfy. Unless one were prepared to believe that a man of Dickens's age and eminence, a writer who had written so movingly of the joys of domestic life, had been unfaithful to his wife, the only other proffered explanation was 'incompatibility of temper'; but that reason, as discussed in so many newspaper accounts, struck many people as almost equally implausible. The appearance of the 'violated letter', however inadvisable it seems in retrospect, at least supplied what had been so conspicuously lacking in the 'Personal' statement: a plausible and specific set of reasons for the separation, beyond mere 'incompatibility', in the form of Catherine Dickens's purported failures as a wife and a mother. The timing of its publication therefore suggests that someone connected with its appearance was responding to the already extensive newspaper coverage of the scandal.

Unlike much of the material about the Dickens scandal that had appeared in the American press in June, the 'violated letter' and its associated documents appeared in their entirety in the British press just as quickly as steamships could bring the American papers to London, appearing first on 30 August in the *Evening Star* under the heading, 'Mr. Charles Dickens and His Wife', before being reprinted all over Britain in the following week. The *Star* was quick to point out that

> the public will, of course, bear in mind that in this painful case MRS. DICKENS has all along remained silent. Her husband's story only has been told. It is possible that she might, if disposed, put a different complexion upon it.[51]

Reynolds's Weekly concurred, adding, 'We do not think that in this instance [her] silence signifies acquiescence in all he says'.[52] The definitive editorial

---

[50] Catherine Waters, *Dickens and the Politics of the Family* (Cambridge: Cambridge University Press, 1997), p. 10.

[51] *Evening Star*, 30 August 1858, p. 3. Interestingly, the *Star* and most of the other British papers give the letter's source as the *New York Tribune*, while others attribute its publication to 'New York papers', but none sources it from the *Herald*, where it first appeared. This anomaly, perhaps derived from the *Herald*'s reputation as a scandal-sheet, doubtless accounts for Forster's later mistake.

[52] *Reynolds's Weekly*, 5 September 1858.

coup de grâce was administered by the *Liverpool Mercury* in a long piece entitled, 'Literary Men and the Public' that was reprinted by many other papers:

> Mr. Dickens some weeks back thought proper to devote a page of his *Household Words* to a statement relative to certain domestic troubles of his, and to certain scandalous rumours to which (as he informed the world) they had given rise. [...] The thing passed off, however, with much less comment than it deserved. Mr. Dickens is a sort of spoiled child of the public, and can take liberties which would be fatal to most men. People stared, wondered, and thought it a piece of abominably bad taste, but were hardly inclined to resent it.
>
> Within the last few days, however, a document of a somewhat different description, attributed to Mr. Dickens, has come before the world—a document which, unless he can satisfactorily clear himself of all responsibility for its publication, must gravely damage him in the estimation of all men whose esteem is worth having. [...] A man who stands at the very head of popular English literature tells all England and America [...] that a lady with whose conduct and temper the public have not the remotest concern is a bad mother and is not quite sane.[53]

A long letter to the editors of the *Evening Herald* and the *Evening Star*, signed 'A Hater of Scandal', archly questioning the authenticity of the letter, arguing sarcastically that Dickens could not possibly have stooped to 'such an unmanly attack' on his own wife and calling upon the novelist to repudiate it.[54] Three weeks later, this letter had re-crossed the ocean and appeared in the *Cleveland Daily Herald*, the *Charleston Courier* and other American papers, reviving another brief round of commentary.[55] By this time, also, the reactions to the 'Personal' statement had begun to appear in the Australian and New Zealand press, a reminder that the circulation of gossip had reached global proportions.

---

[53] *Liverpool Mercury*, 9 September 1858.
[54] *Evening Herald*, 1 September 1858, p. 3. The letter appeared in the *Star* on the same date.
[55] *Charleston Courier*, 1 September 1858, p. 1.

Conclusion

To select items on the same topic from many papers over even a short period of time may leave the impression that newspaper readers during that period were concerned with little else. This was not true, of course, for the world of the newspaper press was an almost incalculably vast and many-sided one. Although it is remarkable how far and how fast the Dickens scandal spread in the summer of 1858, and how varied and extensive were the newspaper commentaries on the subject, from the perspective of twenty-first-century media it is equally remarkable how restrained the coverage was, even in most segments of the American press. Although in his initial statement he had mistakenly estimated the reach of rumour, Dickens had been entirely correct in asserting that his relationship with his reading public had been a long and intimate one and that relationship seems clearly to have acted as a kind of force-field that, together with the conventional limits observed by most newspapers, acted to constrain the response to the scandal.

This protective restraint continued to operate for the rest of Dickens's life, persisting even after his death in 1870. Featured in a New York literary weekly called the *Arcadian*, this obscure article is the only actual eyewitness account we have of this key part of the novelist's life, offering a vivid glimpse of Dickens and Ternan together. "It was evident to nearly all of us", the correspondent wrote of the Manchester performances, "that the two were mutually infatuated. Dickens was constantly at her side." Although quick to add that "[Dickens's] affection for her was said to be purely platonic", the writer matter-of-factly explains that "it was this intimacy which was the final cause of the rupture between Dickens and his wife", adding to his account yet another version of the "misdirected jewels" story.[56] And yet not only did the publication and reprinting of this remarkable report have no measurable impact whatever upon Dickens's reputation in America, it was

---

[56] The article was reprinted in its entirety on 6 August 1874 in the *Daily Whig and Courier* of Bangor, Maine, as well as the *Evening Bulletin* of San Francisco, and discussed in both the *New York Times* and the *Chicago Daily Inter-Ocean*. Although I have not been able to inspect the pertinent issue of this short-lived (1872-78) and scarce periodical, the reprinting dates and the fact that the *Arcadian* was published on Thursdays suggest that it had first appeared on 31 July 1874. As the story appears to originate from someone who was involved in the Manchester productions, and as few among that small circle were still alive and residing in London in 1874, a likely candidate for the authorship of this story is musician Francesco Berger.

afterward so entirely forgotten even in that country that no mention of it has ever appeared in any Dickens biography, or even in any scholarly accounts of Ellen Ternan or the scandal, from that time to this.

The Dickens scandal called forth strong feelings among newspaper writers and readers on both sides of the Atlantic, giving rise to reflections on the nature of marriage as well as the nature of genius and celebrity, and highlighting continuing controversy over the boundaries between public and private life, and between oral and print culture. Close attention to the way in which the scandal was reported upon and discussed in both Britain and America therefore illuminates key nineteenth-century attitudes as well as the winding course of Dickens's reputation and Dickensian biography. Such attention also allows us to begin to trace some portion of the complex and dynamic circulatory system of the mid-Victorian press.

Index